Historical Dictionary of the Puritans

Charles Pastoor
Galen K. Johnson

*Historical Dictionaries of Religions,
Philosophies, and Movements, No. 79*

The Scarecrow Press, Inc.
Lanham, Maryland • Toronto • Plymouth, UK
2007

SCARECROW PRESS, INC.

Published in the United States of America
by Scarecrow Press, Inc.
A wholly owned subsidiary of
The Rowman & Littlefield Publishing Group, Inc.
4501 Forbes Boulevard, Suite 200, Lanham, Maryland 20706
www.scarecrowpress.com

Estover Road
Plymouth PL6 7PY
United Kingdom

Copyright © 2007 by Charles Pastoor and Galen K. Johnson

All rights reserved. No part of this publication may be reproduced, stored in a retrieval system, or transmitted in any form or by any means, electronic, mechanical, photocopying, recording, or otherwise, without the prior permission of the publisher.

British Library Cataloguing in Publication Information Available

Library of Congress Cataloging-in-Publication Data
Pastoor, Charles, 1969–
 Historical dictionary of the Puritans / Charles Pastoor, Galen K. Johnson.
  p. cm. — (Historical dictionaries of religions, philosophies, and movements ; no. 79)
 Includes bibliographical references.
 ISBN-13: 978-0-8108-5085-9 (hardcover : alk. paper)
 ISBN-10: 0-8108-5085-0 (hardcover : alk. paper)
 1. Puritans–Dictionaries. I. Johnson, Galen K. II. Title.
BX9323.P37 2007
285'.903–dc22   2006101374

∞™ The paper used in this publication meets the minimum requirements of American National Standard for Information Sciences—Permanence of Paper for Printed Library Materials, ANSI/NISO Z39.48-1992.
Manufactured in the United States of America.

HISTORICAL DICTIONARIES OF RELIGIONS, PHILOSOPHIES, AND MOVEMENTS
Jon Woronoff, Series Editor

1. *Buddhism*, by Charles S. Prebish, 1993
2. *Mormonism*, by Davis Bitton, 1994. *Out of print. See no. 32.*
3. *Ecumenical Christianity*, by Ans Joachim van der Bent, 1994
4. *Terrorism*, by Sean Anderson and Stephen Sloan, 1995. *Out of print. See no. 41.*
5. *Sikhism*, by W. H. McLeod, 1995. *Out of print. See no. 59.*
6. *Feminism*, by Janet K. Boles and Diane Long Hoeveler, 1995. *Out of print. See no. 52.*
7. *Olympic Movement*, by Ian Buchanan and Bill Mallon, 1995. *Out of print. See no. 39.*
8. *Methodism*, by Charles Yrigoyen Jr. and Susan E. Warrick, 1996. *Out of Print. See no. 57.*
9. *Orthodox Church*, by Michael Prokurat, Alexander Golitzin, and Michael D. Peterson, 1996
10. *Organized Labor*, by James C. Docherty, 1996. *Out of print. See no. 50.*
11. *Civil Rights Movement*, by Ralph E. Luker, 1997
12. *Catholicism*, by William J. Collinge, 1997
13. *Hinduism*, by Bruce M. Sullivan, 1997
14. *North American Environmentalism*, by Edward R. Wells and Alan M. Schwartz, 1997
15. *Welfare State*, by Bent Greve, 1998. *Out of print. See no. 63.*
16. *Socialism*, by James C. Docherty, 1997. *Out of print. See no. 73.*
17. *Bahá'í Faith*, by Hugh C. Adamson and Philip Hainsworth, 1998. *Out of print. See no. 71.*
18. *Taoism*, by Julian F. Pas in cooperation with Man Kam Leung, 1998
19. *Judaism*, by Norman Solomon, 1998. *Out of print. See no. 69.*
20. *Green Movement*, by Elim Papadakis, 1998
21. *Nietzscheanism*, by Carol Diethe, 1999. *Out of print. See No. 75.*
22. *Gay Liberation Movement*, by Ronald J. Hunt, 1999
23. *Islamic Fundamentalist Movements in the Arab World, Iran, and Turkey*, by Ahmad S. Moussalli, 1999
24. *Reformed Churches*, by Robert Benedetto, Darrell L. Guder, and Donald K. McKim, 1999
25. *Baptists*, by William H. Brackney, 1999
26. *Cooperative Movement*, by Jack Shaffer, 1999
27. *Reformation and Counter-Reformation*, by Hans J. Hillerbrand, 2000
28. *Shakers*, by Holley Gene Duffield, 2000
29. *United States Political Parties*, by Harold F. Bass Jr., 2000
30. *Heidegger's Philosophy*, by Alfred Denker, 2000
31. *Zionism*, by Rafael Medoff and Chaim I. Waxman, 2000
32. *Mormonism*, 2nd ed., by Davis Bitton, 2000
33. *Kierkegaard's Philosophy*, by Julia Watkin, 2001
34. *Hegelian Philosophy*, by John W. Burbidge, 2001
35. *Lutheranism*, by Günther Gassmann in cooperation with Duane H. Larson and Mark W. Oldenburg, 2001
36. *Holiness Movement*, by William Kostlevy, 2001

37. *Islam*, by Ludwig W. Adamec, 2001
38. *Shinto*, by Stuart D. B. Picken, 2002
39. *Olympic Movement*, 2nd ed., by Ian Buchanan and Bill Mallon, 2001. *Out of Print. See no. 61.*
40. *Slavery and Abolition*, by Martin A. Klein, 2002
41. *Terrorism*, 2nd ed., by Sean Anderson and Stephen Sloan, 2002
42. *New Religious Movements*, by George D. Chryssides, 2001
43. *Prophets in Islam and Judaism*, by Scott B. Noegel and Brannon M. Wheeler, 2002
44. *The Friends (Quakers)*, by Margery Post Abbott, Mary Ellen Chijioke, Pink Dandelion, and John William Oliver Jr., 2003
45. *Lesbian Liberation Movement: Still the Rage*, JoAnne Myers, 2003
46. *Descartes and Cartesian Philosophy*, by Roger Ariew, Dennis Des Chene, Douglas M. Jesseph, Tad M. Schmaltz, and Theo Verbeek, 2003
47. *Witchcraft*, by Michael D. Bailey, 2003
48. *Unitarian Universalism*, by Mark W. Harris, 2004
49. *New Age Movements*, by Michael York, 2004
50. *Organized Labor*, 2nd ed., by James C. Docherty, 2004
51. *Utopianism*, by James M. Morris and Andrea L. Kross, 2004
52. *Feminism*, 2nd ed., by Janet K. Boles and Diane Long Hoeveler, 2004
53. *Jainism*, by Kristi L. Wiley, 2004
54. *Wittgenstein's Philosophy*, by Duncan Richter, 2004
55. *Schopenhauer's Philosophy*, by David E. Cartwright, 2005
56. *Seventh-day Adventists*, by Gary Land, 2005
57. *Methodism*, 2nd ed., by Charles Yrigoyen Jr. and Susan Warrick, 2005
58. *Sufism*, by John Renard, 2005
59. *Sikhism*, 2nd ed., by W. H. McLeod, 2005
60. *Kant and Kantianism*, by Helmut Holzhey and Vilem Mudroch, 2005
61. *Olympic Movement*, 3rd ed., by Bill Mallon with Ian Buchanan, 2006
62. *Anglicanism*, by Colin Buchanan, 2006
63. *Welfare State*, 2nd ed., by Bent Greve, 2006
64. *Feminist Philosophy*, by Catherine Villanueva Gardner, 2006
65. *Logic*, by Harry J. Gensler, 2006
66. *Leibniz's Philosophy*, by Stuart Brown and Nicholas J. Fox, 2006
67. *Non-Aligned Movement and Third World*, by Guy Arnold, 2006
68. *Salvation Army*, by Major John G. Merritt, 2006
69. *Judaism*, 2nd ed., by Norman Solomon, 2006
70. *Epistemology*, by Ralph Baergen, 2006
71. *Bahá'í Faith*, by Hugh Adamson, 2006
72. *Aesthetics*, by Dabney Townsend, 2006
73. *Socialism*, 2nd ed., by Peter Lamb and James C. Docherty, 2007
74. *Marxism*, by David M. Walker and Daniel Gray, 2007
75. *Nietzscheanism*, 2nd ed., by Carol Diethe, 2007
76. *Medieval Philosophy and Theology*, by Stephen F. Brown and Juan Carlos Flores, 2007
77. *Shamanism*, by Graham Harvey and Robert Wallis, 2007
78. *Ancient Greek Philosophy*, by Anthony Preus, 2007
79. *Puritans*, by Charles Pastoor and Galen K. Johnson, 2007

For Jennifer, Catherine, Ella, and Isabelle
—C. P.

To my wife Lori and daughter Caroline
—G. K. J.

Contents

Editor's Foreword *Jon Woronoff*	ix
Preface	xi
Acknowledgments	xiii
Chronology	xv
Introduction	1
THE DICTIONARY	23
Bibliography	361
About the Authors	405

Editor's Foreword

Sometimes a relatively small, determined group of people can have a disproportionately large impact on history, altering the course of whole countries and in certain ways the world. The Puritans are among such groups, changing not only the religious practices of 16th- and 17th-century England, Scotland, and other areas, but carrying their ways to what became the United States, where the influence was initially rather notable. Although there are no longer any Puritans, in the original sense, their trace can be found in the Reformed or Calvinist churches, from which they sprang, and the Congregationalist, Presbyterian, and Baptist churches that succeeded them. More broadly, although there are no Puritans, the concept of puritanism is still used today very widely, if also very inaccurately. The complicated situation in which the Puritans arose, their trajectory across history, and their legacies are more than adequate reasons to justify a *Historical Dictionary of the Puritans*, but it is the lasting confusion that makes it that much more valuable.

This latest volume in the series on religions, philosophies, and movements, and the different ways in which the Puritans can fit into all these categories, is a good way of learning about them. The introduction places them in the context of the times, and helps to define them, an arduous task, indeed. This done, details are provided in several hundred entries that focus on crucial figures, most of them (but not all) Puritans, as well as the practices and concepts that defined them. Others describe major events, some of momentous consequence, such as the English Civil Wars and Restoration, and the crossing of the Pilgrim fathers in the *Mayflower* and establishment of the early colonies in New England. Because this tale is long and often twisted, it might be useful to resort periodically to the chronology. And it is even more helpful, for those who are curious to learn more, that a comprehensive bibliography is included at the end.

This volume was written by two persons intensely interested in the subject and period, Galen K. Johnson and Charles Pastoor. Both of them teach at John Brown University in Arkansas, Dr. Johnson being assistant professor of theology and Dr. Pastoor, associate professor in the department of English. Both are also specialists on the Puritans, on whom they have published widely. They have written numerous articles and Dr. Johnson authored a book on one of the foremost figures, *Prisoner of Conscience: John Bunyan on Self, Community, and Christian Faith*. This experience was precious in guiding us through the maze of information and disinformation surrounding the Puritans.

Jon Woronoff
Series Editor

Preface

Our goal in composing this book has been to fill a void in the existing literature of Puritanism: an extensive, accessible dictionary of the major persons, terms, and events of the historical Puritan movement. The existing compendia of Puritanism usually compose multiple volumes, tend not to justify as we have sought to do in our Introduction their choice of entries, do not encompass both England and America or both older Puritans and later Nonconformists, and are often out of print. Through consulting other books' listings of Puritans and developing our own sensitivities of who should not be omitted in order to tell the Puritan story, we composed our initial list of terms. Then, through careful research of primary texts and secondary literature, we wrote our entries, expanding our list as we came across additional names that we believed merited inclusion. In the process of making these decisions, we began to think through the questions of general Puritan identity that we have addressed in detail in the Introduction. We have been fascinated by all that we have learned in the process of research and writing, especially taking note of how many Puritans' lives intersected with one another on both sides of the Atlantic. It was amazing to learn, for example, how many notable figures were relatives, friends, or disputants of John Cotton. Generally speaking, the persons or events that we believe were influential in Puritan entries receive longer entries, although there are exceptions. For instance, we do not consider William Vane more germane to Puritan history than William Perkins, but Vane's career in both England and New England was so long and diverse that his entry in our book is the lengthier of the two. Hoping to give our readers the same sense of interconnectedness that we have discovered between so many Puritan lives, we have written our entries with a concerted effort to maximize the possibilities for cross-reference. So, words printed in bold type in the entries direct the reader to separate entries on those words.

Acknowledgments

The authors express their profoundest gratitude to the Institute for Learning Enhancement and Faculty Development Committee of John Brown University for awarding each of us a Shipps Scholar Grant from 2004 to 2006, which provided us with the financial support and course release time needed to write this book. The JBU library efficiently acquired all the resources we requested to facilitate our research. Our students Billy Nye, Samantha Smallwood, and Sarah Tomkinson helped to compile the entries for the bibliography. David Carruth was especially helpful in the early stages of the project. And series editor Jon Woronoff has been a gracious and efficient guide through the publication process.

Chronology

1526 Tyndale New Testament is published. Thomas Cardinal Wolsey burns Lutheran books in England.

1533 Thomas Cranmer becomes Archbishop of Canterbury.

1534 King Henry VIII becomes supreme head of the Church of England.

1536 Tyndale Bible is published. John Calvin publishes *Institutes of the Christian Religion*.

1537 Matthew's Bible is published.

1539 Taverner's Bible is published.

1546 Martin Luther dies (b. 1483).

1547 King Henry VIII dies. Reign of King Edward VI begins.

1548 Great Bible is published. Bishops' Bible is published.

1549 *Book of Common Prayer* is issued.

1552 Second *Book of Common Prayer* is issued.

1553 Forty-two Articles are issued. King Edward VI dies. Lady Jane Grey rules England for nine days. Reign of Queen Mary I begins. Edmund Bonner, Bishop of London, prosecutes Protestants. Marian exiles flee to the continent.

1554 Queen Mary I marries Philip of Spain. Reginald Cardinal Pole reconciles England with the papacy. Marian exiles in Frankfurt divide over use of *Book of Common Prayer*.

1555 John Rogers is burned at Smithfield. John Hooper is killed at Gloucester. Nicholas Ridley and Hugh Latimer are executed at Oxford. John Calvin secures a house of worship for Marian exiles in Geneva.

1556 Thomas Cranmer is executed. Reginald Pole becomes Archbishop of Canterbury. William Whittingham translates Genevan Psalter into English.

1557 John Knox travels back and forth between Geneva and Scotland.

1558 Queen Mary I dies. Reign of Queen Elizabeth I begins. John Knox publishes *The First Blast of the Trumpet against the Monstrous Regiment of Women*. John Calvin censures Knox's regicidal rhetoric.

1559 Matthew Parker becomes Archbishop of Canterbury. Act of Supremacy and Uniformity is issued. *Book of Common Prayer* is slightly revised.

1560 Geneva Bible is published. Roman Catholicism is overthrown in Scotland. John Knox guides the implementation of Reformed Protestantism in Scotland.

1561 First Calvinists settle in England after fleeing Flanders, Holland. Thomas Norton translates John Calvin's *Institutes of the Christian Religion* into English. St. Paul's Cathedral in London is badly damaged by fire. Anabaptist leader Menno Simons dies (b. 1496).

1562 Massacre of Huguenots occurs in France.

1563 The term "Puritan" is used possibly for the first time in England to describe those who wish to further reforms within the Church of England. Forty-Two Articles become Thirty-Nine Articles. John Foxe publishes *Acts and Monuments*. Council of Trent dismisses.

1564 John Calvin dies (b. 1509).

1565 Archbishop Matthew Parker's *Advertisements* causes Puritan protests.

1567 Controversy over wearing vestments arises.

1568 Bishop's Bible is published.

1570 Pope Pius V claims to depose Queen Elizabeth I. Thomas Cartwright preaches on Presbyterian reforms at Cambridge University.

1571 Sir William Cecil is named Lord Burleigh.

1572 John Knox dies (b. 1505). England's first presbytery forms in Wandworth, near London. Archbishop Parker labels as "Puritans" those who challenge ecclesiastical authority.

1576 Edmund Grindal becomes Archbishop of Canterbury.

1577 Edwin Sandys, Archbishop of York, hesitates to prosecute Puritans as directed. John Aylmer, Bishop of London, does suppress Puritans.

1582 Robert Browne first states Congregationalist principles in *A Treatise of Reformation without Tarrying for Any*.

1583 John Whitgift becomes Archbishop of Canterbury. Whitgift's Articles are issued.

1585 England assists Holland in the Eighty Years' War against Spain.

1586 Henry Barrow is imprisoned.

1587 Mary, Queen of Scots, is executed. Her son becomes King James VI of Scotland.

1588 English navy defeats the Spanish Armada. Martin Marprelate tracts appear.

1591 William Perkins publishes *The Golden Chaine*.

1592 William Perkins publishes *The Arte of Prophesying*.

1593 Henry Barrow, John Greenwood, and John Perry are hanged for Separatism. Richard Hooker publishes *Of the Laws of Ecclesiastical Polity*. Henry Barrow dies (b. 1550).

1595 Lambeth Articles are issued.

1602 William Shakespeare's comedy *Twelfth Night* parodies the term "Puritan." William Perkins dies (b. 1558).

1603 Queen Elizabeth I dies. Reign of King James I begins. Millennary Petition is presented. Thomas Cartwright dies (b. 1535).

1604 Hampton Court Conference convenes. John Bancroft becomes Archbishop of Canterbury. *Book of Common Prayer* is revised.

1605 Gunpowder Plot occurs. William Bradshaw publishes *English Puritanisme*.

1607 English settlers arrive in Jamestown, Virginia.

1608 Puritan Separatists from town of Scrooby migrate to Holland.

1609 William Ames is ejected from Cambridge University for Nonconformity. John Smyth rebaptizes himself in Holland. Jacob Arminius dies (b. 1560).

1611 King James (or Authorized) version of the Bible is published. George Abbot becomes Archbishop of Canterbury.

1612 Thomas Helwys founds first Baptist church on English soil. John Smyth dies (b. 1570).

1615 Irish Articles are issued.

1617 King James I issues the Declaration of Sports (Book of Sports).

1618 Synod of Dort convenes (–1619). Thirty Years War begins in Europe (–1648).

1620 English Pilgrims sail to America on the *Mayflower*. Mayflower Compact is written and signed. Plymouth Plantation is founded.

1621 Robert Burton publishes *The Anatomy of Melancholy*. Pilgrims celebrate the first Thanksgiving.

1622 John Donne becomes Dean of St. Paul's Cathedral, London.

1623 George Wither publishes *Hymns and Songs of the Church*, England's first congregational hymn book. Captain John Mason founds colony of New Hampshire.

1624 James I makes Virginia a royal colony.

1625 King James I dies. Reign of King Charles I begins. Charles I marries Henrietta Maria.

1626 William Bradford and other Pilgrim settlers purchase Plymouth from original London investors.

1628 Petition of Right is issued. The Duke of Buckingham is assassinated. William Laud becomes Bishop of London. Oliver Cromwell becomes a Member of Parliament. Patent for Massachusetts Bay Colony is issued.

1629 Charles I dismisses Parliament for third time, thus beginning the king's personal rule (–1640). Charles I charters Carolina colony.

1630 Richard Sibbes publishes *The Bruised Reed and Smoking Flax*. John Winthrop and many others migrate to New England, establish the Massachusetts Bay Colony. Winthrop preaches "A Model of Christian Charity."

1631 Saybrook patent for Connecticut is issued. Roger Williams arrives in Massachusetts.

1632 Charles I charters the colony of Maryland.

1633 William Laud becomes Archbishop of Canterbury. Laud insists that the Book of Sports be read from every English pulpit. William Ames joins Hugh Peter as co-pastor of English Protestant congregation in Rotterdam. William Ames dies (b. 1576). William Prynne publishes *Histrio-Mastix*. John Donne's *Poems* and George Herbert's *The Temple* are published posthumously. John Cotton arrives in Boston.

1634 Anne Hutchinson migrates to Boston. Pequot War begins in New England (–1637).

1635 Roger Williams is banished from Massachusetts. Thomas Hooker founds Hartford, Connecticut. Boston Latin School begins as the first public school in America. Richard Sibbes dies (b. 1577).

1636 Charles I seeks imposition of Anglicanism on the National Church of Scotland. Roger Williams founds Providence colony on the principle of religious freedom. Harvard College is founded in Cambridge, Massachusetts. William Vane is elected the governor of Massachusetts. Antinomian crisis erupts in Massachusetts (–1638).

1637 William Prynne, Henry Burton, and John Bastwick have their ears cut off. John Milton publishes *Lycidas*. Oliver Cromwell boards a ship bound for New England, but royal orders prevent it from sailing. John Winthrop again becomes the governor of Massachusetts. Anne Hutchinson is banished from Massachusetts.

1638 Scottish Presbyterians sign the Scottish National Covenant, abolish episcopacy.

1639 First Bishop's War with Scotland begins.

1640 Short Parliament is both called and dissolved. Long Parliament is called. Second Bishop's War begins. Root and Branch Petition is issued. Et cetera oath is issued. The Bay Psalm Book, the first book printed in America, is published.

1641 Smectymnuus publishes two tracts. Star Chamber is dissolved. Irish rebellion erupts. House of Commons presents Charles I with Grand Remonstrance. Parliament organizes its army under the leadership of Robert Devereux, the Third Earl of Essex. Richard Baxter becomes pastor in Kidderminster. Henry Parker publishes *A Discourse Concerning Puritans*.

1642 First English Civil War begins (–1646). Parliament orders the closing of theaters (–1660). William Ames' *The Marrow of Sacred Divinity* is published.

1643 Westminster Assembly convenes (–1653). Sequestration Ordinance is passed. Solemn League and Covenant is signed. New England Confederation forms between Massachusetts, Plymouth, and New Haven colonies. John Pym dies (b. 1584).

1644 Charles I's Oxford Parliament meets. Parliamentary army wins major victory at Marston Moor but loses at Lostwithiel. The Earl of Essex falls into disfavor with Parliament. New Model Army forms under the leadership of Sir Thomas Fairfax. Samuel Rutherford publishes *Lex, Rex: The Law and the Prince*. John Milton publishes *Areopagitica*. Baptists issue First London Confession. Roger Williams publishes *The Bloudy Tenent of Persecution for Cause of Conscience*.

1645 Archbishop Laud is executed. New Model Army defeats Royalist forces at Naseby. Peace negotiations fail at Uxbridge. Parliament forbids use of *Book of Common Prayer*. Westminster Assembly produces Ordinances for Directory of Worship and Presbyterian Church Government. Royal Society first convenes in London to promote scientific study. John Eliot founds Roxbury Latin School in Massachusetts.

1646 Westminster Confession is issued. Charles I surrenders to Scottish troops. Oxford surrenders to Parliament. Parliament orders the replacement of episcopacy with Presbyterianism. John Geree publishes *The Character of an Old English Puritane or Nonconformist*. Thomas Edwards publishes *Gangraena: Or a Catalogue and Discovery of many* *of the Errours, Heresies, Blasphemies and pernicious Practices of the Sectaries.* George Fox founds the Quakers. Cambridge Synod convenes in Massachusetts (–1648). John Eliot begins first sustained missionary outreach to Indians of Massachusetts.

1647 Second English Civil War begins (–1649). Charles I briefly escapes from custody. Putney Debates occur. John Owen publishes *The Death of Death in the Death of Christ.*

1648 Pride's Purge removes many Presbyterian sympathizers from Parliament. Self-Denying Ordinance is passed. Rump Parliament begins. Cambridge Platform is issued in Massachusetts. John Norton publishes *Responsio ad Gal. Apollonnium*, the first book in Latin published in America.

1649 Charles I is beheaded. Many Roman Catholics flee England. John Milton publishes *The Tenure of Kings and Magistrates.* House of Lords is abolished. Interregnum begins. Levellers are suppressed. England is declared a Commonwealth. Third Civil War begins (–1651). Oliver Cromwell represses Irish revolt. Parliament charters the Society for the Propagation of the Gospel in New England. John Winthrop dies (b. 1588). Thomas Shepard dies (b. 1605).

1650 James Ussher publishes *Annales Veteris et Novi Testamenti*, estimating the year of creation as 4004 B.C. Oliver Cromwell defeats the Scots, orders the dispersion of the Diggers and the Ranters. Command of the New Model Army passes from Sir Thomas Fairfax to Oliver Cromwell. Compulsory attendance at Anglican parishes is abolished. Andrew Marvell publishes *Horatian Ode.* Anne Bradstreet publishes *The Tenth Muse*, the first book of poetry published by an American Puritan woman. William Bradford probably completes *Of Plymouth Plantation.*

1651 Charles II attempts invasion of England from Scotland, is defeated. Fifth Monarchists become active. Thomas Hobbes publishes *Leviathan.* Baptists argue for liberty of conscience in Massachusetts.

1652 John Milton writes "To Sir Henry Vane the Younger." English war with the Dutch begins. Gerrard Winstanley publishes *The Law of Freedom in a Platform.* John Cotton dies (b. 1585).

1653 Oliver Cromwell dismisses Rump Parliament. Barebones Parliament is both convened and dissolved. Instrument of Government becomes new English constitution. Protectorate begins (–1659).

1654 First Protectorate Parliament convenes (–1655). Triers are appointed.

1655 Royalist uprisings occur. Oliver Cromwell forbids Anglican worship services, appoints Major Generals. Thomas Fuller questions the usefulness of the term "Puritan" in *The Church History of Britain*. Jews are readmitted into England.

1656 Second Protectorate Parliament convenes (–1658). The Quaker James Nayler rides into Bristol on a donkey, claiming to be Christ. Richard Baxter publishes *The Reformed Pastor*. Mary Fisher and Ann Austin become first Quaker missionaries in the New World.

1657 Oliver Cromwell declines crown, is reinstalled as Lord Protector. William Bradford dies (b. 1590). John Lilburne dies (b. 1615).

1658 Oliver Cromwell dies (b. 1599). Richard Cromwell becomes second Lord Protector. Independents produce Savoy Declaration. Anti-Quaker laws pass in Massachusetts.

1659 Rump Parliament reconvenes. Richard Cromwell resigns as Lord Protector. Sir George Booth leads failed Royalist rebellion. The Protectorate is dissolved. Four Quaker missionaries are executed in Massachusetts.

1660 General George Monck helps secure the Restoration. Reign of King Charles II begins. Long Parliament dissolves. Declaration of Breda is issued. Convention Parliament convenes. William Juxon becomes Archbishop of Canterbury. Richard Baxter becomes chaplain to Charles II. House of Lords and episcopacy are restored.

1661 Cavalier Parliament convenes (–1679). Clarendon Code is passed (–1665). Savoy Conference convenes. Venner's Uprising of Fifth Monarchists occurs. Samuel Rutherford dies (b. 1600).

1662 Act of Uniformity is issued. Hundreds of Nonconformist clergy are ejected from their livings on St. Bartholomew's Day. Thirty-Nine Articles are reissued. Non-Anglicans are precluded from taking degrees at Oxford and Cambridge. Half-Way Covenant is signed in New England. Henry Vane dies (b. 1613).

1663 Gilbert Sheldon becomes Archbishop of Canterbury.

1664 First Conventicle Act is issued. Triennial Act is issued.

1665 Five Mile Act is issued. Anglo–Dutch War begins. Great Plague kills nearly 70,000 Londoners. First Baptist church organized in Massachusetts convenes.

1666 Great Fire of London occurs. John Bunyan publishes *Grace Abounding to the Chief of Sinners*.

1667 John Milton publishes *Paradise Lost*.

1669 Richard Mather dies (b. 1596).

1670 Second Conventicle Act is issued.

1671 John Milton publishes *Paradise Regained* and *Samson Agonistes*. George Fox visits America and Barbados.

1672 Declaration of Indulgence is issued.

1673 Test Act is issued. Declaration of Indulgence is withdrawn. James, Duke of York and heir to the throne, publicly declares himself a Roman Catholic. Sir Christopher Wren begins the rebuilding of St. Paul's Cathedral in London.

1674 William Coddington becomes the first Quaker governor of Rhode Island. John Milton dies (b. 1608).

1675 King Philip's War begins in New England (–1676). Governor John Leverett of Massachusetts rebukes Increase Mather for preaching on divine judgment.

1676 Fire destroys much of Boston. Roger Williams publishes *George Fox Digg'd Out of His Burrowes*.

1677 Massachusetts makes Sabbath-breaking a civil crime.

1678 John Bunyan publishes *The Pilgrim's Progress*. Popish Plot occurs. William Sancroft becomes Archbishop of Canterbury. Robert Barclay publishes an *Apology* for the Quaker movement.

1679 Exclusion Crisis deals with attempts to block James, Duke of York, from the throne.

1680 Whigs stage anti-papal processions in London.

1681 Charles II rules without Parliament. William Penn secures patent for Pennsylvania.

1682 Mary Rowlandson publishes *The Sovereignty & Goodness of God*, the first published narrative of a former Indian captive in America.

1683 Rye House Plot occurs. Roger Williams dies (b. 1603). John Owen dies (b. 1616).

1684 John Bunyan publishes *The Pilgrim's Progress*, Part II. Massachusetts loses its original charter.

1685 King Charles II dies. Reign of King James II begins. Monmouth Rebellion occurs. Bloody Assizes are conducted. Increase Mather is elected president of Harvard College.

1687 First Act of Indulgence is issued.

1688 Second Act of Indulgence is issued. Glorious Revolution occurs. James II abdicates the throne, escapes to France. William of Orange lands in England. John Bunyan dies (b. 1628).

1689 William and Mary are proclaimed King and Queen of England. Act of Toleration is issued. John Locke publishes *A Letter on Toleration*. Baptists issue Second London Confession. Attempt of Sir Edmund Andros to become royal governor over a consolidated New England is met with revolt in Boston.

1690 Church of Scotland formally constitutes itself. King William's War erupts in America between English and French (–1697).

1691 John Tillotson becomes Archbishop of Canterbury. Massachusetts receives a new royal charter. Massachusetts Bay Colony merges with Plymouth Colony. Richard Baxter dies (b. 1616). George Fox dies (b. 1624).

1692 Witchcraft trials occur in Salem, Massachusetts. Thomas Watson publishes *Body of Practical Divinity*. Cotton Mather publishes *Wonders of the Invisible World*.

1693 College of William and Mary is founded in Williamsburg, Virginia.

1694 Thomas Tenison becomes Archbishop of Canterbury.

1700 Samuel Sewall publishes *The Selling of Joseph*, the first book printed in America to oppose the slave trade. Increase Mather resigns Harvard presidency.

1701 Yale College is founded in New Haven, Connecticut.

1702 Reign of Queen Anne begins. Cotton Mather's *Magnalia Christi Americana* is published.

1707 Isaac Watts publishes *Hymns and Spiritual Songs*. Act of Union consolidates England and Scotland as the Kingdom of Great Britain.

1708 Saybrook Platform is passed in Connecticut.

1712 Final witch trial in England occurs.

1717 Marrow Controversy breaks out in Scotland (–1722).

1718 William Penn dies (b. 1644).

1719 Daniel Defoe publishes *Robinson Crusoe*.

1723 Increase Mather dies (b. 1639).

1726 William Tennent founds Log College. Samuel Willard publishes *The Compleat Body of Divinity*, American Puritanism's only systematic theology.

1727 Smallpox epidemic strikes Massachusetts.

1728 Cotton Mather dies (b. 1663).

1729 Jonathan Edwards succeeds Solomon Stoddard as pastor in Northampton, Massachusetts.

1734 First revival under Jonathan Edwards' ministry occurs in Northampton.

1740 Gilbert Tennent preaches "The Danger of an Unconverted Ministry." George Whitefield preaches for Jonathan Edwards. Great Awakening reaches apex in New England.

1741 Jonathan Edwards preaches "Sinners in the Hands of an Angry God."

1743 Charles Chauncy's *Seasonable Thoughts on the State of Religion in New England* provides impetus for Unitarianism.

1746 College of New Jersey (later Princeton) is founded in Princeton, New Jersey. Jonathan Edwards publishes *A Treatise on Religious Affections*.

1748 Isaac Watts dies (b. 1674).

1750 Jonathan Edwards is dismissed from Northampton congregation.

1754 French and Indian War erupts in America between English and French (–1763).

1758 Old Side/New Side Presbyterians are reconciled. Jonathan Edwards dies shortly after accepting Princeton presidency (b. 1703).

Introduction

Any Internet search for the terms "Puritan" or "puritanical" in the news these days is surely to return multiple derogatory references. For instance, on the date of writing this paragraph, 10 April 2006, upon typing in the word "Puritan" in Google News, one could discover on but the first page of "hits" an interview with Fox News by Hugh Hefner that criticized the hurt and hypocrisy of Puritanism, a London wire report scolding the puritanical censorship of the Rolling Stones in China, a plea that the Anglican communion of Australia not allow Puritan prejudice to bar women and gays from ordination, several websites likening the policies of George W. Bush to those of a Puritan theocracy, and even one newspaper article that blamed Puritanism for making digestion a stressful occurrence for many Americans. In short, the common perception of Puritanism in 21st-century media reflects the lasting appeal of H. L. Mencken's smarting definition: "Puritanism is the haunting fear that someone, somewhere, may be happy."[1]

Such scorn does in fact bear similarity to Puritanism's original detractors in the Church of England four centuries ago, although those critics' motivation to secure a uniform national faith was hardly the same as the preferment of personal liberties championed by Puritanism's detractors today. Lucy Hutchinson's biography of her husband John, for instance, probably written around 1640, reveals that Puritans from the beginning were commonly considered "seditious, factious, hipocrites, ambitious disturbers of the publick peace, and, finally, the pest of [the] Kingdome."[2] The direction of Puritan scholarship in recent years, however, has recognized that a presumption of moral priggishness is not nearly adequate evidence to condemn the Puritans to irrelevancy or even repugnancy. The full story of Puritanism is in fact one of remarkable diversity, vitality, and even allure, and so this dictionary seeks to provide a careful preening of its theological, literary, and historical tapestry.

As explained in the Preface, defining Puritanism properly requires attention to at least four major aspects of its history and influence: chronology, ecclesiology, theology, and politics. Each will now receive some elaboration.

CHRONOLOGY

When composing a dictionary focusing on important persons and events in a historical movement like Puritanism, it is necessary to have at least a working understanding of when the movement began and when it ended. However, unlike a similar work on, say, the Protestant Reformation, whose first great figure was clearly Martin Luther, or on the Russian czars, whose final representative was Nicholas II, Puritanism had no clearly visible doorman, nor any single person who turned out the lights. William Haller speaks representatively for the impression one gets from much Puritan scholarship when he concludes, "Who was the first Puritan and who may prove to be the last are questions one need not try to answer. There were Puritans before the name was invented, and there probably will continue to be Puritans long after it has ceased to be a common epithet."[3] Yet as accurate as this assessment is, it provides absolutely no guidance for a project such as this. One must still adjudicate who to include as the earliest Puritans, thus drawing a line somewhere between any religious predecessors of the group and the group itself, and again whom to consider the latest person or persons deserving to be called "Puritan" with a capital "P." Adding to the difficulty but also the consequence of one's decision-making—especially given that the focus here is on Puritanism in England and America—is the obvious realization that the time span of Puritanism's formal existence in America was clearly different from in the mother country.

According to Leland Ryken, William Tyndale is "often considered the first Puritan," perhaps because William Tyndale's 1525 vernacular Bible made him the first person to disobey the crown for the advancement of English Protestantism.[4] Yet while Tyndale was surely a very recent ancestor of the Puritans, it seems to be rather anachronistic to describe any Englishman as a Puritan before King Henry VIII had even divided the English church from Rome. Following the 1655 claim of Thomas Fuller's *Church History of Britain*, which attributed the first known use of the term "Puritan" to the year 1564, a number of scholars reasonably argue for the beginning of Puritanism as at least some time in the 1560s.[5] This was, after all, the decade when Thomas Cartwright began to promote Presbyterianism at Cambridge, opposition to vestments became an open and divisive controversy, and Robert Browne started to think through the virtues of independency. This is a good rule of thumb; it pinpoints the start of Puritanism to a relatively specific point in time, when multiple significant events occurred, without making any one of those events to stand apart from the others.

Even so, this dictionary considers the incipience of Puritanism as slightly earlier, although the difference really does not add a large number of names to the ledger of early Puritan worthies. It treats as the first Puritans those English Protestants whose entire religious outlook became defined by their reaction to the persecutions of Queen Mary I. It was when so many exiles spent time with John Calvin and other Reformed leaders on the continent from 1553 to 1558 that they collectively developed the theological sensitivities that drove them to campaign for a new Church of England once Elizabeth began her reign and they could return home. The agitation of these returned exiles over Elizabeth's *via media*, as one finds in John Knox, broke out into the first signs of recognizable Puritanism mentioned earlier. Thus, Dan D. Danner claims that Puritanism really organized in Geneva,[6] and Horton Davies agrees that the Puritan manner of intense biblical devotion came into England through Marian repatriates like William Whittingham and Miles Coverdale.[7]

If, then, the approximate start of English Puritanism was the late 1550s, when was its conclusion? The number of presumed answers to this question in the secondary literature is also quite varied. Patrick Collinson draws the line after the Hampton Court Conference of 1604, when the Puritans' failure to draw concessions from King James I marked a clear turning point from intra-church criticism to increasing displays of apologetic dissent.[8] It is impractical to close the book on Puritanism so early because it would exclude many Separatists, however, one may properly reject Collinson's opinion on this matter. B. R. White believes that the Restoration of King Charles II in 1660 was the death knell of Puritanism because the crown's retribution against the Puritans for his father's execution forced English ministers either to return to Anglicanism or preach in private to discombobulated congregations of Nonconformists.[9] There is poignancy in White's observation, for the ultimate triumph of the Stuart dynasty over the Protectorate of Cromwell undeniably signaled Puritanism's wane. Yet John Bunyan, Richard Baxter, John Owen, John Milton, and other notables all made their most lasting contributions to Christian history after the Restoration, and it would be harder to justify their removal from Puritanism than their inclusion.

Instead, it appears that Puritanism breathed its last in England as Enlightenment rationalism began to gather force. The Puritan Dissenters had in fact appeared to gain a second wind when the Act of Toleration once and for all recognized their freedom of worship in 1689. Yet this same Act, reflecting the temperament of John Locke, was really the harbinger of a rising latitudinarian spirit that stretched the accepted bounds of English Christianity so wide that it lost much of its theological depth. It also left Puritans no formal adversary against which to organize their reaction. As Christopher Hill explains, "Locke was a Christian, and he favoured religious toleration; but his Christianity was shorn of everything that had made Puritanism revolutionary—of direct contact with God, of enthusiasm—and his toleration was the rational calculation of the Toleration Act rather than the humanist idealism of a Milton."[10] The minimalist faith of Locke's early brand of Deism posited an absent God, who no longer summoned Puritans to enact his will.

Ironically, then, it was when the remnants of Puritanism finally secured their religious liberty for all future generations in 1689 that the glue that had given them cohesion finally dissolved. There was no enemy for them left to fight, and their toleration was really an indication of how little threat they still posed to the church–state establishment. In a sense, the Act of Toleration had made it so easy to be a Puritan that hardly anyone wanted to be one anymore. Also, many people were weary of the religious conflicts of the previous century and found the stability of the established church a welcome relief. In the end, therefore, "the Puritans lost, more or less, every public battle that they fought."[11] In a new era that valued reason over revelation, Puritanism became not only unappealing but actually disreputable.

Even those figures in the 18th century who still preferred Puritan biblicism to Anglican formalism largely saw that they would have no career outside the state church. Such was the case, for instance, with both John Newton, the former slave trader who became an Anglican priest, and John Wesley, the father of Methodism who never actually left the Church of England. Although both Newton and Wesley drew inspiration from Puritan authors, neither opposed episcopacy nor challenged the authority of the church—even when they were dissatisfied with it. Hence, Newton and Wesley were not Puritans. If there was a last English Puritan, though, their contemporary Isaac Watts (1674–1748) might very well qualify. What else would one call him? Unlike Newton and Wesley, Watts dared to remain a Nonconformist, and he could not attend Oxford or Cambridge because of it. He was a significant influence on American Puritans like Cotton Mather and Jonathan Edwards. And he is buried in the Bunhill Fields Dissenters' cemetery in London, nearby the tombs of John Bunyan, John Owen, Thomas Goodwin, and relatives of Oliver Cromwell. "Watts was a Puritan, an eighteenth-century Puritan," even if his contributions to evangelical hymnody actually helped sound the death knell for the Puritans' most beloved musical form, the psalter.[12]

At least the beginnings of Puritanism in America are fairly easy to identify. The Pilgrims who arrived in the New World in 1620 were mostly Separatists; the much larger Puritan group that came under the direction of John Winthrop in 1630 was more ecclesiastically conservative and began establishing state churches in Massachusetts Bay. Congregationalism was the predominant mode of Puritanism in America, although there were also Presbyterians scattered throughout the northern and middle colonies, and pockets of Baptists and Quakers as well, despite occasional legislation passed against them. Yet the attempt of Boston ministers like John Cotton to perpetuate American Puritanism through a strong church–state alliance obviously collapsed. Basil Hall opines that once the Puritans who had fled the state-regulated worship of England started their own church, they already ceased to be Puritans.[13] But because Puritanism actually originated in the desire to set the course of its nation, it should really be no surprise that even Congregationalists erected state churches when they finally could.

It does certainly appear unfortunate that Massachusetts Congregationalism proved incapable of tolerating persons like Roger Williams and William Penn whose religious outlook grew out of a similar Puritan impulse to promote godliness. But, nonetheless, the banishment of

Williams and Penn, and the antinomian crisis that likewise led to the expulsion of Anne Hutchinson, still proved the unassailable strength of the Puritans' societal vision through at least the 1650s.

It was when the original Puritan settlers had children and grandchildren who could never share their forebears' religious intensity that the older leaders began to see that their cultural grip was slipping away. Some historians locate the beginning of this "declension," and therefore the first concrete sign of American Puritanism's demise, in the Half-Way Covenant of 1662. When Puritan ministers felt compelled to baptize the children of unregenerate parents merely to keep their churches populated, then it became obvious to many that the earlier standards of Puritanism had relaxed.[14]

Michael G. Hall argues that the career of Increase Mather illustrates Puritanism's downfall. Mather was from the "first family" of New England Puritanism and its zealous defender for decades. But after King Charles II revoked the original charter for Massachusetts in 1684, effectively ending Puritan self-governance in that colony, Mather became the only representative of the older generation to sign the second royal charter in 1691.[15] The new royal charter meant that Anglicanism was now the official faith of Massachusetts and that use of the *Book of Common Prayer* was mandatory. The simple Puritan meetinghouse came increasingly to be displaced by the spires and stained glass windows of Anglican parish churches. Voting rights extended to all male landowners, not merely those who had supported the Puritan clergy as before.[16] For all practical purposes, the new charter entailed that "the New England national covenant scheme was broken."[17] That someone of the stature of Increase Mather would resign himself to this change amounted to a concession of Puritanism's defeat.

The reorganization of Massachusetts also allowed for an influx of new colonists who were attracted to the New World not because they cared for John Winthrop's "city upon a hill" but because they sensed economic opportunity.[18] Also, as more and more soldiers arrived to help secure the crown's interests against the French and Indians, Boston grew as a port town that catered to such non-Puritan interests as excess drinking and prostitution.[19] Enlightenment thought began to circulate throughout New England, too, and with it the spirit of Unitarianism. Increase Mather was forced from the Harvard presidency in 1701 and no longer equated New England with the new Israel as he had when he was younger.[20] In 1702, Cotton Mather's *Magnalia Christi Americana* lamented the departure of the "good old Puritans."[21] "The national covenant, once a mainstay of Puritan thought, was yielding to moralistic individualism."[22]

But of course, one cannot fully perform the postmortem report on American Puritanism until one has treated Jonathan Edwards. Indeed, for some scholars, Edwards was such "a deeply orthodox Puritan"[23] and so "loyal to the theology inherited from the 17th-century Puritans"[24] that he was truly "the quintessence of Puritanism."[25] With so much of the historical literature claiming Edwards as a Puritan, it seems hardly worthwhile even to consider a contrary argument, yet the great paradox of Edwards is that American Puritanism's greatest figure may also have been its last.[26] Edwards was a Congregationalist who opposed the ecclesiological compromise of the Half-Way Covenant, continued to defend the holiness of the Sabbath against those who used it for games and business, and ardently promoted orthodox Calvinism against Unitarianism. In other words, he remained entrenched against those main forces that eventually softened the old Puritan hegemony.

Yet Edwards was also influenced by the heightened emphasis on pious feelings—or "religious affections," as he called them—that had come to characterize the English revival movement of Wesley and the mesmeric George Whitefield. Puritans had always recognized the significance of inner transformation to complement outward confession, but they had also tended to be wary of excessive reliance on emotional display for fear that human hearts were so fallen as to be more likely to manufacture idols than obey God. Edwards was himself not a particularly emotive preacher, and he also discouraged reliance on feeling alone as secure evidence of one's salvation. Yet Edwards' openness to the new revivalism, seen supremely in his inviting Whitefield to share both his pulpit and leadership in the Great Awakening of the 1740s, also let into Puritanism the preferment of individual conscience that contributed mightily to the erosion of all established authority—even that of Edwards himself, who was dismissed from his Northampton, Massachusetts, church in 1750. Edwards died in 1758, and since "in many respects Jonathan Edwards was the last true Puritan," that year serves as a passable estimation of Puritanism's demise.[27] For at least by then, it is easy to see that even when "outward forms remained . . . the Puritan spirit was ebbing away."[28]

ECCLESIOLOGY

It would be much easier to define a Puritan doctrine of the church if one could only do so negatively—that is, by pointing out that expression of the church against which nearly all Puritans stood in opposition. Puritans uniformly believed that the Church of England had failed to advance the Protestant Reformation to a condition adequately attuned to the word of God. Thus, "the Puritan goal was to complete what England's Reformation began: to finish reshaping Anglican worship, to introduce church discipline into Anglican parishes, to establish righteousness in the political, domestic, and socio-economic fields."[29] But what alternative vision of the church did God expect? This was a highly volatile question. At first, claims Martyn Bennett, "Few of the Puritans in England were opposed to the episcopate form of church government as a general rule."[30] That is to say, the earliest persons to express dissatisfaction with the pace of reform within the Church of England desired to spur that reform from within, and so they presumed not only that governance by bishops was theoretically consistent with God's bidding, but further that the British monarch was truly the supreme bishop of that state church. According to Basil Hall, who relies on 17th-century sources Thomas Fuller and Richard Baxter, it was not until the outbreak of civil war in England around 1642 that the word *Puritan* came mostly to mean non-Anglicans, particularly Presbyterians and Independents and soon thereafter various types of Separatists.[31] This means that not only were some of the most noted early Puritans, such as William Perkins, William Ames, and John Foxe, lifelong members of the Church of England, but they were also the rule rather than the exception for nearly the first whole century of the Puritan movement, from the mid-16th to mid-17th centuries.

Yet Queen Elizabeth I (1558–1603), King James I (1603–1625), and King Charles I (1625–1649) commonly viewed the Puritans as grating disturbers of the ecclesiastical peace and therefore further as political liabilities. Elizabeth's *via media* between Reformed theology and Catholic liturgy could never admit the more strident Protestantism of those who had left to study with John Calvin during the reign of her half-sister Mary and who desired to reshape England into a reflection of Geneva after they returned. James agreed to receive the Puritans in 1604 at the Hampton Court Conference, but once he declined their Millennary Petition, even the favor of authorizing a new English Bible could not still their resentment. That umbrage accrued to itself a persecution complex once Charles authorized the suppression of Puritan ministers through the policies of Archbishop William Laud and other bishops. What gave particular offense to the Puritans, and correlatively what spurred the ecclesiological splintering of their movement, was the insistence of their superiors that conformity to the national faith required conformity in every minute detail to its liturgy. This was especially true when the Episcopal clergy's interpretation of Scripture on matters of church government was misaligned with the teachings of Geneva.[32]

A telling indication of Puritanism's ecclesial future was the influential refusal of John Hooper to wear vestments for his ordination as Bishop of Gloucester in 1551. Hooper declined to don the formal clerical garb of Anglican priests because it invoked for him both the Old Testament priesthood of Aaron, which had been invalidated by Christ, and, still worse, the suppression of the gospel by Catholic ceremonialism. "Unease over traditional vestments," B. R. White explains, "was not merely a sign of narrow bigotry, [for] it was a recognition that what people habitually saw might often speak more loudly than Protestant sermons."[33] Hooper's belief that he was no less a servant of the English church even for spurning its procedure became one of the clearest Puritan hallmarks, as various persons began to appeal to their own consciences to discover what they needed to uphold or avoid in order to bring about the long-awaited conclusion of the English Reformation. For a number of more radical Puritans, the *Book of Common Prayer*, particularly the more "Romanized" revision of 1559, also became a common target of conscientious objection.[34] John Bunyan became perhaps the most famous and outspoken person to refuse submitting his conscience to the Prayer Book. He lived by the dictum that faith comes not by ceremony but by hearing, for like most Puritans, his preferred manner of worship centered upon preaching. In 1646, John Geree's *The Character of an Old English Puritane* observed that a Puritan "was a man of good spiritual appetite, and could not be content with one meal a day. An afternoon sermon did relish as well to him as one in the morning."[35]

The willingness of Puritan leaders to rescue the church by dissenting from its rules created the fertile environment in which Separatism would later grow. According to White, it was primarily Laud's persecutions of Puritan ministers in the 1630s that made "the whole question of the nature of the church, its constitution and its proper government . . . a live issue for an increasing number of English Christians."[36] The original division of non-Anglican Protestantism was between the Presbyterians, whose church polity was invested in elders rather than bishops, and the Independents, who because they favored a government of congregationally elected ministers, also became known as Congregationalists in America. The Presbyterians and Independents often lived in uneasy coexistence during the English Civil Wars, not only because the Presbyterian leadership in Parliament and the Independent leadership of the army begrudged their dependence on each other, but also because the Presbyterians were unwilling to forfeit the hope that eventually all English Protestants would still coalesce around a Presbyterian-led state church. The Independents could not abide such ambition, but to prevent it they conducted a power play of their own, not only grabbing the nation's executive authority after King Charles' execution through the Protectorate of Oliver Cromwell, but also forcing many of the Presbyterian Members of Parliament out of their seats. Ironically, while these political maneuvers by the Independents effectively blocked the consolidation of a Puritan state church in England, the Congregationalists in America not only created state churches in colonies like Massachusetts Bay and Connecticut, but they so dominated the American Puritan scene that very few studies of American Puritanism even mention Presbyterians like Francis Makemie and Gilbert Tennent, who surely would be recognized as Puritans had they spent their careers in England.

To the left of the Independents were a large variety of religious groups that wanted their share of the spoils from the Puritan victory over the king, but which were increasingly willing to forgo a national church in their image simply for the guarantee of toleration. These groups were Separatists inspired by Robert Browne and Henry Barrow, who denied that it was even possible to maintain godly discipline in a church too closely allied with the state. The Baptists ended up being the most influential of these denominations. Although the Presbyterians and Independents often looked askance at the Baptists for their rejection of infant baptism and similarity in name to the theologically suspicious Anabaptists, and the Baptists in turn criticized the older Puritans for not entirely rejecting a state church, one should certainly consider the Baptists as an important part of the Puritan story because they perpetuated in their own way the Puritan emphasis of a godly churchmanship that preferred testimony to ceremony. White explains, "Their difference from the Puritans was primarily that of the urgency with which they acted rather than the ideals which they maintained."[37] Likewise should one consider the Quakers, perhaps the next most historically influential of the 17th-century Separatist groups, to be in the Puritan family despite their significant differences from other Puritans. The Baptists in large part still considered themselves to be defenders of historic Christian orthodoxy on such doctrines as the Trinity, the two natures of Christ, and salvation by sacrificial atonement, but the Quakers' theology was far more experiential and could treat even the Bible as a lesser spiritual guide than one's own direct encounter with God via the "inner light." Even so, the Quakers not only shared Puritan emphases on simplicity, sincerity, and separateness,[38] but, adds Richard E. Wentz, "latent within Puritanism's struggle to effect the pure life in community with others are the seeds of Quaker teachings."[39] Geoffrey Nuttall also attributes the origins of Quakerism to an "ardent Puritan search for reality."[40]

The American religious historian Winthrop Hudson calls Quakerism "the left-wing of the Puritan movement,"[41] but can one completely dismiss those sects even to its theological left from the Puritan ledger? The Ranters, Levellers, Diggers, Fifth Monarchists, Muggletonians, and similar groups whose agendas could no longer find audiences much after the Restoration of Charles II in 1660 also merit recognition as members of the extended Puritan family. One good reason, according to Harry S. Stout, is that most of these extreme Separatists were in fact disparaged as puritanical during their brief 17th-century existence.[42] Another reason is that these groups, like other Puritans, typically believed that their groups' unique activities could inaugurate the reign of King Jesus on earth in a manner that the lethargically conservative Church of England never could. Thus, although it is always prudent to remember that the first Anglican and Presbyterian Puritans would not have seen themselves as organically connected to the "hotter" secessionists,[43] the two main phases of Puritanism—conformist and nonconformist—have too much in common to be entirely distinguished in a project such as this one. As William Haller expounds, "The relation of the Puritan Presbyterian reformers to the Puritan sectaries and independents, of Puritan orthodoxy overshooting its mark to Puritan individualism running wild, is of importance for the understanding of the Puritan movement."[44] This is simply because all these groups, although their political center could not hold the victory they combined to win over the monarchy, eventually shared the common ecclesiological conviction that their church could be a purer manifestation of the people of God than the Anglicanism directed from the throne of Elizabeth and the Stuarts. In this regard, the later radicals even proved the general rule of their Puritan forebears, from whom they inherited a continuous stream of iconoclasm, which lived to oppose excessively formal religion as papist and antichristian, all for the sake of a more godly society.

THEOLOGY

When one thinks of Puritan theology, one likely thinks immediately of a single theological system, whether pejoratively or appreciatively: Calvinism. Never mind, as Basil Hall says, that most Puritan writers actually did not cite John Calvin very often by name.[45] For the genesis of Puritanism was truly Calvin's influence on those Marian exiles who could not remain satisfied with the religious status quo when they returned to their homeland. Most Puritans on both sides of the Atlantic presumed and preached in common the basic tenets of Calvinist thought: human depravity, divine sovereignty, and predestination unto salvation. Indeed, as fractured as the various ecclesiological expressions and even political ambitions of Puritanism became, Calvinism may very well have provided the vertebrae that held the whole movement together. The secondary literature on Puritanism, therefore, expectedly and rightly recognizes that Puritan thought was "shaped by a theology which was broadly Calvinist in type," even if this Calvinism became adaptable to multiple expressions besides the presbyter-based polity of Geneva.[46]

Calvinism provided the lens through which the majority of Puritans could read the Bible and discern the will of God most clearly, and the creeds of Puritanism, like the Presbyterians' Westminster Confession and the Independents' Savoy Declaration, bear its firm imprint. Calvinism explained adequately to Puritans why the same Christ who invited "whosoever will" to come unto him also declared that no one would in fact come to him unless so drawn by God the Father: so deep was the effect of original sin in human nature that none would respond positively to the gospel call except the elect, and, in turn, only the elect would want to preach for God's glory. There is little question that the major spokespersons of the Puritan movement, like William Perkins, William Ames, John Owen, John Cotton, and Jonathan Edwards, to name but a few, were not only Calvinists but also outspoken opponents of Arminianism's greater emphasis on human decision-making. The Synod of Dort, which met in Holland in 1619, most famously formalized the orthodox Calvinist beliefs of the era.

Yet once again, Puritanism was not a monolithic movement, even in its theology. Not only did some groups like the Quakers on Puritanism's left edge wholly reject Calvinist soteriology, but so did other figures closer to the Puritan center. The Baptists provide the most obvious example. Although the larger portion of Baptists in the 17th century eventually proved to be the Calvinistic kind often called the Particular Baptists, the older pocket of English Baptists were known as General Baptists for their belief that Christ's atonement does not apply only to the individual elect. John Smyth and Thomas Helwys were the first and most visible of these Arminian Baptists. The Presbyterian Richard Baxter, despite his fame for penning *The Reformed Pastor*, was viewed nonetheless by some as promoting an Arminian or Amyrauldian view of salvation that made saving grace dependent upon human acceptance as a kind of work. And John Goodwin, a Puritan preacher who gave vocal support to anti-Royalist forces during the Civil Wars, was an acknowledged Arminian.

Because even in its theology, then, the Puritan mainstream must admit exceptions, some have suggested that Puritanism should be more conveniently understood as a moral force rather than a theological one. A. G. Dickens argues, for example, "In the last resort Puritans were denoted and united less by theological dogma than by attitudes of mind and by a way of life."[47] Typical features of the Puritan morality might include regular church attendance, Sabbath keeping, sexual propriety, and the rejection of gambling and profanity.[48] This is the kind of list that still vilifies the Puritans to many today, although Edmund Morgan wonders if the reason why "we have to caricature the Puritans [is] in order to feel comfortable in their presence."[49]

Yet one ought not to reduce Puritan theology only to a list of ethical rules. First, the Puritans themselves would not have admitted the distinction, believing as they did that rectitude in morality was not only inseparable from but also the expected consequence of rectitude in theology. The willingness to segregate morality and theology is a modern sensibility, and the trustworthiness of observers who reduce Puritanism only to a moral code, ostensibly in order to ridicule it by later standards, is highly suspect. David Daniell explains, "Now, to try to construct a picture of 'Puritanism' from the satirical publications of its enemies is like trying to study Soviet missile strength in the 1950s using only information supplied by the Pentagon."[50] Besides, the Puritans were not necessarily the legalistic killjoys that its critics typically assume.[51] Second, dismissing the Puritans' theology under the pretense of assessing their morality actually provides no advantage for assessing Puritanism as a historical and cultural phenomenon. For although one could certainly adduce a list of frequent Puritan ethical concerns, like that in the previous paragraph, the range of Puritan morality on its more extreme wing was so diverse as to prove less useful for assessing the movement than the simpler theological rubric of Calvinism and its objectors. For some dissenters, like the Levellers and Diggers, for instance, puritanical morality was not about personal asceticism at all but about the redistribution of property. And for the Ranters and the Adamites, scant though their numbers were, sexual mores were actually libertine rather than austere.

The description "Puritan" may never have been a denominational title, but it was always and irreducibly a theological one, even when that theology took unorthodox expressions in the movement's left flank.[52] Hence, while this dictionary is noncommittal and interdisciplinary, it concedes the veracity of Ryken's caution: "The secular interpretation of Puritanism is the product of an irreligious age and overlooks that, even in its political and social and economic manifestations, Puritanism expressed a religious outlook."[53]

POLITICS

Common political opposition to King Charles I was nearly as significant to Puritan identity as was the common ecclesial opposition to a ruthless episcopacy. Of course, Puritanism predates Charles' reign by several decades, and William Bradshaw's *English Puritanisme* was already noting the movement's desire to effect political change in 1605.

But it was not until Charles' reign during the 1630s that Puritanism took on a new dimension that would become integral to the latter half of its existence: the willingness to fight for its religious vision via political power. Indeed, several scholars have observed that while some 17th-century sources defined Puritanism ceremonially, others doctrinally, and still others morally, as often as not they did so politically.[54] There are exceptions to this general trait, like the pacifistic Quakers, but the Puritan temperament did not easily abide disappointment and usually rationalized taking up arms for the cause of national godliness. In the description of Daniel Neal, the Puritans reasoned that, "after so many years' waiting [on the king], it was lawful to act without him, and introduce a reformation in the best manner they could."[55] The Presbyterians were the first to see the opportunity that political influence afforded for removing Charles and his oppressive Archbishop of Canterbury, William Laud. Indeed, the more Laud sought to repress the Puritans, the more he seemed to fuel their ire against both the king and the church.[56] Largely under the leadership of John Pym, the Presbyterians gained control of the Long Parliament and frequently named themselves to military posts in the earliest efforts to control or capture Charles.

Because these politicians rarely had tactical training, army leaders persuaded them to pass the Self-Denying Ordinance and resign their field commissions in 1645. Once the New Model Army arose out of the ashes of the Parliamentary militia, Independent generals proved their abilities by turning the tide of the Civil Wars in the Puritans' favor, and then they used their influence to block Presbyterian ambitions to govern a new state church. The Independent John Milton defended this strategy in "On the New Forcers of Conscience" by cautioning, "New Presbyter is but Old Priest writ large." Milton was concerned that Presbyterians would court other Protestants' help until the king was removed, and then they would make mandatory their own preferred church form. But other groups felt just as wary about Milton's hero Oliver Cromwell once he became Commander-in-Chief and Lord Protector. One sees this concern particularly in the Levellers, who argued to no avail in the Putney Debates of 1647 that the army's leaders never had any desire to protect civil liberties.[57]

Douglas Campbell helpfully describes the Puritans' prevailing political philosophy when he advises, "We should remember that men first get liberty for themselves before they think of it for others."[58] So although it is true that many Puritans on both sides of the Atlantic were primarily concerned with securing their own religious freedom and then imposing their preferences on others in God's name, it was also the same Puritan impulse "to carry inferences from dogma into secular life" that sparked early democratic ideas.[59] The congregational polity of the Independents, for example, was as precious to the Baptists as the sacrament from which they took their name, and from its voluntary principle they developed the conviction that the extraction of the government from gathered churches could actually sanctify the state by maximizing the religious freedom of its most devout citizens. It was in the name of church–state separation, therefore, that Baptists joined in Parliament's "good old cause" against the king in the 1640s, even as their Connecticut heirs petitioned Thomas Jefferson to support disestablishment upon his election as the U. S. president in 1801. It was also as a Baptist—albeit briefly as one—that Roger Williams enshrined religious liberty in his Providence colony in the 1630s.

Williams believed that the godliest state was the one so completely free that no one dared usurp the prerogative of God to persuade a person of his or her theological errors. "There is [also] in Quakerism," reminds Wentz, "a certain continuation of the principle of Christendom and the Puritan desire for the holy commonwealth. Even [William] Penn's experiment [of Pennsylvania in 1682] assumed that toleration and pluralism would permit God's will to effect itself in an ideal society."[60] Perhaps the leftward sects of Puritanism abandoned the formal ideal of a national covenant with God, but their individual relationship with God still inspired their hopes for their nation. Across the Puritan spectrum, concern for the reform of personal lifestyle tended to extend into the realm of "concern for the reform of both secular and ecclesiastical politics."[61]

Even in their nadir, the Puritans still did whatever they could to inject their own serum of godliness into their society. For instance, when the Restoration proved the failure of the Puritans to hold their opportunity to govern England, they still hoped to check the crown by insisting on their religious liberty as the price of Charles II's coronation. That is, to the every end of the Interregnum (1660), the Puritans sought to use whatever political clout they had to maximize their contribution to the national morality. Charles, in fact, promised the requested freedom in his Declaration of Breda, but once in power he did not keep his word, and his revival of persecution against dissenters like Bunyan did much to dissuade a new generation from perpetuating the Puritan cause.

Bunyan himself, imprisoned from 1660 to 1672, seemed to recognize the passing away of the Puritan era, as his character Attentive in *The Life and Death of Mr. Badman* laments, "I will tell you a story of one that died some time since in our Town. The man was a godly old Puritan, for so the godly were called in time past."[62] Yet so long as Bunyan had breath, he never relinquished his hope that theological right might vindicate itself through political might, praying in the posthumously published *Of Antichrist, and His Ruine* that there might yet be a day when future English kings would become "Bout-Hammers" against all demonic forces at work in the world.[63] How could it be that Bunyan could, on the one hand, go to jail for refusing to recognize the king's authority in religious matters, and yet, on the other, plead with God for a king who could be the extension of divine rule on earth? Even the Puritan hagiographer Benjamin Brook explains matter-of-factly of Bunyan and many like him, "Their notions of civil and religious liberty were confused."[64] This confusion may very well have been Puritanism's fatal flaw.

CONCLUSION

Michael Watts wisely cautions students of Puritanism to acknowledge its irreducible internal diversity: "The Puritan desired liberty for self-expression in matters of religion, but not to the point where it would disrupt the decent order of the church; he challenged the rulings of the magistrate in ecclesiastical affairs, but not to the point of denying his authority; he scorned many of the rites of the established church, but not to the point of repudiating the church itself."[65] Yet this essay has also identified general trends that at least provide a general rule by which to measure one's qualifications for inclusion in the Puritan movement. This is possible because "the disagreements that rendered Puritans into Presbyterians, independents, separatists and baptists were in the long run not so significant as the qualities of character, of mind and of imagination, which kept them all alike Puritan."[66] Thus, in sum, Puritanism dated from approximately 1558 to 1689, with a few lingering Nonconformists for the next half century in England, and 1620 to 1758 in America; featured ecclesiological pliability, encompassing groups from reform-minded Episcopalians to Presbyterians to Independents to radicals; gave usual adherence to the doctrines of Calvinism, with a correlatively biblical morality consumed with living for God; and exhibited political ambition, often with a desire to conduct a holy union between church and *polis*.

NOTES

1. Quoted by Leland Ryken, *Worldly Saints: The Puritans as They Really Were* (Grand Rapids, Mich.: Zondervan Publishing House, 1986), 1.
2. Lucy Hutchinson, *Memoirs of the Life of Colonel Hutchinson with the Fragment of an Autobiography of Mrs. Hutchinson*, ed. James Sutherland (London: Oxford University Press, 1973), 44.
3. William Haller, The Rise of Puritanism (New York: Harper Torchbooks, 1957), 3.
4. Ryken, 1.
5. Benjamin Brook, *The Lives of the Puritans* (Morgan, Pa.: Soli Deo Gloria Publications, 1994), I.28–29; Douglas Campbell, *The Puritan in Holland, England, and America: An Introduction to American History* (New York: Harper and Brothers, 1892), I.xxvii; Ellwood Johnson, *The Pursuit of Power: Studies in the Vocabulary of Puritanism* (New York: Peter Lang, 1995), 10; Dan G. Danner, *Pilgrimage to Puritanism: History and Theology of the Marian Exiles at Geneva, 1555–1560* (New York: Peter Lang, 1999), 8–9; John Brown, *The English Puritans: The Rise and Fall of the Puritan Movement* (Geanies House, U. K.: Christian Focus Publications, 1998), 15; Horton Davies, *Worship and Theology in England: From Cranmer to Baxter and Fox, 1534–1690* (Grand Rapids, Mich.: William B. Eerdmans Publishing Company, 1996), I.41; Patrick Collinson, *The Elizabethan Puritan Movement* (London: Jonathan Cape, 1967), 60–61; J. I. Packer, *A Quest for Godliness: The Puritan Vision of the Christian Life* (Wheaton, Ill.: Crossway Books, 1990), 28.
6. Danner, 23, 47.
7. Davies, Horton. *The Worship of the English Puritans*, 3.
8. Collinson, 464–466.
9. Barrington R. White, *The English Puritan Tradition* (Nashville, Tenn.: Broadman Press, 1980), 13.
10. Christopher Hill, *The Century of Revolution, 1603–1714* (New York: W. W. Norton, 1980), 252.
11. Packer, 23.
12. Arthur P. Davis, "Isaac Watts: Late Puritan Rebel," *The Journal of Religious Thought* 13 (Spring-Summer 1956), 124.

13. Basil Hall, "Puritanism: The Problem of Definition," in *Studies in Church History, Volume II: Papers Read at the Second Winter and Summer Meetings of the Ecclesiastical History Society*, ed. G. J. Cuming (London: Thomas Nelson and Sons, 1965), 294–295.

14. David C. Brand, *Profile of the Last Puritan: Jonathan Edwards, Self-Love, and the Dawn of the Beatific* (Atlanta, Ga.: Scholars Press, 1991), 8.

15. Michael G. Hall, *The Last American Puritan: The Life of Increase Mather, 1639–1723* (Middletown, Conn.: Wesleyan University Press, 1988), xiv.

16. Peter W. Williams, *America's Religions: Traditions and Cultures* (New York: Macmillan, 1999), 105.

17. Brand, 8.

18. Williams, 104.

19. Michael G. Hall, 328–330.

20. Michael G. Hall, 305, 351.

21. Harry S. Stout, "Puritanism," in *Dictionary of Christianity in America*, ed. Daniel G. Reid, Robert D. Linder, Bruce L. Shelley, and Harry S. Stout (Downers Grove, Ill.: InterVarsity Press, 1990), 966.

22. Sidney E. Ahlstrom, *A Religious History of the American People* (New Haven, Conn.: Yale University Press, 1972), 280.

23. Richard N. Current, T. Harry Williams, Frank Freidel, and Alan Brinkley, *American History: A Survey*, 7th ed. (New York: Alfred A. Knopf, 1987), 82.

24. George M. Marsden, *Jonathan Edwards: A Life* (New Haven, Conn.: Yale University Press, 2003), 4.

25. Ahlstrom, 312.

26. Roger E. Olson, *The Story of Christian Theology: Twenty Centuries of Tradition and Reform* (Downers Grove, Ill.: InterVarsity Press, 1999), 494.

27. Brand, 1.

28. John Adair, *Puritans: Religion and Politics in Seventeenth Century England and America* (Stroud, Gloucestershire, U. K.: Sutton Publishing, 1998), 247.

29. J. I. Packer, 28.

30. Martyn Bennett, *The Civil Wars in Britain and Ireland, 1638–1651* (Oxford: Blackwell Publishers, 1997), 74.

31. Basil Hall, 289–290.

32. Horton Davies, *The Worship of the English Puritans* (Westminster, U. K.: Dacre Press, 1948), 3.

33. White, 13.

34. White, 17; Michael R. Watts, *The Dissenters: From the Reformation to the French Revolution* (Oxford: Clarendon Press, 1978), 18.

35. Quoted in Watts, 15, and White, 11.

36. White, 22.

37. White, 18.
38. Geoffrey F. Nuttall, *The Puritan Spirit: Essays and Addresses* (London: Epworth Press, 1967), 175.
39. Richard E. Wentz, *American Religious Traditions: The Shaping of Religion in the United States* (Minneapolis, Minn.: Fortress Press, 2003), 101.
40. Nuttall, 18.
41. Winthrop S. Hudson, *Religion in America: An Historical Account of the Development of American Religious Life*, 3rd ed. (New York: Charles Scribner's Sons, 1981), 9.
42. Stout, 964–965.
43. Perry Miller, ed., *The American Puritans: Their Prose and Poetry* (Garden City, N. Y.: Anchor Books, 1956), 3; Basil Hall, 286.
44. William Haller, 147.
45. Basil Hall, 295.
46. White, 12.
47. A. G. Dickens, *The English Reformation*, 2nd ed. (University Park, Pa.: Penn State University Press, 1993), 374.
48. Campbell, I.239.
49. Edmund S. Morgan, *The Puritan Dilemma: The Story of John Winthrop*, ed. Oscar Handlin (San Francisco, Calif.: HarperCollins, 1958), xi.
50. David Daniell, *The Bible in English: Its History and Influence* (New Haven: Yale University Press, 2003), xviii.
51. Ryken, 2–7; Adair, ix.
52. Edward Hindson, ed., *Introduction to Puritan Theology: A Reader* (Grand Rapids, Mich.: Baker Book House, 1976), 17.
53. Ryken, 11.
54. Christopher Hill, *Society and Puritanism in Pre-Revolutionary England* (New York: St. Martin's Press, 1997), 7; Campbell, I.238–239; Daniel Neal, *The History of the Puritans, or Protestant Nonconformists* (New York: Harper and Brothers, 1858), I.218–219.
55. Neal, I.182.
56. Watts, 66.
57. A. S. P. Woodhouse, ed., *Puritanism and Liberty: Being the Army Debates (1647–9) from the Clarke Manuscripts with Supplementary Documents* (Chicago: The University of Chicago Press, 1965), 11.
58. Campbell, I.l-li.
59. Woodhouse, 38.
60. Wentz, 102.
61. White, 10.

62. John Bunyan, *The Life and Death of Mr. Badman*, ed. James F. Forrest and Roger Sharrock (Oxford: Clarendon Press, 1988), 144.

63. John Bunyan, *The Miscellaneous Works of John Bunyan*, vol. 13, ed. W. R. Owens (Oxford: Clarendon Press, 1994), 481.

64. Brook, I.59.

65. Watts, 16.

66. Haller, 17.

The Dictionary

– A –

ABBOT, GEORGE (1652–1633). Archbishop of Canterbury. Abbot was born at Guilford in Surrey, the son of a cloth-worker. He received his early education at the Guilford grammar school and, in 1570, entered Balliol College, **Oxford**. He graduated B.A. in 1582 and M.A. in 1585. In 1583, he was elected to a probationary **fellowship**, at which time he was also probably **ordained**. He received his B.Th. in 1594 and his D.Th. in 1597. He was appointed master of University College in 1597 and dean of Winchester in 1600. Abbot played a prominent role in university affairs and held a variety of university offices, including senior dean and vice-chancellor of the university three times between 1601 and 1606. In 1603, he was a part of the delegation chosen to welcome **James I** to England upon his accession. Abbot gained Parliamentary representation for Oxford in 1604 and was a member of the **Hampton Court Conference**. He opposed the Puritan cause, but he was one of eight Oxford divines who participated in the translation of the **King James Version** of the **Bible**.

Abbot traveled to Scotland in 1608 to promote unification between the churches of Scotland and England, work which brought him to the attention of James I, who appointed him Archbishop of Canterbury in 1611. Abbot distinguished himself by harsh treatment of English **Catholics** and by measured **toleration** of **Nonconformity**. He also demonstrated principled resistance to the royal will, particularly with regard to the divorce of Lady Frances Howard and the **Earl of Essex**, and he opposed James' adoption of the *Book of Sports*. Abbot actively promoted a match between Princess Elizabeth and the Elector Palatine, but his opposition to the projected marriage of the Prince of Wales to the Spanish infanta brought him into conflict with

William Laud and others at the court. A hunting accident in 1622, resulting in the death of a gamekeeper, brought Abbot's authority into question, although he was formally pardoned by James. Abbot attended the king on his deathbed and presided over the coronation of **Charles I**, but conflicts with Charles, Laud, and the Duke of Buckingham led to Abbot's removal from the office of archbishop. He spent his last years in exile from court and died at Croydon.

Abbot was a prolific writer whose work reveals a strong **Calvinist** bent, but he did not join the Puritan call for reformation of the church. His two best-known works are his *Exposition on the Prophet Jonah* (1600) and his *Geography, or a Brief Description of the Whole World* (1599).

ADAMS, THOMAS (c. 1583–c. 1653). English writer and divine. Educated at **Cambridge University**, Adams received his B.A. in 1601, his M.A. in 1606, and was **ordained** in 1604. He served at several rural posts before his licensure as curate of Northill in Bedfordshire in 1605 and his subsequent appointment to the vicarage of Willington in 1611. While at Willington, Adams gained prestige as a **preacher** and began to publish his sermons, including *The Gallants Burden* (1612) and *The White Devil* (1621). In 1614, Adams was appointed vicar of Wingrave, where he remained until 1618. He also held a **lectureship** during this time at St. Gregory's under St. Paul's Cathedral, an appointment he lost when King **James I** began to curtail such lectureships in 1623. Adams served as rector of St. Bennet's from 1619 until the early 1640s, when his endorsement of the monarchy and ecclesiastical hierarchy led to his sequestration. In his last years, Adams relied on the support of his former parishioners, to whom he dedicated his last two published sermons, *God's Anger* and *Man's Comfort* (1653).

Adams's **Calvinist** theology, opposition to enforced ceremony, and strong opposition to **Catholicism** alienated many contemporary high-church **Anglicans**, while his commitment to the crown and the Anglican form of church government earned him the disapprobation of Puritan extremists. Today, he is recognized as a master of pulpit oratory. Called the "prose Shakespeare of Puritan theologians" by Robert Southey, he has also been ranked with John Donne, his friend and patron, as one of the finest writers of 17th-century religious prose. Adams's **preaching** employed theatrical and literary conventions of the day. Most notable is his use of the satiric prose character sketch popularized by Sir Thomas Overbury. In addition to his many published sermons, Adams wrote several treatises, as well as a massive commentary on Second Peter.

ACT OF TOLERATION. Under King William III, **Parliament** passed the Act of Toleration on May 24, 1689, granting freedom to all **Nonconformists**, including **Baptists**, **Congregationalists**, and **Quakers**. The act allowed these groups to maintain their own places of **worship** and their own **preachers**, though it subjected the preachers to oaths of allegiance. Although the act extended freedom of worship to these groups, it continued to deny them certain social and political freedoms, including the right to hold public office. Previous attempts to increase religious liberties under **Charles II** and **James II** (*see* DECLARATIONS OF INDULGENCE) had been revoked because they also extended **religious liberty** to Roman **Catholics**. The Act of Toleration did not allow freedom of worship to Catholics. It also excluded Unitarians.

ACT OF UNIFORMITY. In the 16th and 17th centuries, three Acts of Uniformity were passed to create unity of practice in the Church of England. The first of these was passed in 1552 during the reign of **Edward VI**, requiring the use of the *Book of Common Prayer* in all services of the English Church. After the death of Queen **Mary I**, **Parliament** passed the second Act of Uniformity, which imposed similar measures to those of the 1552 act. It was passed along with the Act of Supremacy, restoring the Church of England as the national church.

The most famous Act of Uniformity was passed in 1662, after the **Restoration** of **Charles II**, as a part of the **Clarendon Code**, which also contained the **Conventicle Act**, the **Five Mile Act**, and the **Corporation Act**. This Act of Uniformity required clergy to swear their assent to everything contained in the *Book of Common Prayer*, the use of which was made compulsory in all church services. It was in many ways a reprisal for the abolition of **Anglicanism** during the **Commonwealth** (1642–60), at which time conforming priests were deprived of their benefices. With Anglicanism restored, the **Cavalier**

Parliament now took measures guaranteed to drive the Puritan **preachers** from their pulpits. The 1662 act led to the eviction of more than 2,000 ministers from their parishes.

ALLEINE, JOSEPH (1634–1668). English minister. Alleine, the son of a Puritan clothier, was born in Devizes, Wiltshire. His older brother Edward preceded him in the ministry but died in 1645, at which time Alleine expressed his desire to pursue a ministerial vocation as well. He entered Lincoln College, **Oxford**, in 1649 but moved to the more Puritan Corpus Christi College in 1651. He received his B.D. in 1653 and remained at Corpus Christi as tutor and then chaplain. Although he was offered high preferment in the state, Alleine declined, instead accepting an appointment to serve as assistant to the eminent Puritan divine George Newton at St. Mary Magdalene in Taunton, a center of Puritanism and the wool trade. Shortly thereafter, he married his cousin, Theodosia Alleine.

While at Taunton, Alleine gained recognition for his **preaching** and for his commitment to saving the lost. He continued in this role until 1662, when he, along with Newton, was ejected from the ministry under the **Act of Uniformity**. Alleine continued preaching, for which he was indicted, fined, and imprisoned. Upon his release, he resumed his preaching despite ill health and was again imprisoned, this time under the **Conventicle Act** and the **Five Mile Act**. He died at age 34, shortly after his second release from prison.

Alleine's enduring work is his enormously popular *Alarm to the Unconverted*, a book Iain Murray calls "a true model of Puritan evangelism." Persons who acknowledge the influence of this book on their own thought and work include **George Whitefield** and Charles Haddon Spurgeon. Alleine's ministry is recorded in Theodosia Alleine's account of her husband's life.

ALSOP, VINCENT (c. 1630–1703). English **Nonconformist** divine. Alsop's father was the rector of South Collingham, Northamptonshire, where Alsop was born. He attended Uppingham grammar school and entered St. John's College, **Cambridge**, as a sizar (a student required to pay minimal fees) in 1648, though there is no record of his graduation. He was **ordained** a deacon in the **Anglican** church and served as assistant-master in the free school of Oakham, Rutland.

By his own account, Alsop lived disreputably until he fell under the influence of Benjamin King, a local minister, whose daughter he later married. He was subsequently ordained for ministry in the **Presbyterian** Church and served as minister in Wilby, Northamptonshire, until 1662, when he was ejected from office under the **Act of Uniformity**. He was imprisoned for six months, for allegedly praying with a sick person.

Alsop achieved fame with a book titled *Antisozzo*, published in 1675, a witty attack on William Shedock, the dean of St. Paul's, whom Alsop depicted as a **Socinian**. The book was written in the manner of **Andrew Marvell**'s *Rehearsal Transposed* and helped its author procure an appointment in Westminster as an **Independent** minister, which he held until his death. He was succeeded in this pulpit by **Edmund Calamy**. An advocate of **religious liberty**, Alsop endorsed **James II's Declaration of Indulgence** in 1687. He was an original manager of the Common Fund, which was established to help aged ministers, poor churches, and to educate candidates for ordination. He served as a **lecturer** at Pinner's Hall and at Salter's Hall. In his later years, Alsop was also active in efforts at ecclesiastical compromise.

Other works by Alsop include *Melius Inquirenduni* (1679) and *Mischief of Impositions* (1680). Noted for their compelling rhetoric and satiric wit, both are considered classics of the Nonconformist movement.

AMBROSE, ISAAC (1604–1664). English **Presbyterian** divine. The son of a clergyman and descendent of a prominent **Catholic** family, Ambrose was born in Ormskirk, Lancashire. His father was Richard Ambrose, the vicar of Ormskirk. Ambrose entered Brasen-nose College, **Oxford**, in 1621; he graduated B.A. in 1624 and was **ordained** the same year. He was appointed to the curacy of Castleton in Derbyshire in 1627 and was made vicar of Clapham, Yorkshire, in 1629. Through the influence of the Earl of Bedford, he was incorporated M.A. at **Cambridge** in 1632. He was also appointed one of the king's four **preachers** in Lancashire, after which he settled in Garstang. In 1633, he was appointed vicar of Preston. Ambrose was arrested and briefly taken prisoner in 1642 and again in 1643 by the king's commissioner of array but was released through the influence of his wealthy supporters.

Ambrose was a prominent leader in the establishment of Presbyterianism in strongly Catholic Lancashire. He was empowered to ordain ministers, served as a moderator of the seventh Lancashire classis, and supported the **Westminster Assembly**. He also served as a disburser of relief after the **English Civil Wars**. He was briefly imprisoned again in 1649 for signing the "Agreement of the People Taken into Consideration." Ambrose remained at Preston until 1654 when he returned to Garstang as minister. During the **Commonwealth**, Ambrose served on the committee for the ejection of "scandalous and ignorant ministers and schoolmasters." In 1662, he was ejected from church office under the **Act of Uniformity**. He died two years later at Preston of apoplexy.

Ambrose is notable among the Puritan writers for his warm and lively prose, which is often striking for its eloquence and depth of feeling. His writing reveals a strong commitment to **Calvinism**, though it is generally not controversial, evincing rather a concern for personal meditation and likeness to Christ. His most popular work is *Looking to Jesus* (1658); other works include *Prima, Media, and Ultima* (1650); and *War with Devils and Ministration of and Communion with Angels* (1661).

AMES, WILLIAM (1576–1633). English divine, theologian, and university professor. The son of William Ames, a merchant, and his wife, Joan Snelling, Ames was born in Ipswich. His parents died when Ames was a child, and he was brought up by his maternal uncle at Boxford, a Puritan stronghold in Suffolk. His uncle provided for his education and sent Ames to Christ's College, **Cambridge**, a center of **Nonconformist** thought, where he studied under the tutelage of **William Perkins**. Ames earned a B.A. in 1598, an M.A. in 1602, and received a teaching **fellowship** the same year. He became a leading figure at Cambridge of the Puritan cause, refusing to wear the **surplice** and eschewing ceremonialism. In 1609, he preached a St. Thomas Day **sermon** denouncing gambling, a pasttime that the **Anglican** Church sanctioned during the Twelve Days of Christmas. The sermon resulted in his suspension from **ordination** and the revoking of his academic degrees. Ames left Christ's College and sought a pastorate, but **George Abbot**, **Archbishop of Canterbury**, refused to grant him a license. He moved to **Holland**, then a refuge for many

English Nonconformists. He briefly joined the congregation in Leiden, where **Henry Jacob** and **Robert Parker** were members. In 1611, he became chaplain to Sir Horace Vere, commander of the English forces in the Netherlands, in whose service he remained until 1619. He also published, along with **William Bradshaw**, a book titled *English Puritanisme* (1610). Ames married while in Holland, and upon the death of his first wife, married again in 1618.

In 1618–19, Ames represented the English **Calvinist** party at the **Synod of Dort**, which formulated the five points of Calvinism in response to the five points of the **Arminian Remonstrants**. He served as paid adviser to the synod president. In 1622, Ames was installed as a professor at Franeker in Friesland. Despite raucous students and contentious colleagues, Ames was prolific during his years at Franeker, building a strong reputation among Reformed theologians, and he served as *rector magnificus,* the university's highest office. Distressed by students' play-going, gambling, swearing, drinking, and Sabbath breaking, he also sought to bring moral reform to the university but with little effect. In his later years, he accepted the call to serve as copastor with **Hugh Peters** to the English Protestant church in Rotterdam. However, he died of pneumonia shortly after his arrival when his house flooded. Peters preached his funeral sermon.

As a writer, Ames was both prolific and influential. His *Medulla Theologiae* (*Marrow of Theology*), published in 1623, is considered the first Puritan work of systematic theology, and his *De Conscientia* (1630) is a principal source of Puritan morality. The posthumously published *Fresh Suit Against Ceremonies* (1633), an exposition of the differences between the Puritan and Anglican parties, influenced **Richard Baxter** to embrace Nonconformity. Ames is seen as a significant influence on English, American, and **Dutch Puritanism**.

AMYRAULDIANISM (also Amyraldism and Amyraldianism). Amyrauldianism, also known as "hypothetical universalism" and "four-point **Calvinism**," derives its name from the French Reformed theologian Moses Amyraut (1596–1664), who taught at the Protestant seminary in Saumer. Although Amyraut maintained the Calvinist doctrines of election and reprobation, he rejected the doctrine of limited atonement, the teaching that Christ's death on the cross atones only for the **sins** of the elect. Instead, he taught that Christ's atonement for sins extends to all of humanity, thus making **salvation** hypothetically universal; however, only the unconditionally elect, or those enabled by the Holy Spirit, could answer the call by repenting and believing. This teaching is seen by some as a moderate position between Calvinism and **Arminianism** and has much in common with Martin Luther's teaching of universal atonement and limited election.

In England, proponents of Amyrauldianism in various forms included **Richard Baxter**, **James Ussher**, and **John Davenant**. At the **Westminster Assembly**, **Edmund Calamy**, **John Arrowsmith**, and others represented the Amyrauldian position. Although the assembly did not include Amyrauldian views in either the catechism or confessions, neither did it specifically repudiate them.

ANABAPTIST(S). The term "Anabaptist," which literally means "rebaptizer," was originally a derogatory term applied to those who reject the practice of infant **baptism** and endorse the baptism of adult believers, usually with an insistence upon immersion. Though during the Reformation the term was often used to designate members of any radical Reformation group, the origins of the movement belong to early 16th-century Switzerland, Germany, and the Netherlands. The Hutterites, Mennonites, and Amish are modern-day descendants of the Anabaptist movement. The extent to which Anabaptists influenced the development of the **Baptist** movement is a matter of debate among church historians. The early Baptist leader **John Smyth** was for a time associated with Anabaptists.

In addition to adult baptism, Anabaptist groups commonly share a number of beliefs and practices. They seek to restore the church to what they believe to be its apostolic or primitive form. They believe that government is a worldly institution and that the church must be antithetical to it; hence, the holding of civic offices is prohibited, as is military service. They oppose capital punishment and the swearing of oaths. They are non-creedal, embracing **Scripture** alone as the absolute standard of truth. Anabaptists place great emphasis on living a holy life; they believe in the necessity of works, as well as faith. Furthermore, they advocate free will. A common practice of Anabaptist groups is the sharing of communal property.

During the Reformation, Anabaptists were persecuted by both **Catholics** and Protestants. Anabaptist activity in England seems to have begun in the 1530s, when adherents from the continent fled to England in the hopes of avoiding persecution. In this, they were disappointed. **Henry VIII** actively persecuted Anabaptists, and subsequent monarchs also took varying and generally effective measures to suppress the movement. Even at the height of the Anabaptist movement, the majority of Anabaptists in England are thought to have been refugees from other countries.

ANGLICANISM. The term "Anglican" denotes the beliefs and practices of the Church of England. The Anglican Church claims apostolic succession from the first followers of Jesus to the **ordination** of the first **Archbishop of Canterbury**, St. Augustine, in the sixth century. However the formation of a national church distinct from the Roman **Catholic** Church occurred in the 1530s when **Henry VIII**, seeking an annulment of his marriage to Catherine of Aragon, signed the Act of Supremacy, making himself, rather than the pope, the head of the Church of England.

It would have suited Henry had this alteration, along with the dissolution of the monasteries, proved to be the extent of the reformation of the English church. However, its theology and practice began to take a more Protestant turn under the leadership of **Thomas Cranmer**, whom Henry appointed Archbishop of Canterbury in 1533. Under Cranmer, celibacy of the priesthood was abolished, as was the doctrine of transubstantiation. During the brief reign of **Edward VI**, Cranmer and others continued to take the church in a Protestant/ **Calvinist** direction and produced the *Book of Common Prayer* (1549,1552), which not only sets forth the church's liturgy but serves as a practical rule of Anglican life and beliefs. Anglicanism was abolished during the reign of Queen **Mary I** from 1553 to 58, but when Queen **Elizabeth I** ascended to the throne, she restored the Church of England, with herself as its supreme governor.

Elizabeth faced the warring claims of the Puritans, who hoped to reform the church along **Presbyterian** lines, and the Catholic clergy who sought a restoration of the Catholic Church as the national church. In what is known as the **Elizabethan Settlement**, Elizabeth proposed a via media, or middle way, between these opposed forces.

The Anglican Church would continue to be an **episcopacy**; that is, it would continue to be governed by archbishops and bishops. All **worship** services would follow a fixed form set forth in the *Book of Common Prayer*, and the service would also retain some of the traditional elements of the Catholic service, including kneeling, genuflecting, and the wearing of **vestments** and **surplices** by the priest. However, the church would allow its members to believe anything not contrary to **Scripture**. In other words, it allowed for considerable differences in theological opinions. The basic principles and practices of Anglicanism were codified in the **Thirty-Nine Articles**, The Act of Supremacy, and the **Act of Uniformity**.

Under **James I** and **Charles I**, the Anglican Church remained the national church of England and tenuously maintained its middle road between **Catholicism** and Puritanism. During the reign of Charles I, the restrictive high-church policies of **Archbishop of Canterbury William Laud** alienated the Puritans. During the **Interregnum**, the Puritan faction effectively abolished Anglicanism as the national church, but the **Restoration** of the monarchy in 1660 also brought about the restoration of the Anglican Church. The Act of Uniformity, in 1662, as well as other ordinances, drove thousands of dissenting ministers from their pulpits. Only with the passing of the **Act of Toleration** in 1690 did the Anglican Church begin to take on its present form, still the national church but not the exclusive church of England.

ANNESLEY, SAMUEL (1620–1696). English minister. Annesley was born at Hasely, Warwickshire. His father died when he was four, but his mother saw to his education, and, in 1635, he entered Queen's College, **Oxford**, where he earned his B.A. in 1639. By 1644, Annesley appears to have been **ordained** as both **Anglican** and **Presbyterian** clergy. He may have been **lecturer** at Chatham. He served as a chaplain at sea to the Earl of Warwick, after which he was appointed to a prestigious and lucrative incumbency at Cliffe, in Kent. The previous minister had been ejected for his Royalist sympathies, and his devoted parishioners initially treated Annesley with hostility, although he seems to have eventually earned their goodwill.

During the **Interregnum**, Annesley established himself as a lead figure in the Puritan movement. In 1648, he was asked to preach a fast day **sermon** before the House of Commons; he was also granted the degree of Doctor of Laws by Oxford University, and was once again at sea in the service of the Earl of Warwick. In 1657, **Oliver Cromwell** appointed Annesley as lecturer at St. Paul's Cathedral, and, in 1658, **Richard Cromwell** appointed him to the vicarage of St. Giles, Cripplegate. In 1660, he served as a **trier** for the approbation of ministers, and, in 1661, he edited *The Morning Exercise at Cripplegate,* a popular sermon collection. However, with the **Restoration** of the monarchy (1660) and the issuing of the **Act of Uniformity** in 1662, Annesley was ejected from office. He continued to preach privately, and on one occasion had his personal property seized for keeping a **conventicle**. In 1672, he erected a meetinghouse in Spitalfields. Licensed as a Presbyterian, he preached there until his death.

Annesley's funeral sermon was preached by **Daniel Williams**, and he is the subject of an elegy by **Daniel Defoe**, who was a member of his congregation. He was also the father of Susanna Wesley, the mother of John and Charles Wesley.

ANTINOMIANISM. From the Greek *anti* (against) and *nonos* (law). Antinomianism is the belief that because Jesus has freed Christians from the moral law, they are not obliged to obey it. While antinomianism was often attacked as a warrant for **sin** and lawlessness, most individuals accused of holding antinomian views believed that the individual was bound to obey promptings of the Holy Spirit, and that such submission would keep him or her from sin.

Antinomian teachings seem to have been current as early as the apostolic era, leading the Apostle Paul to clarify his teachings on the law in Romans and his first letter to the Corinthians. It was Martin Luther, however, who coined the term to characterize the teachings of Johannes Agricola. Luther taught justification by faith alone but that the law was still essential for revealing sin, leading the individual to repentance, establishing social order and decency, and giving the Christian a rule of life. Agricola opposed these teachings, claiming that the law had no essential function for the redeemed soul, a position he ultimately recanted.

In England and America, the term "antinomian" was often used to label any individual whose teachings tended to minimize the importance of the law in the Christian life. Many members of the Puritan clergy labeled a popular devotional work by **Edward Fisher** titled *Marrow of Modern Divinity* as antinomian (*see* MARROW CONTROVERSY). In Massachusetts, **Anne Hutchinson** was banished in 1636 for teaching what authorities considered a form of antinomianism. Both Fisher and Hutchinson claimed that obedience to the law was not a necessary part of one's preparation for conversion.

ARCHBISHOP OF CANTERBURY. The primate of all England, highest ecclesiastical position in the Church of England. The first Archbishop of Canterbury was Augustine in the sixth century. Prior to the English Reformation, the archbishop was head of the Roman Catholic Church in England and thus also served as the English representative of the pope. When **Henry VIII** declared himself the head of the English Church in 1534, he replaced then archbishop William Warham with **Thomas Cranmer** (1533–56), a cleric with strong Protestant convictions who was executed as a heretic by Queen **Mary I**. Mary's choice for Archbishop was Reginald Pole (1553–56), who helped reimpose **Catholicism** on England and who died within hours of Mary. During the period from the restoration of the Church of England under Queen **Elizabeth I** (1558) to the **Glorious Revolution** (1689) a principal issue of the office was the question of how much latitude to give to **dissenters** and **Nonconformists**.

Three men served as Archbishop of Canterbury under Queen Elizabeth. The first, Matthew Parker (1559–76), reluctantly accepted the position and bore the difficult task of instituting Elizabeth's via media, or "middle way," between Catholicism and the Puritan movement. Parker laid out the regulations for the church service in his "Advertisements" and generally enforced strict conformity, though he yielded somewhat on the issue of wearing **vestments**. Following Parker, Edmund Grindal (1576–83) showed considerable tolerance to Nonconformists and was ultimately suspended from his office for refusing to suppress Puritan prophesyings and **preaching**. After Grindal, Elizabeth selected John Whitgift (1583–1604) who, more than his predecessor, conscientiously sought to maintain Anglican uniformity, though he later made some concessions to the Puritans, such as signing the **Lambeth Articles** and approving the translation of the **King James Bible**.

The first Archbishop of Canterbury chosen under the Stuart dynasty was Richard Bancroft (1604–11), who continued the strict enforcement of uniformity, resulting in many clergy being deprived of their offices. Bancroft was succeeded by **George Abbot** (1611–33), who vigorously suppressed extremists, but on the whole was also fairly tolerant of moderate Puritans. He himself refused to read the *Book of Sports* from his pulpit. Abbot was replaced with **William Laud** (1633–45), a radical **Anglican** who enforced strict conformity and exercised sometimes brutal suppression of dissenters. Of all the Archbishops of Canterbury between 1558 and 1689, Laud bore the greatest antipathy to the Puritan movement and contributed more than any other to the polarization of the English Church. During the **English Civil Wars**, **Parliament** ordered his execution and abolished the **episcopacy**.

When the episcopacy was restored under **Charles II**, William Juxon (1660–63) was selected as the new Archbishop, but age and declining health prevented him from taking an active part in church affairs. After Juxon, Gilbert Sheldon (1663–78) sought to unify the Church of England by supporting the **Act of Uniformity**, which led to the ejection of over 2,000 ministers from the church. William Sancroft (1678–89) continued his predecessor's policy of suppressing Nonconformity, opposing legislation aimed at reconciling dissenters with the established church. He also opposed the **Declaration of Indulgence** (1687), for which he was committed briefly to the Tower. However, having sworn his allegiance to **James II**, Sancroft refused to do the same to William and Mary and was thus deprived of office in 1690. His successor, John Tillotson (1691–95), was the first Archbishop of Canterbury to oversee the English Church during the era of relative **religious liberty** created by the **Act of Toleration**.

ARMINIANISM. Designation for a set of beliefs that originated in the Netherlands and is named for Jacobus Arminius (1559–1609), a professor of theology at Leiden. In Arminius' view, the **Calvinist** doctrine of **predestination**, particularly as it was developed by John Calvin's followers, such as Theodore Beza and Hugo Grotius, led to the conclusion that God is the author of evil. Arminius offered a modified form of Calvinism that he believed was more compatible with human reason. In 1610, a year after Arminius' death, his followers, calling themselves the Remonstrants, developed five points based on Arminius' teachings and intended to revise then-accepted **Reformed theology**: conditional election (election is conditional upon human belief, foreseen by God); universal atonement (Christ died for all of humanity, creating the possibility of **salvation** for all but assurance for none); free will (human beings possess free will, despite the fall, and must freely embrace the offer of the gospel); resistible grace (human beings have the ability to reject the offer of grace); and uncertain perseverance (a Christian can lose his or her salvation after conversion). At the **Synod of Dort** (1618–19), Calvinist theologians met to develop their response; the result was the five points of Calvinism, as laid out in the Canons of Dordt. Accordingly, Calvinism and Arminianism became the two dominant, yet opposed, theological views of the Reformed movement.

Arminianism in many ways hearkens back to the teachings of the **Catholic** theologian Thomas Aquinas. In 16th-century England, it was especially popular among the members of the clergy who hoped to bring the English church back to its Anglo–Catholic traditions. Thus, it exerted its greatest influence during the reign of **Charles I** and after the **Restoration**. John Wesley, the founder of the Methodist movement, also embraced many of Arminius' teachings, as did the leaders of the General **Baptist** movement. Most Puritans, however, were Calvinistic in their theology and strongly opposed Arminianism.

ARROWSMITH, JOHN (1602–1659). Master of St. John's College, **Cambridge**, vice-chancellor of Cambridge University. Arrowsmith was born near Newcastle-on-Tyne, Northumberland, and entered St. John's College, Cambridge, in 1616. He graduated B.A. in 1619, M.A. in 1623, and was elected **fellow** of St. Catharine's Hall, Cambridge. In 1631, the same year he married, Arrowsmith became curate of St. Nicholas Chapel, King's Lynn. In 1642, he was one of two Norfolk ministers to be consulted on church affairs. In 1643, he was appointed as a member of the **Westminster Assembly**, where, along with **Edmund Calamy** and several others, he acted as an advocate of **Amyrauldianism**. Arrowsmith received his D.D. in 1644 and was appointed master of St. John's College, Cambridge in the same year. In 1645, he became rector of St. Martin Pomeroy, Ironmonger Lane.

When the **Long Parliament** established **Presbyterianism** as the Church of England in 1647, Arrowsmith served as a member of the Sixth London Classis. In the same year, he was appointed vice-chancellor of Cambridge University. In 1651, he was made Regius Professor of Divinity and in 1653 master of Trinity College. He was appointed one of the **triers** for examination of candidates for the ministry in 1654.

Arrowsmith was a leading Presbyterian in Cambridge and London during the **English Civil Wars**, and he was the author of many published **sermons**. Among his best-known works is *A Chain of Principles*, originally intended to illustrate 30 spiritual aphorisms, though Arrowsmith died after completing his treatment of only six. His *Tactica Sacra* (1657) urges a renewed commitment to church discipline and religious uniformity. *Theanthropos,* published in 1660, is a detailed exposition of John 1:1–18. Other published works include *Covenant-Avenging Sword Brandished* (1643), *England's Ebenezer* (1645), and *A Great Wonder in Heaven* (1647).

ASHE, SIMEON (c. 1597–1662). English **Nonconformist** minister. Ashe's date and place of birth are not known. He was educated at **Emmanuel College, Cambridge**, and **ordained** in 1619. Where he spent the first years of his ministry is not known, but in 1627, he was appointed Vicar of Rugely, Staffordshire. In 1633, he was ejected from office for refusing to read the ***Book of Sports*** or conform to established ceremonies. Under the protection of Sir John Burgoyne, he preached at a public chapel in Wroxhall, Warwickshire, where he was free from diocesan control. He was also able to preach under the protection of Lord Brook. Ashe remained in Warwickshire until 1639, when he was appointed military chaplain to the Earl of Manchester, whom Ashe would later defend in several pamphlets. He also was a **lecturer** at St. Bartholomew's Exchange (1641–42), St. Bride's (1642–46), and St. Michael's, Bassishaw (1646–52). He was nominated as a member of the **Westminster Assembly** of Divines, replacing Josiah Shute, who died before the Assembly began. He also preached frequently before **Parliament**.

Ashe opposed the trial and execution of **Charles I** and joined 58 other ministers in signing *A Vindication of the Ministers of the Gospel in and About London.* He stood on the scaffold at the execution of

Christopher Love in 1651. In 1655, Ashe received the rectorship of St. Augustine's in London and was a lecturer at St. Peter's, Cornhill. Under **Richard Cromwell**, he served as a **trier** for the approbation of ministers. When the monarchy was restored in 1660, Ashe was among the ministers sent to Breda to welcome **Charles II** back to England. Ashe died a few days before the passing of the **Act of Uniformity** in 1662, under which he would most likely have been ejected from the ministry.

Ashe is the author of several published **sermons**, and he served as editor to the works of other divines, such as **John Ball**, to whose works he also wrote many prefaces. He was the editor of a collection of funeral farewells, including sermons by **Edmund Calamy**, **Thomas Manton**, **William Jenkyn**, and **Thomas Watson**.

– B –

BABINGTON, GERVASE (1550–1610). Bishop of Llandaff, Exeter, and Worcester. Babington was born in Nottinghamshire. He matriculated at Trinity College, **Cambridge**, where he became a protégé of John Whitgift. He graduated B.A. in 1571, was appointed junior **fellow** in 1573, and received his M.A. in 1575. He was incorporated at **Oxford** in 1578 and became a university preacher at Oxford in 1580.

Babington was personal chaplain to the Earl of Pembroke. In this capacity, he is said to have helped Mary Sidney, the Countess of Pembroke and one of the first **women** in England to gain a literary reputation, with her translations of the Psalms. In 1588, through the influence of his patrons, Babington was presented with the prebends of Llandegla and Wellington. He became treasurer of Llandaff in 1589–90, and Bishop of Llandaff in 1591. In 1594, he was translated to the see of Exeter, and in 1597, Queen **Elizabeth I** nominated him as Bishop of Worcester, in which capacity he established himself as an energetic administrator and a constant preacher. He was appointed as a representative of the **episcopacy** at the **Hampton Court Conference** in 1604, though some suspected that Babington himself had turned Puritan. He was also the vice-president of the Royal Council in the Welsh Marches (1605). Babington died of a fever in 1610 and is buried in the cathedral of Worcester.

The strongly **Calvinist** Babington was sympathetic to the Puritan cause and was a voice of moderation between the Puritans and the established church. His collected works were published in 1615 and include annotations on the Pentateuch, The Ten Commandments, and The Lord's Prayer.

BALL, JOHN (1585–1640). English divine. Ball was born in Cassington, Oxfordshire. He was educated at the private school in nearby Yarnton and at the age of 15 entered Brasen-nose College, **Oxford**, as a servitor. He transferred to St. Mary's Hall and graduated B.A. in 1604, after which he took a post as tutor to the children of Lady Cholmondeley in Cheshire. In this capacity, he came to embrace Puritan ideals. He was **ordained**, without subscription, in 1610 and subsequently served as minister in Whitmore, a small, low-paying curacy near Newcastle, in Staffordshire, where he remained for the next 30 years. Ball also taught school and, in 1612, he married Ellen Buckenhall, with whom he had seven children.

Although he opposed separation from the Church of England, Ball was a committed **Nonconformist**. He frequently appeared in the ecclesiastical courts for refusing subscription, keeping **conventicles**, and, in one instance, for keeping a fast on Ascension Day. According to some sources, Ball was deprived of office by John Bridgeman, the Bishop of Chester.

Most of Ball's writings were published only after his death through the efforts of his literary executor and personal friend **Simeon Ashe**. They include *A Short Treatise Containing All the Principal Grounds of Christian Religion*, which went through 14 editions by 1632, and *A Friendly Trial of the Ground Tending to Separation* (1640), in which Ball argued against separation from the established church. His *A Treatise of the Covenant of Grace* (1645) is an early Puritan exposition of Covenant Theology.

BAPTISM. *See* SACRAMENTS.

BAPTIST(S). The Baptists originated as English **Separatists** who first called themselves the Baptized churches, or Churches of the Baptized way, before adopting the pejorative appellation "Baptists" as their own by the 1640s. Their distinctive religious beliefs were a rejection of any biblical warrant for infant **baptism** and an insistence on the separation of church and state. Yet although these twin emphases have broadly defined Baptists from the early 17th century to the present, the Baptists have also remained a remarkably diverse denomination. This is in large measure because there is no single founder of the Baptist faith, and so scholarly dispute exists over the full story of the Baptists' origins, and especially the degree of their relationship to the continental **Anabaptists**. However, most scholars of Baptist history agree that Baptists in England segregated largely along two tracts, the General Baptists and the Particular Baptists.

Many consider that English Baptist history begins with the dissenting minister **John Smyth**. Once an **ordained** minister in the Church of England, Smyth developed sympathy for **Nonconformity** and the idea that no government had a divine right to impose religious belief. Smyth gathered a congregation in Gainsborough, where one of his members for a brief time was **John Robinson**, who became the pastor to the group of Puritans who became known as the **Pilgrims**. Smyth became so reactionary against the formalities of **Anglicanism** that he forbade even the liturgical reading of **Scripture** in **worship** lest the extemporaneous movement of the Holy Spirit be quenched. For fear of government suppression of their illegal worship meetings, Smyth and **Thomas Helwys** left England for Amsterdam, **Holland**, in 1607. While in Holland, Smyth became convinced that his infant baptism had been invalid since the normative New Testament administration of baptism was for conscientious believers. In 1609, in the absence of any other true Christian body that could administer to him true baptism, Smyth rebaptized himself, probably by the affusion of water over the head, and then baptized the others. However, Smyth soon developed second thoughts over his actions after he met a group of Mennonites. Convinced that the Mennonites, one expression of the Anabaptists, did indeed have a true church, Smyth and a few of his members submitted themselves for membership in the Mennonite church. Believing to the contrary that they needed no verification for their actions by any other Christian body, Helwys and some other members decided to return to London to develop their newly organized faith in their own homeland. The church started by Helwys is now recognized as the first Baptist church on English soil. For arguing in *A Short Declaration of the Mistery of In-*

iquity (1612) that the crown had no right to interfere in the administration of his or any church body, Helwys was sentenced to Newgate prison, where he died.

The Baptist heirs of Smyth and Helwys are known as General Baptists for their advocacy of theological **Arminianism**, specifically its idea that the saving atonement of Christ is offered in a general way to all who voluntarily believe in him, and not only to the foreordained elect. Their doctrine was set forth most capably by Thomas Grantham in the Orthodox Creed of 1679. They rejected that any are **predestined** to damnation but affirmed that one could lose one's assurance of **salvation**. The General Baptists were not connected to the Anabaptists organically, but they did share common tenets and came at least for a short time under the influence of the Mennonites. The Particular Baptists, on the other hand, were proponents of **Calvinism** and expressly distanced themselves from the Anabaptists in their London Confession of 1644, which was modeled on the **Presbyterians' Westminster Confession** except for changes on baptism and church/state relations. The roots of the Particular Baptists appear to have been in the Separatist congregation of **Henry Jacob** in the Southwark section of London. Although Jacob himself did not become a Baptist, the history of his church under his successors John Lathrop and Henry Jessey tended increasingly in that direction. In 1638, some of the members of this church (known as the JLJ church, from the last name initials of its ministers), led by Samuel Eaton and Richard Blunt, formed England's first Particular Baptist church. In time, the Particular Baptists outgrew their General Baptist predecessors in both England and America. The insistence that believer's baptism should be in the mode of full immersion became commonplace among all Baptists by the mid-1640s, largely through the persuasiveness of writers like John Spilsbury. Perhaps the most famous Baptist of all was **John Bunyan**, the author of *The Pilgrim's Progress*, although Bunyan himself shied away from any denominational label and upset other Particular Baptists like **William Kiffin** by admitting to communion or even church membership persons who had not been baptized as adults or by immersion. A third group of early English Baptists, the Seventh-Day Baptists, insisted that true **worship** of God should take place on Saturday in accordance with the fourth commandment (Exodus 20:8). Because they had been committed to

millenarianism, in the hope that the **English Civil Wars** might augur the second coming of Christ, these Baptists did not survive in large numbers after the **Restoration** of the Stuart monarchy in 1660.

Roger Williams founded the first Baptist church in America at his Providence colony in 1639. Williams did not remain a Baptist but for a few months, however, and became one of those **Seekers** who doubted that any true church existed on earth. John Clarke founded another Baptist church in Newport in 1641. The earliest Baptist confession in America, the Philadelphia Confession, was Calvinist in theology and became in turn the guiding principle for the first association of Baptist churches, the Philadelphia Association, in 1742. The New Hampshire Confession of 1833 was more Arminian in nature.

BAREBONES (BARBON or BAREBONE), PRAISE GOD (c. 1596–1679). English leather seller, lay preacher, and Parliamentarian. Barebones was a member of the congregation established by **Henry Jacob**. When this church split in 1640, Barebones became pastor of one of the halves. In 1641, his **sermon** against the bishops and the *Book of Common Prayer* led to a riot when passersby overheard his oration and proceeded to smash the windows of the building, owned by Barebones, in which the service was being held. A number of Barebones' congregation were arrested.

Meanwhile, Barebones thrived in the leather sellers' trade and took an active part in local politics, serving as a common councilman from 1650–51 and as a member of the Committee of Safety in 1651. In 1653, Barebones was summoned to serve in the short-lived assembly that consequently came to be known as the **Barebones Parliament**. He was considered a radical, but although he shared the millennial views of the **Fifth Monarchists**, he did not directly support their movement. He did, however, actively oppose the **Restoration** of the Stuart monarchy in 1660, resulting in his seven-month incarceration for treason in the Tower of London. His later years brought financial trouble with the loss of his place of business in the great fire of London (1666).

Barebones wrote two books defending the practice of infant **baptism**: *A Discourse tending to prove . . . Baptism . . . to be the ordinance of Jesus Christ. As also that the Baptism of Infants is war-*

rantable (1642) and *A Reply to the Frivolous and Impertinent answer of R. B. and E. B. to the Discourse of P. B.* (1643). His millennial views are expressed in *Good Things to Come* (1675).

BAREBONES PARLIAMENT. *See* PARLIAMENT.

BARROW, HENRY (or Barrowe) (c. 1550–1593). Separatist and pamphleteer. Barrow was born in Shipdam, Norfolk, and entered Clare Hall, **Cambridge**, as a fellow-commoner, receiving his B.A. in 1570. He was a member of **Gray's Inn** but never came before the bar. He also initially sought preferment at the court, but around 1580 heard a **sermon** that caused him to retire to the country and devote himself to spiritual study. During this time, he developed strict Puritan views, which he held to for the rest of his life. He also became intimate friends with **John Greenwood**, a leader of the Separatist movement who influenced Barrow to embrace a radical form of **Congregationalism**.

In 1587, Barrow visited Greenwood, who was then incarcerated at the Clink, and was himself arrested and brought before Archbishop Whitgift. He refused to take the ex officio oath before the High Commission and was committed to the Gatehouse at Westminister. After several months in jail, Barrow faced a tribunal of privy councilors and ecclesiastical commissioners and was formally indicted, along with Greenwood, for recusancy. Neither could afford to pay the heavy bail imposed by the court, and Barrow spent the remaining six years of his life in prison. During his confinement, Barrow wrote extensively defending Congregationalism. His works include *A True Description of the Visible Congregation of the Saints* (1589) and *A Brief Discovery of the False Church* (1591). Though they were frequently labeled **Brownists**, Barrow and Greenwood endorsed a congregational position more extreme than that of **Robert Browne**, denying that the established church was a "true" church. Their followers came to be known as **Barrowists**.

In 1590, the bishops sent several conforming Puritan ministers to persuade Barrow and Greenwood to refrain from further writing, but to no avail. In 1593, he and Greenwood were charged with "devising and circulating seditious books," found guilty, and sentenced to death. After several reprieves, they were hanged on 6 April of the same year.

BARROWISTS. Early **Independents** or **Congregationalists**. The Barrowists followed the teachings **Henry Barrow** and **John Greenwood**, both of whom were executed in 1593. They held to many of the same principles as the **Brownists**, with the difference that the Barrowists utterly repudiated the Church of England as a false church, not even admitting the legitimacy of its **sacraments** or clergy. As such, Barrow, Greenwood, and their followers represent a radical extreme in early Congregationalism.

BASTWICK, JOHN (1593–1654). Physician and pamphleteer. The son of a wealthy yeoman, Bastwick was born in Writtle, Essex, and raised by his mother and his stepfather, Robert Cotton, who was a gentleman. Bastwick studied with the Puritan **lecturer Richard Rogers** and entered **Emmanuel College, Cambridge**, in 1614. However, in 1616, he left for the continent to study medicine, first at Leiden and later at Padua, where he received his M.D. in 1622.

Upon returning to England in 1624, Bastwick settled in Colchester, where he established a medical practice, but by 1625, he had moved to London, married Susanna Poe, the daughter of the prominent physician Leonard Poe, and set up practice anew. His association with the radical **Alexander Leighton**, as well as the publication of his anti-**Catholic** *Elenchus Religionis Papisticae* (1624), led him into conflict with the authorities. He was arrested and brought before the high commission and king's bench. In 1635, he was fined £1,000, excommunicated, banned from medical practice, and his books were burned. Bastwick was also committed to the Gatehouse prison until he would recant. Undaunted, he resumed his writing in prison, and with the help of **John Lilburne** produced a satirical self-defense titled *Litany of Dr. John Bastwicke* (1636), in which he called the bishops "the tail of the beast" and described them as lecherous gluttons. This publication earned Bastwick an appearance before the **Star Chamber**, along with **William Prynne** and **Henry Burton**. The Chamber fined him £5,000, sentenced him to life imprisonment, and ordered that his ears be cut off. Sympathetic onlookers strewed the path to the pillory with flowers. Bastwick produced his own scalpel, and after the penalty was exacted, he proclaimed, "As I have now lost some of my blood, so am I ready and willing to spill every drop in my veins . . . for maintaining the truth of God, and the honor of the King."

In 1640, the **Long Parliament** ordered Bastwick's release. He fought for the Parliamentary army in 1642 and was taken prisoner by Royalist forces at Leicester. Released in 1644, he returned to London, where he embraced **Presbyterianism** and produced a long attack on **Independency** titled *Independency Not God's Ordinance* (1645). In his later years, Bastwick sought a seat in **Parliament** but was unsuccessful; he alienated many of his friends, such as Lilburne, with his attacks on Independents, and was plagued by financial troubles. He died in 1654 and was buried in an unmarked grave.

BATES, WILLIAM (1625–1699). English **Presbyterian** divine. The son of a gentleman, Bates was born in London. He entered New Inn Hall, **Oxford**, in 1641, but transferred to **Emmanuel College, Cambridge,** to which he was admitted as a pensioner in 1643. He earned his B.A. from Queens' College in 1645 and his M.A. in 1648. In 1649, Bates was first appointed vicar of Tottenham in Middlesex; he then became vicar of St. Dunstans-in-the-West, London, and served as a commissioner at the **Savoy Conference** in 1658, where he argued in favor of Presbyterianism. Bates actively supported the **Restoration** of **Charles II** to the throne and served as a royal chaplain. He was offered the deaneries of Lichefield and Coventry but declined them and would likely have been made a bishop had it not been for his dissenting opinions. In 1662, Bates was forced to resign from his position at St. Dunstans under the **Act of Uniformity**. He continued his ministry illegally as the pastor of a dissenting congregation in Hackney, London; though he avoided prison, he did incur heavy fines. He also delivered Tuesday **lectures** at Salter's Hall in London.

A moderate **Nonconformist**, Bates was respected by advocates of the **episcopacy**, as well as by his fellow Presbyterians. He worked with **Richard Baxter**, **Thomas Manton**, and other to develop terms of religious accommodation, though these efforts were unsuccessful. He also stood by Baxter during his trial, and, upon the accession William and Mary, delivered a congratulatory address on behalf of the **dissenters**. In 1694, he was certified as preacher to a congregation in Mare Street, Hackney.

Bates's biographers note his learning, amiableness, and eloquence. His published works include *Considerations on the Existence of God and the Immortality of the Soul* (1676), *Four Last Things* (1691), and *Spiritual Perfection* (1699).

BAXTER, RICHARD (1615–1691). English minister. Baxter was born and raised in Rowton. At the time of Baxter's birth, his father, who had compromised the family estate by gambling, came under religious conviction, with the result that Baxter was raised in a strongly Puritan environment. Although at an early age he rebelled against strict Sabbath observance—a rebellion at least partly occasioned by the publication of the ***Book of Sports***—he himself converted at the age of 15 while reading an old Puritan tract titled *Bunny's Resolutions*. Rather than attend a university, Baxter chose to study with Richard Wickstead at Ludlow Castle, who, though he gave little direction to Baxter's studies, gave him full access to the castle library. Although he considered pursuing a career at court, Baxter decided to return home and study under the **Nonconformist** clergymen Joseph Symonds and Walter Cradock.

In 1638, Baxter took the position of headmaster at the grammar school in Dudley, Worcestershire. He also took divine orders and accepted an invitation to preach at Bridgnorth, Shropshire, where he refused to take the **Et Cetera Oath** and embraced a position of moderate **Nonconformity**. In 1641, he accepted the call to Kidderminster, where his teachings on original **sin** caused controversy among his parishioners, as did his Parliamentary sympathies. In 1645, Baxter accepted the call to serve as chaplain of the Parliamentary forces. In this role, he sought to mediate differences between various radical elements within the army but with limited success. His career as chaplain was cut short by illness in 1647, at which time he returned to Kidderminster, where he served for another 13 years. During this time, Baxter wrote some of his most important work, and his ministry flourished. In 1660, he accepted the call to serve as a chaplain in ordinary to King **Charles II**, in which capacity he frequently addressed **Parliament**.

He participated in the **Savoy Conference** of 1660, which, over the objections of Baxter and 11 other Puritan divines, composed the **Act of Uniformity**, demanding from all ministers strict adherence to the

Book of Common Prayer. Baxter was among the 2,000 Puritan preachers ejected from the clergy for refusing to subscribe. What followed was a long period of illness, financial difficulty, transience, and imprisonment. Baxter was variously accused of and either fined or imprisoned for keeping a **conventicle**, **preaching** without a license, and libeling the church in his *Paraphrase of the New Testament* (1685). It was also during this period that Baxter married Margaret Charleton, whose virtues he recorded in *Breviate of the Life of Mrs. Margaret Baxter* (1681). After 1687, when **James II** issued his **Declaration of Indulgence**, Baxter was able, despite declining health, to devote himself to writing, unmolested by the authorities.

Baxter is considered one of the most influential Nonconformists and a voice of **religious toleration**. His theology was a source of controversy among fellow Puritans, since his strong opposition to **antinomianism** led him to adopt a modified form of **Amyrauldianism**. Baxter is considered the chief proponent of Amyrauldian theology in England. Nevertheless, according to J. C. Ryle, he was "a man of most eminent personal holiness . . . one of the most powerful preachers that ever addressed an English congregation . . . and one of the most diligent theological writers the world has ever seen." He was a prolific writer whose practical and devotional works include *A Christian Directory* (1673), *A Call to the Unconverted* (1658), *The Saints' Everlasting Rest* (1658), and *The Reformed Pastor* (1656).

BAY PSALM BOOK. The *Bay Psalm Book* was the common **psalter** of the **Massachusetts Bay Colony** and was the first book to be printed on American soil. A printing press was purchased from England for the specific purpose of producing the book, which appeared in 1640, 20 years after the first **Pilgrims** arrived at Plymouth Rock. The owner of the printing press was Stephen Day; the translators included over 30 ministers, among them **John Cotton**, **Richard Mather**, Thomas Weld, and John Eliot. The preface is commonly attributed to Mather, but some scholars believe Cotton to be the author.

The *Bay Psalm Book* replaced several other psalters brought by the colonists, which they considered insufficiently literal translations from the Hebrew. The translators sought to provide as literal a translation as possible into vernacular English, such as would be appropriate for singing in **worship** services. They were less concerned with creating elegant poetry, and the verses are often awkward and labored as a result.

The *Bay Psalm Book* remained in use by colonial churches for the next hundred years and was also adopted by some churches in England and Scotland. A version published in 1651 provided major revisions, primarily aimed at improving the poetry. Known as *The New England Psalm Book*, it appeared in multiple editions both in New England and Britain. Prior to the ninth edition, the psalm book did not include **music** but indicated the appropriate tunes to be sung from Ravenscroft Psalter. The ninth edition, with music, appeared in 1698.

BAYNES, PAUL (c. 1560–1617). English **Congregationalist** divine. Baynes was born in London and educated at Wethersfield, Essex. He entered Christ's College, **Cambridge**, as a pensioner in 1590, graduating B.A. in 1594 and M.A. in 1597. In 1600, he was elected **fellow**. Baynes' behavior at Cambridge was "irregular," so much so that his father, unbeknownst to Baynes, left him a trust fund of £40 a year on the condition that he give up his evil ways, which Baynes ultimately did. He succeeded **William Perkins** as the **lecturer** at St. Andrews in Cambridge, and it was under Baynes' **preaching** that **Richard Sibbes** was converted.

In 1608, Baynes was silenced for preaching without a license. His appeal, according to Brooks, was denied because the black fringe on his cuffs offended the archbishop. He was later tried by the **Privy Council** for keeping **conventicles**, but the charges were dismissed. Deprived of his benefice, Baynes spent his last years moving about, often supported by the local gentry, preaching when he was able, and writing. He died in Cambridge.

A Congregationalist, Baynes was critical of the established church, but he also opposed the **Brownist** movement toward **Separatism**. Sibbes called Baynes his "father in the gospel." His best-known works are a commentary Colossians (1635) and *The Diocesans Tryall* (1621).

BEHMENISTS. Behmenists were the followers of the teachings of Jacob Boehme, a shoemaker from the German town of Görlitz. Boehme set forth a form of Protestant mysticism in which the world can only be understood through the drawing of oppositions. Good and evil, for instance, can only be understood in relation to each other. These kinds of oppositions are a basic part of human nature, and all people carry both Heaven and Hell in them. The same is true of God, who contains and reconciles all opposing elements of the cosmos in his character. Boehme also taught that God is in all who believe, and thus the word written in believers' hearts takes precedent over what is taught in the **Bible**.

Boehme's teaching exerted considerable influence in England. His works were the subject of a commentary by John Pordage (1607–81), the rector of Bradfield, Berkshire. Pordage and Jane Leade (1623–1704) organized a group called the Philadelphians that embraced many of Boehme's teachings. William Law (1686–1761) translated several of Boehme's books into English. Although the Behmenists did not constitute a formally organized sect, Boehme's teachings are thought to have influenced the **Quaker** movement, the **Muggletonians**, and the **Familists**.

BERNARD, RICHARD (1568–1641). English minister. Bernard was born in Epworth, Lincolnshire. Two daughters of Christopher Wray, the Lord Chief Justice of England, took an interest in Bernard as a youth and sent him to Christ's College, **Cambridge**, where he received his B.A. in 1594–95, and his M.A. in 1598. Also in 1598, he published a Latin edition of the works of Terence, with an English translation, and was made rector of Epworth. In 1601, he was presented to the vicarage of Worksop in Nottinghamshire.

For several years, Bernard was involved in the **Separatist** movement but later became vehemently opposed to the cause and wrote several pamphlets denouncing Separatism. However, he refused to conform to the practices of the **Anglican** Church and was silenced by the bishop for **Nonconformity**. In 1613, he became vicar of Batcombe in Somersetshire, where he remained for the rest of his life. He was succeeded at Batcombe by Richard Alleine.

Bernard wrote in a range of styles on a variety of subjects. *The Faithful Shepherd*, published in 1607, is a treatise on the subject of pastoral ministry that has been compared to **Richard Baxter**'s *The Reformed Pastor*. He also wrote an extended allegory titled *Isle of Man, or Proceedings in Manshire* (1627) that may have influenced **John Bunyan**'s *Pilgrim's Progress*. He wrote a commentary on the

Book of Ruth titled *Ruth's Recompense*. Other works include *The Fabulous Foundation of Popedome* (1619) and *Look Beyond Luther* (1623). In addition to his anti-Separatist tracts, he wrote treatises against the use of ceremonies in **worship** and on **witchcraft**. His works feature occasional instances of humanistic concern—appeals on behalf of Jews, the poor, and prisoners.

BIBLE. *See* BISHOPS' BIBLE; GENEVA BIBLE; KING JAMES BIBLE; MATTHEW'S BIBLE; TYNDALE BIBLE; SCRIPTURE.

BISHOPS' BIBLE. An English translation of the **Bible**. Officials of the English Church, most notably Matthew Parker, the **Archbishop of Canterbury**, sought to produce a revised version of the **Great Bible**, the first authorized English translation. It was hoped that such a version would supplant the **Geneva Bible** in popular esteem. Church officials objected to the Geneva Bible's strongly **Presbyterian** marginal glosses and notes. Parker and several other bishops did the translating, and in early printings the translators initialed their work. The first printing appeared in 1568, featuring short exegetical notes. In 1571, a convocation at Canterbury ordered copies of the Bishops' Bible to be placed in every cathedral, and every archbishop, bishop, dean, and other church dignitary to make a copy available in his home for the use of his servants and strangers.

The Bishops' Bible received the royal warrant and was used in **Anglican worship** services; however, the Geneva Bible remained more popular for private devotional use. While the Geneva Bible went through 150 printings by 1606, the Bishops' Bible was reprinted a mere 20 times. The Bishops' Bible remained the official translation of the Anglican Church even after the 1611 publication of the **King James Bible**, or Authorized Version. The Bishops' Bible is also known as the "Treacle Bible" for its translation of Jeremiah 8:22: "Is there not a treacle in Gilead?"

BISHOPS' WARS. The Bishops' Wars were a series of conflicts between England and Scotland from 1639 to 1640. They were occasioned by **Charles I's** decision to impose **episcopacy** on the Scottish Church, which had adopted the **Presbyterian** model of **worship** and church government in 1560. Attempts to use the ***Book of Common***

Prayer in services at the Cathedral of St. Giles in Edinburgh led to riots and to ratification of the National Covenant in 1638. The Scots vowed not only to abolish episcopacy but raised an army to prevent any attempt at its reimposition. Undaunted, Charles himself led an army of 18,000–20,000 soldiers to Scotland in 1639; however, his forces were overmatched by the more experienced, better organized, better supplied, and deeply motivated Scottish army. Led by Alexander Leslie and Lord Rothers, the Scots seized control of all major ports and strongholds. When Charles' forces met Leslie's at Berwick-upon-Tweed, neither side wanting to fight, they signed the Treaty of Berwick, bringing to an end the First Bishops' War.

Charles, however, did not abandon his hope of bringing uniformity to Scotland. Realizing that he would need funds to match the Scots on the battlefield, Charles decided to summon **Parliament**, ending his 11-year-long personal rule. Parliament responded with a series of demands that Charles rejected. Consequently, he dismissed it after three weeks, hence its nickname, the **Short Parliament**. Meanwhile, the Scots, sensing their advantage, invaded England and occupied two northern counties. Proceeding without the needed funds from Parliament, Charles once again led a force against the Scottish army, which soundly defeated him at the Battle of Newburn, then advanced to Newcastle and seized the coal supplies there. Charles was forced to sign the Treaty of Ripon, in which he agreed to pay the Scottish troops an indemnity of £850 per day pending a permanent settlement. Unable to meet these demands on his own, the penniless king was again driven to recall Parliament, to whose demands he was now forced to yield. These demands included the impeachment and eventual execution of the Earl of Strafford and **William Laud**. This Parliament, nicknamed the **Long Parliament**, was not formally dissolved until 1660.

BLOOD, THOMAS (c. 1618–1680). Parliamentary army colonel, **Fifth Monarchist**. Blood was born in Ireland in the County Clare. He served in the Parliamentary army, for which service he received a magistracy and lands in Ireland, both of which he lost at the time of the **Restoration**. Apparently in an attempt to reclaim these privileges, he participated in an unsuccessful attempt to kidnap the Duke of Ormond and seize Dublin Castle, after which he fled to **Holland**. When he returned to England, Blood joined the Fifth Monarchists and later the Covenanters in Scotland.

Blood was involved in several other daring exploits, the most famous of which was his failed attempt to steal the crown jewels. Even though he and his accomplices killed the keeper of the jewels and a yeoman, Blood—apparently through the influence of the Duke of Buckingham—received a pardon from **Charles II**.

BLOODY ASSIZES. "Bloody Assizes" is the name given to the trials of the followers of the Duke of Monmouth in his ill-fated Protestant rebellion against the **Catholic James II**. After the defeat of Monmouth's forces at the Battle of Sedgemoor (1685), James II sent Lord Chief Justice George Jeffreys to the west country to dispense justice to the defeated rebels. Jeffreys was a notoriously harsh judge who had also presided over the trial of **Richard Baxter**. Although many of the gentry who had supported Monmouth were able to avoid execution by paying substantial bribes, Jeffreys ordered the execution of over 400 rebels, mostly peasants, many of whom pleaded guilty because they had been promised mercy. Some were drawn and quartered. Another 800 were transported to the West Indies.

James elevated Jeffreys to lord chancellor for his services. In 1689, one of the rebels, John Tutchin, published a partly fictionalized version of the events titled *The Protestant Martyrs, or the Bloody Assizes*. The event increased public distrust of James, helping pave the way to his deposition and the ascendancy of William of Orange (1688). *See also* MONMOUTH REBELLION.

BOLTON, ROBERT (1572–1631). English Puritan divine. Bolton was born in Blackburn, Lancashire; his father, Adam Bolton, was a yeoman. Bolton was educated at the Blackburn school and, in 1592, his parents sent him to Lincoln College, **Oxford**. With the death of his father a short time later, Bolton was unable even to afford his books. He transferred to Brasen-nose College, where he was awarded the Nowell scholarship, and graduated in 1596. In 1602, he became a **fellow** at Brasen-nose. Bolton was a gifted academician who excelled in philosophy, logic, and languages, but he was equally well known for card playing, play-going, swearing, and Sabbath breaking; moreover, he was suspected of holding **Catholic** sympathies. Dismissive of the leaders of the Puritan movement, he called **William Perkins** a "barren, empty fellow." However, Bolton was eventually converted through the influence of Thomas Peacock and settled on a ministerial vocation, earning a Bachelor of Divinity in 1609. In 1610, he married and became rector of Broughton in Northamptonshire, where he remained for the rest of his life. Known for his patriotism, stern demeanor, and religious zeal, Bolton was an influential preacher. He also held a **lectureship** at Kettering. He died after a prolonged illness at the age of 60 and was buried in the church at Broughton.

Bolton's published works demonstrate a deep concern for both public morality and the inner, spiritual life of the Christian. They include *General Directions for a Comfortable Walking with God*, *Instructions for a Right Comforting Afflicted* **Consciences**, *A Cordiall for Christians in the Time of Affliction*, and *The Four Last Things: Death, Judgment, Hell, Heaven*, which contains the last **sermon** he preached before his death. He also wrote *The Carnal Professor* and *Discourse about the State of True Happiness*.

BOLTON, SAMUEL (1606–1654). English Puritan divine. The son of William Bolton, Bolton was born in Lancashire and educated at Manchester School. He entered Christ's College, **Cambridge**, in 1625, graduating B.A. in 1629 and M.A. in 1632. He married Elianor Little in 1633 and became curate of Harrow, Middlesex, the following year. He subsequently served as minister at St. Martin's Church in Ludgate Street and at St. Saviours, Southwark. He was also appointed **lecturer** at St. Anne and St. Agnes, Aldersgate.

Bolton was a member of the **Westminster Assembly** in 1642 and, in 1645, was chosen as master of Christ's College, though he continued to preach frequently at St. Andrew's, Holborn. From 1650–52, he served as vice-chancellor of Cambridge. Bolton's published works include a collection of fast **sermons** titled *A Tossed Ship Making to Safe Harbor, or, A Word in Season to a Sinking Kingdome* (1644), *The Arraignment of Error* (1646), *The True Bounds of Christian Freedom* (1645), and *The Guard of the Tree of Life* (1645), a treatise on the Lord's Supper.

BOOK OF COMMON PRAYER. The *Book of Common Prayer* sets forth the liturgy for **worship** services in the Church of England, as well as the administration of the **sacraments** and other rites and ceremonies of the church. The earliest version appeared in 1549 during the reign of **Edward VI**. Produced under the direction of **Thomas Cranmer, Archbishop of Canterbury**, *The First English Prayer Book* combined many of the traditional elements of the **Catholic** liturgy with Reformed doctrines and practices. It retained the old order of the Latin mass and the doctrine of transubstantiation; however, vernacular English replaced Latin as the language of the service. The new prayer book emphasized **Scripture** as the basis for worship and eliminated some ceremonial elements. It also simplified the service, the single volume replacing the missal, breviary, manual, and pontifical used in the Roman Catholic liturgy. Although the Latin mass was observed in a variety of ways throughout England, the prayer book provided a common form to be used in all services.

Parliament adopted the *First Book of English Prayer* as the only legal form of worship in the English church; however, Protestant opposition led to the production of a second prayer book in 1552, once again under the direction of Cranmer, though Peter Martyr, **Nicholas Ridley**, and **John Knox** may also have contributed. This version eliminated the teaching of transubstantiation and any language implying **salvation** through works. Clerical **vestments** were simplified, and communion tables replaced altars. This version remained in use for only eight months until the accession of Queen **Mary I**, who reinstituted **Catholicism**, banned the prayer book, and executed Cranmer.

When Queen **Elizabeth I** ascended to the throne in 1558, she reestablished the Church of England and also commissioned a new version of the *Book of Common Prayer*. As a part of the **Elizabethan Settlement**, this version incorporated more Catholic elements than the previous edition, such as the suggested use of vestments by the priest and the observance of saints' days. Prayers against the pope, which appeared in the 1552 version, were removed. These changes became a source of contention with many Puritans, but it remained the official prayer book until 1645, when it was outlawed by the Puritan-controlled **Long Parliament**. With the **Restoration** of the monarchy in 1660, however, a slightly modified version of the book appeared. The **Act of Uniformity** (1662) required all preachers to give assent to this version of the *Book of Common Prayer*, leading to the ejection of over 2,000 ministers from their pulpits.

The *Book of Common Prayer* was a major cause of religious controversy during the 16th and 17th centuries in England, but its required use and the beauty of its language also made it one of the most influential books in the development of the English language.

BOOK OF SPORTS. In 1617, **James I** issued a declaration that certain sports were permissible on Sundays and other holy days. These activities included "leaping, vaulting, or any such harmless recreation," along with "May-games, Whitsun-ales and Morris-dances, and the setting up of May-poles," as long as they did not conflict with regular Sabbath **worship**. Other activities were prohibited, including bear-baiting, bull-baiting, "interludes," or **dramatic** entertainments, and bowling.

James made the declaration at the request of Thomas Morton, Bishop of Chester, in response to a growing controversy in Lancashire, where the Puritan clergy sought to enforce strict observance of the Sabbath, or **Sabbatarianism**. Despite opposition from **Archbishop of Canterbury George Abbot**, James ordered that the declaration be read by all ministers from their pulpits; however, reaction to the order was so strong that James was forced to withdraw his command. On 18 October 1633, **Charles I** reissued the declaration as *The King's Majesty's declaration to his subjects concerning lawful sports to be used*, with the command that any minister who refused to read it from the pulpit would be deprived of his position. Among the ministers who resigned or were ejected from office under this declaration were **Richard Capel** and **Simeon Ashe**. With the rise of the Puritan party during the period leading up to the **English Civil Wars**, opposition to the declaration grew. By 1640, all attempts to enforce it had ceased, and, in 1643, **Parliament** ordered that it be publicly burned.

BOSTON, THOMAS (1676–1732). Scottish **Presbyterian** divine. Boston was born in Duns, a small town in the Border country of Scotland. His father was John Boston, a minister and covenanter who was imprisoned for **Nonconformity**. At age 11, Boston was converted under the **preaching** of Henry Erskine. He attended the grammar school at Duns from 1685 to 1689, and entered the University of Edinburgh in 1691, graduating M.A. in 1694. **Ordained** in 1699, he became preacher at the tiny parish of Simprin and married Katharine Brown, with whom he had 10 children, six of whom died in infancy. His son Thomas became founder of the Relief Church. In 1707, Boston accepted the call to serve as minister in the parish of Ettrick. Here, he found that **Separatism** had caused such deep division among the people of the church that for the first three years of his ministry he refused to administer the Lord's Supper. However, during his tenure at Ettrick, Boston greatly increased the number communicants: in 1710, the first time he administered the **sacrament**, 60 people received it, whereas at his last communion in 1731, the number had risen to 777.

Though he described himself as "timorous," Boston was a prominent figure in a number of early 18th-century religious controversies. He opposed the abjuration oaths of 1712 and 1719, and he stood against the teachings of University of Glasgow professor of divinity John Simson, who was eventually suspended from his position for teaching Arianism. But Boston is best known for his involvement in the so-called **Marrow Controversy**. While at Simprin, Boston first read **Edward Fisher**'s *The Marrow of Modern Divinity*, a book that stresses the unconditional nature of **salvation** but that many considered an expression of **antinomianism**. A "Marrow Man," Boston openly acknowledged the book's influence on his own preaching and writing, and actively promoted its publication in Scotland. Additionally, he affirmed the controversial Auchterarder creed, which stated that "it is not sound and orthodox to teach, that we must forsake **sin** in order to our coming to Christ." Boston's best-known works are *Human Nature in it Fourfold State* (1720, 1729) and *The Crook in the Lot* (1737), a treatise on **providence**. Other works include *Body of Divinity and Miscellanies* and *The Art of Man-Fishing*. He also penned his well-known and highly regarded spiritual *Memoirs* (1776).

BRADFORD, WILLIAM (c. 1590–1657). Governor of the Plymouth Colony. Bradford was born in Austerfield, Yorkshire, to yeoman parents. Both his parents died when Bradford was a child, and he was reared by his grandfather and uncles. Rather than receiving a formal education, Bradford was apprenticed to a farmer. He became a **Separatist** when, at the age of 12, he began to visit the Separatist church in the nearby town of Scrooby and heard the **preaching** of Richard Clyfton. In 1609, he emigrated to Amsterdam and then to Leiden to join the Scrooby Separatists who had gone there to avoid religious persecution. While in **Holland**, Bradford supported himself as a weaver. He married his first wife, Dorothy May, in 1613.

In 1620, Bradford, along with 101 other passengers, many of them members of his own congregation, set sail for northern Virginia; however, bad weather forced them to land first at Cape Cod, and finally at Plymouth, Massachusetts. En route, Bradford, along with other members of the party, composed the **Mayflower Compact**. Bradford also suffered personal tragedy: his wife Dorothy drowned when she fell overboard while the ship was anchored in Provincetown Harbor.

In 1621, John Carver, the first governor of Plymouth, died, and Bradford was elected to replace him. As governor, Bradford served as the financial manager of the colony, as judge, as negotiator with the Dutch in New Amsterdam, as overseer of trading posts, and as chief diplomat to the Native American population. In 1623, he married Alice Carpenter Southworth, a widow with three children. During his time as governor, Bradford began his work on what would eventually be published as the *History of Plymouth Plantation*, a detailed and precise account of the colony up to the year 1646. Bradford continued to serve as governor until shortly before his death at age 67.

BRADSHAW, WILLIAM (1571–1618). English **Congregationalist** minister. Bradshaw was born at Market Bosworth, Leicestershire, and received his early schooling at Worcester. He entered **Emmanuel College, Cambridge**, in 1589 and received both his B.A. and M.A. degrees; however, he was denied a **fellowship**, which instead went to **Joseph Hall**. **Laurence Chaderton**, the master of Emmanuel College, procured Bradshaw a position as tutor to the family of Sir Thomas Leighton, the governor of Guernsey. While serving the Leighton family, he met the Puritan leader **Thomas Cartwright**, with whom he became lifelong friends, and James Montague, who became the first master of Sidney Sussex College, Cambridge, in 1599. Montague granted Bradshaw a fellowship at Sidney Sussex. Bradshaw also took orders and began to preach in villages near Cambridge. However, a controversy over his publication of the works of John Darrel, who had been tried for conducting exorcisms, led to Bradshaw's departure from Cambridge in 1601.

Once again through the influence of Chaderton, Bradshaw received an appointment, this time as **lecturer** at Chatham, in Rochester. Although the congregation responded enthusiastically to his **preaching**, a charge of heresy led to a summons to appear before Archbishop Whitgift. When obliged to take the ex officio oath before the High Comission, Bradshaw refused and was suspended from his ministry. He stayed with the Redich family in Derbyshire, near Stapenhill, where he preached at the Redich's private chapel and in Stapenhill Church. After his marriage, he moved to Stanton Ward, where his wife supported him with needlework and teaching.

After the failure of the Puritans to achieve their objectives at the **Hampton Court Conference**, Bradshaw published *English Puritanisme* (1605). The book argued for the purification of church doctrine and a revision of church polity, allowing greater autonomy to individual congregations. Although Bradshaw strongly endorsed submission to civil authority, the book was considered dangerous; his lodgings in London were raided and searched. Bradshaw was absent at the time, but his wife was brought before the High Commission. Bradshaw retreated to Derbyshire, which remained his home base, though he continued to travel and preach for the rest of his life. He died during a visit to Chelsea and is buried in Chelsea Church. **Thomas Gataker** preached his funeral **sermon** and wrote his biography.

English Puritanisme established Bradshaw as one of the intellectual leaders of the early Puritan movement. He was also a prolific writer and, along with Henry Jacob, one of the earliest **Non-Separatist** advocates of Congregationalism. Joseph Hall described Bradshaw as "very strong and eager in argument, hearty in friendship, regardless of the world, a despiser of compliment, a lover of reality."

BRADSTREET, ANNE (1612–1672). English and American poet. Bradstreet was born in Northampton. Her father was Thomas Dudley, a soldier under Queen **Elizabeth I** and steward to the Earl of Lincoln. Her mother, Dorothy Yorke, was an educated gentlewoman. In her childhood, Bradstreet was tutored in Greek, Latin, French, Hebrew, and English. At the age of 16, she married Simon Bradstreet, a 25-year-old assistant in the Massachusetts Bay Company and a ward of the Dudley's.

Three years later, in 1630, the Dudleys and the Bradstreets emigrated to New England. The three-month journey aboard the *Arbella* was exceptionally difficult, with bad weather and disease claiming the lives of several passengers. Within a short time of their arrival, Bradstreet's family soon became one of the most influential in the colony. Her father served as deputy-governor under Governor **John Winthrop**. Bradstreet's husband Simon served as chief administrator under Winthrop and twice as governor. After brief stays in several towns, Bradstreet and her family settled in Ipswich and later in Andover.

Bradstreet bore eight children, all of whom survived into adulthood. Her poems indicate that her marriage to Simon was happy, though punctuated by lengthy separations when his official duties required travel about the colonies and to England. In addition to other hardships, she experienced frequent illness, including smallpox and tuberculosis, and the threat of Indian attacks. Nevertheless, she maintained an active intellectual life and read widely in history, literature, and **science**. She was also a personal friend of **Anne Hutchinson**, who was banished from the colony in 1638.

In 1650, a collection of Bradstreet's poetry, surreptitiously copied by her brother-in-law, was published in England under the title *The Tenth Muse Lately Sprung Up in America*, making her the first published American poet. The volume sold well and features her earlier, more formal, imitative poetry. Bradstreet is now remembered and appreciated primarily for her later work—poems that explore her spiritual life, as well as her experiences as a mother and wife. Along with spiritual devotion, her poems demonstrate striking intellectual freedom. The standard edition of her works was published by Twayne in 1981. *See also* WOMEN.

BREWSTER, WILLIAM (c. 1560–1644). Printer, cofounder of the colony at Plymouth Rock. William Brewster was born in Scrooby, Nottinghamshire. From 1580 to 84, he studied at Peterhouse, **Cambridge**, but left without taking a degree. He then entered the service of William Davison, Queen **Elizabeth I**'s ambassador to the Low Countries. He remained in this position until 1587, when Davison's involvement in the trial and execution of Mary Queen of Scots incurred Elizabeth's disfavor.

Brewster returned to Scrooby, where he served as postmaster, a position of some importance, and became a ruling elder of the **Separatist** congregation at Scrooby.

In 1607, Brewster joined other members of the Scrooby congregation who decided to emigrate to **Holland** to flee persecution, but the group was betrayed by the skipper whose sloop was to transport them. Brewster and other leaders were imprisoned. The next year, the group successfully departed from Hull and arrived in Amsterdam.

While in Holland, Brewster taught English at the university and set up a printing press, printing religious works prohibited by the English authorities. In 1619, he obtained a land grant in Virginia, and he and **William Bradford** were the two chief leaders of the company of **Pilgrims** who set sail aboard the *Mayflower* in September 1620.

Brewster served as preacher and teacher of the Plymouth colony until 1629, when Ralph Smith arrived to serve as the congregation's regular pastor. In his later years, he continued to preach occasionally for the congregation and serve as an adviser to Bradford.

BRAINERD, DAVID (1718–1747). American missionary. Brainerd was born in Haddam, Connecticut. His father, a Puritan clergyman, died during Brainerd's infancy, and his mother died when he was 14. In 1739, Brainerd entered Yale University but was expelled in 1741 for criticizing one of the tutors. He was licensed to preach in 1742; in 1743, under the sponsorship of the Scottish Society for Promoting Christian Knowledge, he began his ministry among Native Americans. Brainerd's first missionary post was at Kaunaumeek, 20 miles from Stockbridge. Later, and for the rest of his life, he worked among the Delaware tribes in Pennsylvania and New Jersey.

Brainerd worked tirelessly on behalf of Native Americans, despite his poor health and fits of depression. He died of tuberculosis at age 29 in the home of **Jonathan Edwards** in Northampton. In 1749, Edwards published *An Account of the Life of the Late Rev. David Brainerd, chiefly taken from his own Diary and other Private Writings*. It remains Edwards' most popular work and served as a major inspiration for the 18th- and 19th-century **missionary** movements.

BRIDGE, WILLIAM (c. 1600–1670). English **Congregationalist** divine. Bridge entered **Emmanuel College, Cambridge**, as a sizar (a student required to pay minimal fees) in 1619. He graduated B.A. in 1623, M.A. in 1626, and was then elected a **fellow** at Emmanuel. He was ordained in 1627 and served as a lecturer for five years in Essex before his appointment to the parish of St. George's Tombland in Norwich. Bridge remained at St. George's until 1637, when he was ejected from office and excommunicated under the articles and injunctions of Bishop Wren. Bridge then fled to **Holland** and settled in Rotterdam, where, with fellow Congregationalist **Jeremiah Burroughs**, he served as pastor to an **Independent** English congregation.

Bridge returned to England in 1642 at the beginning of the **English Civil War**. He was frequently invited to speak before **Parliament**. He was also elected to the **Westminster Assembly** of Divines. Bridge, Burroughs, **Philip Nye**, **Thomas Goodwin**, and **Sidrach Simpson** made up the "**Five Dissenting Brethren**," representing Congregationalist concerns to the assembly. Bridge eventually settled at Yarmouth, where he served as pastor until ejected again from office, this time under the 1662 **Act of Uniformity**. He continued his ministry by **preaching** occasionally at Clapham in Surrey and at **conventicles**. He died at Yarmouth.

Bridge published many tracts and several collections of **sermons**. Among these is his series of 13 sermons on Psalm 42:11, published under the title *A Lifting up of the Downcast*. The work treats the subject of spiritual depression and was reprinted in 1979 by Grace and Truth Books. His pamphlet *A Word to the Ages* was republished in 2003 by Soli Deo Gloria Press, which also published his five-volume works in 1989.

BROOKS, THOMAS (1608–1680). English divine. Brooks's place of birth is unknown. He entered **Emmanuel College, Cambridge**, as a pensioner in 1625. Nothing is known of his life for the next 20 years, though biographers speculate that he served as a chaplain to Parliamentary commanders during the **English Civil Wars**, both at land and sea. In 1648, he became preacher at St. Margaret's, New Fish-Street Hill. Here he found himself in conflict with his flock, apparently over his attempts to transform the church into an **Independent** congregation. During the **Interregnum**, his strong support of **Congregationalism**

and the army, as well as his opposition to the **Fifth Monarchists** and **Levellers**, brought him to the attention of **Oliver Cromwell**.

Ejected from the ministry under the **Act of Uniformity** in 1662, Brooks continued to preach on occasion, though he was never imprisoned. He remained in London during the year of the plague (1655) and the Great Fire (1666), an event that he described in his book titled *London's Lamentations*. In 1672, Brooks was granted a license to preach in Lime Street. He outlived his first wife and married his second several years before his death. Brooks was buried in **Bunhill Fields**.

Brooks was the author of 16 works of devotion and edification, including *Precious Remedies Against Satan's Devices*, *The Mute Christian under the Smarting Rod*, and *Apples of Gold for Young Men and Women*.

BROWNE, ROBERT (c. 1550–1633). English **Congregationalist** minister and **Separatist**. The son of an influential gentry family, Browne was born in Tolethorpe near Stamford and graduated B.A. from Corpus Christi College, **Cambridge**, in 1572. After serving as a schoolmaster in Southwark, London, Browne obtained a **lectureship** at Islington. He then served as chaplain to Duke of Norfolk. During his chaplaincy, he began to preach openly against the **Anglican** hierarchy and ceremonies. In 1581, he was appointed to serve as minister to a church in Norwich, where he drew a large congregation. Browne's church distinguished itself by adopting a covenant precluding communion with "wicked persons," and he continued to condemn openly the practices of the state church, leading to his imprisonment in 1581 by Bishop Freake of Norwich. Released through family influence, he was imprisoned two more times in 1581.

In 1582, Browne led his faithful to establish a new church, based ostensibly on the model of the New Testament church, in the more tolerant environs of Middleburg, Zeeland, but the fellowship dissolved after two years because of internal strife. After a brief attempt to establish a church in Scotland, Browne returned to England in 1584–85, where he continued to preach against the established church, appear before ecclesiastical courts, and undergo imprisonment and release. While **preaching** at Norwich, he was summoned to appear before Bishop Lindsell of Peterborough, who, according to some late sources, threatened Browne with excommunication. In any event, Browne renounced his Separatist opinions and ultimately obtained the rectorship of Achurch-cum-Thorpe Waterville in Northamptonshire. Scholars dispute whether Browne performed these duties himself or leased his benefice. In either case, he remained in Northamptonshire for 42 years. However, he continued to be involved in legal disputes and was excommunicated in 1631. At age 82, Browne was brought before the local magistrate for assaulting the parish constable and jailed. He died in prison. It was, by his own reckoning, the last of 32 separate incarcerations during his life.

Browne is best known as one of the first Separatists and the figure from whom the **Brownist** movement derived its name. He was also an early proponent of Congregationalism who influenced many of the early American Puritan settlers. Browne's best-known works are *A Treatise of Reformation without Tarrying for Any* and *A Booke Which Sheweth Forth the Life and Manners of All True Christians*. See also DUTCH PURITANISM.

BROWNISTS. Early **Congregationalists** or **Independents**. In the narrow sense, the term "Brownists" refers to the followers of **Robert Browne**, such as those who settled with him at Middleburg, but the term is also used for anyone who came to embrace Browne's teachings, the central tenet of which is the autonomy of the individual congregation. The Brownists are generally considered **Separatists** who strongly opposed not only the ecclesiastical hierarchy of the **Anglican** Church but its forms of **worship** and its ceremonies. In spite of this opposition, Brownists still recognized the Anglican Church as a true church with valid **sacraments**. In this they were less extreme than the **Barrowists**, who believed that the established church was a wholly lost cause. Many of the early New England settlers were influenced by Browne's teachings.

BULKELEY, PETER (1583–1659). English and American clergyman. Peter Bulkeley was born in Odell, Bedfordshire. His father was Dr. Edward Bulkeley, the rector of Odell, and his mother was Olive Irby. Bulkeley entered St. John's College, **Cambridge**, graduating B.A. in 1605 and M.A. in 1608. He was also appointed a **fellow** of the college. He was **ordained** at Ely and made prebendary of the cathedral in 1609. In 1610, he was named university preacher at Cambridge and, upon his father's death, became his successor as the rector of Odell. He also received a sizable inheritance from his father's estate and was incorporated at **Oxford**.

Bulkeley was a **Nonconformist** but was discreet in his views, and he served under John Williams, Bishop of Lincoln and a Puritan sympathizer. But by 1635, **Archbishop of Canterbury William Laud** had silenced Bulkeley for his Nonconformity. Bulkeley sold his property and moved his family to New England, where, in 1636, he cofounded Concord, Massachusetts, and established a church there. In 1637, he was appointed pastor.

Bulkeley earned a reputation for being an earnest, diligent, and exacting spiritual leader. According to **Cotton Mather**, his "great exactness of piety" alienated some members of his flock, but he was also affable and drew their respect with his zeal and character. He baptized the children of partial members, a liberal practice that anticipated the **Half-Way Covenant**. Although he played a limited role in the civic life of the colony, Bulkeley did participate in the synod that condemned **Anne Hutchinson** in 1638.

Bulkeley's most important published work is *The Gospel-Covenant, or, The Covenant of Grace Opened* which first appeared in 1646. A collection of **sermons** preached in response to the **antinomian** controversy, the book also provides an early exposition of New England **covenant theology**. Bulkeley may also have contributed to the *Bay Psalm Book*.

BUNHILL FIELDS. Dissenter burial ground in London. Located in the borough of Islington, the cemetery occupies about four acres between City Road and Bunhill Row. Though Bunhill Fields has seen varied uses throughout its history, its use as a burial ground dates back to Saxon times. In 1498, part of the land was designated for military training. In the mid-16th century, bones from St. Paul's charnel house were removed to Bunhill Fields, piled up, and covered with topsoil. The resulting elevation is the "bone hill" from which the cemetery derives its name, and was high enough to serve for a time as the location for three windmills. In 1665, the land was designated as a common burial place. Because it was never consecrated as holy ground by the Church of England, it became a popular cemetery for

Nonconformists. The last burial took place in 1854, and, in 1869, the City of London established Bunhill Fields as a community garden. The cemetery is final resting place to over 120,000 souls. **John Bunyan**, **Daniel Defoe**, **John Milton**, **Isaac Watts**, **John Owen**, and **John Goodwin** are among the many well-known Nonconformists buried there. A **Quaker** burial ground adjoins Bunhill Fields, in which **George Fox** and thousands of other Quakers are buried.

BUNYAN, JOHN (1628–1688). English **Nonconformist** minister. Bunyan was born in the small hamlet of Elstow in Bedfordshire. His father Thomas Bunyan was a tinker or brasier, one who mends pots and pans for a living, but his mother and sister, each named Margaret, died in his 16th year. Bunyan appears to have been disgruntled by the quick remarriage of his father, and he joined the **New Model Army** garrison at Newport Pagnell largely as a diversion. There is no evidence that Bunyan was involved in any significant military engagement during the **English Civil Wars**, although he recalled how another soldier died who at the last moment went to the front lines in his place. Shortly before his time in the army ended, Bunyan married for the first time, but there is no surviving record of his wife's name. In his autobiography *Grace Abounding to the Chief of Sinners* (1666), Bunyan only says that she came from a Puritan family and that her father could only supply Arthur Dent's *The Plain Man's Pathway to Heaven* and Lewis Bayly's *The Practice of Piety* as a dowry. She bore him four children, including a blind daughter, Mary.

Returning to Bedfordshire, Bunyan took up his father's trade to support his growing family. Through the influence of his wife and some embarrassing episodes in which villagers known for immorality chastised him for swearing, Bunyan began to pursue a religious transformation. Although, as he describes in *Grace Abounding*, he at first made progress only haltingly because he took pride in his own righteousness rather than the righteousness of Christ, at last he began to understand **salvation** by grace after reading Martin Luther's *Commentary on Galatians*. In 1653, Bunyan joined the **Separatist** church of John Gifford in Bedford and was rebaptized in the River Ouse. Gifford's successor John Burton asked Bunyan to preach on occasion, and once made aware of his persuasive gifts, Bunyan also took to theological argumentation in print. His first published work, *Some*

Gospel-Truths Opened (1656), contended fiercely against the **Quakers** and their allegedly subjectivist reliance on the inner light above the bloody sacrificial atonement of Christ on Calvary. In 1658, Bunyan's wife died, but like his father, he remarried quickly—the following year, he wed Elizabeth, who would become his most outspoken defender when Bunyan later became the target of state repression.

In 1659, Bunyan published probably his most influential dogmatic work, *The Doctrine of the Law and Grace Unfolded*, which defended the covenant theology of **Calvinism** against the **Latitudinarianism** of Edward Fowler. Bunyan's fame as a preacher and writer grew so widely that he caught the attention of King **Charles II**. Accused of holding **conventicles** in defiance of the state-sponsored church, Bunyan was arrested after the **Restoration** in 1660 and was sent to jail in Bedford in January 1661. There he would remain, excepting a brief respite and occasional weekend releases, until 1672, making his imprisonment the longest such sentence of any Nonconformist in the Stuart dynasty. He continued to write while in prison, however, beginning with *Profitable Meditations* in 1661. Bunyan was at last released from jail under the **Declaration of Indulgence** of 1672, and he registered legally as a **Congregationalist** minister. He became the pastor of his church in Bedford, following the ministry of Samuel Fenn and John Whiteman while he was in prison. Because of his preference for believer's **baptism**, Bunyan led his church into fellowship with the **Baptists**, yet he always remained suspicious of denominational labels, saying in *A Confession of My Faith* (1672) that they came "from hell and Babylon." Bunyan also refused to make one's mode of baptism a test for church membership or even reception of the Lord's Supper. He defended his position against stricter Baptists like **William Kiffin** in *Differences in Judgment about Water-Baptism, No Bar to Communion* (1673), and *Peaceable Principles and True* (1677).

Bunyan faced a second imprisonment around 1677–78, during which time he probably finished the imaginative work that brought him lasting fame. *The Pilgrim's Progress* is the allegorical tale of the protagonist Christian's arduous trek from the City of Destruction to the Celestial City, and its adventuresome plot and scriptural underpinning made it a favorite nonbiblical text of many homes for the following two centuries. It went through 11 printings and 100,000 copies in its first decade, which was also the final 10 years of Bunyan's life. From 1678–88, Bunyan preached widely throughout central England, earning the nickname of "Bishop Bunyan." He also penned three more fictional works, *The Life and Death of Mr. Badman* (1680), *The Holy War* (1682), and *The Pilgrim's Progress, Part II* (1684), and one of the earliest attempts at Christian children's literature, *A Book for Boys and Girls* (1686). In August 1688, Bunyan was on a **preaching** trip in London when asked to effect reconciliation between an estranged father and his son. On the journey, Bunyan got caught in a heavy rainstorm, and although he preached the next day, he quickly became ill and died on August 31, in the home of John Strudwick. He was buried in London's **Bunhill Fields**. Several political writings appeared posthumously over the next few years after his death, including *Of Antichrist, and His Ruine*, a **prayer** for godly monarchs willing to yield to the higher kingship of Christ. *See also* MECHANICK PREACHERS.

BURGESS, ANTHONY (?–1664). English **Presbyterian** minister. Burgess studied at St. John's College, **Cambridge**, and then became a **fellow** at **Emmanuel College**. He became the pastor of a church in Sutton Coldfield, Warwickshire, but he fled from there to Coventry when early fighting from the **English Civil Wars** broke out nearby. He was invited to attend the **Westminster Assembly** in 1646 and **preached** alongside **Stephen Marshall** for **Parliament**. The most common opponents in his **sermons** and writings were **Catholicism** and **antinomianism**. After the **Restoration** of King **Charles II** that ended the Puritan stronghold on English government, Burgess was one of the Protestant ministers who lost their ecclesiastical positions on **Saint Bartholomew's Day** of 1662. He lived his final two years in seclusion.

BURROUGHS, JEREMIAH (1599–1646). English **Congregationalist** divine. Burroughs was educated at **Emmanuel College, Cambridge**. Upon taking his degree, he entered the ministry, first at Bury St. Edmunds, where he served with **Edmund Calamy**, then as rector of Titshall in Norfolk. Burroughs remained at Norfolk for several years until, in 1637, he was deprived of his benefice under the articles and injunctions of Bishop Wren. After staying for some time in the home of the Earl of Warwick, he left England to serve with **William Bridge** as minister to an English congregation in Rotterdam. While in **Holland** he also met **Thomas Goodwin**, **Philip Nye**, and **Sidrach Simpson**.

Burroughs remained in Rotterdam until the **English Civil Wars** began, whereupon he returned to England. He was appointed minister at Stepney and subsequently at Cripplegate in London—two of the largest churches in England. In 1643, Burroughs was appointed to serve as an **Independent** in the **Westminster Assembly** of Divines, where he, along with Goodwin, Simpson, Nye, and Bridge formed the group known as the "**Five Dissenting Brethren**." He died before the Assembly was concluded.

Burroughs was the author of 20 works, including a four-volume commentary on Hosea. His best-known work is the devotional classic, *The Rare Jewel of Christian Contentment*.

BURTON, HENRY (1578–1648). Clergyman and pamphleteer. Burton was born at Birdshall in Yorkshire. He was educated at St. John's College, **Cambridge**, and later incorporated at **Oxford**. After taking his degrees, Burton was appointed tutor to the sons of Robert Carey, later the Earl of Monmouth. Most likely through Carey's influence, Burton was made clerk of the closet to Prince Henry in 1612, and, after Henry's death, clerk of the closet to the future king, Prince Charles. Burton expected to continue in that office after Charles became king; however, Richard Neile, the Bishop of Durham and clerk under King **James I**, retained the position. This disappointment led Burton, in 1623, to write to the king, accusing both Neile and **William Laud** of being inclined to "popery." Charles consequently banished him from court.

Soon after, Burton became rector of St. Matthew's, Friday Street, where he preached vehemently against the bishops and Episcopal practices. He also wrote inflammatory pamphlets, such as *The Baiting of the Pope's Bull*, *Babel No Bethel*, *The Grand Impostor Unmasked*, and *Truth Shut Out of Doors*. Church authorities sought several times to bring charges against Burton but were unsuccessful until 1636, when he preached two **sermons** that, in effect, accused the bishops of involvement in a papist conspiracy. Burton was summoned by the ecclesiastical commissioner to answer, under oath, a charge of sedition. After refusing to take the oath and locking himself in his study, Burton was finally apprehended. He was indicted by the **Star Chamber** along with **William Prynne** and **John Bastwick**. Burton was deprived of his rectory, his degrees were revoked, he was fined £5,000, his ears were chopped off, he was pilloried and sentenced to life imprisonment, with no access to friends, family, pen, ink, or paper. The sentence was carried out despite large demonstrations of public support for Burton.

In 1640, Burton was released by the **Long Parliament**. During his remaining years, he served as pastor to an **Independent** congregation in St. Matthew's and as a Tuesday **lecturer** at St. Mary's Aldermanbury. He also continued to write polemical pamphlets.

– C –

CALAMY, EDMUND (1600–1666). English **Presbyterian** divine, called Edmund Calamy, the Elder. Calamy was born in London and educated at Pembroke Hall, **Cambridge**. While at Cambridge, Calamy opposed the influential **Arminian** party and was thus excluded from a **fellowship**. However, he drew the attention of Nicholas Fenton, the Bishop of Ely, who made him his chaplain and granted him his first living at St. Mary's, Swaffham Prior. Calamy resigned this post in 1626 to serve at Bury St. Edmunds, where he labored with **Jeremiah Burroughs**. Here, he remained for 10 years until he, along with Burroughs and 30 other ministers in the diocese, resigned rather than subscribe to Bishop Wren's articles and injunctions. Calamy then served for a short time as rector, or possibly **lecturer**, at Rochford in Essex, but the climate damaged his health, leading him to resign this position also.

In 1641, Calamy was appointed to the **Westminster Assembly** of Divines, where he distinguished himself as a moderate in support of Presbyterianism and as an advocate of **Amyrauldianism**. He was also one of the ministers who wrote under the acronym **Smectymnuus**, in response to Bishop **Joseph Hall**'s defense of **episcopacy**. Calamy opposed the execution of **Charles I**, kept a low profile during the years of the **Commonwealth**, and supported the **Restoration** of **Charles II**. In 1660, he was selected as one of the divines sent to retrieve the Charles from Holland.

After the Restoration, Calamy was offered the bishopric of Coventry and Lichfield, but he rejected the offer. In 1662, he was ejected from office under the **Act of Uniformity**. He remained in London during his latter years, surviving the Great Fire of London in 1666, but dying shortly thereafter.

Calamy's published works are mostly **sermons**. His *Monster of Sinful Self Seeking Anatomized* has been republished by Kessinger. His son, Edmund Calamy the Younger, was also ejected from the ministry in 1662. His grandson, Edmund Calamy III, was an early historian of the Puritan movement.

CALVINISM. The theological system set forth by the 16th-century reformer John Calvin and further developed by such theologians as Ulrich Zwingli, Théodore Beza, and Heinrich Bullinger. A central tenant in Calvinist theology is the sovereignty of God over all creation. Because God is sovereign, human **salvation** is best understood as a gracious initiative undertaken by God. Thus, Calvin and his followers subscribed to the doctrine of **predestination**; that is, they believed that God in his mercy chooses to save some (the elect) and not others (the reprobate).

The basic principles of Calvinist theology were set forth in five concise points at the **Synod of Dort** in 1619.

- **Total Depravity**. As a result of the fall, all human beings are born corrupt and enslaved to **sin**. Because of this fallen nature, human beings are unable to choose voluntarily to follow God and thus stand condemned before him.
- **Unconditional Election**. God chooses whom he will save before time. Because human beings cannot in themselves do anything to affect their own salvation, faith is best understood not as a condition for salvation but as a proof of one's election.
- **Limited Atonement**. Salvation through the sacrifice of Jesus on the cross does not extend to all human beings but only to the elect.
- **Irresistible Grace**. God's sovereign grace, extended only to the elect, is always efficacious. Those whom God elects have no

power to resist his grace and thus are brought to saving faith in him.
- **Perseverance of Saints**. Because salvation is foreordained by God, those who are saved can never lose their salvation. The term "saints" includes all who are chosen by God.

The "Five Points of Calvinism" were developed in response to the teachings of Jacobus Arminius, who sought to modify what he considered to be the harsher elements of accepted Calvinist doctrines (*see* ARMINIANISM). Another theologian who worked to devise a more moderate form of Calvinism was Joseph Amyraut (*see* AMYRAULDIANISM).

Calvinism came to have an overwhelming influence on the English Reformation. This development is due, in part, to the harsh suppression of Lutheranism under **Henry VIII** and the subsequent persecution of Protestants under Queen **Mary I**. During the rule of Mary, many Protestant refugees fled to Switzerland and **Holland** (*see* MARIAN EXILES), where they imbibed Calvinist ideas. They then brought this influence back to England when Mary's sister **Elizabeth I** ascended the throne, their hope being to establish a national Church in England, based upon the model they had seen in Geneva and elsewhere. A commitment to the doctrine of God's sovereignty, as well as the principles of **covenant theology**, led many Puritans to seek reforms that extended beyond the church and into all areas of civic life. Their theocratic vision came to its fullest fruition during the **Interregnum** in England and in colonial New England.

Most of the Puritans embraced some form of Calvinism, as did many prominent non-Puritans. The **Thirty-Nine Articles** and the **Westminster Confession** are two of the most important doctrinal statements of English Calvinism. **John Knox** was the central figure in the spread of Calvinism to Scotland.

CAMBRIDGE. *See* CAMBRIDGE UNIVERSITY.

CAMBRIDGE PLATFORM. The Cambridge Platform is a document declaring the principles of church government and discipline for New England **Congregationalists**. It sets forth all the elements of Congregationalist polity, in addition to its fundamental principle: the independence of the local congregation. Accordingly, while the Platform allowed for church leaders to meet together in councils and synods, those groups would have no binding power. Because the Platform affirmed the union of church and state, it established that Congregationalist polity would be preserved by the civil government, which would also oversee matters of church doctrine. Representatives from 29 churches helped draft the Platform, which was adopted by the Congregational synod at Cambridge, Massachusetts, in 1648. Although the Cambridge Platform represents a rejection of the **Presbyterian** form of church government set forth by the **Westminster Assembly**, which had met two years before, it incorporated the **Westminster Confession**, the doctrinal statement of that Assembly.

CAMBRIDGE PLATONISTS. *See* CUDWORTH, RALPH.

CAMBRIDGE UNIVERSITY. A commonly accepted point of origin for Cambridge University is the year 1209, when scholars migrated from **Oxford** to Cambridge (50 miles northeast of London) to escape riots that had broken out between the scholars and citizens of Oxford. Hugo de Balsham, the Bishop of Ely, founded the university's first college, Peterhouse, in 1284. Over the next 300 years, 15 more colleges were added. In 1318, Pope John XXII recognized Cambridge as *studium generale*, making it, along with Oxford, one of the most prestigious universities in Europe. Its first professorship of divinity, the Lady Margaret Chair, was founded in 1502. Erasmus, the third Lady Margaret Professor, taught at Cambridge from 1511–14, and in that time helped bring the new learning of the Renaissance to England. Under Queen **Elizabeth I**, Cambridge was granted a revised body of statutes in 1570, under which the heads of the colleges were granted much of the governance of the university. **Parliament** formally incorporated the institution in 1571.

By the late 16th century, Cambridge had become known as a Puritan stronghold through the influence of such men as **Thomas Cartwright**. This reputation was heightened in 1584 when Sir **Walter Mildmay** founded **Emmanuel College** as a school for the training of Puritan ministers. For many decades, Cambridge continued to produce hundreds of ministers who spread the principles of Puritanism throughout England. Many of the intellectual, civil, and religious leaders of early New England received their education at Emmanuel, as well. Newtowne, Massachusetts, was renamed "Cambridge" in the university's honor, and **Harvard College**, located at Cambridge, was founded on the model of Emmanuel College.

CAPEL, RICHARD (1586–1656). English minister. Capel was the son of an alderman and a member of an ancient family of Hereford. He was born at Gloucester and entered St. Alban's Hall, **Oxford**, as a commoner in 1601. Capel graduated B.A. in 1605, and M.A. in 1607 from Magdalen College and was nominated a perpetual **fellow** of the College in 1609.

Capel served for a time as an attendant at court to the Earl of Somersby. In 1613, he was presented to the rectory of Eastington, where he became a leader of the Puritan party. When required to read the *Book of Sports* aloud before his congregation in 1633, Capel refused and resigned from the ministry. He then obtained a license to practice medicine and settled at his estate in Pitchcombe, near Stroud. In 1641, he was reinstated as a minister and resumed his ministry at Pitchcombe, where he remained for the rest of his life. Capel's chief work is *Tentations: Their Nature, Danger, and Cure* (1658).

CARTWRIGHT, THOMAS (1535–1603). English minister. Called the "Father of the Puritans," Cartwright was born in Hertfordshire and studied divinity at St. John's College, **Cambridge**, until he was forced to leave the university during the reign of Queen **Mary I**. During this period, he worked as a clerk, resuming his studies when Queen **Elizabeth I** ascended the throne. Cartwright was granted a **fellowship** at St. John's College and later at Trinity College, Cambridge, where his rhetorical skills earned him the distinction of debating against **John Preston** before the queen during a state visit in 1564. He served as the chaplain to the Archbishop of Armagh from 1565–67, and was also appointed Lady Margaret Professor of Divinity at Cambridge.

One of the first **Presbyterians**, Cartwright used his position at the university to criticize the structure and hierarchy of the Church of England. Thus, when John Whitgift became the vice-chancellor of Cambridge, he deprived Cartwright of both his professorship and fellowship, whereupon Cartwright left England to study with Theodore

Beza in Germany. Cartwright returned to England in 1572 with the hope of being appointed to a professorship of Hebrew but was denied the appointment for having expressed sympathy with John Field and Thomas Wilcox's "Admonition to **Parliament**." He fled England once again to avoid arrest and served as minister to English congregations in Antwerp and Middleburg. He also helped to organize Hugenot churches on the Channel Islands.

Cartwright drew the attention of James VI of Scotland (later **James I** of England), who offered him a chair at the University of St. Andrews, but Cartwright declined and returned, without permission, to London in 1585, where he was briefly imprisoned. He was appointed as Master of the Earl of Leicester's Hospital in Warwick, where he continued to preach, and was again imprisoned briefly in 1590 and 1591. He died in Warwick.

Cartwright is notable for his deep learning and his at times combative personality. As one of the early Puritans, he helped to establish the basic issues and tone of the movement. *See also* DUTCH PURITANISM.

CARYL, JOSEPH (1602–1673). English **Congregationalist minister**. Caryl was born in London and graduated from Exeter College, **Oxford**, after which he served as a preacher at Lincoln's Inn and also frequently preached before **Parliament**. Caryl was a member of the **Westminster Assembly** of Divines (1643) and served as a **trier** for the approbation of ministers. He was among the ministers who attended **Charles I** during his confinement at Holmby House, served as a commissioner in the Treaty of the Isle of Wight (1648), and was appointed by **Oliver Cromwell** to a **lectureship** at Oxford, along with **Edward Reynolds** and **Thomas Goodwin**. He was chosen, along with **John Owen**, to accompany Cromwell to Scotland in March 1650. An **Independent**, Caryl was also a member of the **Savoy Conference** of Congregational elders (1658).

Caryl served as minister at St. Magnus near London Bridge until he was ejected from the ministry under the **Act of Uniformity** in 1662. However, he continued to preach to an Independent congregation in London until his death. His successor in this position was John Owen.

The writing for which Caryl is best remembered is his massive 12-volume commentary on the Book of Job.

CATHOLICISM. From the Synod of Whitby in 664, the Roman Catholic Church was the official church of England. It remained so until 1534, when, through the Act of Supremacy, **Henry VIII** declared himself the head of the Church of England, dissolved the monasteries, and appropriated all church property. By the end of Henry's reign (1547), many Reformation ideas had taken hold, and, under King **Edward VI**, the Church of England continued to take shape as a Protestant denomination, particularly in its theology. However, the Catholic Church was restored during the reign of Queen **Mary I** (1553–58), and many Protestants were burned at the stake for heresy. After the Protestant Church of England was restored under Queen **Elizabeth I**, the memory of this persecution intensified anti-Catholic sentiment among English Protestants for generations. Also, Pope Gregory XIII proclaimed in 1580 that the assassination of Elizabeth, who had been excommunicated in 1570 as a heretic, would not be a mortal **sin**. The Elizabethan government responded by making it treason to be a Catholic priest and establishing laws and restrictions intended to eradicate the old faith. Nevertheless, certain areas of England, particularly Northern England, remained Catholic strongholds.

From this point to well into the 19th century, Roman Catholics were the victims of sometimes intense persecution. For many Puritans, anti-Catholic sentiment was also the basis of their opposition to the ***Book of Common Prayer*** and the practices of the **Anglican** church. The wearing of the **surplice**, the making of the sign of the cross, the use of images in **worship**, the observance of saints' feast days, and even the Episcopal form of church government, were seen as traces of the papist tradition they so despised. Even during the reigns of **Charles II**, who was secretly Catholic, and **James II**, who was openly Catholic, popular animosity toward Catholicism prevented its legalization. Although Protestant **Dissenters** stood to gain religious freedom under the **Declarations of Indulgence** proposed by Charles and James, most were so hostile to the idea of tolerating Catholics that they opposed these acts. And it was largely fear of the establishment of a Catholic dynasty that led to the **Glorious Revolution**.

CAVALIER. Name for supporters of **Charles I** during the **English Civil Wars**. The Parliamentarians coined "cavalier" as a derogatory term for the king's supporters. The stereotypical image of the cavalier was that of a swaggering, overdressed courtier with ringleted hair. The Royalists responded with their own derogatory term, "**Roundheads**," for supporters of the Parliamentarian cause. *See also* PARLIAMENT.

CAVALIER PARLIAMENT. *See* PARLIAMENT.

CHADERTON, LAURENCE (c. 1536–1640). Master of **Emmanuel College, Cambridge**. The exact date of Chaderton's birth is not known. He was the son of a wealthy and devout Roman **Catholic** gentleman, and he received his early education from Laurence Vaux, the author of a Catholic catechism. Chaderton entered Christ's College, Cambridge, in 1564–65. Here, he came to embrace Protestant principles, for which his father withdrew all financial support; however, Chaderton was able to continue his studies by obtaining a scholarship. He graduated in 1567 and was elected a **fellow** of Christ's College, where he served at various times as dean, tutor, and lecturer. Chaderton was also influential as an afternoon **lecturer** at St. Clement's Church in Cambridge, a lectureship he maintained for 50 years. In 1576, he married the daughter of Nicholas Culverwell and, in 1578, received his B.D.

In 1584, Sir **Walter Mildmay** invited Chaderton to become the first master of Emmanuel College, Cambridge. He held the position for 50 years and was instrumental in establishing Emmanuel College as a center of Puritan teaching. He was also one of the ministers chosen to present the Millenary Petition to King **James I** in 1604. From 1607–11, he was active in the production of the **King James Bible**. When he finally did resign as master of Emmanuel College, it was to ensure that a **Calvinist**—**John Preston**—would succeed him. Chaderton was noted for his keen and active intellect, even in old age. He died at the age of nearly 100 and is buried in Emmanuel Chapel.

Throughout his very long career, Chaderton distinguished himself as a moderate Puritan, respected and admired even by those who disagreed with him. His friends included more radical Puritans, such as **Thomas Cartwright** and **William Perkins**.

CHARLES I (1600–1649). King of England. Charles was born in Dunfermline, Fife, Scotland, the second son of King James VI of Scotland and Anne of Denmark. His father became King **James I** of England, the first English monarch of the Stuart dynasty in 1603. Charles joined his father in England the following year. When his elder brother Henry died in 1612, Charles became the heir apparent to the thrones of England, Ireland, and Scotland. He assumed the throne in 1625 after his father's death, and like his father, he asserted the divine right of kings. Unable to convince **Parliament** to concede to his position, Charles sought to govern strictly by personal rule and dismissed the Short Parliament after less than a month in May 1640, but Parliament's resistance to his policies eventually precipitated the **English Civil Wars**. Charles was ruthless to his political enemies, often bringing them up for charges without any hope of defense at the **Star Chamber**. Largely through his **Archbishop of Canterbury**, **William Laud**, Charles also pressed liturgical changes in the Church of England that angered the Puritans for evidence of popery; these included the required wearing of **vestments**, use of a revised *Book of Common Prayer*, and preaching that favored **Arminianism** over **Calvinism**.

Although Charles' attempts to implement these same reforms in Scotland at first met with resistance during the **Bishops' Wars**, such opposition softened when he begrudgingly recognized **Presbyterianism** as the Scottish national faith. However, this Royalist support from the north was not enough for Charles to overcome the combined animosity of the Long Parliament and the **New Model Army** in England, whose common distrust of Charles was greater than their mutual suspicion of each other. War commenced in 1642, and after Charles was able to avoid capture for several years either by holing up in Oxford or staying on the move, in 1647, Scottish troops captured Charles and handed him over to the army. Although Charles escaped for a time, and Royalist forces continued to fight, in January 1649, Charles finally stood trial. Following Charles' beheading at

Whitehall on 30 January, the **Protectorate** of **Oliver Cromwell** began. Charles' elder surviving son was crowned as King **Charles II** in May 1660, the date of the **Restoration** of the Stuart dynasty. His younger surviving son followed his brother to the throne in 1685 as King **James II**.

CHARLES II (1630–1685). King of England. Charles was the elder surviving son of King **Charles I** and Henrietta Maria of France. During the **English Civil Wars**, which culminated in the execution of his father by order of **Parliament**, Charles fought for a short time with Royalist forces, but he left England in 1646 to join his mother in France. In 1648, he moved to The Hague, where he fathered James Crofts, the future Duke of Monmouth, by Lucy Walter. After his father's death in January 1649, Charles received recognition by the Church of Scotland as Scotland's king upon subscribing to the **Solemn League and Covenant**. He and his Scottish allies were unable to overthrow **Oliver Cromwell**'s rule over England, however, and so he returned to France. After the death of Cromwell and the resignation under pressure of **Richard Cromwell** as the lord protector, General **George Monck** forced the Long Parliament to dissolve itself and give way to the Convention Parliament, which would end the **Interregnum** and recall Charles as England's ruler. After issuing the **Declaration of Breda**, which assured his tolerance of **Nonconformity**, Charles arrived in London and commenced the **Restoration** of the Stuart dynasty on 29 May 1660. Almost immediately, Charles ordered the execution of his father's living enemies and disinterred the bodies of Oliver Cromwell and his son-in-law **Henry Ireton**. His **Test Act** required all citizens to partake of communion in the Church of England. He ignored Breda and presided over a harsh persecution of **dissenters**, the most famous of whom was **John Bunyan**, who remained in the Bedford jail until Charles at last issued the **Declaration of Indulgence** in 1672. Charles was received into the Roman **Catholic** Church on his deathbed, and when his Catholic brother **James II** outmaneuvered Monmouth to take the throne in 1685, this only confirmed to many Puritans that Charles had supported a "**Popish Plot**" that would secure a Catholic successor on the throne.

CHARNOCK, STEPHEN (1628–1680). English Puritan divine. Charnock was born in the parish of St. Catherine Cree, London, and attended **Emmanuel College, Cambridge**, where he was converted under the influence of William Sancroft, later the **Archbishop of Canterbury**. Upon graduating, Charnock served for a short time as minister to a congregation in Southwark, until 1649, when he was granted a **fellowship** at New College, **Oxford**. He was subsequently appointed senior proctor (1652). In 1655, Charnock left Oxford to serve as chaplain to Henry Cromwell, son of **Oliver Cromwell**, in Ireland.

With the death of Cromwell and the **Restoration** of **Charles II**, Charnock lost this position and was unable to secure one elsewhere. He returned to London, where he continued his studies, although his entire library was lost in the Great Fire of London (1666). He also made occasional trips to France and **Holland**. In 1675, he was appointed joint pastor with **Thomas Watson** of a **Presbyterian** church in Bishopsgate, London.

Charnock published little during his lifetime, yet he is best remembered for his writings. His best-known work, *Discourses on the Existence and Perfections of God*, is a classic Puritan exposition on the doctrine of God and was reprinted by Baker Books in 1979. Charnock's other works include *A Treatise on Divine Providence*, *On Regeneration*, *On Man's Enmity to God*, and *On Reconciliation*.

CHAUNCY, CHARLES. English and American **Nonconformist** minister, second president of **Harvard College**. Chauncy was born in Yardlebury, Hertfordshire, to an old and prominent family. He graduated from Trinity College, **Cambridge**, and was then appointed to a lectureship in Greek. Chauncy held two vicarages, at Ware, Hertfordshire, and Marston, St. Lawrence, North Hamptonshire. He resisted the regulations imposed upon the clergy by Archbishop Laud and was brought before the High Commission in 1630 and 1634. The second time, he was suspended and imprisoned. After several months in prison, Chauncy chose to submit and recant his Nonconformist beliefs. However, in 1637, he penned a retraction of his submission, shortly before his departure to the Massachusetts colonies. The retraction was published in 1640.

For a year after his arrival in Plymouth, Chauncy served as assistant to the Reverend John Reyner. In 1641, he accepted the call to serve as minister in the nearby settlement of Scituate, where, despite maintaining the meager living his work provided, he remained for the next 12 years.

In 1654, Chauncy was called by his former church at Ware to return to its pulpit. Given the comparative religious freedom of the **Interregnum**, Chauncy accepted and was about to return when he received the invitation to become the second president of Harvard College. He served as president of Harvard until his death.

Chauncy wrote many works, including *The Doctrine of the **Sacrament**, with the Right Uses Thereof* (1642), *The Plain Doctrine of the Justification of a Sinner in the Sight of God* (1659), and *Thoughts on the State of Religion in New England* (1743).

CLARENDON CODE. The Clarendon Code consisted of four legal statutes passed by **Parliament** between 1661 and 1665. It took its name from Edward Hyde, the first Earl of Clarendon, and Lord Chancellor of England under **Charles II**. Clarendon himself opposed some of the provisions of the code, though he supported enforcement of the statutes after their passage. The code served to reestablish the authority of the **Anglican** Church and stifle **Nonconformity**.

The Corporation Act (1661) required all municipal officials to be members of the Anglican communion and to reject the 1643 **Solemn League and Covenant**, thus excluding Nonconformists from public office.

The 1662 **Act of Uniformity** required clergy to swear their assent to everything contained in the ***Book of Common Prayer***, the use of which was made compulsory in all church services. This act led to the ejection of more than 2,000 nonconforming ministers from their pulpits.

The **Conventicle Act** (1664) prohibited gatherings of more than five people for **worship** outside the auspices of the established church.

The **Five Mile Act**, passed in 1665, prohibited Nonconformist preachers from coming within five miles of any incorporated town where they had previously held a living, and it forbade them from teaching in schools.

Charles II sought to suspend penalties imposed under the Clarendon Code by issuing the 1662 **Declaration of Indulgence** but was unsuccessful in doing so. The effect of the code was to deepen religious divisions in post-**Restoration** England and severely restrict **religious liberty** for both Roman **Catholics** and Protestant **Dissenters**. *See also* TEST ACT.

CLARKSON, DAVID (1622–1686). English **Nonconformist** divine. Clarkson was born at Bradford, Yorkshire, and educated at Clare Hall, **Cambridge**, to which he was elected **fellow** in 1645. His pupils included John Tillotson, future **Archbishop of Canterbury**, who succeeded him in his fellowship in 1651. Clarkson was granted the perpetual curacy of Mortlake in Surrey, which he held until 1662, when he was ejected under the **Act of Uniformity**. Following his ejection, he became assistant to **John Owen** in an **Independent** congregation in London, and when Owen died in 1683, Clarkson succeeded him as pastor.

Clarkson's complete works were published in 1846. A three-volume collection of his works has been republished by Banner of Truth.

CLARKSON (or CLAXTON), LAURENCE (1615–1667). Ranter leader, member of multiple sects. Clarkson was born in Preston, Lancashire, and raised in the Church of England. He developed Puritan convictions early on and was particularly opposed to the desecration of the Sabbath with "maypoles, dancing and rioting." As a young man, Clarkson set out to explore the various English sects, including **Presbyterians, Independents**, and **antinomians**. He also entered the ministry, first holding a benefice in Pulham Market, Norfolk. Clarkson became minister of an **Anabaptist** congregation in 1644 and was imprisoned in 1645, until he recanted the practice of **baptism** by immersion. He was subsequently appointed minister of Sandridge Hertfordshire, where he remained for less than a year.

During this time, Clarkson began his prolific career as a pamphleteer; his early titles included *The Pilgrimage of Saints by Church Cast Out, in Christ Found, Seeking Truth* (1646) and *True Discovery Who Are the Troublers of True Israel* (1646). After unsuccessfully seeking to rejoin the Presbyterians in 1648, he joined a group of Ranters, of which he became the principal leader. According to

Clarkson's own claims, his principal qualification was his own unbridled licentiousness.

As a Ranter, Clarkson published a pamphlet titled *A Single Eye, All Light no Darkness, or Light and Darkness One* (1650), which the House of Commons deemed "impious and blasphemous." Its publication led to a month-long prison stay for its author. He was also banished, but the proclamation was never carried out. Upon his release, Clarkson became minister at Terrington St. John in Marshland, Norfolk. In 1658, he left Norfolk and moved to London, where he joined a group led by John Reeve and **Lodowick Muggleton**. Clarkson wrote several pamphlets defending Reeve's teachings and his own autobiography, *The Lost Sheep Found, or, The Prodigal Returned to His Fathers House, After Many a Sad and Weary Journey through Many Religious Countreys* (1660). However, with the death of Reeve, Clarkson came into conflict with Muggleton and sought to draw followers of his own out of the Muggletonian group. He was unsuccessful in doing so and eventually humbled himself before Muggleton, admitted his fault, and became a faithful disciple.

In his later years, Clarkson wrote works of practical morality. After the London Fire of 1666, he sought to establish a relief fund for the fire's victims, but the enterprise brought him to financial ruin. He was thrown into Ludgate prison for debt, where he remained for a year until his death.

COLLINGES, JOHN (1623–1690). English **Presbyterian** minister. The son of Edward Collinges, a clergyman, John Collinges was born in Boxted, Essex, and, until the age of 16, was educated at the grammar school of nearby Dedham, where he came under the **preaching** of **John Rogers** and, afterward, Matthew Newcomen. He attended **Cambridge**, and, at age 22, became preacher at Bures, Essex. While at Bures, he stayed with the family of Isaac Wyncoll and married the oldest daughter. In 1651, he accepted a call to St. Savior's parish in Norwich and, in 1653, to St. Stephens. He was appointed a commissioner of the **Savoy Conference** in 1661. In 1662, he was ejected from the ministry under the **Act of Uniformity**. For a brief time before his death, Collinges also served as minister of a Presbyterian chapel at Colgate.

Collinges was a voluminous writer. Many of his early works are polemical tracts on subjects such as lay-preaching, church government, Sabbath observance, and the celebration of Christmas. He wrote many devotional and pastoral works, including *Five Lessons for a Christian to Learn* (1650), *A Cordial for a Fainting Soul* (in three parts, 1649, 1650, and 1652), a commentary on Song of Solomon titled *Intercourses of Divine Love Between Christ and His Church* (1676), and a spiritual guide for weavers titled *The Weaver's Pocketbook, or Weaving Spiritualized* (1675). Collinges also wrote a significant number of the annotations for **Matthew Poole's** *Commentary on the Bible*.

COMMONWEALTH. After the execution of **Charles I** and the abolition of the monarchy in 1649, the **Rump Parliament** declared England a Commonwealth with a republican form of government. The term "Commonwealth" is often used to refer to the English government during the whole **Interregnum**, though the establishment of the **Protectorate** in 1653 marked a departure from the principles upon which the Commonwealth was established.

With the abolition of the monarchy, there were few checks on **Parliament's** legislative power. It created the Council of State, which replaced the **Privy Council** and which fulfilled many of the responsibilities of the former monarchy, but most members of the Council of State were also members of Parliament. Parliament replaced the Episcopal national church with a **Presbyterian** church; however, it allowed most dissenting groups to **worship** as they chose. It also enforced moral codes that prohibited plays, alehouses, Christmas celebrations, and that enforced strict Sabbath observance. These measures, along with high taxation necessary to fund military campaigns in Ireland and Scotland, contributed to the Rump's unpopularity, but the only real check to Parliament's authority lay with the army. **Oliver Cromwell**, the leader of the army, had served Parliament by crushing the Irish Rebellion in 1649 and defeating the Scots in 1650, but his distrust of the body led him to dismiss it forcibly on 26 April 1653, bringing the Commonwealth to an end.

CONGREGATIONALISM OR INDEPENDENCY. Congregationalism is a form of church governance in which individual congregations are self-governing and independent. Early Congregationalists (in England, early Congregationalists called themselves Independents) rejected not only the hierarchy of bishops who controlled the **Anglican** state church but the system of district assemblies proposed by **Presbyterians** as well.

In 1582, the principles of Congregationalism were first set forth by the **Separatist Robert Browne**, who is considered the father of Congregationalism, and whose followers were known as **Brownists**. Other early Congregationalist leaders, such as **Henry Barrow** and **John Greenwood**, were even more extreme in their rejection of established church government and practice. Their followers were known as **Barrowists**. The Elizabethan government took extreme measures to prevent the spread of Congregationalism, believing that tolerance would lead to civil and ecclesiastical anarchy. Greenwood and Barrow were executed, and other Congregationalists also faced death, imprisonment, or banishment. As a result, many early Congregationalists sought refuge in **Holland**. The largest congregation rose up in Leyden, where **John Robinson** was pastor. Members of this church comprised the group of **Pilgrims** that set sail on the Mayflower in 1620.

In New England, where Congregationalism was allowed to flourish without external hindrance, its principles led to the formation of a strict but thriving theocracy. Although early New England colonies developed into prosperous communities, they did so to the virtual exclusion of any dissenting views.

In England, varying degrees of government restraint under the Stuarts limited the growth of Congregationalism. However, during the **English Civil Wars**, Congregationalists grew in number and influence. **Oliver Cromwell** himself was a Congregationalist. In 1643, they were represented at the **Westminster Assembly** of Divines by **Thomas Goodwin**, **Philip Nye**, **Jeremiah Burroughs**, **William Bridge**, and **Sidrach Simpson**, known collectively as the **Five Dissenting Brethren**. In 1658, Congregationalist leaders met to compose the **Savoy Declaration**, a modified version of the **Westminster Confession**, expressing the basic principles of Congregationalism. The declaration was adopted as the authoritative statement of beliefs for Congregationalists churches both in England and in New England.

According to the Savoy Declaration, the elect are called by God to "walk together in particular Societies or Churches, for their mutual edification and the due performance of Public **Worship**." Each of these societies is a fully realized miniature version of the universal church and is not subject to external jurisdiction of any kind. Rather, all decisions regarding church governance, doctrine, and discipline are to be made by members of the church leadership, which consists of pastors, teachers, elders, and deacons. These officers are elected by members of the church body and **ordained** by the laying on of hands. Members are allowed into the church only by the consent of the church itself. Each church has the authority to discipline its members, including the authority to excommunicate, but such actions may only be taken against individual members. Churches may belong to synods or councils, but such bodies serve in an advisory capacity; they hold no authority over individual churches. A dissatisfied member may peaceably leave one church and join another.

Although the Congregationalists enjoyed religious freedom and growing influence during the **Interregnum**, the **Restoration** of the monarchy in 1660 led to their renewed persecution. Such edicts as the **Corporation Act** (1661), the **Act of Uniformity** (1662), the **Conventicle Act** (1663, 1670), the **Five-Mile Act** (1665), and the **Test Act** (1673) suppressed Congregationalism, as well as all other forms of dissent. Congregationalists achieved their freedom with the passing of the **Act of Toleration** in 1689, which suspended all penal laws in ecclesiastical matters.

CONSCIENCE. The Puritan idea of "conscience" is closely related to the teachings of John Calvin and Martin Luther on the subject. According to this idea, the conscience is the principal means by which God makes His word effectual in the lives of human beings. It is a rational faculty, providing the individual with self-knowledge, and a part of the image of God that human beings retain despite their fallen condition. As such, it speaks with the authority of God's voice. Of course, the conscience for most Puritans did not speak as the sole authority and was not itself trustworthy for **salvation**; it was always subject to God's will as revealed in the **Bible**. The **Quaker** reliance on the Inner Light was objectionable to many other Puritans for the reason that it seemed to privilege the conscience over God's Word.

The cultivation of a sensitive conscience was an essential part of the Godly life, and each believer was responsible for acting in accordance with it. **Preaching** filled an important role by consistently applying God's revealed truth to the consciences of its hearers.

The Puritans employed an impressive range of metaphors to express the function of the conscience in the life of the believer, describing it as a watchman, spokesman, mentor, preacher, God's deputy, and his spy. According to **Richard Sibbes**, the conscience served as a kind of court within each individual, acting variously as register, witnesses, accuser, judge, and executioner. **William Perkins** and **William Ames** helped form the Puritan idea of conscience with book-length examinations of the subject—*Cases of Conscience,* by Perkins, and *Conscience with the Power and Cases Thereof,* by Ames. Other Puritan works on the subject of conscience include **Robert Bolton**'s *Instructions for a Right Comforting Afflicted Consciences,* **Timothy Cruso**'s *The Blessedness of a Tender Conscience,* and **William Fenner**'s *The Soul's Looking Glasse, with a Treatise of Conscience.*

CONVENTICLE(S)/CONVENTICLE ACT. According to the Conventicle Act of 1664 (16 **Charles II** c. 4), a conventicle is a religious assembly of more than five people outside the auspices of the Church of England. Such gatherings were common among **Nonconformists**, who would often hold meetings in private homes or in the open country to **worship** according to the dictates of their **conscience**. One of several statues that comprised the **Clarendon Code**, The Conventicle Act prohibited such gatherings, which were often led by deposed ministers. Well-known Puritans who led conventicles include **Joseph Alleine**, **Samuel Annesley**, **Richard Baxter**, **Paul Baynes**, **William Bridge**, **John Flavel**, **William Jenkyn**, and Edward Laurence. The penalties for leading such gatherings included imprisonment and heavy fines. The penalties were lightened somewhat under the 1672 **Declaration of Indulgence**, and the law was finally repealed in 1689 with the passing of the **Act of Toleration**.

COPPE, ABIEZER (1619–1672). English **Ranter**, doctor. Coppe was born in Warwick. He was educated at the Warwick grammar school and, in 1636, entered All Souls, **Oxford**, as a servitor. While at Oxford, he served as the postmaster of Merton and led, by his own account, a grossly immoral life. He left the university upon the outbreak of the **English Civil Wars** without taking a degree. Like the other principal figure of the Ranter movement, **Laurence Clarkson**, Coppe was associated with several churches and sects. He first joined the **Presbyterians**, then became an **Anabaptist**, and served as a chaplain in the **New Model Army**.

Around 1650, Coppe became a Ranter and supposedly preached in the nude, which may account for his 14-week sojourn in the Warwick prison. He also published his best-known work, *A Fiery Flying Roll*, which was an extended tirade against social injustice and hypocrisy. The book so incensed the authorities that they banned it and ordered all copies to be burned by the common hangman. Its author was committed to the prison at Coventry and later to Newgate Prison. While at Newgate, Coppe wrote a remonstrance of his beliefs and, upon his release, preached a **sermon** of recantation at Burford, Oxfordshire. In his later years, Coppe changed his name to Higham and practiced medicine in the parish of Barnes, Surrey, while occasionally continuing to preach in **conventicles**.

CORPORATION ACT (1661). *See* CLARENDON CODE.

COTTON, JOHN (1585–1652). English and American Puritan divine, grandfather of **Cotton Mather**. John Cotton was born in Derby, England, and educated at Trinity College, **Cambridge**. He served as a **fellow**, head lecturer, dean, and tutor at **Emmanuel College**, Cambridge, before taking the vicarage of St. Botolph's in Boston, England, in 1612. He remained at St. Botolphs for the next 21 years. An extremely popular preacher, Cotton began at this time to develop Puritan sensibilities, which led him to forsake the observance of legally authorized ceremonies. When the High Commission Court began to take action against him, Cotton fled in disguise to London, where he remained hidden for several months until, eluding the watch set for him by civil authorities, he boarded a ship bound for the **Massachusetts Bay Colony** in 1633. In Massachusetts, Cotton accepted the call to serve as minister at the First Church of Boston, where his **preaching** was enthusiastically received.

Cotton had an enormous impact on the ecclesiastical and civil life of New England. Although he opposed democratic ideas and religious freedom, he played a central role in all major theological and political controversies of the period. He initially supported the cause of **Anne Hutchinson**, who was a member of his own congregation, but later withdrew his support and argued for her expulsion, as he did for **Roger Williams**.

As a writer, Cotton was both learned and prolific. Several of his works provide an exposition of New England **Congregationalism**, including *The Keys to the Kingdom of Heaven and the Power Thereof*, *The Way of the Churches of Christ in New England*, and *The Way of Congregational Churches Cleared*. He was also a contributor to the ***Bay Psalm Book***.

COVENANT THEOLOGY. Also known as **Federal Theology**. According to Covenant theology, God's relationship with humankind throughout history is best understood as a series of agreements set forth either explicitly or implicitly in the **Bible**. God established the first of these covenants with Adam, who acted as the representative of the entire human race. With this covenant, God promised eternal life as long as humanity lived in obedience to him but death if it disobeyed. Adam and Eve disobeyed God by eating the forbidden fruit; thus, all humanity stands condemned before God by imputation.

But God in his mercy established a second covenant in place of the first. This is the Covenant of Grace, in which God promises eternal life and blessings to all who believe in him. In the Old Testament, this agreement serves as the basis for the covenants established with Noah, Abraham, Moses, and David. In the New Testament, the New Covenant extends to all who believe in Christ, the second Adam, as the sacrifice by which God reconciles humanity to himself. Covenant theology also posits a third Covenant of Redemption between God the Son and God the Father. In this covenant, the Father appoints the son to serve as the substitutionary sacrifice that makes the Covenant of Grace possible.

Although Martin Luther and John Calvin both taught covenant theology in substance, later reformers, such as Caspar Olevianus, Zacharias Ursinus, Herman Witsius, and Heinrich Bullinger, are responsible for developing a full system of covenant theology. In

England, William Ames's *Marrow of Sacred Divinity* was an important work in the spread of this system. By the 17th century, the covenant was an established part of **Reformed theology**, expressed in both the **Westminster Confessions** and Catechisms.

For many Puritans, the **sacraments** were signs of the New Covenant and replaced or superseded signs of the old covenants established before the birth of Christ. They viewed the Lord's Supper as the replacement for the Passover, and **baptism** as the new circumcision. Paedobaptists based the practice of baptizing children on the belief that the covenant is established not only with believers but with their children as well.

The idea that covenants are collective in nature became a key element in the civic life of colonial New England. Early settlers in New England saw the covenant as extending beyond families and households to whole communities. They viewed themselves and their neighbors as bound together with God and with each other in a covenant relationship that assured their mutual prosperity. This conception of covenantal ties explains in part the strict guidelines governing virtually every aspect of human behavior among early American Puritans. One of the most extensive Puritan treatments of Covenant theology is Francis Roberts' *The Mystery and Marrow of the Bible*.

COVERDALE, MILES (c. 1488–1568). Bible translator. Little of Coverdale's early life is known. He was born in Yorkshire, studied theology at **Cambridge University**, and was **ordained** as a priest at Norwich in 1514. He entered the convent of Austin Friars at Cambridge, and, under the influence of the prior, Robert Barnes, and Thomas Cromwell, he came to embrace Reformed ideas. He left the convent in 1528 to become a secular priest and began to preach against transubstantiation, the use of images in **worship**, and making confessions. In 1528, having come to the attention of the bishops, he fled to the continent.

Accounts of Coverdale's life for the next seven years vary. He may have visited Hamburg and assisted William Tyndale in his translation of the Pentateuch. He may also have worked as a proofreader for the Antwerp printer Martin de Keyser. He was, at any rate, in Antwerp in 1534, and had begun work on a translation of the entire Bible. The first version of this Bible appeared in 1535, with a dedication to the king, and a revised version appeared in 1537. The Coverdale Bible was the first complete version of the Bible to be published in English.

In 1535, Coverdale returned to England, where he helped edit the **Great Bible** and translated tracts by Martin Luther and other continental reformers. He also published *Goostly Psalms and Spirituall Songs Drawen Out of the Holy Scriptures,* the first book of metrical Psalms rendered into English. But with the shift to a conservative regime in the English Church and the adoption of the Act of Six Articles in 1639, Coverdale fled England again. Before leaving, he also married, in direct violation of the Six Articles. During his second exile, he spent three years at Strasbourg. He translated works from Latin and German and wrote a defense of Barnes, who was burned at the stake as a heretic. He was made Doctor of Theology at Tubingen and became assistant minister at the Church of St. Thomas in the small town of Bergzabern, where he was also headmaster of the town school. Meanwhile, Coverdale's works were burned in England.

Coverdale returned to England a year after the accession of **Edward VI**. He was appointed an almoner of Queen Katherine Parr and a royal chaplain. He may also have been a consultant for the ***Book of Common Prayer***. When rebellion broke out in Cornwall and Devon over the adoption of the prayer book, Coverdale served as preacher to Lord Russell's force that put the rebellion down. Coverdale also became a popular preacher during this time, and, in 1551, was appointed Bishop of Exeter. In the meantime, he continued to translate works, such as Erasmus's *Paraphrases of the New Testament*.

With the accession of Queen **Mary I**, Coverdale was deprived of his bishopric and imprisoned but was eventually released through the influence of the King of Denmark, who also granted him amnesty. After a brief sojourn in Denmark, Coverdale returned to Bergzabern, staying for two years, after which he traveled to Arau. By 1558, he had settled in Geneva, where he very likely helped with the production of the **Geneva Bible**.

With the accession of Queen **Elizabeth I**, Coverdale returned to England in 1559. He was offered his old see but refused, choosing instead to minister to the church of St. Magnus, near London Bridge in 1564. Two years later, he resigned the pulpit, most likely in opposition to **Archbishop of Canterbury** Matthew Parker's rules regarding the wearing of **vestments**. Coverdale continued to be a popular preacher in his last years. He died at age 81 and is buried in the chancel of St. Bartholomew by the Exchange. *See also* MARIAN EXILES.

CRANMER, THOMAS (1489–1556). Archishop of Canterbury. Cranmer was born in Aslacton, Nottinghamshire. He went to **Cambridge** and was elected fellow of Jesus College in 1515. Around 1520, Cranmer began to develop an interest in Lutheran theology as he entered the church and pursued his theological studies. His rise to prominence began in the late 1520s, as **Henry VIII** began to seek the means by which he could divorce his first wife, Catherine of Aragon, and marry her lady-in-waiting, Anne Boleyn. In a chance meeting with two of Henry's advisers, Cranmer suggested a consultation with European divines. When the suggestion was conveyed to Henry, he summoned Cranmer for an interview, then commissioned him to write a treatise defending the proposed annulment. After Cranmer performed this service, Henry employed him on several diplomatic missions. While on one of these missions in Germany, Cranmer married.

When William Warham, the Archbishop of Canterbury, died in 1533, Henry selected Cranmer as his successor. As Archbishop, he dutifully approved the king's multiple marriages and divorces. All the while, Cranmer's own growing Protestant convictions put him at odds with Henry's policy of keeping the English church essentially **catholic**, despite its separation from the Roman Catholic Church. Cranmer opposed the Act of the Six Articles, especially because it forbade clergymen to marry and required that he send his own wife back to Germany. He also unsuccessfully pled for the lives of Anne Boleyn, Thomas More, and Thomas Cromwell, all of whom were beheaded at Henry's command.

With the death of Henry and the accession of **Edward VI**, however, Cranmer was able to pursue reforms of church theology and practice, moving the church in a strongly Protestant direction. Among other reforms, he allowed clergy to marry and repudiated the doctrine of transubstantiation. The beliefs of the church were set forth in the Forty-Two Articles, which were later revised under **Queen Elizabeth I** to the **Thirty-Eight Articles**. Cranmer also produced the *Book of*

Common Prayer, which provided a set liturgy in English, and an **Act of Uniformity**, requiring use of that liturgy in all churches.

Cranmer supported the succession of Lady Jane Grey after the death of Edward in 1553 and was charged with treason when **Mary I** acceded to the throne instead. After Mary revived the heresy laws, Cranmer was given the opportunity to recant, which he initially refused to do. However, after being forced to watch the burning of **John Hooper** and **Nicholas Ridley**, Cranmer made six recantations. These were deemed insufficient to spare him from execution, and he was brought to the stake on 22 March 1556. Instead of recanting his heresies publicly as was expected, Cranmer disavowed his former recantations and announced that his right hand should burn first for having signed them. Accordingly, before his body was consumed, he thrust his right hand into the flames.

Cranmer is recognized as one of the main architects of Anglicanism, and the story of his heroic martyrdom became a rallying point for Protestant dissidents during the reign of Queen Mary. When **Elizabeth I** came to the throne, she reinstated the church along the lines established by Cranmer, but many of her subjects had by then developed more radical Protestant views, and they viewed his reforms as too limited. Thus, while Cranmer's work endured, much of the Puritan movement gathered its force in opposition to the principles and practices he helped to establish.

CRISP, TOBIAS (1600–1643). English Puritan divine. Crisp was born in London to one of England's wealthiest families. His father, Ellis Crisp, was an alderman and sheriff of London. Crisp was educated first at Eton College, then at **Cambridge University**, where he received his B.A. He received his M.A. and D.D. from Balliol College, **Oxford**.

In 1627, Crisp became the rector at Brinkworth, Wiltshire. His **preaching** was well-received; furthermore, as a man of independent means, he gained a reputation for generosity and hospitality. Crisp supported the Puritan cause during the **English Civil Wars** and, as a result, was driven from the country by the king's soldiers and forced to take up residence in London, where his views on divine grace led him into conflict with other divines. Crisp died at age 43 of smallpox.

During his early days, Crisp was ostensibly inclined to **Arminianism**. His later repudiation of Arminian doctrine was so severe that many of his contemporaries suspected him of **antinomianism**. Others, including Augustus Toplady and Charles Spurgeon, dispute this claim. Crisp published nothing during his own lifetime, but 52 of his **sermons** were published after his death under the title *Christ Alone Exalted, in the Perfection and Encouragement of His Saints, Notwithstanding Their Sins and Trials*.

CROMWELL, OLIVER (1599–1658). Lord Protector of England. Born at Huntingdon to Robert and Elizabeth Cromwell, Oliver Cromwell entered Sidney Sussex College, **Cambridge**, in 1616 and married Elizabeth Bourchier in 1620. He represented Huntingdon in **Parliament** in 1628 and then made his living as a local administrator and collector of rents in Huntingdon, St. Ives, and Ely. In 1640, he again became a Member of Parliament, this time for Cambridge. He was one of the more outspoken **Independents** amidst the **Presbyterian** majority of both the Short and Long Parliaments.

Cromwell's landmark military career began in 1643 when he became a colonel in the Eastern Association of Parliament's army. His administrative capabilities were immediately obvious, and quickly he became both a lieutenant-general and the governor of the Isle of Ely. He participated in the important campaigns of Marston Moor in 1644, which secured the north of England for Parliament against King **Charles I**, and of Naseby in 1645, which won the south and southwest. Also in 1645, he signed the **Solemn League and Covenant** in order to win Scottish Presbyterian aid in the war effort, yet he fully supported the **Self-Denying Ordinance**, which excluded many Presbyterian Parliamentarians from holding military posts in the restructured **New Model Army**. Cromwell rose to second-in-command by the request of captain-general, Sir **Thomas Fairfax**. For the next several years, his primary responsibility was to quell Royalist uprisings in Scotland and Ireland. He signed the death warrant for the king and became a member of the Council of State in 1649.

In 1650, Fairfax resigned his commission, and Cromwell acceded to leadership of the army, leaving his son-in-law **Henry Ireton** in charge of affairs in Ireland. Although Cromwell was wary of some of the more politically radical **dissenters**, like the **Levellers**, he also believed that the Presbyterian leadership of Parliament was not interested in including even moderate Independents like himself in the future government of the **Commonwealth**. In 1653, the same year that he married his second wife Frances Russell, he showed his political and military might by dismissing the Long Parliament. On 16 December 1653, he became the Lord Protector of England under the Instrument of Government and ruled England and its territories as a military governor.

Cromwell immediately involved himself in both the political and religious affairs of the nation. He redrew the voting districts and placed them under the charge of majors-general. He summoned two **Protectorate Parliaments** for assistance in raising money to fight the Dutch, but he also quickly dismissed both for being disagreeable even though their makeup was largely shaped by his own political influence. He appointed **triers** of ministers to ensure Puritan orthodoxy across the land, and he discontinued for a time all use of the *Book of Common Prayer*. Yet he was largely tolerant of the many varieties of Protestantism, meeting personally with **Nonconformist** leaders, such as **George Fox**, and receiving the encouragement of **John Milton** to continue to defend liberty of **conscience**. In 1657, Cromwell decided to resist taking the crown, as offered under the Humble Petition and Advice. Instead, he received a second installation as Lord Protector. When he died in September 1658, he received a state funeral at Westminster Abbey, and his son **Richard Cromwell** began a mere eight-month rule in his stead that ended in resignation and made way for the **Restoration**. When **Charles II** took the throne, he ordered that Cromwell's body be disinterred and publicly mutilated at Tyburn. A large statue of Cromwell now stands in front of the Parliament building in London.

CROMWELL, RICHARD (1626–1712). Lord Protector of England. Richard Cromwell was the third son of Elizabeth and **Oliver Cromwell**. He served in the Parliamentary Army during the First **English Civil War** (1642–46) and became a member of Lincoln's Inn in 1647. Cromwell married Dorothy Mayor (or Major) in 1649. He was elected to **Parliament** for Hampshire in 1654 and was appointed a member of the Committee for Trade and Navigation in

1655. Cromwell also served as Member of Parliament for **Cambridge University** from 1656–68; in 1657, he was appointed to the Council of State and to the Upper House in Parliament. Cromwell showed less interest in statesmanship during the first part of his father's **Protectorate** than in hunting and field sports, and he suffered financial troubles through mismanagement of his estate. However, as the oldest surviving son of Oliver Cromwell, he succeeded his father as Lord Protector upon Oliver's death on 3 September 1658. He held the position for a mere eight months.

Cromwell had the support of the Third Protectorate Parliament, which he summoned in January 1659. But many in the army had reservations about the new lord protector, especially in his role as military commander-in-chief. Already smoldering hostilities between the army and Parliament intensified when Parliament questioned the army's treatment of **Fifth Monarchists** and **Cavaliers**. Matters worsened as members of Parliament moved to impeach Major General William Boteler for actions performed under the authority of Oliver Cromwell. The army responded by establishing an Army Council, which stood in direct opposition to Parliament. Parliament, in turn, prohibited meetings of the council. When Cromwell was informed of an army plot to seize him at Whitehall, he responded famously, "I will not have a drop of blood spilt for the preservation of my greatness, which is a burden to me." The army rendezvoused at St. James' on 21 April, and army officials demanded that Cromwell dissolve Parliament—a demand with which he ultimately complied.

Although the chief army officers intended for Cromwell to remain lord protector, pressure from junior officers and members of the republican party ultimately led them to recall the Long Parliament, which voted to abolish the Protectorate on 7 May 1659. Cromwell resigned on 24 May. Deeply in debt and in danger of being arrested by his creditors, Cromwell fled to France in 1660, where he assumed the alias "John Clarke" and lived on his wife's inheritance of £600 per year. He remained on the continent until 1680, when he returned to England. Cromwell took up residence in the house of a Sargeant Pengelly in Cheshunt, where he quietly spent his remaining years.

CRUSO, TIMOTHY (c. 1656–1697). Presbyterian minister. Cruso was born in Newington Green, Middlesex, and studied for the ministry at Newington Green Academy under Charles Morton, future vice-president of **Harvard College**. **Daniel Defoe** was a fellow student at Newington, and a nominal connection has been suggested between Cruso and Defoe's *Robinson Crusoe*. Cruso received his M.A. in Scotland and, by 1688, was pastor to a Presbyterian congregation at Crutched Friars.

Cruso earned a reputation not only as a sound practical preacher but as a noncontrovertialist. When tension between Presbyterians and **Independents** led to the withdrawal of several Presbyterian ministers from the Pinner's Hall merchant **lectureships**, Cruso was invited to fill one of the vacancies. He is said to have enjoyed "the pleasures of the table" and such enjoyment may have contributed to his early death. He is buried in Stepney Church.

Two works for which Cruso is especially remembered are his *Sermons on the Rich Man and Lazarus* (1696) and *The Blessedness of a Tender Conscience* (1691).

CUDWORTH, RALPH (1617–1688). Philosopher. Cudworth was born in Aller, Somersetshire. The son of the rector, he entered **Emmanuel College, Cambridge,** in 1632, took his master's degree in 1639, and was appointed **fellow** and tutor in 1639. In 1645, he was appointed master of Clare College and professor of Hebrew.

In this capacity, he became known as one of the leaders of the **Cambridge Platonists**, a group of theologians, philosophers, and scientists that included Henry More, Benjamin Whichcote, **Peter Sterry**, and John Worthington. The Cambridge Platonists used platonic philosophy to demonstrate the compatibility of faith and reason. They opposed the tendency of thinkers, such as John Hobbes and René Descarte, to remove God from natural processes or assign him a secondary role. At the same time, they opposed the Puritan notion of non-rational, passive spiritual revelation. Reared as a Puritan, Cudworth embraced certain **Nonconformist** ideas, such as the freedom of individual choice over authoritarian rule in matters of religious practice.

In 1646, Cudworth earned his bachelor of divinity. His **sermons**, such as the one preached before the House of Commons in 1647, advocated tolerance in the charged religious and political atmosphere of the decade. He served as rector of North Cadbury, Somerset, from

1650–54, and was appointed master of Christ's College, Cambridge. He married in 1658; his daughter, Demaris, would later become a friend of John Locke. In 1662, he was made rector of Ashwell, Herts.

In 1678, the same year he was appointed to the Prebendary of Gloucester, Cudworth published his major philosophical work, *The True Intellectual System of the Universe*, an anti-deterministic argument for the existence of a supreme being. The work opposes two forms of atheism: Hobbesien atomism and hylozoism, which attributes life to matter. Cudworth also sought a synthesis of mechanistic atomism and Platonic metaphysics, employing the concept of the Plastic Medium, essentially a revival of Plato's concept of World Soul.

Two of Cudworth's works were published after his death: *A Treatise Concerning Eternal and Immutable Morality* (1731) and *A Treatise of Free Will* (1838). He was also the author of several theological works, including *A Discourse Concerning the True Nature of the Lord's Supper* and *The Union of Christ and the Church* (1642).

CULPEPER, NICHOLAS (1616–1654). English physician. Born in London 13 days after his fathers' death, Culpeper was reared by his mother in her parents' home in Essex. At age 16, he was sent to **Cambridge** to prepare for the ministry. While at Cambridge, he made plans to marry secretly, but his fiancée died when her coach was struck by lightning. Culpeper's family cut off their support when they heard of the affair; consequently, he left Cambridge and went to London, where he became an apprentice to an apothecary. In 1640, he set up his own thriving medical practice in Spital Fields. During the **English Civil Wars**, he fought on the Parliamentary side and suffered a severe chest wound in the Battle of Newbury.

In 1649, Culpeper published an English translation of *A Physical Directory*, the physicians' pharmacopoeia. Previously available only in Latin, the publication of the *Directory* posed a direct challenge to the medical establishment, enabling common readers to diagnose and treat their own illnesses without the guidance of a doctor. In 1653, Culpeper published *The English Physician, or Herball*, for which he is best known. It is the first guide to the medicinal use of native plants and herbs to be published in English.

Culpeper died of tuberculosis at age 37. He left behind over 70 unfinished manuscripts, many of which were published after his death.

– D –

DAVENANT, JOHN (1572–1641). Bishop of Salisbury. The son of a wealthy merchant, John Davenant was born in Watling Street, London. He attended Merchant Taylors' School and entered Queens' College, **Cambridge**, as a pensioner in 1587. He graduated B.A. in 1591, M.A. in 1594, and was admitted a **fellow** of the college in 1597. Davenant received his B.D. in 1601, his D.D. in 1609, and was appointed Lady Margaret Professor of Divinity, a post he held until 1621. He also held the rectorships of Fleet, Lincolnshire, and Leake, Nottinghamshire. Through the influence of wealthy patrons, such as the Earls of Rochester and Salisbury, Davenant was appointed president of Queens' College in 1614. In 1618, King **James I** made Davenant one of his royal chaplains and sent him as part of the English delegation that attended the **Synod of Dort**. Davenant presented the case for hypothetical universalism, also known as **Amyrauldianism**, and exerted considerable influence over the synod's decisions. In 1620, he was made rector at Cottenham, Cambridgeshire. In 1621, he succeeded his brother-in-law Robert Townson as Bishop of Salisbury.

As a prominent member of the clergy, Davenant conformed to the practices of the established church; however, he was also a staunch defender of **Calvinist** theology and a strong opponent of the **Arminian** theology that held sway in the church during the rule of **William Laud**. In 1630, he was brought before the **Privy Council** for teaching **predestination** in a Lent **sermon** preached at court. Let go with a warning from the King **Charles I**, he continued to promote Reformed principles, working with Thomas Morton and **Joseph Hall** to create a union of Reformed churches in England and on the continent. In 1640, Davenant unsuccessfully urged **Parliament** to adopt a canon suppressing Arminianism. He did, however, assent to the canons in their final version, as well as to the *Et Cetera* **Oath**, though he had reservations concerning its wording. Davenant died in the same year that the canons were approved.

DAVENPORT, JOHN (1597–1670). English and American **Congregationalist** minister, founder of New Haven, Connecticut. Davenport was born in Coventry, the son of the mayor. He entered **Oxford** in 1613, and in 1615, became chaplain at Hilton Castle near Durham. He returned to Oxford in 1625 to receive his M.A. and was appointed vicar of St. Stephen's Church in Coleman Street, London. Along with **William Gouge**, **Richard Sibbes**, and others, Davenport participated in a scheme to purchase **lay impropriations**, the profits of which would support the ministers of poor congregations. The plan was thwarted by **Archbishop of Canterbury William Laud**, who considered it a means of promoting **Nonconformity**. Up to this point, Davenport had outwardly conformed to the practices of the church. Along with **Thomas Goodwin**, **Philip Nye**, and **William Twisse**, Davenport even met with **Thomas Hooker** and **John Cotton** to urge them to conform to the practices of the **Anglican** Church as well. Instead, the reverse happened: Cotton convinced Davenport and some of the others that conformity came at too high a price. Davenport subsequently removed to the Netherlands, where he served two unofficial congregations in Rotterdam and Amsterdam. He returned to England briefly before sailing for New England in 1636.

Sailing on the *Hector*, Davenport arrived in Boston in 1637, just in time to participate in the Cambridge synod at which **Anne Hutchinson** was tried. In 1638, he left Boston to found a colony at Quinnipac, later called New Haven. Davenport played a central role in the creation of the Colony's constitution, which stipulated that only church members could vote or hold office. It also called for the creation of a governing body called the "Seven Pillars of State," of which Davenport was one. For the next 30 years, he stood as a major figure in the civil and religious life of the colony. When William Goffe and Edward Whalley fled to New England to avoid prosecution for their part in the execution of **Charles I**, Davenport concealed them in his house. He also led the failed opposition to the charter that united the New Haven Colony with Connecticut.

In 1668, Davenport accepted a call to serve as pastor to First Church in Boston. Here, he found himself in opposition to the **Half-Way Covenant**, adopted by that church in 1662. The conflict led to an acrimonious split and the formation of Old South Church. The controversy continued long after Davenport's death two years later. He is buried in John Cotton's tomb.

DECLARATION OF BREDA. The proclamation in which **Charles II** set forth the conditions under which he would return to England as king. Charles drew up the declaration with help from three advisers: Sir Edward Hyde, the Marquis of Ormond, and Sir Edward Nicholas. In it, he offered general pardon to the enemies of his father, the deposed and executed **Charles I**; only those directly involved in the former king's execution would be held to account. The declaration expressed Charles' desire to ease restrictions on **religious liberty**; it offered full payment of arrears to soldiers, and promised fair settlement of land disputes. Charles also accepted legislation of the first two years of the **Long Parliament**. Finally, he recognized the right of **Parliament** to levy taxes and extended the full exercise of justice to the common courts.

Charles and his advisers issued the Declaration of Breda on 4 April 1660. Copies were sent to House of Lords, House of Commons, the Fleet, the Council of State, and the City of London. Both houses of Parliament responded by voting for the **Restoration** of the monarchy under Charles. Despite the assurances of toleration provided in the Declaration, the Restoration brought about new measures, such as the **Clarendon Code**, that curtailed religious liberty.

DECLARATION OF INDULGENCE. Five Declarations of Indulgence were issued between 1660 and 1688. The first three were issued by **Charles II** and the latter two by **James II**. To a greater or lesser extent, the aim of these declarations was to provide greater religious freedom by suspending Parliamentary legislation aimed at those who refused to **worship** according to the established practices of the Church of England.

Charles' declarations served two purposes: they were intended to ease conflict between the **Anglican** and Puritan factions, but as a secret **Catholic**, Charles also hoped to create freedom of worship for the sake of Roman Catholics in England, and he was under pressure from abroad to do so, as well. In the **Declaration of Breda**, Charles had announced his desire to establish religious freedom in England upon his accession. The first Declaration of Indulgence (1660) exempted offenders from prosecution for their refusal to conform in minor matters of ceremony. It was hoped that this declaration, along with the calling of the **Savoy Conference**, would build a rapprochement between members of the Puritan and Anglican parties. But negotiations between the two sides at the conference broke down and the declaration quickly died.

The second Declaration of Indulgence was issued in 1662, in response to the passing of the **Clarendon Code**, a set of acts established by the new **Cavalier Parliament** to demand uniformity of practice in all English churches. Charles intended that his declaration would suspend prosecutions under the Clarendon Code, but Parliamentary opposition forced him to withdraw the declaration the following year. Charles issued his third and most famous Declaration of Indulgence in 1672. Opposition to this declaration was so fierce that Charles was not only forced to withdraw it but to approve further restrictions on the right of English Catholics to hold public office.

The openly Catholic James II hoped, like his brother, to make England a place where his fellow Catholics would be free to worship. On 4 April 1687, he made his first Declaration of Indulgence, in which he suspended all penal laws in ecclesiastical matters, permitted individuals to worship in churches other than the established church, and ceased to require religious oaths for civil and military offices. When this declaration was generally ignored, James made another Declaration in 1688, and required that it be read in all churches on two consecutive Sundays. Opposition to this last declaration helped foment the **Glorious Revolution**.

DECLARATION OF SPORTS. See BOOK OF SPORTS.

DEFOE, DANIEL (c. 1660–1731). Satirist, novelist, and journalist. Defoe was born in Cripplegate, London. His father, John Foe (Daniel added the "de") was a butcher and a **dissenter**. Defoe was educated at the academy of the Puritan teacher Charles Morton in Newington Green, just north of London. Although Morton's school chiefly trained young men for the **Presbyterian** ministry, Defoe exhibited greater interest in business and, in 1685, set up shop in London as a merchant and as a seller of marine insurance. By 1692, he was bankrupt, due in part to England's wars in France. Defoe would continue to be plagued by financial trouble throughout much of his life.

In 1685, Defoe joined the ill-fated **Monmouth Rebellion** against **James II**. He was a staunch supporter of William of Orange, whose army he joined in 1688. When some expressed scorn for William's Dutch origins, Defoe responded with a satiric poem titled *The True-Born Englishman* (1701), in which he asserted that William's pedigree was perfectly suited to England, a nation of mongrels, the offspring of generations of European scum. The next 25 years saw Defoe publishing a vast number of pamphlets, journals, articles, and satires, making him one of the most influential and prolific political commentators of the early 18th century. One of his most controversial pieces was the satiric essay "The Shortest Way with Dissenters" (1702). Written in response to the growing concern over "occasional conformity," the essay suggested that the best way to deal with **dissenters** was simply to execute or banish them. Unfortunately, the satiric nature of the proposal eluded many readers. Extreme Tories endorsed it, while Defoe's fellow dissenters viewed him as a traitor to their cause. Furthermore, the essay led to charges of libel against the Church of England. After a period of hiding, Defoe was fined, pilloried, and imprisoned; however, his popularity became evident when onlookers garlanded the pillory with flowers, formed an honor guard around him, and drank to his health. While at Newgate prison, Defoe wrote the mock Pindaric ode, *Hymn to the Pillory* (1703).

With incarceration and failing business ventures, the husband and father of five faced financial destitution. Deliverance from these woes came in the form of an offer from Whig leader Robert Harley. In exchange for release from prison and a pension, Defoe would provide "several honorable, though secret, services." These included traveling to Scotland undercover to meet with the party favoring union. Defoe also seems to have carried his responsibilities as a government agent into his work as the founder of *A Review of the Affairs of France, With Observations on Transaction at Home* (1704). Defoe served as the principal writer, editor, and publisher of the paper, which appeared three times a week for the next nine years. At the outset, Defoe used the *Review* to endorse Whig policies; however, he allowed his opinions to shift with changes in government, endorsing the Tory's policies, as well, when they, in turn, held power.

Defoe continued to publish the *Review* until 1715, when he was charged with libel. He avoided a prison sentence by agreeing to edit the pro-Tory newspaper, *The News Letter*. As a government agent, he also served as managing editor of the Jacobite *Mist's Journal*. Eventually, however, his connections to the government led to the ruin of his reputation as a journalist, and this partly appears to be the reason that he turned to the writing of novels.

Defoe's first novel, *Robinson Crusoe*, based loosely on the true story of castaway Andrew Selkirk, was published in 1719. The immediate success of the book led to the publication of two sequels, and, within five years, nine more novels. The plots of Defoe's novels typically involve protagonists who, either by choice or necessity, are drawn into lives of vice and crime. Their adventures are usually recounted in first person and sometimes in lurid detail; and their wicked ways often lead not only to penitence but also to financial success. His novels include the still widely read *Moll Flanders* and *Roxana*, both of which feature a female narrator/protagonist. Defoe also published an account of the 1664–65 London plague epidemic, *A Journal of the Plague Year* (1722). The book is notable for its careful historical research—Defoe himself was only five years old in 1664—and its graphic, realistic narrative.

In his last years, Defoe seems to have achieved, like many of his characters, a level of prosperity, but in a letter to his son-in-law a year before his death, Defoe wrote that he was in hiding, living in fear of "a wicked, perjured, and contemptible enemy." No single person has ever been identified as Defoe's nemesis, though his work as a journalist and government agent certainly earned him a fair share of enemies.

Defoe died near his place of birth in Cripplegate and is buried in **Bunhill Fields**. He is recognized not only as one of the 18th century's most prolific writers but as one of the first English novelists, several of whose works are still widely read. Also, although hardly an exemplar of journalistic integrity, he is remembered as one of the fathers of modern English journalism.

DEVEREUX, ROBERT (1591–1646). Third **Earl of Essex**, Commander of the Parliamentary forces in the **English Civil Wars**. Born in London, Devereux was the son of Robert Devereux and Frances Walsingham.

His father, a favorite of Queen **Elizabeth I**, was executed for treason in 1601. His inheritance, of which he was initially deprived, was restored by **James I** in 1604, and the younger Devereux was educated alongside James' son Henry, Prince of Wales. James arranged Devereux's marriage to Lady Frances Howard in 1606, but the marriage was annulled in 1613, after Lady Frances was found to be having an affair with Robert Carr, one of James' favorites.

Devereux retired to his house at Chartley and played no role in public affairs until 1620, when he served with a volunteer force in support of Frederick V of Bohemia. In 1625, he led an unsuccessful naval assault on Cadiz. When **Charles I** sought to impose forced loans after the dissolution of the second **Parliament**, Devereux was among those who refused to consent. He also signed the **Petition of Right**. In 1631, he contracted his second marriage, but this marriage also ended in separation as a result of his wife, Elizabeth Paulet's, alleged infidelity. In anticipation of the First **Bishops' War**, Devereux was appointed lieutenant general of the army in 1639, but a truce was signed and the army disbanded before he could lead his force into battle. He was subsequently discharged from his position and denied further promotion.

In 1640, Devereux was appointed to the commission that negotiated with the Scots at Yorkshire. He urged the king to convene Parliament. In 1641, Charles appointed him to the **Privy Council**, but in this capacity he acted against the king by voting for the condemnation of the Earl of Strafford, one of Charles' most trusted advisers. When the First **English Civil War** broke out in 1642, he sided with Parliament, became a general of the Parliamentarian army, and was proclaimed a traitor by Charles. Devereux fought successfully at Edgehill; he also captured Reading and relieved Gloucester in 1643. However, he failed to bring about a decisive victory at Newbury, Essex, and was unsuccessful in his attempt to take **Oxford**. He also suffered defeat at Lostwithiel, Cornwall in August 1644. **Oliver Cromwell** roundly criticized Devereux before Parliament, and Devereux, in turn, opposed the formation of the **New Model Army**. Under the **Self-Denying Ordinance**, he was forced to resign his commission. However, in 1645, Parliament recognized his contributions and granted him an annuity of £10,000. Devereux died a year later and was buried at Westminster.

DIGGERS OR TRUE LEVELLERS. The Digger movement arose in response to the dire economic conditions of England near the end of the **English Civil Wars** and in early years of the **Interregnum**. It consisted of a number of groups that appear to have sprung up simultaneously throughout central and southern England. These groups comprised individuals who banded together to cultivate common lands and share their property.

One of the first Digger communities took root around 1648. It published a tract titled *Light Shining in Buckinghamshire*, in December of that year, followed by *More Light Shining in Buckinghamshire*, in 1649. The most famous Digger community rose up in April 1649, when a group of about 15 men gathered at St. George's Hill, Surrey, to collectively farm common wasteland. The group's leaders were William Everard and **Gerard Winstanely**. The same month the group published its manifesto, *The True Leveller's Standard Advanced*. Winstanley became the spokesman for the movement and wrote a number of pamphlets, such as *The New Law of Righteousness* (1648), *The New Law of Righteousness Budding Forth* (1649), and *A Declaration from the Poor Oppressed People of England* (1649). These works laid out an agenda for the Diggers that called for "the leveling of all estates," or the abolition of private property rights, which Winstanely equated both with the fall of humankind and the Norman Conquest. In its place, he proposed a form of utopian communism.

The Diggers at St. George's Hill were thwarted in their efforts by local landowners and clergymen who accused them of trespassing and incited mobs to tear down the Diggers' houses and trample their crops. Its number having grown to about 50, the group relocated to nearby Cobham Heath, where similar problems led to its dispersal in 1650. Other Digger communities rose up in various locations, including Dunstable in Bedfordshire, Barnet in Hamptonshire, Bosworth in Leicestershire, Entfield in Middlesex, and Wellingborough in Northamptonshire. All met a similar demise to that of Winstanely's group. In 1652, Winstanley published *The Law of Freedom in a Platform* with a dedication to **Oliver Cromwell**; however, by this point, most Digger communities seem to have been broken up. Digger ideas had virtually no impact on domestic policy during the **Commonwealth** or **Protectorate**. However, the socialist, communist, and anarchist movements of the 19th and 20th centuries do bear their influence. *See also* LEVELLERS.

DINGLEY, ROBERT (1619–1660). English minister. Dingley entered Magdalen College, **Oxford**, in 1634, received his B.A. and his M.A., and then took holy orders. Although he initially held strong **Anglican** views, he became a staunch Puritan and supported **Parliament** at the outbreak of the **English Civil Wars** (1642). He was presented to the rectory of Brightstone on the Isle of Wight, where he earned a reputation for outstanding **preaching**. He was also zealous in the cause of removing ignorant and scandalous schoolmasters and ministers from their positions. Dingley died at Brightstone and is buried in the chancel of his church. He is best remembered for his work *The Spiritual Taste Described, or a Glimpse of Christ Discovered* (1649), republished as *Divine Relishes of Matchless Goodness* (1651).

DISSENTER(S). The early use of the term "dissenters" generally includes all persons, whether **Catholic** or Protestant, who separated themselves for the sake of religious principle from communion with the established churches of England or Scotland. Only later did it come to denote exclusively Protestants who dissented. The term is often used interchangeably with "**Nonconformists**," but "dissenters" can refer not only to those who oppose the teachings and practices of the national church but also those who oppose the very idea of a national or state church.

DOD, JOHN (c. 1549–1645). English Puritan minister. Dod was born as Shotlidge, near Malpas, Cheshire. He was the youngest in a family of 17, and his parents were moderately wealthy country gentlefolk. Dod received his early education at Westchester, and when he was 14, his parents sent him to Jesus College, **Cambridge**. He graduated B.A. in 1576, was appointed **fellow** in 1579, and proceeded M.A. in 1580. During a dispute with a college steward over an unpaid bill, Dod flew into such a rage that he became ill, and in a fever experienced a profound recognition of guilt, ultimately leading to his conversion. While at Cambridge, he began delivering **lectures** at the nearby town of Ely. Despite offers from other colleges, Dod remained at Jesus College until 1585, when he was presented with the vicarage of Hanwell in Oxfordshire, a position he occupied for the next 20 years. While at Hanwell, he married the stepdaughter of **Richard Greenham,** Ann Bownd, with whom he had 12 children.

In 1604, Dod was suspended by the Bishop of **Oxford** for **Nonconformity**. He resumed **preaching** at Fenny-Compton, Warwickshire, and, after that, at Canons Ashby, Northamptonshire, until he was silenced by **Archbishop of Canterbury George Abbot** at the command of **James I**. Subsequently, he was offered the rectory of Fawsley, where he remained for he rest of his life.

Noted for his wit, directness of speech, and deep religious conviction, Dod was one of the most popular and influential preachers of his day and a major early figure of the Puritan movement. He preached at **Thomas Cartwright**'s funeral and was a friend of **Richard Sibbes**, **Arthur Hildersham**, **John Preston**, and many others. His works include *A Plain and Familiar Exposition of the Lord's Prayer*. With Robert Cleaver, he co-wrote *A Treatise or Exposition on the Ten Commandments* (1603) and *A Brief Explanation of the Whole Book of the Proverbs of Solomon*.

DOOLITTLE, THOMAS (c. 1630–1707). **Nonconformist** minister and tutor. Doolittle was the son of a glover. Born at Kidderminster, he grew up under the **preaching** of **Richard Baxter**, who encouraged him to enter the ministry. The series of **sermons** later published by Baxter under the title *The Saint's Everlasting Rest* led to Doolittle's conversion. He was apprenticed for a time to a lawyer but refused to do copywork on Sunday. He then entered Pembroke Hall, **Cambridge**, as a sizar (a student required to pay minimal fees), graduating B.A. in 1653, and M.A. in 1655. Having been **ordained** as a **Presbyterian** minister, he was chosen to be pastor of St. Alphage, London Wall. Doolittle was a popular preacher, but, in 1662, he was ejected from his pulpit under the **Act of Uniformity**.

Doolittle supported himself by opening a boarding school in Moorfield; his students included **Edmund Calamy**, **Matthew Henry**, and other distinguished Puritans. But despite the success of the school, various relocations—sometimes to avoid arrest and seizure of goods—made its operation difficult. After the London Fire of 1666, Doolittle illegally erected churches in **Bunhill Fields** and Mugwell Street, for which he narrowly avoided arrest. In 1689, under the **Declaration of Indulgence**, he was able to return to his ministry at Mugwell Street, where he remained for the rest of his life. Doolittle and his wife, Mary, had three sons and two daughters. A son, Samuel Doolittle, followed his father into the ministry. Doolittle's works include *A Treatise Concerning the Lord's Supper* (1665), *A Call to Delaying Sinners* (1683), *The Saint's Convoy to and Mansions in Heaven* (1698), and *A Complete Body of Practical Divinity* (1723).

DOWNAME (OR DOWNHAM), GEORGE (d. 1634). Bishop of Derry. George Downame was son of William Downame, Bishop of Chester. George was most likely born in Chester, though the date of his birth in not known. In 1585, he was elected a **fellow** of Christ's College, **Cambridge**, where he was later taught logic. He also received the prebendaries of Chester (1594), St. Paul's (1598), and Wells (1615). In 1616, **James I** made Downame one of his chaplains and elevated him to the bishopric of Derry in Ireland. Downame's strong **Calvinist** beliefs were a special asset in this position, making him particularly acceptable to the Scots who settled in Ulster after the adoption of the **Irish Articles**.

In 1631, Downame published a **sermon** titled *The Covenant of Grace*, which featured an attack on **Arminianism**. To it was appended *A Treatise of the Certainty of Perseverance*, a defense of the 38th Irish Article. When the book came to the attention of **William Laud**, he sought to have it suppressed in England and Ireland; however, it appeared in Dublin before the order could be carried out.

Downame was a signatory to the protestations of popery, but he did show tolerance to **Presbyterians** within his bishopric and provided clergy who could preach and catechize in Irish. Downame died in Derry and is buried in the cathedral. Other works by Downame include his *Treatise Concerning the Antichrist Against Bellarmine* (1603), *The Christian's Sanctuary* (1604), and *A Treatise of Justification* (1633).

DRAMA. Concurrent with the rise of Puritanism in late 16th-century England was the rise of the English professional theater, particularly in London. Although it would be inaccurate to say that all Puritans were opposed to drama or that the opposition to drama was exclusively Puritan, many of the best-known attacks on the theater came from its Puritan critics.

The Puritan antitheatrical bias was caused in part by the stage's early connection to the Roman **Catholic** church. During the Middle Ages, English drama consisted almost entirely of mystery plays, which recounted the history of humankind from the creation to the final judgment, and allegorical morality plays. These church-sanctioned productions were a primary means of religious instruction for a largely illiterate populace, but the association of English drama with Catholicism was enough to render the largely secular plays of the late 16th century suspect. The dramatic representation of biblical events was associated with the Catholic use of images in **worship**, which the Puritans considered idolatry. Hence, by extension, secular drama bore the taint not only of Catholicism but was considered a violation of the second commandment.

The theater's critics drew from early church fathers, such as Cyprian and Tertullian, who wrote against the Roman stage, and certain arguments became the basis for virtually every published attack on drama from the late 1570s to the early 1640s. In addition to being idolatrous, drama offered graphic depictions of **sin** and vice and thus served to promote immoral behavior. The exclusion of **women** from the stage led to the practice of men dressing and acting the parts of women, a violation of Mosaic Law. The common practice of staging performances on Sundays drew people away from church and violated the fourth commandment. And the theater's critics were quick to make the connection between play-going and the plague—God's judgment on England for its unrighteousness and its love of worldly entertainments. The theater's critics sought not to reform the theater but to abolish it, and so did the magistrates of London, with the result that the theaters operated under the constant threat of closure. However, acting companies, such as Shakespeare's, continued to survive, largely through the support of Queen **Elizabeth I**, who herself enjoyed drama and required plays to be performed at court during the Christmas season.

The arguments against drama were enumerated in countless **sermons** and pamphlets. Some of the best-known early attacks on the stage include Stephen Gosson's *School of Abuse* (1579) and Philip Stubbe's *Anatomie of Abuses* (1583). The only learned divine to give extended treatment to the question of drama was **John Rainolds**, in his tract, *Th' Overthrow of Stage-Playes* (1599). These attacks resulted in a flurry of defenses of the theater by such writers as Thomas Heywood, Thomas Nashe, and Thomas Lodge. The Puritan also became a stock figure of the Elizabethan and Stuart stage, with such dramatists as Ben Jonson and **Thomas Middleton** depicting Puritans as narrow-minded, self-righteous hypocrites. One of the most famous Puritan stage caricatures is Zeal-of-the-Land-Busy in Jonson's play, *Bartholomew Fair*.

Under **James I** and **Charles I**, the hostilities between the stage and its Puritan critics intensified, as the main acting companies came under the direct patronage of the crown and many Puritans became leaders in the formation of the anti-Royalist party. In 1625, **William Prynne** published his 1,100-page attack on the theater titled *Histriomastix* and was accused of sedition, sentenced to life imprisonment, and had his ears cut off. However, with the execution of Charles I in 1649, and with the Puritan party in ascendancy, the theaters were all closed and all dramatic performances were prohibited. They remained so until the **Restoration** of the monarchy in 1660. *See also* MUSIC.

DURANT (OR DURANCE), JOHN (c. 1620–1689). Independent minister. Durant was born in Bodmin, Cornwall. His father was the mayor of Bodmin, and as a youth, Durant was apprenticed to a soapmaker. He may have been educated at Pembroke Hall, Cambridge, but by 1641, he had begun his preaching career. Durant was appointed to a **lectureship** at St. Peter's, Sandwich, in 1644. Within a year or two, he removed to Canterbury to serve as preacher to an Independent congregation. During the **Interregnum**, Durant was a strong advocate of the **Commonwealth**. He held several lectureships and became one of six preachers at Canterbury Cathedral. After the **Restoration** of the monarchy in 1660, Durant was ejected from the cathedral pulpit.

Calamy called Durant an "excellent practical preacher," and his works show evidence of his knowledge of Greek, Hebrew, and Latin. He is best remembered for his works of spiritual consolation, including *Comfort and Counsel for Dejected Souls* (1651) and *Sips of Sweetness, or Consolation for Weak Believers* (1651). After the death of his own daughter, Durant wrote *Altum Silentium, or Silence the*

*Duty of Saints under Every Sad Providence, a **Sermon** Preached after the Death of a Daughter by Her Father* (1659). He also published *The Spiritual Seaman, or a Manual for Mariners* (1655), republished in 1658 as *The Christian's Compass.*

DUTCH PURITANISM. Along with England and America, the Netherlands comprised one of the major international centers of Puritanism. Strong economic, political, and religious ties had bound England and the Netherlands together since the early part of the 16th century; by the mid-1600s, England was serving as home to many Dutch craftsmen and refugees driven abroad by the Spanish Inquisition. In 1581, when the Netherlands declared its independence from Spain, it, in turn, developed tolerant policies that welcomed people of all creeds, making the country a haven for anyone fleeing religious persecution. During the 16th century, it served as home to six English congregations, one of the most important being the Merchant Adventurers Church, which first met in Antwerp and then moved to Middleburg. Its ministers included **Thomas Cartwright**, **Walter Travers**, and **Dudley Fenner**. **Separatists** also settled in Middleburg, founding an important but chronically divided church, led by such well-known figures as **Robert Browne**, **Francis Johnson**, and **Henry Jacob**. The chaplains for the army posts in the towns of Flushing and Brielle also contributed to the Puritan presence among the Dutch.

In the 17th century, the number of English churches in the Netherlands rose to 34, representing a range of Puritan beliefs and practices including **Presbyterian**, Separatist, **Congregationalist**, and **Anabaptist**. Amsterdam, The Hague, Rotterdam, and Zeeland were among the many cities that hosted these congregations. At the university at Franeker, William Ames made significant contributions to the development of Puritan theology. In Leiden, **John Robinson** led a group of Congregationalists, many of whom set sail on the *Mayflower* in 1620. Some Puritans, including those at Leiden, found the Dutch policy of **toleration** distressing and worried that their children would be fully assimilated into Dutch society. Many Puritans who had settled in the Netherlands returned to England at the end of the **English Civil Wars** in 1649 to enjoy the relatively free religious climate of the **Interregnum**. At the same time, the Netherlands saw an influx of **Anglicans** who were disenfranchised by the new Puritan government. **Quaker** missionaries also appeared in the Netherlands during this period. With the **Restoration**, the Anglicans returned to England, and some Puritans made their way back to the Netherlands. After 1689, many who had settled in the Netherlands continued to maintain a presence there, for economic rather than religious reasons. *See also* NYE, PHILIP; PARKER, ROBERT; PETERS, HUGH; PILGRIMS; POOLE, MATTHEW.

DYER, WILLIAM (c. 1632–1696). Nonconformist English minister. Little of Dyer's early life is known. He began his preaching career in Chesham, then accepted a call to minister at Cholesbury in Buckinghamshire. By 1662, he had vacated his pulpit, most likely in response to the **Act of Uniformity**. Dyer preached at St. Anne's, Aldersgate Street, London, in 1665, and the **sermons**, in which Dyer claimed the plague was God's punishment on London, were published under the title *Christ's Voice to London* (1666). In later life, Dyer is thought to have been sympathetic to **Quakers** and may have converted to Quakerism. He is buried in a Quaker cemetery in Southwark. Dyer's writing has been compared stylistically to **John Bunyan**'s and **John Saltmarsh**'s. His best-known work is *A Cabinet of Jewels, or a Glimpse of Sion's Glory* (1663).

DYKE, DANIEL (c. 1580–1614). Nonconformist English minister. Dyke was born in Hampstead, Essex, the son of a nonconforming minister. He entered St. John's College, **Cambridge**, where he graduated B.A. in 1595–96. He received his M.A. from Sidney Sussex College in 1599 and was appointed a **fellow** of Sidney Sussex in 1606, the same year he received his B.D. He accepted the call to serve as minister at Cogeshill, Essex, but was suspended for Nonconformity. He then became minister at St. Albans, where his ministry was very successful, but his involvement in efforts to reform the church, as well as his refusal to take orders or wear the **surplice**, led to his suspension by the Bishop of London. His parishioners and Lord-Treasurer Burghley (William Cecil) petitioned unsuccessfully on his behalf. He was also accused of incontinency, though his accuser later recanted. Dyke's works were published posthumously by his brother Jeremiah. They include *The Mystery of Self-Deceiving* (1615) and *Two Treatises, the One of Repentance, the Other of Christ's Temptations* (1616).

– E –

EDWARD VI (1537–1553). King of England from 1547–53. Edward was the only son of **Henry VIII** and his third wife, Jane Seymour, who died 12 days after giving birth. His tutors included such first-rate scholars as Roger Ascham, Sir John Cheke, Richard Cox, and Barnaby Fitzpatrick. Educated alongside his half-sister, Elizabeth (*see* ELIZABETH I), the future king demonstrated a precocious intelligence and a mastery of French, Latin, and Greek by the age of 13.

In 1547, Henry VIII died, and nine-year-old Edward became king of England and Ireland. Before his death, Henry had provided for a Regency Council to govern England during Edward's minority, but Edward's maternal uncle, Edward Seymour, the Duke of Somerset, established himself as Protector of the Realm. When Somerset left for Scotland to negotiate the king's marriage to Mary, Queen of Scots, another uncle, Thomas Seymour, along with the Earl of Warwick, used the opportunity to increase their influence. Somerset was deprived and eventually executed. After the proposed marriage to Mary fell through, Edward was betrothed to the daughter of the French King Henry II in 1551. However, he died of consumption before the marriage could take place. Shortly before his death, Edward tried to exclude his sisters from succession and supported the claim of Lady Jane Grey.

Despite his youth, Edward possessed strong Protestant convictions and, through **Archbishop of Canterbury Thomas Cranmer**, moved the English Church in a more Protestant direction than was allowed under Henry: the worship service was simplified, members of the clergy were allowed to marry, and the doctrine of transubstantiation was abolished. Under Edward, Cranmer also developed the ***Book of Common Prayer***, which provided a vernacular English order of worship, and he developed a clear statement of Anglican beliefs in the Forty-Two Articles, which were reduced under Elizabeth to the **Thirty-Nine Articles**. The reforms made under Edward were abolished during the reign of his sister **Mary I**, but they served as the foundation of Anglican theology and worship when Anglicanism was restored under Elizabeth I.

EDWARDS, JONATHAN (1703–1758). American **Congregationalist** preacher and theologian. Widely considered America's greatest native theologian, Edwards was born in East Windsor, Connecticut, to the Reverend Timothy and Esther Edwards. His mother was the daughter of **Solomon Stoddard**, the longtime pastor of the Congregationalist church in Northampton, Massachusetts. Edwards received his undergraduate and master's degrees from Yale College and then in 1722 preached briefly for a **Presbyterian** church in New York City. In 1723, he moved to Bolton, Connecticut, and then he returned to Yale as a tutor in 1724–25. Edwards kept carefully organized notebooks on several academic disciplines, including not only theology but philosophy, politics, and biology. In 1727, he married Sarah Pierpont and became an apprentice minister under his grandfather. In 1729, he became the Northampton church's sole pastor after Stoddard's death.

In his **sermons**, Edwards became an inveterate opponent of **Arminianism**, Unitarianism, and **antinomianism**. Although his homiletic style was plain, consisting of reading prepared notes while rarely raising his gaze from the lectern, Edwards observed a dramatic increase in religious fervor in his town about 1734. He attributed this to a sovereign work of God that turned local citizens away from private vices toward an intense and public quest for holiness. He explained how a keen sense of divine **providence** enlivened his own devotion in his *Personal Narrative* (1739) and how a public desire for the same suddenly spread throughout adjacent towns in *Faithful Narrative of the Surprising Work of God* (1737). Edwards also befriended the vibrant evangelist and fellow **Calvinist George Whitefield**, and invited him to preach in Northampton. With the combined ministry of Edwards and Whitefield serving as agents, the **Great Awakening** spread throughout New England in the 1740s. While a famous sermon of 1741, "Sinners in the Hands of an Angry God," asked unconverted **sinners** to think of themselves as spiders dangling by a thread over the fires of Hell, the chief message of the revival was the necessity of a "new birth" in the hearts and minds of Christian believers. Edwards explained this vital need in *Some Thoughts Concerning the Revival* (1743) and *Treatise Concerning Religious Affections* (1746).

Yet despite Edwards' international reputation, he fell into controversy with his church members in 1750. Edwards repudiated the

Half-Way Covenant long espoused by Stoddard, which permitted the **baptism** of children whose parents did not give evidence of regenerate faith. Edwards also refused to grant the Lord's Supper to such parents. The church dismissed Edwards, and he became a missionary to Native American Indians in Stockbridge, Massachusetts. Indian **missions** had long been a matter of interest to Edwards, and he had written a biography of the missionary **David Brainerd** in 1749. Without having to prepare weekly sermons on a regular basis, Edwards poured his energies into penning new theological works, mostly notably a rejection of human autonomy called *Freedom of the Will* (1754). In 1757, Edwards agreed to become the president of the College of New Jersey (later Princeton), succeeding in that office Aaron Burr Sr., the husband of his daughter Esther. However, Edwards died within three months of moving to Princeton because of a contaminated smallpox inoculation. His *Original Sin* appeared in the same year as his death, 1758. Edwards' most important posthumous publication was *A History of the Work of Redemption* (1774), based upon a series of lectures he had given at Northampton.

Jonathan Edwards Jr. (1745–1801), the ninth of Edwards' 10 children, attended Princeton and continued his father's legacy as one of the leading figures of the **New England Theology**. He later became the president of Union College in Schenectady, New York. Edwards' descendants, in fact, include 13 college presidents, 65 college professors, three United States senators, and one vice president of the United States, Aaron Burr Jr.

ELIOT, JOHN (1592–1632). Parliamentarian. Eliot, the son of a wealthy landowner, was born in St. Germans, Cornwall. He was educated at Blundell's School, Tiverton, Exeter College, **Oxford**, and at the Inns of Court. While traveling on the continent, he met George Villiers, court favorite and the future Duke of Buckingham. Through Villiers' influence, Eliot obtained the post of Vice-Admiral of Devon 1619. In 1623, he apprehended the famous pirate John Nutt, but Nutt's patron, Sir George Calvert, had him pardoned, and Eliot himself was imprisoned for four months on a trumped-up charge.

In 1624, Eliot was elected to **Parliament**, where he distinguished himself as a masterful orator, demanding the restoration of Parliamentary liberties revoked by **James I**. Eliot supported Buckingham's warlike policies against Spain, but, in 1625, he opposed King **Charles I**'s policy of extending tolerance to **Catholics**, which eventually put him at odds with Buckingham as well. The following year, Charles sought to remove his most vociferous critics in Parliament by making them sheriffs and thus excluding them from the new assembly. This act brought Eliot to the front of the opposition, where he called for an inquiry into Buckingham's failed military expedition to the port of Cadiz. Eliot also convinced the Commons to issue a remonstrance demanding that royal councilors be examined and approved by the House. When he carried Buckingham's impeachment to the House of Lords and delivered the charges against him, Charles sent Eliot to the Tower, but Parliament demanded his release. Charles finally yielded to their demand but then dissolved Parliament in order to save Buckingham. Eliot was dismissed from office and incarcerated again in the Tower, but the need to reconvene Parliament once again led to his release.

When Parliament reconvened in 1628, Eliot was, along with Sir Edward Coke, one of the most active promoters of the **Petition of Right**. After Buckingham's assassination in 1629, Eliot directed his attacks against **Arminian** theology and the rituals in the Church of England. When Charles ordered the Commons to adjourn, Eliot read a protest against arbitrary taxations and religious innovation while the speaker was held down in his chair. Charles dissolved Parliament again and, once again, threw Eliot, along with eight other opposition leaders, in the Tower. Eliot refused to answer the charges brought against him, was fined £2,000, and imprisoned at the king's pleasure. He rejected the offer of release in exchange for a confession of wrongdoing and remained in the Tower until his death, three years later, from tuberculosis. Eliot's supporters viewed him as a martyr, and his death became a rallying point for the Puritan opposition.

ELIZABETH I (1533–1603). Queen of England from 1558 to 1603. Elizabeth was the daughter of **Henry VIII** and his second wife, Anne Boleyn. Her mother was executed on trumped-up charges of adultery when Elizabeth was less than three years old. Along with her older half-sister, Mary (*see* MARY I), Elizabeth was deprived of her status as a princess and declared illegitimate. For her first 10 years, Elizabeth was brought up in Hatfield and Hertfordshire, but when Henry married for the sixth and last time, the new queen, Katherine Parr, convinced Henry to restore his daughters to their former status. Elizabeth then began to study alongside her younger half brother Edward (*see* EDWARD VI) under some of England's finest intellects: Roger Ascham, Sir John Cheke, and Richard Cox. Like her brother, Elizabeth was an excellent scholar and was fluent in Latin, Greek, French, and Italian. When Edward became king, he took measures to exclude both Mary and Elizabeth from succession, granting it instead to their cousin, Lady Jane Grey. However, the majority of Englishmen supported Mary's claim, and Elizabeth rode alongside Mary on her triumphant entry to London in 1553. However, as Mary's attempts to impose Catholicism on England grew increasingly unpopular, Mary suspected Elizabeth of being involved in Protestant plots against the throne. Elizabeth was, for a time, confined in the Tower of London on suspicion of treason.

When Mary died in 1558, Elizabeth, then 25, acceded to the throne amidst general adulation, but the nation was also deeply divided, especially along religious lines. Her Roman Catholic subjects hoped that the English Church would remain catholic, while the Protestants held a range of hopes and expectations. Many who had sojourned in Holland and Geneva (*see* DUTCH PURITANISM) during the reign of her sister (*see* MARIAN EXILE) had embraced **Calvinist** theology, a **Presbyterian** form of church government, and a form of worship that bore no traces of the Catholic mass. Such were the reforms they hoped to introduce to the England Church. Elizabeth, however, pursued a course of compromise by reinstating a church along the lines established during the reign of Edward. It would be essentially Protestant in theology while retaining an **episcopal** form of church government (*see* ANGLICANISM), and services would follow a slightly revised version of the ***Book of Common Prayer***. These policies were established in the **Act of Uniformity** and the Act of Supremacy, as well as in the **Thirty-Nine Articles**. Protestant dissatisfaction with this arrangement, also known as the **Elizabethan Settlement**, led to the rise of the Puritan movement.

Elizabeth was a gifted and generally popular politician, and she is remembered as one of the greatest English monarchs. During her 45-year reign, England remained an independent power and grew in economic strength. Elizabeth never married, despite pressure from

Parliament and her advisers, but shortly before her death, she granted her favor to the succession of James VI of Scotland, later **James I** of England.

ELIZABETHAN SETTLEMENT. *See* ANGLICANISM; ELIZABETH I.

EMMANUEL COLLEGE. *See* CAMBRIDGE UNIVERSITY; MILDMAY, WALTER.

ENDECOTT, JOHN (c. 1589–1665). Also **Endicott.** Governor of the Massachusetts Bay Colony. Very little is known about the early life of Endecott. In 1628, along with five other men, he bought a patent for some land on the **Massachusetts Bay** from the Plymouth council and led the first expedition there, which was followed by a larger group of settlers, led by John Winthrop, in 1630. Endecott's company settled at Naumkeed, which it renamed Salem. He imposed strict rules on the settlement; in an incident made famous by Nathaniel Hawthorne, Endecott tore down the maypole erected by members of an earlier settlement at nearby Merrymount (now Quincy). Endecott served as governor of the Massachusetts Bay Colony from 1629–30 and several times after that (1644, 1649, 1651–53, 1655–64). He was appointed sergeant major general of the militia and, in 1636, led an attack on the Pequot Indians that helped precipitate the **Pequot War**. Endecott is also remembered for his persecution of **Baptists** and **Quakers**, three of whom were executed under his administration. However, he did defend **Roger Williams**, of whose congregation he was a member, and he also helped found **Harvard College**.

Endecott is noted for his able, albeit harsh and intolerant, leadership of the Massachusetts Bay Colony, which experienced considerable growth during his administration.

ENGLISH CIVIL WARS. The English Civil Wars were a series of conflicts between Royalist and Parliamentary forces that led ultimately to the execution of the king in 1641. The conflict began when Charles was compelled to summon the **Long Parliament** after the debacle of the **Bishops' Wars**. Parliament responded by making numerous demands on the king, including the execution of the Earl of

Stafford. They then proceeded to adopt various aggressive measures, declaring themselves indissoluble without their own consent, arresting **Archbishop of Canterbury William Laud**, and abolishing prerogative courts, to name a few. When the Irish rebelled in November 1641, Charles was once more compelled to request support from Parliament to put down the rebellion, but instead of providing him with the necessary soldiers and funds, Parliament responded by delivering The **Grand Remonstrance** (1 December 1641), a document laying out what it considered decades of abuses by the king's counselors and its demands for reform. On 4 January 1642, Charles responded by sending armed troops to **Parliament** in order to arrest **John Pym**, John Hampden, and three other radical Parliament leaders; however, the intended victims were forewarned and escaped. Charles then left London to gather support and plan his offensive. He raised the royal standard at Nottingham on 22 August 1642.

The first Royalist strike occurred at Edgehill on 23 October, but proved unsuccessful. Over the next year, Charles and his commanders followed a strategy of circling London and slowly tightening their grip. Parliament meanwhile negotiated a treaty with the Scots, and their joint forces defeated the main Royalist army at Marston Moor on 2 July 1644. The main force in the victory was the army of the Eastern Association, led by **Oliver Cromwell**. On 14 June 1645, Cromwell's army faced the Royalist forces again, this time at Naseby, and won a decisive victory.

Charles retreated to **Oxford** and then turned himself over to the Scots in May 1646. A year later, the Scots agreed to hand Charles over to Parliament, but on 3 June 1647, Parliamentary forces seized him and held him at Hampton Court, from which he eventually escaped. Charles then fled to the Isle of Wight, where he carried on negotiations with both Parliament and the Scots. Hoping that the Scots' disappointment over their dealings with Parliament would help make them his allies, Charles negotiated an agreement whereby **Presbyterianism** would be instituted for three years in England in exchange for Scottish help in restoring him to his throne. The Scottish attempt to invade England occurred in August 1648 but was easily repelled.

Some members of Parliament still hoped to negotiate with the king, but Cromwell opposed any such attempts. On 6 December 1648, a file of soldiers under Colonel John Pride expelled more than a hundred of the king's supporters in Parliament, a move known as **Pride's Purge**. The remaining members, known as the **Rump Parliament**, tried the king for treason and executed him on 30 January 1649.

EPISCOPACY. *See* ANGLICANISM.

ERASTIANISM. Erastianism is the idea that the civil government has absolute authority over the church. It takes its name from Thomas Erastus (1524–83), a Swiss Protestant theologian in Heidelberg. Erastus argued that **Scripture** does not authorize the church to excommunicate its erring members but that the exercise of church discipline belongs to the state. More broadly, however, the term "Erastianism" came to signify a belief in the supremacy of the state in ecclesiastical matters. The church has no power to exercise punitive measures; even the question of who is eligible to receive the **sacraments** is under the jurisdiction of civil magistrates.

The Erastians comprised a small but vocal minority at the **Westminster Assembly** of Divines in 1643. Principal proponents of the Erastian view were ministers **John Lightfoot** and Thomas Coleman. Erastian lay assessors included John Selden and Bulstrode Whitelocke. Though the Erastians were in the minority, they naturally had the support of **Parliament**, which had called the Assembly in the first place. Many in Parliament feared that a new form of ecclesiastical government operating in its own separate sphere would make the **Presbyterian** ministers and elders just as powerful as the bishops they replaced.

ESSEX, EARL OF. *See* DEVEREUX, ROBERT.

***ET CETERA* OATH.** One of 17 canons published by the Convocation of Bishops in 1640, after the dissolution of the **Short Parliament**. The Convocation required all members of the clergy to swear never to give consent "to alter the government of this Church, by archbishops, bishops, deans, archdeacons, *et cetera*, as it stands now established." When the **Long Parliament** was summoned later that year, opponents of the *Et Cetera* Oath responded by presenting the **Root**

and **Branch Petition**, which bore 15,000 signatures. **Charles I** suspended the oath in October of the same year.

– F –

FAIRFAX, THOMAS (1612–1671). Third Baron Fairfax of Cameron, Parliamentarian army general. Thomas Fairfax was born in Denton, Yorkshire, and educated at St. John's College, **Cambridge**, and **Gray's Inn**. He received early military training in the low countries under Horace Vere, Baron of Tilbury. Returning to England in 1632, he married Vere's daughter Anne in 1637 and was knighted in 1641. Fairfax fought for **Charles I** during the **Bishops' Wars**, but at the beginning of the **English Civil Wars** in 1642, he sided with the Parliamentarian cause and was appointed second in command to his father and General of Horse.

Fairfax earned his first important victory in January 1643, when he captured the town of Leeds. In May of the same year, he achieved even greater renown at Wakefield. Believing the town to be garrisoned by, at most, 900 soldiers, Fairfax took only 1,500 of his own men. The town was in actuality held by over 3,000 Royalist infantry, as well as several troops of horse. Despite his miscalculation, Fairfax led his force to victory. This success was followed by defeat in Adwalton Moor (30 June 1643), after which Fairfax was sent to Lincolnshire. Serving under the Earl of Manchester, he helped rout the Royalist army at Winceby (11 October). He captured Gainsborough on 2 December, and led a successful campaign against Sir John Byron at Nantwich (29 January 1644), where he took 1,500 prisoners, including Colonel **George Monck**. Fairfax also participated in the storming of Selby (11 April). At the decisive battle of Marston Moor (2 July), Fairfax led the cavalry on the right. He was wounded twice: at Marston Moor and again during the siege of Helmsley the following August.

Fairfax was appointed commander of the **New Model Army** in January 1645. He led the army into battle at Naseby on 14 June, where he captured an enemy color personally. He then ventured into the West Country to relieve the besieged city of Taunton. He won decisive victories against Royalist forces at Bridgewater (23 July),

Bristol (10 September), Torrington (16 February 1646). Exeter (9 April), and finally at the Royalist capital of **Oxford** (24 June). When the Scots handed Charles I over to the Parliamentarian forces, Fairfax escorted the defeated king to London. He then withdrew from military life, in part to recover his health. However, with the Royalist uprisings in 1648, Fairfax returned to battle as commander of the New Model Army. He defeated the Royalist forces in South Wales, Kent, and Essex, and put down the Scottish invasion as well.

Fairfax was named as a judge in the trial of Charles I, but he did not participate after the preliminary session. He was also nominated to the Council of State and reappointed army commander but chose instead to retire in 1650. During the **Protectorate**, Fairfax withdrew for the most part from military and political life but was active in bringing about the **Restoration** of the monarchy under **Charles II**. After the Restoration, he spent his remaining years in quiet retirement and died at Nunappleton.

FAMILISTS. The English term for members of a mystical religious sect called *Familia Charitatis,* or the Family of Love. The group was established around 1540, in the town of Emden, by Hendrick Niclaes, a wealthy merchant from the city of Münster. Originally Roman **Catholic**, Niclaes proclaimed himself a prophet, having received a special outpouring of "the spirit of the true love of Jesus Christ." Combining elements of German mysticism and **Anabaptist** beliefs, Niclaes taught that the "Family" was above the **Bible**, creeds, liturgy, and law. He also taught a form of impeccability, meaning that members of the church hierarchy, including Niclaes himself, could attain spiritual and moral perfection. The group practiced adult **baptism** and a form of communism, with a hierarchical structure based on that of the Roman Catholic Church. Many of the sect's beliefs are laid out in Niclaes's book *An Introduction to the Holy Understanding of the Glass of Righteousness.* Niclaes used his frequent business travels to spread his beliefs and gained adherents in France, Germany, Flanders, and England, but because he did not establish any specific forms of **worship**, many of his followers continued to worship in established churches.

In 1560, Niclaes was forced to leave Emden. He settled in England, where he seems to have already gained followers during his previous visits. Familist societies formed in Guilford, Surrey, Ely, and elsewhere. Charged with **antinomianism**, the Familists were suppressed under the reigns of Queen **Elizabeth I** and King **James I** but continued to exist longer in England than anywhere else. They survived the **Commonwealth**, dying out only in the late 17th and early 18th centuries, when they were absorbed into other groups, such the **Quakers**. Because membership was secret, it is impossible to know how widespread Familism was at its height.

FAMILY LIFE. The **covenant theology** of **Presbyterians, Independents**, and **Congregationalists** permitted the **baptism** of infants upon the belief that God's grace works through families. These Puritans pointed to the privilege of circumcision in ancient Israel as a precedent and contended that God's grace to parents must be at least as permissive under the new covenant of Christ. Disputes in New England arose when the parents of baptismal candidates did not appear themselves to be regenerate, but the **Half-Way Covenant** was devised in Connecticut to legitimate the continuation of the practice. Although Puritans recognized the importance of allowing younger children to enjoy play, they strongly instilled discipline and the avoidance of idleness in the older ones. So **Cotton Mather** advised, "Better whipt, than Damn'd." Puritans took seriously the education of their children because being able to read and understand the **Bible** was the centerpiece of their cultural vision. Puritans taught their children catechisms and wrote books especially geared to young persons' understanding, such as the *New England Primer* (1690), which included Mather's *Good Lessons for Children* and rhymes by **Isaac Watts**. *See also* MARRIAGE; WOMEN.

FEDERAL THEOLOGY. *See* COVENANT THEOLOGY.

FELLOW/FELLOWSHIP. The term "fellow" in the university system of the 16th and 17th centuries denotes the status of a senior scholar, one who has completed his degrees and is no longer required to pay tuition. Upon receiving their Bachelors degrees, especially gifted young academicians were often elected fellows, typically by the colleges from which they had graduated. Fellows received a stipend in exchange "for teaching of youths not on the foundation" (Oxford English Dictionary).

FENNER, DUDLEY (c. 1558–1587). Nonconformist English minister. Fenner was born in Kent to a wealthy family and entered Peterhouse, **Cambridge**, in 1575. He was a supporter of **Thomas Cartwright** in the **Presbyterian** cause and was consequently forced to leave Cambridge without taking a degree. He may have served as assistant to Richard Fletcher, vicar of Cranbrook, Kent, but soon followed Cartwright to Antwerp. When Edmund Grindal was appointed **Archbishop of Canterbury** in 1575, Fenner returned to England, anticipating greater tolerance of Puritan views. He was appointed curate of Cranbrook, but when John Whitgift replaced Grindal as archbishop in 1583, Fenner was one of 17 ministers who refused to subscribe to **Whitgift's articles**. Despite several appeals and petitions, Fenner was arrested and spent three months in prison. He finally subscribed, only to gain his liberty and leave England. He served as pastor to a church in Middleburg, where he remained until his death before the age of 30.

Fenner is considered one of the ablest exponents of Puritan views. His works include *The Artes of Logic and Rhetoric* (1584), *Sacra Theologica* (1585), and *A Short and Profitable Treatise on Lawful and Unlawful Recreations* (1587, 1590). *See also* DUTCH PURITANISM.

FENNER, WILLIAM (1600–1640). English minister. Fenner was educated at Pembroke College, **Cambridge**, where he received his B.A. in 1618 and his M.A. the following year. He was appointed a member of **Oxford University** in 1622. Fenner took holy orders and may have served as chaplain to the Earl of Warwick at Sedgley, Staffordshire. However his Puritan principles led to his removal from Sedgley, after which Fenner preached in various places and was apparently especially admired by the nobility. In 1627, he received his B.D. and two years later was presented to the living of Rochford in Essex, where he remained until his death.

Fenner's writing has been noted for it plain manner and zealous tone. His works include *The Soul's Looking Glasse, with a treatise of* **Conscience** (1640) and *Christ's Alarm to Drowsie Sinners* (1646).

FIENNES, WILLIAM (1582–1662). First Viscount of Saye and Sele, Parliamentarian, colonial administrator. Fiennes was born at Broughton Castle, Oxfordshire, and educated at New College, **Oxford**, where he became a **fellow** in 1600. In 1613, upon the death of his father, he became the eighth Baron of Saye and Sele. During a brief period of friendship with the Duke of Buckingham, he was elevated as the first Viscount of Saye and Sele. As a member of the House of Lords, however, he established himself as an opponent of the crown and an enemy of Buckingham. In 1622, he spent six months in prison for objecting to King **James I**'s imposition of benevolence, a tax without Parliamentary consent, and continued to lead the opposition throughout his career. Clarendon called Fiennes "the oracle of those who were called Puritans in the worst sense." King **Charles I** gave him the nickname "Old Subtlety." Fiennes opposed proposed amendments to the **Petition of Right** in 1628. He also refused to pay the forced loan and resisted the imposition of ship money—means by which Charles tried to collect funds without the consent of **Parliament**.

During Charles I's personal rule (1629–40), Fiennes was active in establishing colonies in America. He collaborated in the founding of Saybrook, Connecticut, and Providence Island in the West Indies, and he bought a plantation at Cocheco, New Hampshire. However, his proposal for the introduction of hereditary aristocracy into New England government was rejected, and Fiennes himself chose to remain in England.

Upon the outbreak of the First **Bishops' War** in 1639, Fiennes reluctantly joined Charles' expeditionary force against the Scots; however, his refusal to take an oath requiring him to defend the king with his life led to Fienne's dismissal and his return home. In 1640, as Charles prepared to call Parliament for the first time in 11 years, Fiennes was one of several Parliamentarian leaders who barely avoided impeachment. In 1641, Charles made the conciliatory gesture of appointing Fiennes privy councilor and a commissioner of the treasury, but Fienne's continued opposition to the crown became evident when he was appointed to the Committee of Safety and made lieutenant of Oxfordshire, Cheshire, and Gloucestershire. When the **English Civil Wars** broke out in 1642, Fiennes raised forces for Parliament. As a member of the **Westminster Assembly**, he helped pass the **Self-Denying Ordinance** in 1647. In the conflict between Parliament and the army, he supported the army, and he opposed the trial and execution of Charles. After Charles' execution, Fiennes retired from public life. When the monarchy was restored in 1660, he resumed his seat in Parliament and served as a privy councilor to **Charles II** and Lord of the Privy Seal. He died at Broughton Castle.

FIFTH MONARCHISTS. The Fifth Monarchists derived their name from prophecies in the Book of Daniel, chapter 2. These prophecies tell of the rise and fall of four kingdoms in history—which many have seen as the Assyrian, Persian, Greek, and Roman Empires. Daniel says that these kingdoms will be replaced by a Fifth Kingdom set up by God that would last for a 1,000 years. The Fifth Monarchists believed that this turning point in history was upon them and that they must prepare the way by overthrowing the established order, by violence, if necessary, and establishing Christ's Kingdom in its place. Thus, they supported the trial and execution of **Charles I** in 1649.

The movement began between 1649 and 1651. Its first major meeting occurred at The Church of All-Hallows-the-Great, London in December 1651, led by two radical preachers named John Simpson and Edmund Feake. Supporters were primarily tradesmen and craftsmen, and many came from **Baptist** and **Independent** churches. Fifth Monarchist ideas also found much support among soldiers in the **New Model Army**. The main leader of the movement in the army was Major-General **Thomas Harrison**, who also signed Charles' death warrant.

The Fifth Monarchists saw **Oliver Cromwell**'s dissolution of the **Rump Parliament** in April 1653 as a crucial step toward the ushering in of Christ's kingdom, which they believed would be established by King Jesus himself when he returned in 1666. They were further encouraged by the creation of the Nominated Assembly, or **Barebones Parliament**, in December of the same year. The Nominated Assembly included many Fifth Monarchists as delegates. They also viewed the prosecution of the Anglo–Dutch War as a part of the fulfillment of prophecy, the means by which their revolution would spread throughout Europe and ultimately to Rome, where it would topple the papacy.

Cromwell's dissolution of the Nominated Assembly and his establishment of the **Protectorate** in December 1653 were blows to the Fifth Monarchist movement. When several prominent leaders, including Simpson and Feake, denounced Cromwell's actions, they were thrown in prison. Harrison was dismissed from the army, imprisoned twice under Cromwell, and executed after the **Restoration**.

The Fifth Monarchist continued their opposition throughout the years of the Protectorate. In 1657, a plot to overthrow Cromwell was discovered and **Thomas Venner**, the leader of plot, was imprisoned. Though released after the Restoration, Venner led another uprising of the Fifth Monarchists in 1661. During the fighting between these insurgents and the army, more than 40 lost their lives. Venner and other leaders were hanged, and new legislation was passed to repress all sects. The suppression of Venner's Rebellion signaled the end of the Fifth Monarchist movement, whose members most likely merged eventually with other less radical **millenarian** sects.

FISHER, EDWARD (c. 1626–1648). English Puritan writer. Little of Fisher's life is known. He may have been a barber and appears to have belonged to a gathered congregation in London. Fisher was the author of *The Marrow of Modern Divinity*, published in 1645, a popular book that sparked off what came to be know as the **Marrow Controversy** in Scotland. He also wrote *A Touchstone for the Communicant* (1647) and *London's Gate to the Lord's Table* (1648).

FIVE DISSENTING BRETHREN. The leading representatives of the small but vocal **Congregationalist/Independent** minority in the **Westminster Assembly**. The group included **Thomas Goodwin**, **Philip Nye**, **Jeremiah Burroughs**, **William Bridge**, and **Sidrach Simpson**. All had been silenced under **Archbishop of Canterbury William Laud** and had gone into exile in the Netherlands during the 1630s. The Five Dissenting Brethren were moderate Congregationalists; they rejected **Separatism** and, unlike the **Brownists** and **Barrowists**, were amenable to intercommunion with other churches. As the minority, they were also naturally advocates of religious tolerance. In February 1644, the Brethren published a treatise laying out their position, titled *An Apologetical Narration, Humbly Submitted to the Honorable Houses of Parliament*.

FIVE MILE ACT (1665). *See* CLARENDON CODE.

FLAVEL, JOHN (c. 1630–1691). English **Presbyterian** minister. The son of **Richard Flavel**, an eminent Puritan minister, John Flavel was born in Bromesgrove, Worcestershire, and educated at University College, **Oxford**. In 1650, while still at Oxford, Flavel was appointed to serve as probationer and assistant to the minister at Diptford in Devon County, where he was subsequently **ordained** and became a minister. Flavel then obtained a curacy in the seaport town of Dartmouth, where he served until he was ejected from the ministry under the **Act of Uniformity** in 1662. He continued to reside in Dartmouth and minister privately to members of his congregation until the passing of the **Five-Mile Act** in 1665. He removed to Slapton, exactly five miles from Dartmouth. While at Slapton, Flavel preached in **conventicles** and frequently returned secretly to Dartmouth to minister to his congregation.

Flavel lived for a time in London, where he narrowly avoided arrest. He returned to Dartmouth and was placed under house arrest. When **James II** issued his **Declaration of Indulgence** in 1687, Flavel resumed his public ministry and assumed a demanding **preaching** schedule, despite his poor health. Himself a Presbyterian, Flavel worked to reconcile the Presbyterians and **Independents** of Devonshire, where he died, survived by his fourth wife.

Flavel wrote works of practical theology that are notably accessible and anecdotal. They include *Navigation Spiritualized* (1682), *A Token for Mourners* (1674), *The Method of Grace* (1681), and *Pneumatologia, A Treatise on the Soul of Man* (1685).

FLAVEL, RICHARD (c. 1607–1655). English Puritan divine, father of **John Flavel**. Richard Flavel served as minister in several parishes: Bromesgrove, in Worcestershire; Hasler and Willersey, in Gloucestershire. In 1660, he was ejected from the ministry because his position at Willersey was sequestered with a living incumbent. Flavel removed to London, where, in 1665, during an outbreak of the plague, he was arrested, along with his wife, for holding a private **prayer** meeting. They and their followers were imprisoned at

Newgate. Flavel and his wife contracted the plague and died shortly after their release.

FOX, GEORGE (1624–1691). Founder of the Society of Friends (**Quakers**). Fox was born at Fenny Drayton in Leicestershire. He was the son of Christopher Fox, a Puritan churchwarden and weaver, and Mary Lago. He was tutored by his mother, educated at the village school, and afterward was apprenticed to a cobbler and a grazier. As a youth, Fox was pious, serious-minded, and inquisitive. In 1643, he began a period of wandering from town to town, consulting with various religious scholars, clergymen, and **dissenters**. Toward the end of this period, Fox began to have a series of religious "openings" in which he felt God speaking directly to him. From these experiences, he developed his teaching of the "Inner Light"—the means by which God communicates directly to the individual without the necessity of **sacraments** or ministers. By 1648, Fox had begun to preach his beliefs. He and his followers, who called themselves the Society of Friends, were frequently beaten, stoned, and imprisoned. Fox himself was imprisoned on seven different occasions between 1650 and 1674.

In 1652, Fox preached before a large group in Yorkshire, many of whom embraced his teachings. In the same year, he established his headquarters at Swarthmoor Hall, home of the Puritan judge Thomas Fell, whose wife, Margaret, was one of Fox's most devoted followers. In 1653, while under arrest, Fox was brought before **Oliver Cromwell**. He met with Cromwell on two other occasions using these opportunities to petition the Lord Protector for relief from persecution for himself and his followers. In 1669, he also married the now widowed Margaret Fell, who became a Quaker leader in her own right.

Fox spent his final years laying out the basic organization, **worship**, beliefs, and behavior of the Society of Friends. He continued to preach and traveled widely to destinations including Ireland (1663), Barbados and America (1671), the Netherlands (1677), and Germany (1684).

Fox kept a journal which provides a spiritual autobiography and history of **Quakerism** from its beginning through 1675. It was completed after his death by several editors and published in 1695. Fox died in London and is buried in the Quaker cemetery adjoining **Bunhill Fields**. *See also* MECHANICK PREACHERS.

FOXE, JOHN (1516–1587). Martyrologist. Foxe was born in Boston, Lincolnshire. The son of a middle-class family, Foxe lost his father at an early age. His mother remarried, and she and Foxe's stepfather, Richard Melton, sent Foxe to Brasen-nose College, **Oxford**, in 1534. He received his B.A. in 1537, was made **fellow** two years later, and was awarded his M.A. in 1543. During his time at Oxford, Foxe came to embrace Reformation ideas; he was especially opposed to celibacy of the priesthood. Consequently, he refused **ordination** and, along with several others, resigned his fellowship in 1545.

Foxe spent a year as tutor to the Lacy family in Warwickshire, where he married Agnes Randall. However, by 1547, he had moved to London, where he became tutor to the children of Henry Howard, Earl of Surrey, a statesman and poet who had been executed for treason earlier the same year. Foxe's charges included Charles Henry, future Lord Admiral of England, and the 11-year-old Thomas Howard, future fourth Duke of Norfolk, who would become Foxe's patron and lifelong friend. While serving the Howard family, Foxe was **ordained** as a deacon (1550). He began to write tracts in support of the Reformation movement, and he also pled for the lives of the **Anabaptist** Joan Bocher and other Protestant extremists persecuted during the reign of **Edward VI**.

With the accession of Queen **Mary I** in 1553, Foxe fled to the continent. He took with him an uncompleted manuscript of a work titled *Commentari rerum ecclesia gestarum* (Commentary on Affairs within the Church). Published in Strasbourg in 1554, the *Commenatri Rerum* was an early version of Foxe's masterwork, *The Acts and Monuments*. From Strasbourg, Foxe went to Frankfurt, where he found the English Protestant exiles, led by **John Knox** and **Thomas Lever**, divided over the use of the ***Book of Common Prayer***. Foxe sought unsuccessfully to reconcile the two groups, then moved to Basel, where he worked for several printers, but primarily for Johan Oporinus. Here, he was occupied with the publication of manuscripts sent from England, continued to expand his work on Protestant martyrs, and, in 1557, published *Christus triumphans*, an appeal to English nobility on the behalf of Protestants suffering under Mary. He remained in Basel until 1559, a year after Mary's death, to oversee publication of his second Latin martyrology.

Upon his return to England, Foxe spent several years in the home of his former pupil, now the Duke of Norfolk. He was ordained to the **Anglican** priesthood by Edmund Grindal, but while he preached frequently, he did not accept any church office. Instead, he devoted himself to the production of an English translation of his account of the English martyrs. This work, Foxe's *magnum opus*, was published by John Day in 1563, under the title *Acts and Monuments of These Latter and Perilous Days*, though it came to be known more commonly as *Foxe's Book of Martyrs*. Foxe dedicated the book to Queen **Elizabeth I**, who ordered that a copy be placed in every collegiate church. It went through four editions in Foxe's own lifetime.

In the year that *Acts and Monuments* was published, Foxe received the Prebend of Shipton under Wynchwood in Salisbury Cathedral. Though he generously maintained a vicar for Shipton, he refused to contribute a tithe to the repair of the cathedral or wear the **surplice**. His absence during a bishop's visitation in 1568 led authorities to declare him "contumacious." By 1570, he had returned to London, where his principal means of support was a stipend provided by the Duke of Norfolk. He continued to preach, and in 1571, published an edition of Thomas Cramner's 1552 code of ecclesiastical law, titled *Reformatio Legum Ecclesiasticarum*. When the Duke of Norfolk was accused for his role in a planned uprising, Foxe visited him in prison and accompanied him at his execution. In 1575, he wrote a letter to Elizabeth I, urging her to show leniency to Anabaptists and generally opposing the death penalty for heresy. In his last years, he oversaw the revision and fourth edition of *Acts and Monuments*.

After the **Bible**, *Acts and Monuments* was the most widely read book of its day and for at least a century following. While critics have noted weaknesses in Foxe's historiography and have blamed the work for stirring up anti-**Catholic** and anti-Spanish feeling, it remains not only a primary text of the English Reformation but a moving account of those who died for the sake of religious **conscience**. *See also* MARIAN EXILES.

– G –

GATAKER, THOMAS (1574–1654). Moderate Anglican divine. Gataker was the son of Margaret Piggott and Thomas Gataker, rector of St. Edmund the King, Lombard Street. He was born in London and educated at St. John's College, **Cambridge**. Gataker graduated B.A. in 1584, M.A. in 1597, and was made a **fellow** of Sidney Sussex College in 1599, where he became friends with **William Bradshaw**. However, he returned to London in 1600 to serve as domestic chaplain to Sir William Cook. In 1601, Gataker was appointed preacher to the society of Lincoln's Inn. He proceeded B.D. in 1604 and remained at Lincoln's Inn until 1611, when he accepted the call to serve as rector at Rotherhithe. While at Rotherhithe, Gataker published many tracts and **sermons**, including a folio version of his collected sermons in 1637.

In 1642, Gataker was summoned as a member of the **Westminster Assembly** of Divines, at which he argued for a moderated **episcopacy**. He also annotated the books of Isaiah, Jeremiah, and Lamentations for the assembly. And he was also one of 47 London ministers who came out in opposition to the trial and execution of **Charles I** in 1649.

Gataker wrote on a variety of subjects. His work, *The Nature of Lots,* led to accusations that he approved games of chance. He wrote tracts against transubstantiation, astrology, and **antinomianism**. In addition to his many religious writings, Gataker is also noted for his work as an early classicist and linguist. He carried on a regular correspondence with **James Ussher**, with whom he shared an interest in publishing ancient texts. Gataker produced an edition of *Marcus Aurelius*, which is the "earliest edition of any classical writer published in England with original annotations," according to Henry Hallamand, and several treatises on linguistics. Other works include *Dissertatio de stylo Noel Tesamenti* and *Cinnus, alec Adversaria miscellanea*. Gataker's *Opera Critica* was published in 1698.

GENEVA BIBLE. An English translation of the **Bible**. The Geneva Bible was the work of English Protestant exiles (*See* MARIAN EXILES) residing in Geneva during the reign of Queen **Mary I**. **William Whittingham** supervised the translation, and contributors included **Miles Coverdale, Christopher Goodman, Thomas Sampson, Anthony Gilby**, and William Cole. It was based on scholarly editions of the Hebrew **Scriptures** and the Greek New Testament, and drew heavily from the work of William Tyndale, with nearly all of its New Testament taken from the **Tyndale Bible**.

The Geneva Bible first appeared in 1560, with revisions in 1576 and 1599. By 1644, it had been reprinted more than 150 times. The marginal glosses and extensive cross-references, as well is its stylistic force and vigor, made it the most popular Bible for private use. It was the version read by William Shakespeare. But its glosses also reflected the Puritan beliefs of its translators, earning it the disapproval of church officials and King **James I**, whose dislike of the translation led to the authorization of the **King James Bible**. Even so, the Geneva version's popularity endured for decades after the 1611 publication of the King James Version. During the **English Civil Wars**, copies of the Geneva Bible were distributed to soldiers of the **New Model Army**. Only after the **Restoration** did the King James Bible replace the Geneva in popular esteem.

The Geneva Bible was the first English Bible to use verse numbers. It is also known as the "Breeches Bible" for its translation of Genesis 3:7, in which Adam and Eve "sewed figge tree leaves together, and made them selves breeches."

GILBY, ANTHONY (?–1585). English Puritan divine. Gilby was born in Lincolnshire and educated at Christ's College, **Cambridge**, where he received his B.A. in 1531 and his M.A. in 1535. He held a living in Leicestershire until the accession of Queen **Mary I**, at which time he left England to avoid persecution. Gilby joined the Protestant exiles at Frankfurt, where he was a central figure in the controversy over order of **worship** and use of the *Book of Common Prayer*. He left Frankfurt with **John Knox, Christopher Goodman,** and others to form another English church in Geneva and served as pastor to that church in Knox's absence. With his knowledge of Greek and particularly Hebrew, Gilby was an important contributor to the **Geneva Bible**.

With the accession of Queen **Elizabeth I** in 1558, Gilby returned to England. His friend the Earl of Huntington presented Gilby with the living of Ashby-de-la-Zouch in Leicestershire, where he remained for the rest of his life and enjoyed a distinguished reputation but where his opinions also led to controversy. The zealously **Calvinistic** Gilby was a vocal opponent of ceremonies and **vestments**, and in 1571, **Archbishop of Canterbury** Matthew Parker ordered Archbishop of York Edmund Grindal to prosecute Gilby for **Nonconformity**. Grindal claimed that Gilby's parish was outside his jurisdiction. Although Gilby was able to avoid prosecution, he responded to the charges against him in a tract titled *A View of the Antichrist, His Laws and Ceremonies in Our English Church, Unreformed*. Gilby translated works by John Calvin and Theodore Beza, and was himself the author of several treatises, including two commentaries on Micah.

GLORIOUS REVOLUTION. The designation for events surrounding the abdication of **James II** and the crowning of King William III and Queen Mary II. James, who assumed the crown in 1685, was unpopular, principally because he was openly Roman **Catholic**. In 1689, James issued the **Declaration of Indulgence**, which extended religious freedom to people of all faiths, including Catholics. Opponents saw this as a first step toward the reinstatement of Catholicism as the national church of England, and seven of England's 26 bishops refused to read the declaration from their pulpits. Their arrest and eventual acquittal only deepened popular animosity toward James.

Of even greater concern, however, was the fact the James II had produced a legitimate heir, James Francis Edward, born on 10 June 1688, and baptized as a Catholic. The prospect of a Catholic heir to the throne and the establishment of a Catholic dynasty were unwelcome to many in England. Thus, seven prominent English leaders extended an invitation to William of Orange, a Dutch prince and son-in-law to James, encouraging him to come to England in defense of "Protestantism and Liberty." Assured of popular support, William crossed the channel in November and met with no opposition from Royalist forces. James fled to France, was captured, and then allowed to escape. William and Mary were crowned joint monarchs of England on 13 February 1689.

James and his supporters, known as Jacobites, did not, however, give up hope of his restoration to the English throne. Scottish Jacobites staged a rebellion against England's new rulers, but the rebellion was defeated on 27 July 1689, at the Battle of Killiecrankie. Meanwhile, James sailed for Ireland. Accompanied by French soldiers, he hoped to use French and Irish support to retake the crown. Unable to ignore the threat posed by James, William sent his forces to Ireland, himself landing at Carrick Fergus on 14 June 1690. He defeated James on 1 July at the Battle of the Boyne, thus bringing the Glorious Revolution to its definitive end.

GOODMAN, CHRISOPHER (c. 1520–1603). English Puritan divine. Goodman was born in Chester to an old family. He entered Brasennose College, **Oxford**, where he received his B.A. in 1541 and his M.A. 1544. In 1547, he became a senior student at Christ's Church and was appointed Lady Margaret Professor of Divinity.

In 1554, Goodman left England to avoid persecution under the rule of Queen **Mary I**. He first went to Frankfurt, where a congregation of English Protestant refugees had gathered. A rift in that church over the use of the *Book of Common Prayer* led to the formation of a new English church in Geneva, where Goodman served as co-pastor with **John Knox**. Goodman helped Knox write the *Book of Common Order*, and he was one of the principal translators of the **Geneva Bible**. In 1558, he published a tract virulently attacking the rule of Mary and of **women** in general, a publication that earned Goodman the disfavor of the future Queen **Elizabeth I**. When she ascended to the throne the same year, Goodman did not immediately return to England. In 1559, he accepted an invitation from Knox to come to Edinburgh and remained in Scotland for six years, first as a preacher in Ayr and then at St. Andrews.

Goodman returned to England in 1565, but he left the next year, traveling to Ireland as chaplain to Lord Deputy Henry Sidney. In 1570, he accepted a call to serve as minister at Alford near Chester, but by 1571, he had been ejected from his pulpit for **Nonconformity**. Goodman was summoned by the ecclesiastical commissioners at Lambeth, before whom he made a full recantation of his published beliefs and affirmed the government of the queen. In June of the same year, he was examined before Archbishop of Canterbury Matthew Parker, beaten, and forbidden to preach.

Goodman may have returned to Scotland for some time, but he appears to have spent most of his remaining years in Chester. In 1584, he refused to subscribe to **Whitgift's articles**, but because he held no living, no measures were taken against him. Late in life, Goodman was visited by **James Ussher**, who held him in high regard. Goodman was the author of a commentary on Amos.

GOODWIN, JOHN (c. 1594–1665). English Puritan minister. Goodwin was born in Norfolk and educated at Queens' College, **Cambridge**. He graduated B.A. in 1616, was elected fellow in 1617, and proceeded M.A. in 1619. Goodwin left Cambridge to marry, took orders, and served in several parishes, including Raynham, Lynn, Yarmouth, and Norwich. In 1633, he was appointed to the vicarage of St. Stephens, Coleman Street, London. He remained in this position until 1645, when he was ejected from the pulpit for refusing to administer the **sacraments** without discrimination. Goodwin promptly formed an **Independent** congregation that also met in Coleman Street.

Throughout his career, Goodwin was involved in various political and theological controversies. In 1648, he published a tract titled *Might and Right Well Met*, defending **Pride's Purge**. He also wrote several tracts in defense of the trial and execution of **Charles I**. Consequently, at the **Restoration,** he was ordered into custody but eventually released.

Calamy describes Goodwin as a man who "was against every man, and had every man against him." He wrote a vast number of treatises and pamphlets, including attacks on **Presbyterians**, **Fifth Monarchists**, Cromwellian **triers**, and **Baptists**. He, in turn, was frequently attacked for, among other things, his own **Arminian** leanings.

GOODWIN, THOMAS (1600–1680). English **Congregationalist** divine. Goodwin was born in Rollesby, Norfolk, and enrolled at the age of 12 in Christ's College, **Cambridge**. He transferred to St. Catharine's Hall in 1619 and became a **fellow** and lecturer of St. Catharine's in 1620, at which time he was converted. In 1625, Goodwin was appointed **lecturer** at Holy Trinity Church, Cambridge. In 1630, he obtained the vicarage of Trinity; however, during this time, he also came to embrace Congregationalist ideas and subsequently resigned as vicar in 1634, to be succeeded by **Richard Sibbes**. He also resigned his lectureship and fellowship and moved to London, where he married and began **preaching** at various Congregationalist churches. In 1639, the threat of prosecution caused Goodwin to flee to **Holland**, where he met fellow Independents **Jeremiah Burroughs**, **William Bridge**, and **Sidrach Simpson**. He served as co-pastor with **Philip Nye** to a small congregation at Arnheim.

Goodwin returned to London in 1641 at the onset of the **English Civil Wars** and formed a church at St. Dunstan's-in-the-East, near Thomas Street in London. He preached frequently before **Parliament**. In 1643, he was selected as a member of the **Westminster Assembly** of Divines (1642) and served as a leader of the "**Five Dissenting Brethren**," which also included Nye, Burroughs, Bridge, and Simpson. In 1649, Goodwin was appointed chaplain to the Council of State and in 1650, president of Magdalen College, **Oxford**. While at Oxford, he also organized an Independent congregation of which Stephen Charnok was a member. He served as a member of the Board of Visitors, a Cromwellian **trier**, and a member of the **Savoy Conference** of Congregational Elders (1658).

Upon the **Restoration** of **Charles II**, Goodwin was ejected from the presidency at Oxford and returned to London, serving as pastor to Fetter Lane Independent Church, where he remained until his death. He served his flock through the 1665 outbreak of the plague and the Great Fire of London (1666), though he lost half his library in the fire. Goodwin is buried in **Bunhill Fields**.

Goodwin is considered one of the great theological minds of the Puritan movement. His exegetical and doctrinal works include *A Child Walking in Darkness*, *Return of **Prayers***, *Trial of a Christian's Growth*, *Vanity of the Thoughts*, *Aggravation of **Sin***, and *Christ Set Forth*.

GOUGE, THOMAS (1589–1681). **Nonconformist** divine, philanthropist, son of William Gouge. Gouge was born in London and educated at Eaton. He entered King's College, **Cambridge**, in 1625. He graduated B.A. and M.A. and was admitted a **fellow** of King's College in 1628. Having taken orders, he was presented to the rectory of Couldsen, Surrey, in 1634 and in 1638 was appointed vicar of St. Sepulchre's, London. He was one of 58 ministers who signed *A Vindication of the Ministers of the Gospel in and About London*, opposing the trial and execution of **Charles I**.

Gouge was more noted for his charity than his **preaching**. He gave money to the aged poor who attended his catechism classes and employed his poor parishioners in the linen trade at his own expense. However, he was ejected from the pulpit under the 1662 **Act of Uniformity**. Rather than forming an **Independent** congregation of his own, he retired to Hammersmith and raised support for other members of the ejected clergy.

While at Hammersmith, Gouge read the biography of **Joseph Alleine** and was inspired to follow his example by undertaking **mission** work in Wales. He preached in Wales, at first illegally, and founded the Welsh Trust, which established English schools for Welsh children and published and circulated Welsh translations of the **Bible** and other religious books. At home, Gouge continued his work by teaching catechism to children at Christ's Hospital. He lived in good health, even in advanced age, and died in his sleep at age 92. His funeral **sermon** was preached by John Tillotson, future **Archbishop of Canterbury**.

GOUGE, WILLIAM (1575–1653). English Puritan divine. Gouge was born in Bow, near Stratford, in Middlesex. He received his early education at Paul's School in London, Felstad in Essex, and Eton School. He entered King's College, **Cambridge**, graduating B.A. in 1598, M.A. in 1601 or 1602, and received his D.D. in 1628. Gouge was **ordained** in 1604 and became the minister at Blackfriar's Church, London, where he served for his remaining 45 years. He was greatly admired for his **preaching**; his Wednesday morning **lectures**, which he gave for more than 35 years, were very popular. In 1642, Gouge was appointed as a member of the **Westminster Assembly** of Divines and wrote the Assembly's annotations for the books of the **Bible** from I Kings through Esther. However, he opposed the trial and execution of **Charles I** and subscribed to *A Vindication of the Ministers of the Gospel in and About London* (1649).

Gouge was, according to Brook, a paragon of the Puritan virtues of discipline, exactitude, and conscientiousness. His admirers called him "the father of the London Divines and the oracle of his time," while his detractors referred to him an "arch-puritan." His run-ins with ecclesiastical authorities included a nine-week imprisonment for the republication of Finch's *The Calling of the Jews*.

Gouge's works include his massive *Commentary on Hebrews*, published after his death, *The Whole Armour of God* (1615), *Of Domestical Duties* (1622), *The Saint's Sacrifice* (1632), and *A Guide to Go to God* (1626), an exposition on the Lord's Prayer. *See also* LAY IMPROPRIATIONS.

GRAND REMONSTRANCE. A list of abuses and recommendations for reform presented to **Charles I** by **Parliament** on 22 November 1641. The Remonstrance was originally the idea of Charles Digby, Member of Parliament for Dorset, who proposed the creation of the document shortly after Charles, compelled by the debacle of the **Bishops' Wars**, summoned the **Long Parliament** in November of 1640. **John Pym** took up the idea, and he and his followers drafted the document between August and November 1641.

A lengthy document, the Grand Remonstrance featured over 200 clauses, laying out abuses in religion and politics, though it placed most of the blame on Charles' advisers rather than on the king himself. It recommended the summoning of an Assembly of Divines to develop reforms of the church, demanded Parliamentary approval of the king's ministers, and sought Parliamentary control over the army.

After a long night of contentious debate that nearly devolved into a riot, the Grand Remonstrance was approved by a vote of 159 to 148 on 22 November 1641. It was then presented to the king on December 1. Charles initially made no reply, so Parliament decided to force his hand by publishing the document. When Charles finally did reply on 23 December, he rejected all of Parliament's recommendations, though he adopted a conciliatory tone, hoping to strengthen his support. Because the Remonstrance had polarized Parliament, Charles also hoped decisive action might resolve the conflict. Thus, on 4 January, he sent 400 royal guards to Parliament in an attempt to arrest Pym and four other Parliamentary leaders. Though the attempt failed, it marked the complete collapse of relations between the crown and Parliament and helped precipitate the **English Civil Wars**.

GRAY, ANDREW (1634–1656). Scottish **Presbyterian** divine. Gray graduated M.A. from the University of St. Andrews in 1651 and was licensed to preach in 1654, the same year he married Rachel Baillie. The couple had a son who died in childhood. Gray served as minister at the Outer High Kirk in Glasgow. Despite his death from a fever at age 22, he was a popular and influential preacher who emphasized the importance of growth in grace in the Christian life. His **sermons** have been collected and published in several volumes, including *Directions and Instigations to the Duty of **Prayer*** (1669), *The Mystery of Faith Opened Up* (1659), *Great and Precious Promises* (1669), and *The Spiritual Warfare* (1671).

GRAY'S INN. Gray's Inn is one of four Inns of Court in London by which any barrister in England must be certified in order to practice law. The others are **Lincoln's Inn**, the Inner Temple, and the Middle Temple. Each of the inns has a chapel and a library, and the records of Gray's Inn go back the farthest of all, dating to 1422. Prominent Puritans who either studied or preached at Gray's Inn include **Richard Cromwell**, **Thomas Gataker**, **William Penn**, **John Preston**, **William Prynne**, **Edward Reynolds**, **John Thurloe**, **Peter Wentworth**, and **George Wither**. King **Charles II** also visited Gray's Inn multiple times after the **Restoration**.

GREAT AWAKENING. The Great Awakening was a series of Protestant revivals that swept through the American colonies during the mid-1700s. In the middle colonies, early stirrings of religious revival were felt in the 1620s under the preaching of Dutch Reformed minister Theodore Frelinghuysen, but the movement began to gather much greater force among **Presbyterians** during the 1640s, beginning with the ministry of **Gilbert Tennent** in New Brunswick, New Jersey. Tennant, his father **William Tennent**, and his three brothers, all of whom were Presbyterian ministers, became leading figures in the awakening as it spread throughout New York, Pennsylvania, and New Jersey.

The primary figure of the awakening in New England was **Jonathan Edwards**, a **Congregationalist** minister in Northampton, Massachusetts. Edwards lamented what he saw as a decline in piety among youth and a gradual lapse into secularism and rationalism among New England Congregationalists, and his fiery **sermons**, such as the famous "Sinners in the Hands of an Angry God," led to many conversions in and around Northampton. A major voice in the Southern colonies was Samuel Davies, Presbyterian minister at Hanover,

Virginia. The movement reached its height with the appearance of English Methodist preacher **George Whitefield**, who made a series of visits to the colonies beginning in 1739. Whitefield's preaching drew such massive crowds that he was often obliged to preach outdoors, and his appearances throughout the colonies led to thousands of conversions.

An important innovation of the Great Awakening was its dramatic, emotional **preaching**, often by itinerant lay preachers. The desired effect of this preaching was to bring the listener to a state of high emotional and spiritual excitement. Some within the movement, such as James Davenport and his followers, placed great emphasis on the outward expression of spiritual rebirth, in the form of weeping, crying, convulsions, or fainting. In fact, the emotionalism associated with the awakening became one of the chief objections of those who attacked the revivals on the pulpit and in print. Whitefield and Gilbert Tennant responded in kind, accusing the established clergy of spiritual deadness, of being themselves unconverted, and of leading their church members into eternal damnation. Those who promoted and supported the movement came to be known as the "New Lights"; its opponents, such as Boston clergyman Charles Chauncey, as the "Old Lights." As hostilities intensified, Edwards came forth as a moderate, defending the revivals but urging the movement's leaders to caution and restraint.

Over 350 new churches were formed, according to some estimates, as a result of the Great Awakening. It especially contributed to the growth and influence of **Baptists** and Methodists. The movement led to the establishment of a number of schools, including Princeton, Brown, Rutgers, and Dartmouth. Also the Great Awakening inspired many individuals to devote themselves to **mission** work in the Southern colonies and among Native Americans.

GREAT BIBLE. The Great Bible was the first vernacular edition of the **Bible** to be authorized by the English government. King **Henry VIII** ordered its use in the Church of England in 1539. Its chief editor was Miles Coverdale, who reported to the king's secretary and vicar general, Thomas Cromwell. Most of the first printing was conducted in Paris, but hostility from French authorities meant that some of the final first editions had to be printed in London. The Great Bible received its name from its large-size pages, and it underwent six revised editions from 1640–41. It is sometimes called either the Cromwell Bible for Thomas Cromwell, the Chained Bible for its standard presence in some corner of every **Anglican** chapel, or the Cranmer Bible for the preface to the second edition written by **Archbishop of Canterbury Thomas Cranmer**. Cranmer's preface also appeared in the **Bishops' Bible** of 1568, which would have been familiar to some of the first Puritans. The New Testament and portions of the Old Testament in the Great Bible came from translations by William Tyndale, while other portions of the Old Testament were translated by Coverdale from Latin and German editions.

GREENHAM, RICHARD (c. 1535–c. 1594). English **Nonconformist** divine. The birth date and place of Greenham are not known. He entered **Cambridge** in 1559. He was offered a **fellowship** in 1570, but declined, choosing instead to accept the call to preach at Dry Drayton, a poor parish near Cambridge. There, he distinguished himself as a passionate preacher who was tireless in the performance of pastoral duties. He was especially noted for his ability to minister to afflicted **conscience**s. Young men preparing for the ministry were often sent to live with Greenham, including **Robert Browne** and **Henry Smith**. He was suspended briefly for nonsubscription and for not wearing **vestments**. A strict **Sabbatarian**, Greenham expressed his views on Sabbath observance in his best-known work, titled *A Treatise on the Sabbath* (1599).

In spite of his exemplary service to his congregation, Greenham considered his ministry at Dry Drayton ineffectual. After 21 years, he went to London, where he preached in several places, eventually settling at Christ Church in London. He died two years later, according to Fuller, during a plague year, though whether he died of the plague or some other malady is not known. **Richard Baxter** lists Greenham as one of his "practical affectionate English writers."

GREENHILL, WILLIAM (c. 1597–1671). Independent English minister. William Greenhill was most likely the son of a husbandman from Middlesex. He was educated first at Harlington School, then at Gonville and Caius College, **Cambridge**, where he graduated B.A. in 1619 and M.A. 1622. Greenhill was **ordained** at Lincoln in 1628 and became rector of Oakley, Suffolk, in 1629. Probably through the influence of **John Preston**, Greenhill then began to develop Puritan convictions; consequently, in 1633, he refused to read the *Book of Sports* from his pulpit and was deprived of his living by Matthew Wren, Bishop of Norfolk.

Greenhill migrated with fellow Independent **Jeremiah Burroughs** to Rotterdam and joined the Independent congregation of which **William Bridge**, **Sidrach Simpson**, and other notable **Congregationalists** were members. While in Rotterdam, Greenhill and Burroughs made several trips to England to smuggle seditious books. They returned to England in 1641, where they were appointed to a joint **lectureship** by the church at Stepney in London. With the outbreak of the **English Civil Wars** the following year, Greenhill sided with **Parliament** and was invited to preach fast **sermons** before Parliament for the next several years. Greenhill accepted the pastorate of a gathered congregation in Stepney and worked closely with other Independent ministers, becoming one of the most prominent figures in Independent circles. He was appointed to the **Westminster Assembly** of Divines and was affiliated with the **Five Dissenting Brethren**, though he did not sign their "Apologetical Narration." It was during this time that Greenhill began his best-known work, a commentary on the Book of Ezekiel. The first volume appeared in 1545, followed by four more volumes that appeared between 1649 and 1662.

In 1647, Greenhill stood with a group of Independent and **Baptist** ministers who supported the House of Commons in its dispute with the **Levellers**. He supported the execution of **Charles I** but served as chaplain to the royal children and pled on behalf of **Christopher Love**, who was accused of and ultimately hanged for his involvement in a plot to restore the monarchy. In 1652, he was one of nine ministers who met with Parliament to condemn the Racovian Catechism. Greenhill also actively supported **missionary** work in Wales and among the Native Americans.

Greenhill was appointed to the vicarage of Stepney in 1657. He served as governor of Harrow School from 1653–57. He was a **trier** for the approbation of ministers and a member of the committee that ejected unfit members of the clergy. He was also one of six ministers who drafted the **Savoy Declaration** in 1658. Greenhill was himself ejected from the pulpit in 1660; however, he continued to preach secretly in Stepney until the passing of the **Conventicle Act** in 1670, shortly before his death.

GREENWOOD, JOHN (c. 1650–1593). English **Separatist** minister. The date and place of Greenwood's birth are not known. He entered Corpus Christi College, **Cambridge**, as a sizar (a student required to pay minimal fees) in 1577, and graduated with a B.A. in 1581. A strict Separatist, Greenwood first served as chaplain to Lord Rich at Rochford, Essex, and was made deacon by John Aylmer, Bishop of London, but he renounced his **ordination** and became one of the leaders of the Separatist movement in London. Jailed in 1586, he wrote several pamphlets with **Henry Barrow**, most notably, *An Answer to George Gifford's Pretended Defense of Read Prayers*. In 1592, Greenwood was elected teacher of the Separatist church in London, but by 1593, he was back in prison, arrested, along with Barrow, for "devising and circulating seditious books." After two respites, both men were hanged on 6 April of the same year.

Greenwood and Barrow espoused a form of **Congregationalism** that was more extreme that that of **Robert Browne**. Their followers became known as **Barrowists**.

GRINDLETONIANS. The term "Grindletonian" derives from the town of Grindleton, a small community in Northwest Yorkshire, a region of England where a number of unorthodox sects flourished. Grindleton lies at the foot of Pendle Hill, where **George Fox** received a series of visions that led to the founding of **Quakerism**. The Grindletonians are the only known English sect to derive its name from a place, though the movement may have spread to neighboring communities as well.

Grindletonian beliefs are closely aligned with those of other sects, particularly the **Familists**; in fact, there is a contemporary reference to the group as the "Grindletonian Familists." Their beliefs include the privileging of the spirit over the **Bible**; they denied the importance of **ordination**—anyone who possessed the inner light could preach. They also believed that it is possible to live without **sin** and attain Heaven in this life. The Grindletonians seem to have retained some elements of **Calvinism**, however, since they refused to pray for the king, on the basis that they did not know if he was to be counted among the elect.

The main leader of the Grindletonians was Roger Brearley, who was curate at Grindleton from 1615–22, though it is possible that Grindletonian ideas predate his arrival. In 1617, Brearley and his congregation were charged with 50 heretical teachings. Brearley left Grindleton to serve at Kildwick, 10 miles east, where he remained until 1631. He was replaced by John Webster who continued to preach in the Grindletonian vein.

GUNPOWDER PLOT. The Gunpowder Plot of 1605 was a failed Roman **Catholic** plot to kill King **James I** and leading Protestant nobles by blowing up the **Parliament** building when all were present. The conspirators wished to place the king's daughter Elizabeth on the throne and press for her conversion to Catholicism. Parliamentary officials received an anonymous letter that alerted them to the plot, which was orchestrated by Robert Catesby and about a dozen others. The explosives expert for the plot was Guy Fawkes, who is still burned in effigy on the festive Guy Fawkes Day, each 5 November. The Gunpowder Plot stirred anti-Catholic sentiment throughout England and helped to produce the great suspicion against Catholic government that colored English politics for the rest of the Stuart dynasty, raising mistrust of **Charles I**, **Charles II**, and **James II**.

GURNALL, WILLIAM (1616–1679). English Puritan divine. Gurnall was born at Lynn in Norfolk County, a Puritan stronghold. He attended the town's grammar school and, with the Lynn scholarship, entered **Emmanuel College, Cambridge**, in 1631. He received his B.A. in 1635 and his M.A. in 1639, though he was never elected to a **fellowship**.

The date of Gurnall's **ordination** is not known. His first post was in Sudbury, perhaps as curate. In 1644, he was appointed to the rectorship of Lavenham in Suffolk, where he served for his remaining 35 years. Though a Puritan in doctrine, Gurnall subscribed to the 1662 **Act of Uniformity**. By doing so, he retained his position at Lavenham, but he also earned the disapprobation of his fellow Puritans, 2,000 of whom refused to sign and were ejected from their ecclesiastical offices. In 1665, Gurnall was the subject of an attack in print, titled *Covenant Renouncers Desperate Apostates*. The author of this tract accused Gurnall of "hateful defilements, hateful to the word of God and his saints," and called him a member of an "order of anti-Christian priesthood."

Gurnall is best known as the author of the Puritan devotional classic, *The Christian in Complete Armour*. Originally published in three volumes, it consists of a series of **sermons** on Ephesians 6 and is notable for its concreteness and accessibility, as well as its pithy, graphic style. In its sense of proportion, J. C. Ryle compares Gurnall's work to **John Bunyan**'s *Pilgrim's Progress*. The book was so popular that it went through six editions in Gurnall's own lifetime. It was most recently republished in excerpted form by Moody Press in 1999.

GUTHRIE, WILLIAM (1620–1665). Scottish Presbyterian divine. Guthrie was born in Pitforthy, Scotland. He was one of five sons, four of whom entered the ministry. He attended St. Andrews University, where he studied under his cousin, James Guthrie. After taking his M.A., Guthrie began his preparation for the ministry under Samuel Rutherford. He was licensed to preach in 1642, but rather than embarking on his ministerial career right away, he spent two years as tutor to the son of the Earl of Loudon. In 1644, he was appointed the first pastor to the new parish of Fenwick, where he remained for the rest of his career. The size of his parish and the lack of adequate roads rendered travel difficult and limited church attendance. Guthrie is said to have bribed some of his parishioners to attend services and visited others incognito, encouraging them to attend. In addition to being an avid hunter and fisherman, he was considered a great practical preacher—one of the most admired in 17th-century Scotland.

Under **Oliver Cromwell**, in 1645, Guthrie was appointed chaplain to the army; he also served as a **trier** for ministers. However, with the **Restoration** of the monarchy, he was forced out of the ministry in 1664 for resisting the establishment of **episcopacy** on the Church of Scotland.

For his eccentricities, Guthrie's detractors labeled him the "Fool of Fenwick," an appellation he used on the title pages of his published **sermons**. His most significant contribution to Puritan literature is a short work titled *The Christian's Great Interest* (1659). **John Owen** credited it with containing "more divinity" than all of his own writings put together.

– H –

HALF-WAY COVENANT. Drafted by **Richard Mather** in 1657 and adopted by many New England **Congregationalist** churches in 1662, the Half-Way Covenant allowed church members who could not provide evidence of conversion to have their children baptized. Prior to the adoption of the Half-Way Covenant, the privilege of having one's children baptized was extended only to those who could make public affirmation of their faith by reporting an experience of conversion. Among the first generation of New England settlers, this prerequisite was not an issue, but many second- and third-generation Puritans hesitated to make their declaration of such an experience; consequently, full church membership began to decline, especially among men, and in the New England theocracy, many prominent families were denied positions of leadership.

The Half-Way Covenant extended the rite of **baptism** to children of the unconverted, while denying them other prerogatives of full membership, such as partaking of the Lord's Supper and voting on church matters. However, it did make baptized children of the unconverted eligible to seek full membership in the churches when they reached adulthood and might be ready, themselves, to testify to a conversion experience.

Not all churches adopted the Half-Way Covenant, and in some congregations where it was adopted, its opponents seceded, forming new settlements, such as Newark, New Jersey. In the mid-18th century, **Jonathan Edwards** opposed the Half-Way Covenant, and during the **Great Awakening**, with its emphasis on personal conversion, many churches abolished it. However, during the late 17th and early 18th centuries, the Half-Way Covenant advanced the influence of the churches in New England and also extended political and religious rights to a broader constituency.

HALL, JOSEPH (1574–1656). Anglican bishop, satirist, and poet. Hall was born at Ashby-de-la-Zouch and received his early education at the Ashby grammar school. He attended **Emmanuel College**, Cambridge, graduating B.A. in 1592, M.A. in 1596, B.D. in 1603, and D.D. in 1612. In 1598, Hall published the first three books of his verse satire, *Virgidemiarum*. These works, which Hall himself described as "toothless," were followed by three "biting" satires in the same year. Together, they are among the first English satires based on Latin models, though Hall's claim to be the first English satirist is doubtful. They are also early examples of the use of the heroic couplet, which would become the dominant verse form of the 18th century. In 1599, **Archbishop of Canterbury** John Whitgift judged the books licentious and scurrilous and ordered that they be burned.

After taking holy orders, Hall was presented in 1601 with a living at Halsted by Sir Robert and Lady Drury, who were also the patrons of Hall's friend, John Donne. Married in 1603, he traveled in 1605 to Spain and the Netherlands. Around this time, he also published a work of fantasy travel literature titled *Mundus Alter Idem* (*The World Different and the Same*) that would influence Jonathan Swift's masterpiece *Gulliver's Travels*. Hall also published two collections of Christian/Senecan aphorisms and reflections titled *Meditation and Vows* (1605) and *Characters of Virtues and Vices* (1608). In 1606, Hall was appointed chaplain to Prince Henry. After serving as curate of Waltham-Holy-Cross, Essex, and receiving the prebend of Willenhall in the collegiate church of Wolverhampton, Hall was nominated Dean of Worcester. He also traveled to Scotland with **James I** and served as an English delegate to the **Synod of Dort** (1618). In 1627, he was appointed Bishop of Exeter.

Hall was active in the controversy between **Calvinism** and **Arminianism** in the English Church. An Anglican with strong Calvinist leanings, He sought a compromise between the two parties. His efforts at mediation drew the admiration of **Charles I** but also caused Archbishop **William Laud** to suspect Hall of Puritan tendencies and to place him under surveillance. Hall was forced on three separate occasions to answer Laud's accusations before the king. But if Laud considered Hall a crypto-Puritan, more radical Puritans treated him with equal hostility. In 1640–41, Hall wrote two tracts in defense of the Episcopal polity: ***Episcopacy** by Divine Right* and *An Humble Remonstrance to the High Court of Parliament*. These works provoked a flurry of responses, including those of **Smectymnuus** and several pamphlets by **John Milton**, who attacked not only Hall's views on church polity but his earlier satires as well.

Despite his conflicts with Laud, Hall was translated to the see of Norwich in 1641, and also served as a member of the Lord's Committee on religion. But upon the outbreak of the **English Civil Wars** in the same year, Hall, along with 13 other bishops, was impeached and, from New Years through Whitsuntide (the seventh day after Easter) 1642, imprisoned. After his release, Hall was installed at Norwich, but, in 1643, he was deprived of his Episcopal revenues. Hall continued to carry out his duties as bishop, despite these difficulties, until 1646, when townspeople of Norwich desecrated the cathedral and ejected Hall and his wife from the palace. Hall retired to Higham near Norwich, where, despite his poverty, he spent his last years **preaching** when he could and writing devotional works.

As a stylist, Hall earned the admiration of Thomas Fuller, who called him "our English Seneca." His devotional writings include *Contemplations upon the Principal Passages of the Old and New Testaments* (1612–34) and *The Art of Divine Meditation* (1606).

HAMPTON COURT CONFERENCE. The Hampton Court Conference met on 14, 16, and 18 January 1604. King **James I** called the meeting in response to the **Millenary Petition**, which laid out the Puritan agenda for major reforms in the doctrines, **worship**, and government of the English Church. James himself selected representatives for the Puritan position—they included **John Rainolds**, who served as the principal spokesman, **Laurence Chaderton**, **Thomas Sparke**, and **John Knewstubs**. Representing the high church were over 50 clergy, including deans, bishops, and **Archbishop of Canterbury** John Whitgift. The king presided over the conference.

The Puritans chose to present four main points of reform: the purification of church doctrine; the establishment of a **preaching** ministry; revision of church government along **Presbyterian** lines; and alteration to the ***Book of Common Prayer***, including the incorporation of the **Lambeth Articles** into the **Thirty-Nine Articles**. However, James' hostility to the Puritan cause was evident throughout the proceedings. On the second day, Rainold's use of the word "Presbytery" so incensed the king that he dismissed the gathering. On the third day, he announced that with only a few minor concessions to the Puritan position, the practices and teachings of the church would remain unaltered.

Although the Hampton Court Conference led to no significant changes in the English Church, it did lead to one important development—James agreed to the Puritan proposal of a new English translation of the **Bible**. The result was the Authorized, or **King James Bible**.

HARRIS, ROBERT (1581–1658). President of Trinity College, **Oxford**. Harris was born at Broad Campden, Gloucestershire. The son of poor parents, he was educated at the free schools of Chipping Campden and Worcester. He then entered Magdalen College at age 15, supporting himself by tutoring in Greek and Hebrew. He received his B.A. in 1600 and his B.D. in 1614.

After serving as assistant to the rector of Chiselhampton, near Oxford, Harris was **ordained** by 1607 and introduced to the living of Hanwell, Oxfordshire, where he replaced the incumbent, **John Dod**. He also preached at various London churches and gained a large following. In 1642, he was chosen as a consultant to **Parliament**. Harris remained in Hanwell until 1644, when Royalist troops forced him from his home, despite his neutral position in the **English Civil Wars**. He returned to London and was appointed to the **Westminster Assembly**. He also received the call to serve as minister at St. Botolph's, Bishopsgate. In 1646, Harris was ordered to Oxford as one of six divines commissioned to preach in any pulpit of their choosing. He also served as a Parliamentary visitor to the university from 1647–58.

In 1648, Harris both received his D.D. and was made president of Trinity College; as a part of his responsibilities, he was appointed to the living of Garsington, Oxfordshire. Harris served as president of Trinity until his death. Two volumes of his **sermons** were published in 1654. He also published a tract on the **sin** of drunkenness titled *The Drunkard's Cup* (1630).

HARRISON, THOMAS (1616–1660). Parliamentarian, soldier, and **Fifth Monarchist**. Harrison was born at Newcastle-under-Lyme in Staffordshire. The son of a wealthy butcher, he was educated at a local grammar school and placed as a clerk to an attorney at Clifford's

Inn. Upon the outbreak of the **English Civil Wars** in 1642, Harrison joined the **Earl of Essex**'s life guard. He fought in several important battles and earned a distinguished reputation, rising to the rank of major by 1644. An **Independent**, Harrison was a friend to several influential people, including **Oliver Cromwell**, with whom he served at Marston Moor and Naseby.

Harrison was made Member of **Parliament** for Wendover in 1646. He served in Ireland in 1647, and when he returned, sided with the army in its dispute with Parliament. Harrison sought the abolition of the House of Lords and opposed negotiations with **Charles I**. Now a colonel, Harrison also fought with distinction in the Second Civil War, during which he was severely wounded. He initially supported the **Levellers** and urged a compromise, but when the Leveller soldiers mutinied, he helped Cromwell and Ireton crush the rebellion. He also escorted Charles to London and signed his death warrant.

In 1649, Harrison received a military command in Wales, where he became involved with extreme Puritan sects, most notably the Fifth Monarchists. He served as commander of forces in England during Cromwell's campaign against the Scots in 1650; he fought against the Scots and **Charles II**, and at the Battle of Worcester. Elected to Council of State in 1651, Harrison urged the dismissal of the **Long Parliament**. When this goal was accomplished in 1653, he became an influential member of the **Barebones Parliament**, which represented his hopes for a government of God-fearing men chosen by congregations.

Such hopes, however, were dashed by the creation of the **Protectorate**, which Harrison so vigorously opposed that he was stripped of his commission in 1653 and, in 1654, confined to his father's house in Staffordshire. During the Protectorate, Harrison was suspected of involvements with various extremist groups in plots to overthrow the government and was imprisoned several times. Upon the **Restoration**, Harrison was drawn and quartered at Charing Cross for his involvement in the execution of Charles I.

HARVARD, JOHN (1607–1638). Minister, benefactor of **Harvard University**. Harvard was born in Southwark, London, to Robert Harvard, a prosperous butcher, and his second wife, Katharine. Harvard received his early education at the St. Saviour grammar school. In

1625, his father and five of his siblings died during an outbreak of the plague. Harvard's mother remarried and sent him to **Emmanuel College, Cambridge**, where he earned his B.A. in 1631 and M.A. in 1635. He married Anne Sadler in 1636; his mother died the same year, and his brother the following, leaving Harvard the sole heir of his family estate.

In 1637, Harvard and his wife sailed to Massachusetts, carrying on board Harvard's library of approximately 300 books. He accepted a call to serve as minister to First Church, Charlestown, but died a year later of tuberculosis. In his will, Harvard bequeathed half of his estate and his collection of books to the college established the year before in Newtowne, later called Cambridge. In 1638, Harvard College was officially named after him.

HARVARD COLLEGE. The oldest educational institution in the United States, Harvard (now Harvard University) was founded in 1636 at Newtowne, Massachusetts, later renamed Cambridge. In 1639, the school was named after **John Harvard**, who had bequeathed his books and half his estate to the fledgling institution. The founders of Harvard modeled it after **Emmanuel College, Cambridge**, where many of them had been educated. Although the school was not affiliated with any church, its primary purpose was to educate young men for ministry in the Puritan churches of New England. Harvard graduated its first class in 1642.

It was not long, however, before the unifying vision of the Puritan founders of Harvard began to crumble. The school's first president, Henry Dunster, was removed from office in 1654 for questioning infant **baptism**. Likewise, Leonard Hoar, the third president, was forced to resign in 1675 for his supposedly radical views. **Increase Mather**, the seventh president of Harvard, viewed with dismay what he perceived as the institution's decline into liberalism, a view that brought him into conflict with much of the Harvard faculty and led to his resignation in 1701. Increase and his son **Cotton Mather** considered the original mission of Harvard as wholly compromised and gave their support to the Collegiate School, later renamed Yale University, in New Haven, Connecticut, hoping it would continue the work of maintaining Puritan orthodoxy.

HELWYS, THOMAS (c. 1550–c. 1616). English **Baptist** preacher. Helwys was born in Nottinghamshire to a prominent family and educated at **Gray's Inn**. After several years in London, he returned to his Nottinghamshire home, Broxtowe Hall, which subsequently became a haven for early **dissenters**. Helwys joined a group of **Separatists** led by **John Smyth** and followed Smyth to Amsterdam in 1606. After this church excommunicated Smyth for his denial of infant **baptism** and his teaching of free will, Helwys became a member of the new congregation Smyth established. He was appointed this congregation's pastor after Smyth died in 1612. However, he returned to England the same year, along with many members of his congregation, and established a church at Pinner's Hall, which is considered the first General Baptist church in London. Helwys was a popular preacher and gained many converts.

In 1615, Helwys published a treatise called "Persecution for Religion Judged and Condemned." The work was a defense of Baptist beliefs, an attack on the **prelacy**, and an appeal for unrestricted **religious liberty**. As a consequence of this publication, many members of the congregation, along with Helwys, suffered intense persecution. Helwys died in 1616, according to some sources, in Newgate Prison.

HENRY VIII (1491–1547). King of England from 1509–47. The second son of Henry VII, Henry became heir to the throne after the death of his older brother, Arthur, in 1502. As a young man, Henry was a gifted student, athlete, and musician, and when he acceded to the throne upon his father's death in 1509, such admirers as Erasmus and Thomas More hailed him as a humanist monarch. Several weeks before his coronation, Henry married Catherine of Aragon, Arthur's widow, but because of the prohibition in Leviticus 20:21 against a man marrying his sister-in-law, the union required a special dispensation from the pope. One of Henry's primary concerns was to produce a male heir to the throne, but by 1527, the marriage had produced only a female heir, the future **Mary I**. Furthermore, Henry had fallen in love with Anne Boleyn, and, through his principal adviser, Cardinal Thomas Wolsey, petitioned the Vatican for an annulment of his marriage to Catherine. When Wolsey failed to procure the annulment, Henry settled the matter by separating the Church of England from the Church of Rome. This move not only provided Henry with the divorce he wanted but also brought all church assets into possession of the crown; consequently, he dissolved all of the monastic houses in England and seized their property.

Henry's marriage to Anne Boleyn in 1533 produced another female heir, the future **Elizabeth I**, but no male offspring. Within three years, Anne was executed on trumped-up charges of adultery, and Henry had married again. His third wife, Lady Jane Seymour, produced the long-sought-for son, the future **Edward VI**, in 1537, but she died within several days of giving birth. Henry's fourth marriage, this time to the German princess Anne of Cleves, ended in divorce after only six months. His fifth wife, Catherine Howard, was beheaded for marital infidelities after 18 months of marriage. Henry's last wife, Katherine Parr, encouraged Henry to restore Mary and Elizabeth to their status as princesses, of which they had both been deprived.

In his later years, Henry suffered from ill-health, and his uneven temper led to the execution of some of his closest advisers, such as Thomas Cromwell. Henry retained a firm control of the government until his death, but his failed wars with France and Spain had depleted the exchequer, and his domestic policies had caused deep religious divisions within the country. Such was the condition of England when the nine-year-old Edward VI succeeded his father to the throne in 1547.

By establishing an independent Church of England, Henry set the English Reformation into motion; however, Henry himself was hostile to most Reformation ideas and took measures to prevent them from spreading. He actively sought to prevent Tyndale's work of translating the **Bible** into English, and though he later commissioned the **Great Bible** and ordered a copy to be placed in every parish church, he also sought to limit its use. Henry opposed marriage of the clergy and strictly enforced the teaching of transubstantiation, particularly through the adoption of the Statute of the Six Articles in 1539. But Henry's choice of **Thomas Cranmer** as **Archbishop of Canterbury** helped move the English Church in a Protestant direction after his death and throughout the reign of Edward VI.

HENRY, MATTHEW (1662–1714). English **Presbyterian** divine, **Bible** commentator. Henry was born at Broad Oak in Shropshire, to Katherine and Philip Henry, a minister who was ejected from his pulpit in the year of his son's birth. A sickly youth, Henry received most of his early education from his father. From 1680–82, he attended the private academy of **Thomas Doolittle** in Islington, and, in 1685, went to **Gray's Inn** to study law. However, his mind was already set on a vocation in the ministry and, in 1685, he began to preach in the environs of Broad Oak and Chester. After his **ordination** in 1687, Henry began his career as the minister of a church in Chester, where he remained for the next 25 years. The construction of a meeting house in 1699–1700 and its subsequent expansion in 1706 attest to the success of Henry's ministry. While at Chester, Henry began work on a commentary of the Bible.

After declining calls from several London congregations, Henry finally accepted a call to a church in Hackney, London, in 1712, a move that gave him access to libraries and printers to aid him in the production of his commentary. He died of a stroke two years later in Nantwich, and is buried in Trinity Church, Cheshire.

Henry's massive, extremely popular commentary, *The Exposition of the Old and the New Testaments*, is his best-known work. Henry himself completed the work through the book of Acts. Other **Nonconformist** ministers, recognizing its importance, completed the sections on Romans through Revelation. Major religious figures who acknowledged the influence of the commentary on their own faith and ministry include **George Whitefield**, Charles Wesley, and Charles Hadden Spurgeon.

HILDERSHAM, ARTHUR (1563–1632). English Nonconformist minister. Hildersham was born at Stetchworth, Cambridgeshire. His parents were devoted Roman **Catholics** of royal descent who planned for their son to enter the priesthood, but while at the grammar school of Saffron Walden, Essex, Hildersham came under the influence of a Protestant schoolmaster. He entered Christ's College, **Cambridge**, in 1576, but when he refused to recant his Protestant principles and go to Rome as his family planned, they disinherited him. Through the help of his mother's second cousin, Henry Hastings, the Earl of Huntingdon, Hildersham was able to complete his studies at Cambridge, graduating M.A. in 1583. He was denied a **fellowship** but served as a reader of divinity, and, in 1587, through Huntingdon, was presented with a **lectureship** at Ashby-de-la-Zouch. His messages were strongly Puritan, and he was soon brought before the High Commission for **preaching** without a license or orders. He apparently took orders so that he could resume his lectures.

Over the course of his career, Hildersham was silenced and suspended on numerous occasions. He was suspended in 1590, but reinstated a year later, and, in 1593, was appointed vicar at Ashby. He was also one of the ministers who delivered the Millenary Petition to **James I** upon his accession in 1603. Silenced for **Nonconformity** in 1605, he joined **William Bradshaw** and other ministers to conduct twice weekly lectures at Burton on Trent, in Staffordshire. Restored to the pulpit of Ashby in 1609, he was again suspended in 1613, this time on a false accusation of teaching the heresy of soul sleep. In 1615, he was imprisoned for three months for refusing to take the ex officio oath and, in 1616, faced prosecution as a schismatic, the principal charge being that he refused to kneel in order to receive communion. Hildersham avoided imprisonment by hiding in the Hampstead home of Catherine Redich.

In 1625, he was granted a license to preach and resumed his ministry in Ashby. But by 1630, he was suspended again, this time for refusing to wear a **surplice**. Restored to the pulpit in 1631, he died a year later of scorbutic fever and is buried in the chancel of the church at Ashby.

Hildersham was a prominent early figure in the Puritan movement. His friends and followers include William Bradshaw, **William Gouge**, **John Preston**, and **John Cotton**. He wrote two works on the Lord's Supper, titled *A Briefe Forme of Examination* (1619) and *The Doctrine of Communicating Worthily in the Lord's Supper* (1619).

HOLLAND. *See* DUTCH PURITANISM.

HOOKER, THOMAS (1586–1647). English and American Puritan divine, founder of Connecticut. Hooker was born at Marfield, Leicester. He received his B.A. in 1608 and M.A. in 1611 from **Emmanuel College**, **Cambridge**, and remained there as a **fellow** for several years. Subsequently, he preached in Esher, Surrey, then served as **lecturer** at St. Mary's Church in Chelmsford, Essex. When **Archbishop of Canterbury William Laud** sought to abolish church lectureships in 1629, and threatened Hooker with arraignment for **Nonconfor-**

mity, Hooker retired to Little Baddow, where he acted as master of the grammar school while giving counsel to other ministers. When summoned to appear before the High Commission in 1630, Hooker instead fled to **Holland**, where he served first as a minister to the **Nonconformist** church at Delft, then as assistant to **William Ames** in Rotterdam. Thereafter, he sailed to Massachusetts (1633), on the same ship that carried **John Cotton** and **Samuel Stone**.

In Massachusetts, Hooker first pastored the church at Newtowne (subsequently renamed Cambridge), settled by his former parishioners from Chelmsford, who called themselves "Mr. Hooker's Company." In 1636, Hooker left Cambridge and led a group of emigrants to found Hartford, Connecticut, where he remained as pastor until his death. Although the cause for Hooker's departure is not certain, his discontent with Massachusetts' government is a likely cause. Hooker objected to the policy that denied suffrage to non-church members. In his 1638 address to the General Court of Connecticut, he set forth three political doctrines: "That the choice of public magistrates belongs unto the people by God's own allowance; That the privilege of election which belongs unto the people must not be exercised according to their humour, but according to the blessed will of God; And that they who have the power to appoint officers and magistrates, it is in their power also to set the bounds of the power and the place unto which they call them." Hooker helped draft the "Fundamental Orders" that served as the constitution of Connecticut.

Although Hooker did not advocate the separation of church and state, his political philosophy paved the way for democratic government in New England. *See also* MASSACHUSETTS BAY COLONY.

HOOPER, JOHN (?–1555). Bishop of Gloucester and Worcester. Hooper was probably born in Somerset in the 1490s, though the date and place of his birth are not known. He was educated at **Oxford**, earning his B.A. in 1518. Hooper joined the Cistercian monastery at Cleeve, Somerset, where he remained until the dissolution of the monasteries (1536–40). He then entered the service of Sir Thomas Arundel, at which time he began to read the works of Ulrich Zwingli and Heinrich Bullinger. Having embraced fully the Protestantism of these writers, Hooper fled England in 1639, when **Parliament** passed the Six Articles that reaffirmed **Catholic** dogma, such as the teaching of transubstantiation and celibacy of the clergy. He traveled to Strasbourg, where he married, then to Basel and Zurich. While in Zurich, he frequently met with Bullinger and made contact with other Continental reformers.

With the repeal of the Six Articles under **Edward VI**, Hooper returned to England (1649). He became chaplain to Edward Seymour, the Earl of Somerset and Lord Protector; afterward, he served as chaplain to John Dudley, the Duke of Northumberland. Hooper established a reputation not only as a popular preacher but as one of the leading proponents of more extreme Protestant views. In 1550, he was offered the Bishopric of Gloucester, but despite pleas from **Thomas Cranmer** and **Nicholas Ridley**, Hooper refused on the basis of his own objection to the wearing of **vestments** and the oath to the saints required for the office. He changed his mind, however, after spending several weeks in the Fleet prison, and was consecrated in 1551. The sees of Gloucester and Worcester were amalgamated the following year, and Hooper became bishop of both. As bishop, Hooper was known for vigorous fulfillment of his responsibilities, **preaching** several times a day and exercising considerable oversight. With the accession of Queen **Mary I** in 1553, however, Hooper was deprived of his bishopric, imprisoned in the Fleet, and excommunicated for his refusal to recant his Zwinglian beliefs. He remained in the Fleet until the revival of the heresy laws and was burned at the stake in 1555. His martyrdom is recounted in **John Foxe**'s *Book of Martyrs*. A significant influence on later Puritans, Hooper's works include *A Godly Confession and Protestation of the Christian Faith* (1550), *A Declaration of Christ and his Office* (1547), and *A Declaration of the Ten Holy Commandments* (1548).

HORROCKS, JEREMIAH (c. 1618–1641). Astronomer. Horrocks was born in Toxteth, a Puritan community near Liverpool, and entered **Emmanuel College, Cambridge,** as a sizar (a student required to pay minimal fees) in 1632. Given his upbringing and education, he was, most likely, a Puritan, though there is no record of his exact spiritual convictions. Though he left Cambridge after three years without taking a degree, Horrocks developed a friendship with William Crabtree, a Broughton drapier, who helped him nurture a love of astronomy and introduced him to the work of Johannes Kepler.

As a tutor in Toxteth, and subsequently as a curate at Much Hoole, Horrocks pursued his astronomical studies and observations. In studying Kepler's *Rudolphine Tables*, he realized that Kepler had overlooked a solar transit of Venus, which Horrocks predicted would occur just before sunset on Sunday, 24 November 1639. By using a telescope to project an image of the sun onto a piece of paper, Horrocks was able to view this transit. His observations allowed him to calculate the size of Venus and estimate, more accurately than any previous scientist, the distance between the earth and the sun.

In his very brief scientific career, cut short by his death at age 22, Horrocks established himself as a brilliant astronomer. He developed a new dynamical theory accounting for planetary motions, a new lunar theory that would later be improved by Newton, and accurate measures for the diameters of several celestial bodies. He also improved the measure of the horizontal solar parallax. His *Venus in Sole Visa* was published in 1662 and his *Opera posthuma* was published by members of the Royal Society in 1672–73.

HOWE, JOHN (1630–1705). English **Presbyterian** divine. Howe was born in Loughborough, Leicestershire. He entered Christ's College, **Cambridge**, as a sizar (a student required to pay minimal fees) in 1647. At Cambridge, Howe came under the influence of **Ralph Cudworth** and the **Cambridge Platonists**, which may account for the strain of Platonism that runs through his theology. In 1648, he was admitted as a **Bible** clerk to Brasen-nose College, **Oxford**, graduating B.A. in 1650. He received his M.A. from Magdalen College in 1652, where he was appointed a **fellow** and a chaplain. **Ordained** by Charles Herle, the Puritan rector at Winwick, Howe was then introduced to the curacy of Great Torrington in Devon in 1654.

On a trip to London in 1657, Howe met **Oliver Cromwell**, who was so taken with Howe that he made him his domestic chaplain. In this capacity, Howe distinguished himself as a voice for religious **toleration** and mutual forbearance between **dissenters** and conformists. With the **Restoration** of **Charles II** to the throne in 1660, Howe returned to Great Torrington and remained there until he was ejected under the **Act of Uniformity** in 1662. Despite his ejection from church office, Howe continued to preach secretly and published *The Blessedness of Righteousness* in 1668. This work brought him to the attention of Lord Massarent, who invited Howe to serve as his domestic chaplain in Antrim, Ireland.

In 1676, Howe received an invitation to serve as joint pastor to a **Nonconformist** congregation in Haberdasher Hall, London. During this time, he published the first part of his *The Living Temple*. However, with the increasing intolerance of Nonconformity in the early 1680s, Howe again departed from England, and after traveling abroad with Lord Wharton, he settled in Utrecht, where he conducted services in the English chapel and met privately several times with William of Orange. When **James II** issued the **Declaration of Indulgence** in 1687, Howe returned to England and, in 1688, headed the deputation of Nonconformist ministers who welcomed William of Orange to England as the new king. For the remainder of his life, Howe continued to preach and write. He also served as a voice of mutual tolerance between **Congregationalists** and **Presbyterians**.

Howe was respected and admired by both fellow Puritans and non-Puritans. A prolific writer, his works include many popular devotional and theological treatises, including *Inquiry into the Doctrine of the Trinity* and *The Divine Presence*. His best-known work is *The Living Temple*, considered a masterpiece of Puritan natural theology.

HUBBARD, WILLIAM (c. 1621–1704). English and American clergyman and historian. The son of a husbandman, Hubbard was born in Essex. He emigrated to New England with his family in 1635 and was a member of the first graduating class of **Harvard College** in 1642. Hubbard married in 1646, became a full church member in 1653, and was **ordained** in 1658. He was appointed assistant pastor and then pastor of the **Congregationalist** church at Ipswich, a position he held until shortly before his death. Hubbard was married twice, though his second marriage met with opposition from his church, which objected to his bride's supposedly inferior social status. In 1684 and 1688, Hubbard was appointed to serve as acting president of Harvard. Throughout his career, Hubbard established a reputation as a political and religious moderate. He supported the **Half-Way Covenant** and opposed the Salem **witchcraft** trials, even testifying on behalf of one of the accused. He urged religious freedom and obedience to the Navigation Acts, and he took a generally optimistic view of the state of New England, in contrast to **Increase Mather** and other ministers who lamented its corruption.

Hubbard is best known as the author of *History of New England*, the first authorized history of the colonies, for which he relied heavily on the journals of Governor **John Winthrop** and **William Bradford**'s *Of Plymouth Plantation*. The state of Massachusetts promised to pay him £50 for this work, though it is not known whether he ever received the payment. It was first published in 1815. Other works by Hubbard include *A Narrative of Troubles with the Indians* (1677) and *Testimony of the Order of the Gospel in Churches* (1701). In 1703, he co-wrote a petition to clear the names of all who had been accused in the Salem witchcraft trials of 1692.

HUMPHREY, LAWRENCE (1527?–1590). English Puritan minister. Humphrey took the B. A., M. A., and D.D. degrees from Magdalen College, **Oxford**, where he studied with the renowned **Reformed theologian** Peter Martyr Vermigli. He became one of those **Marian exiles** who took refuge in various European cities, such as Basel, Zurich, and Geneva, following the coronation of Queen **Mary I** in 1553. After Mary's death and the coronation of Queen **Elizabeth I**, Humphrey returned to England and received appointment as regius professor of divinity at Oxford in 1560. In 1561, he became the president of Magdalen. Humphrey was well known for his Puritan sympathies and opposition to the Jesuit order of **Catholicism**. He and **Thomas Sampson**, dean of Christ Church, were brought to trial before the **Archbishop of Canterbury** Matthew Parker for their refusal to wear **vestments**. Humphrey was able to escape any formal censure at the time, although he later softened his resistance to donning the surplice. He eventually became the dean of Gloucester (1571) and the dean of Winchester (1580). He was buried at his alma mater Magdalen.

HUTCHINSON, ANNE (c. 1591–1643). Midwife, religious leader. Hutchinson was born Anne Marbury in Alford, Lincolnshire, England. Her father was Fancis Marbury, a dissenting Anglican minister, and her mother was Bridget Dryden. Anne married William Hutchinson, a merchant, in 1612. She bore 14 children, 12 in England and two in New England. While in Alford, the Hutchinsons came under the **preaching** of **John Cotton**, a minister in nearby St. Botolph's, and became devoted followers. When Cotton fled to New England in 1633, after being suppressed by ecclesiastical authorities, Anne and her family followed, settling in Boston.

The Hutchinsons were a prominent Boston family, and Hutchinson's services as nurse and midwife gave her much influence among Boston **women**. She began to host devotional meetings in her home, discussing theology and Cotton's **sermons**. It was in these meetings that she began publicly to express her view that in order to receive grace, one need merely be receptive—the performance of good works and the living of a godly life were not prerequisites. These teachings led Hutchinson's critics to accuse her of **antinomianism**. She also drew a distinction between those who were under a covenant of grace, such as Cotton, her brother-in-law John Wheelwright, and herself, and those, such as John Wilson, the pastor of the Boston Church, who were under the covenant of works. Furthermore, she made a claim to special inspiration and a peculiar indwelling of the Holy Spirit, bringing her into conflict with established Puritan teaching. The meetings grew increasingly popular, drawing as many as 60 people. Men also began to attend, among them **Henry Vane**. In 1636, Vane unseated **John Winthrop** as governor of Massachusetts. When Winthrop returned to power a year later, he brought Hutchinson to trial on charges of having traduced the ministers. She was found guilty, banished, and excommunicated.

Hutchinson and several of her followers settled in Aquidneck, now Rhode Island; however, the leadership of Massachusetts continued their attempts to silence her through deputations. When William Hutchinson died in 1642, Anne moved, along with her six youngest children, to Long Island Sound, near what is now New Rochelle in Westchester County, New York, an area then controlled by the Dutch. A year later, Hutchinson was killed by Native Americans. Only one of her remaining children, a daughter, survived the attack. Winthrop viewed her demise as divine justice.

A statue of Anne Hutchinson stands in front of the State House in Boston. The inscription calls her a "Courageous Exponent of Civil

Liberty and Religious **Toleration**." *See also* MASSACHUSETTS BAY COLONY.

– I –

INDEPENDENCY. *See* CONGREGATIONALISM.

INTERREGNUM. The "Interregnum" is the period of English history between the execution of **Charles I** and the accession of **Charles II**. It was the first time since the inception of the Puritan movement that the Puritans found themselves in a dominant position, both politically and religiously. However, with their main adversaries eliminated, the Puritans found themselves divided against each other, with **Presbyterians** and **Congregationalists** in particular vying for dominance.

After the execution of Charles I in 1649, the **Rump Parliament** declared England a **Commonwealth**, governed as a republic, principally by the Rump Parliament itself. In 1653, **Oliver Cromwell**, the leader of the Parliamentarian Army, forcibly dissolved **Parliament** and established the **Protectorate**, himself serving as Lord Protector. When Cromwell died in 1658, his son **Richard Cromwell** assumed the position of Lord Protector, until the **Restoration** of the monarchy under Charles II in 1660.

IRETON, HENRY (1611–1651). English general. Ireton was the eldest son of German Ireton from Attenborough, Nottinghamshire. He completed his B.A. from **Oxford** in 1629 and began to study law at the Middle Temple. Little is known of Ireton's young adult life until he joined the **New Model Army** in 1642 at the battle of Edgehill, one of the first major engagements of the **English Civil Wars** between **Parliament** and King **Charles I**. For his tactical prowess on the battlefield, Ireton was named by **Oliver Cromwell** to be deputy general of the Isle of Ely in 1643 and commissary-general in 1645. He rose to command the entire left flank of the army's forces, with Cromwell himself commanding the right, despite his brief capture and imprisonment by royalist forces. Late in 1645, he was also received election to Parliament as a representative of Appleby. On 15 June

1646, Ireton married Cromwell's daughter Bridget in Oxford. The couple would have one son and three daughters.

At first, Ireton spoke against the political demands of the **Levellers** at the **Putney Debates** and cautioned against regicide, but, by 1649, he had begun to alter his beliefs on both issues. After the execution of the king, Ireton took command of the army's battalions in Ireland and repressed **Catholic** protests against Cromwell's new **Protectorate**. Ireton died of a fever. When King **Charles II** resumed the Stuart kingship with the **Restoration** of 1660, he exhumed and posthumously executed the remains of both Ireton and Cromwell.

IRISH ARTICLES OR DUBLIN ARTICLES. These 104 articles were approved by a convocation of the Irish Church in 1615. The principal author of the Irish Articles was **James Ussher**, the vice-chancellor of Trinity College, Dublin. Clergy were required to subscribe to the articles, which served as "a rule of public doctrine" for the Irish Church. Any clergy whose teachings opposed what was set forth in the articles was subject to expulsion from the ministry. In this sense, the Irish Articles performed the same function for the Irish church that the **Thirty-Nine Articles** served for the English Church. But the Irish Articles provided a much stronger and more systematic expression of **Calvinist** theology than did the Thirty-Nine, and a stronger denunciation of the papacy. **Presbyterian** influence on the Irish Articles is apparent in the omission of reference to either the threefold ministry or the need for Episcopal **ordination**.

In 1635, **Archbishop of Canterbury William Laud** called another convocation of the Irish Church in order to replace the Irish Articles with the Thirty-Nine Articles. The convocation approved the adoption of the Thirty-Nine, but Ussher, now Archbishop of Armagh and primate of the church in Ireland, circumvented this replacement by requiring clergy to subscribe to both sets of articles.

Although the Irish Articles gradually fell into disuse after the **Restoration** (1660), they served as the primary model in the composition of the **Westminster Confession** (1646). The **Westminster Assembly** adopted both the basic structure and some of the language of the Irish Articles for what would become the most influential document in the development of Presbyterianism.

J –

JACOB, HENRY (1563–1624). English **Congregationalist** divine. The son of a yeoman, Jacob was born in Cheriton, Kent. He attended St. Mary's Hall, **Oxford**, earning his B.A. in 1583 and his M.A. 1586. He also served as a precentor, or choir leader, at Corpus Christi College, **Cambridge**.

Around 1590, Jacob joined a group of **Brownists**, and his allegiance with this movement led him to migrate to **Holland** in 1593. He returned to England in 1597, where he challenged Bishop Bilson for his defense of the clause in the Apostle's Creed that states that Christ descended into Hell. Jacob opposed the teaching. He returned to Holland and established a church in Middleburg, Zeeland. Jacobs distinguished himself from the more radical Congregationalists by arguing that the Church of England was, despite its need for reform, still a true church, an opinion he expressed in a tract titled *A Defense of the Churches and Ministry in England* (1599). A journey to Leyden in 1610 brought Jacob into contact with **John Robinson**, who significantly influenced Jacob's views on church government.

In 1616, Jacob returned to London and established in Southwark what is considered the first Congregationalist church in England. He published a manifesto of the group, *A Confession and Protestation of the Faith of Certain Christians in England*, in the same year. Jacob also traveled to Virginia in 1620 to encourage the spread of Congregationalism there and founded a religious community named Jacobopolis. He returned to England and died in the parish of St. Andrew Hubbard, London. *See also* DUTCH PURITANISM.

JAMES I (1566–1625). King of England. James was born in Edinburgh, the only child of Mary, Queen of Scots, and the Lord Darnley, Henry Stuart. On 24 July 1567, he became King James VI of Scotland after Protestant rebels arrested his mother and forced her abdication of the Scottish throne. James was educated by **Presbyterians** in the Church of Scotland, and his rule proceeded with little difficulty despite his advocacy of the divine right of kings, which he espoused in *The True Law of Free Monarchies* and *Basilikon Doron*. His mother was executed for sedition by order of England's Queen **Elizabeth I** in 1587, but when Elizabeth died in 1603, James was the closest living relative (his great grandmother was the sister of Elizabeth's grandfather Henry VII) to the virgin queen, and so he became as well King James I of England. As King of England, Scotland, and Ireland, James considered himself the first monarch of Great Britain.

With their **Millennary Petition**, the English Puritans asked for James' concessions to their desires for reforms, but James eventually spurned them at the **Hampton Court Conference** of 1604. His relationship with **Parliament** was much more difficult than anything he had experienced in Scottish politics, and though it left him deeply in debt, James governed with no Parliament at all for seven years. The so-called **Gunpowder Plot** of 1605 was an attempt led by Guy Fawkes to assassinate James and replace him with his daughter Elizabeth, who would presumably rule as a Catholic. Fawkes was tortured and executed, but James was more conciliatory toward Catholics thereafter. James also sought to appease the Puritans by paying for the enormously influential **King James Version** of the **Bible**. Yet he died with few political supporters and was beset by dementia in his final months. His son **Charles I** followed James as the second monarch of the Stuart dynasty in England, and his grandsons **Charles II** and **James II** were the last two kings of the Stuart line after the **Restoration**.

JAMES II (1633–1701). King of England. James was born in London, the grandson of King **James I** and younger surviving son of King **Charles I** and Henrietta Maria of France. He stayed in the city of Oxford while his father held the fort there during the **English Civil Wars**, but, in 1648, he joined his older brother, the future King **Charles II**, at The Hague. He lived in France during most of the **Interregnum** but returned to England following the coronation of his brother and the **Restoration** of the Stuart dynasty in 1660. James received multiple appointments from Charles, including lord high admiral of the navy. In 1685, James succeeded his brother to the throne because Charles had no legitimate heirs. One of his first orders of business was to suppress the **Monmouth Rebellion** that had challenged his royal claim, and he followed that up by authorizing the **Bloody Assizes** of Judge George Jeffreys against **Nonconformists** who feared his rule. James Roman **Catholicism** was publicly known and a source of great anxiety for many English Protestants. In 1687,

James issued a **Declaration of Indulgence** in the hopes that greater toleration of dissenters would soften their antipathy toward Catholics as well. In June 1688, in the so-called **Glorious Revolution**, Parliament forced James to abdicate the throne and flee to France. His Protestant daughter, Mary II, and her husband, William III of Orange, succeeded him as monarch.

JANEWAY, JAMES (1636–1674). The son of a curate, Janeway was born at Lilley, Hertfordshire. He entered Christ's College, **Oxford**, in 1655, and graduated B.A. in 1659. Janeway served as tutor to a family in Windsor and is listed by Calamy as one of the ministers ejected under the **Act of Uniformity**, although it is not known whether he was **ordained** before 1662. In any case, Janeway began his ministry as a **Nonconforming** minister around 1665. With the passing of the **Declaration of Indulgence** in 1672, his followers built him a meetinghouse at Jamaica Row, Rotherhithe. Janeway gained a wide reputation as an excellent preacher, despite a **melancholy** temperament. The meetinghouse was torn down when the declaration was revoked in 1673, but a larger sanctuary was built later in its place. Janeway escaped arrest on two occasions. He died of tuberculosis at age 38 and is buried in the church of St. Mary, Aldermanbury.

Janeway is best known for his work, *A Token for Children: Being an Exact Account of the Conversion, Holy and Exemplary Lives and Joyful Deaths of Several Young Children* (1671). The book was a collection of accounts of conversions of children in Janeway's own parish. Intended as a book of exemplary spirituality for children, it became, along with **John Foxe**'s *Book of Martyrs* and **John Bunyan**'s *Pilgrims Progress*, one of the most popular works of Puritan literature. **Cotton Mather** imitated it with his *A Token for the Children of New England* (1645).

JENKYN, WILLIAM (1613–1685). English **Presbyterian** minister. Jenkyn was born at Sudbury, the son of the vicar of All Saints, Sudbury. In 1628, he entered St. John's College, **Cambridge**, where his tutor was **Anthony Burgess**. When Burgess moved to **Emmanuel College**, Jenkyn followed. He received his B.A. in 1632 and his M.A. in 1635. After graduating, Jenkyn held a **lectureship** at St. Nicholas Acons, London, before being presented to the rectory of St.

Leonard's, Colchester, in 1641. Shortly after that, he received the vicarage of Christ Church, Newgate and a lectureship at St. Anne's, Blackfriars, where **William Gouge** was rector.

Jenkyn was among the London Presbyterian ministers who opposed the trial of **Charles I**. As a result, his living was sequestrated in 1650, and he was suspended from the ministry. Jenkyn joined **Christopher Love**'s plot to restore **Charles II** to the throne and was imprisoned in the Tower; however, unlike Love, he avoided execution. Upon his release, his suspension was removed, and he conducted Sunday morning lectureships at Christ Church and St. Anne's. Eventually, he succeeded Gouge as rector of St. Anne's upon Gouge's death in 1654 and returned to the vicarage of Christ Church in 1655. Jenkyn resolved to avoid controversial subjects in his **sermons**; subsequently, his ministry prospered, and he was invited on several occasions to preach before **Parliament**.

Although Jenkyn supported the **Restoration** of the monarchy in 1660, he was ejected again from the ministry, this time under the 1662 **Act of Uniformity**. He continued to preach at **conventicles** and served as treasurer of a public trust for support of ejected clergy. With the passing of the Conventicle Act, Jenkyn left London in 1664, returning only with the passing of the **Declaration of Indulgence** in 1672. He became pastor of a congregation on Jewyn Street and was invited by a coalition of **Independent** and Presbyterian ministers to participate in the lectureship at Pinner's Hall.

When the Declaration of Indulgence was revoked a year later, Jenkyn once again found himself in conflict with the authorities. His **worship** services were disrupted by soldiers, and he was arrested in 1684, while leading a **prayer** meeting. It is said that Jenkyn would have escaped arrest but that he stopped for a woman whose train blocked the stair. He was imprisoned in Newgate, where he remained, despite poor health and several petitions, until he died. Some 150 coaches attended his funeral, and his daughter gave mourning rings with the inscription "Mr. William Jenkyn, murdered at Newgate." Jenkyn's best-known work is his *Exposition on the Epistle of Jude* (1656).

JEWEL, JOHN (1522–1571). Bishop of Salisbury. Jewel was born in Buden, Devon. He was educated at Barnstaple school and entered

Merton College, **Oxford**, but then transferred to Corpus Christi College, earning his B.A. in 1540, his M.A. in 1545, and his B.D. in 1552. He was a **fellow** of Corpus Christi College and also held the vicarage of Sunningwell.

As a public orator of the university, Jewel wrote a commendatory epistle upon the accession of Queen **Mary I** in 1553. Despite having signed the **Catholic** articles, Jewel's Protestant views were well known, and he fled first to London and then to Frankfurt, where he joined the congregation of Protestant exiles gathered there. Jewel sided with Richard Cox in his controversy with **John Knox** over order of **worship** and the use of the *Book of Common Prayer*. While at Oxford, Jewel had become a disciple of Peter Martyr and now left Frankfurt to join Martyr in Strasbourg. He also traveled with Martyr to Zurich and after that spent time in Italy.

With the accession of Queen **Elizabeth I** in 1558, Jewel returned to England. In 1559, he was selected as one of the Protestant disputants at the Westminster conference. Jewel adopted the Puritan position at Westminster, urging for a low-church settlement, but with his appointment to the bishopric of Salisbury in 1560, he became one of the chief proponents of the **Elizabethan Settlement**. He is best known for his *Apologia ecclesiae Anglicanae* (An Apology in Defense of the Church of England), published in 1562, the first systematic defense of the English Church. He carried on spirited and sometimes acrimonious written debates with the Romanists Henry Cole and Thomas Harding. Jewel's position also brought him into conflict with such Puritan leaders as **Thomas Cartwright**.

As bishop, Jewel built the cathedral library at Salisbury and founded a school in the bishop's palace for poor but academically gifted boys. He died at age 49 and is buried in the cathedral at Salisbury.

JOHNSON, EDWARD (1559–1672). English and American historian. Johnson was born in Kent. He was the son of William Johnson, clerk of St. George's Parish, Canterbury, and Susan Porredge. Little is known of his life until 1630, when, bound for Massachusetts, he boarded the *Arbella* with **John Winthrop** and company. Landing in New England, he remained only briefly before returning to England to gather his wife and children. Upon their arrival, Johnson and his family first settled in Charlestown and then helped to establish the town of Woburn. During the course of his career, Johnson served in various civic posts, including deputy to the General Court and captain of Charlestown militia. He helped draft the **Cambridge Platform**, which was adopted by the **Congregationalist** synod in 1648. He also served as an occasional surveyor and mapmaker.

Johnson is best known for *A History of New England from the English Planting in the Yeere 1628 until the Yeere 1652*, subtitled *Wonder-Working Providence of Sion's Saviour in New England*. The book was published in 1653 and is one of the principal sources for the early history of the Massachusetts colony. Like Winthrop and **William Bradford**, Johnson viewed the **Pilgrims** as appointed by God to establish the New Jerusalem in the wilderness of America. But whereas Winthrop and Bradford focus on the lives of eminent men, Johnson's work focuses on the experiences of the colonists as a whole. His history was one of the main sources for *Magnalia Christi Americana*, **Cotton Mather**'s masterful history of the Puritans in America.

JOHNSON, FRANCIS (1562–1617). English **Congregationalist** minister. Francis Johnson was born in Richmond, Yorkshire. His father, John, was a woolen draper and also served as an alderman and town sheriff. Johnson entered Christ's College, **Cambridge**, as a pensioner in 1579, receiving his B.A. in 1582. Johnson proceeded M.A. in 1585, was elected a **fellow** of Christ's College, and **ordained** both as a deacon and a priest. In a **sermon** preached at Cambridge in 1589, he advocated **Presbyterianism**; consequently, university officials demanded that he take the ex officio *mero* oath. He refused and was imprisoned. In 1590, he was expelled from the university for refusing to affirm the queen's regulation of the church. Johnson then left England for Middleburg in the Netherlands, where was appointed minister of the English Merchant Adventurers Church.

In 1591, Johnson obtained a volume that contained two defenses of Congregationalism: **Henry Barrow**'s *A Plain Refutation* and **John Greenwood**'s *A Brief Refutation*. These treatises convinced Johnson to adopt **Separatist** beliefs. He tried to convert his congregation to Separatist views as well, but the ensuing controversy led him to abandon the pulpit in 1592. He returned to England and while in London met Greenwood and Barrow, then became pastor of a London Separatist congregation. Johnson was arrested twice; the second time he was committed to the Fleet prison along with his brother George, where he remained for more than four years. Johnson refused to recant his Separatist beliefs and while in prison wrote two works: *A Treatise of the Ministry of the Church of England*, a response to **Arthur Hildersham**'s defense of the established church, and *A True Confession of Faith*.

Upon their release from prison, the two brothers made an abortive attempt to establish a colony in the Magdalen Islands, after which they arrived in Amsterdam and joined a congregation of exiles there. A variety of controversies plagued the congregation, some of which were occasioned by conflicts between Johnson's brother and Leigh Tomison, Johnson's wife. Johnson ultimately pronounced his brother excommunicated and also excommunicated his own father who had come to Amsterdam to reconcile his two sons.

In the meantime, Johnson had become one of the main spokesmen for the radical Protestant movement. In 1603, he traveled to England with other Separatists, hoping to present to the newly crowned King **James I** petitions urging religious **toleration.** The effort was rebuffed, with the result that Johnson redoubled both his attacks on the English Church and his defenses of Separatism. When Johnson's disciple **John Smyth** united with the **Anabaptists**, Johnson directed his attention toward the Anabaptists, attacking their practices and defending infant **baptism**. He also modified his own theory of church government, giving final authority to the elders, rather than to the congregation. This shift caused a schism in Johnson's Amsterdam congregation, with both sides publishing defenses. Johnson's faction lost ownership of the meetinghouse, and he and his followers moved to Emden, Germany, in 1613. He returned to Amsterdam three years later. His last work, *A Christian Plea*, a critique of Anabaptism, was published in 1617, the year of his death. *See also* DUTCH PURITANISM.

JUSTIFICATION. *See* SALVATION.

– K –

KEACH, BENJAMIN (1640–1704). English **Baptist** preacher. Keach was born at Stoke-Hammond, Buckinghamshire. He was converted at the age of 15 and became a member of a Baptist church, where he began **preaching** three years later. In 1664, he published a book called *The Child's Instructor*, in which he argued against infant **baptism** and advocated a 1,000-year reign of Christ. The self-educated Keach also asserted that the gift of preaching came directly from God and could not be taught by men or universities. As a result, Keach was tried, imprisoned for two weeks, fined £20, and placed in the pillory in the marketplaces of Aylesbury and Winslow, where the hangman burned his book before his face. In 1668, Keach was invited to pastor Horsleydown Church in Southwark, where he remained for the rest of his life. The congregation met secretly in private houses to avoid detection by authorities until the 1687 **Declaration of Indulgence**, after which they erected one of the first public meetinghouses for Baptists.

Keach was initially an **Arminian** but later embraced **Calvinist** doctrines, and, along with **William Kiffin** and **Hanserd Knollys**, was one of the leaders of the Particular Baptist movement. In addition to his polemics on various topics, including baptism and the laying on of hands, he wrote several lengthy poems, including the pre-revolution *Zion Distressed, or the Groans of the Protestant Church*, and the post-revolution *Distressed Zion Relieved*. An early advocate of congregational singing, he also published a collection of hymns titled *Spiritual Melody*. Other works include *Tropologia: A Key to Open Scripture Metaphors* (1682), *Gospel Mysteries Unveiled* (1701), two allegories titled *Travels of True Godliness* and *The Progress of Sin: or the Travels of Ungodliness* (1684), and a collection of **sermons** called *A Golden Mine Opened* (1694). *See also* MUSIC.

KIFFIN, WILLIAM (1616–1701). Leather seller, Particular **Baptist** minister. A leader of the early Particular Baptist movement, Kiffin was born in London. His parents died of the plague in 1625, and four years later, he was apprenticed to a glover. After two years, he resolved to run away from his master, but a **sermon** by Thomas Foxley on the subject of servants' duties to their masters changed his mind.

Kiffin began to attend church regularly and heard some of the most influential Puritan ministers of his day. In 1631, he also joined a group of apprentices who met together to read **Scripture**, **pray**, and offer each other spiritual encouragement. He married in 1638.

By the time of his marriage, Kiffin had become convinced of the errors of the Anglican Church and joined an **Independent** congregation, later known as Devonshire Square Baptist Church. Despite having no formal theological training, Kiffin was invited to preach, the pulpit then being vacant, and was eventually chosen as pastor. By 1642, he had led his congregation to embrace a Baptist stance, which he also defended in a public debate with Daniel Featley in the same year. In 1644, he helped draft the First London Confession of Faith, a statement of six London congregations, laying out Particular Baptist theology and ecclesiology and affirming their essential **Calvinism**. In the late 1640s and 1650s, Kiffin became one of the leading figures in the Baptist movement, appearing in a public debates with prominent religious figures, defending Baptist principles in print, and actively promoting the planting of Baptist churches outside London. He also played a crucial role in disassociating Particular Baptists from the **Fifth Monarchist** movement.

Meanwhile, Kiffin also achieved extraordinary success in the leather and cloth trades, bringing him to the center of London's civil and political life during the **English Civil Wars** and the **Interregnum**. He joined other London citizens in providing horses and riders for the Parliamentary cause and was appointed an officer of the London militia. From 1656 to 1658, he served as member for Middlesex in **Oliver Cromwell**'s last **Parliament**. In the first three years of the **Restoration**, however, Kiffin was arrested and briefly imprisoned. He used his influence to help other **dissenters**, including 12 General Baptists who had been condemned for holding **conventicles**. In 1670, he was elected sheriff of London and Middlesex but was denied the position on account of his **Nonconformity**. He became master of leather sellers in 1671.

With the **Declaration of Indulgence** in 1672, Kiffin obtained a license to preach. He debated the divinity of Christ with **Quakers** in 1674. He also carried on disputes in print with Thomas Collier on the subject of original **sin** (which Collier denied) and with **John Bunyan** on whether the unbaptized should be admitted to the Lord's Supper and granted other privileges of church membership. Kiffin's *A Sober Discourse of Right to Church Communion*, published in 1681, is a definitive early text advocating closed communion. This period of his life was marked by personal tragedies for Kiffin, including the death of his wife, a daughter, and two grandsons who were executed for their involvement in the **Monmouth Rebellion**. In the last weeks of his reign, **James II** appointed a reluctant and heart-broken Kiffin as an alderman of the City of London.

With the **Act of Toleration** in 1689, Kiffin and other Baptist leaders summoned the first national assembly of Particular Baptists, which adopted the Second London Confession of Faith. The same assembly disintegrated in the 1690s over the issue of hymn singing; Kiffin favored the singing of psalms exclusively in **worship**. His later years were marred by an unfortunate second marriage: his wife was charged with defrauding and slandering him, and the Devonshire Square Church barred her from communion. His son William died in 1698. Kiffin himself died three years later and was buried in **Bunhill Fields**.

KING JAMES BIBLE OR AUTHORIZED VERSION. An English translation of the **Bible**. The King James Version was commissioned by King **James I** at the **Hampton Court Conference** in 1604, where representatives of the Puritan party were invited to air their grievances. The only major point on which both the Puritans and the representatives of the high church agreed was the need for a new translation of the Bible. The Puritans sought a more accurate translation than was at that time available, whereas James and officials of the Anglican Church hoped that a new translation would replace the **Geneva Bible** as the most popular version among the laity. The Geneva Bible gave offense for certain translational choices, as well as marginal notes and glosses that affirmed Puritan theology and a **Presbyterian** form of church government. James stipulated that the new version follow the **Bishops' Bible** as closely as possible but that other previous English translations were to be consulted as necessary. He also directed that the Bible be published without notes and glosses and that the translation adopt language supportive of **episcopacy**.

Fifty-six scholars undertook the work of translation. They were divided into six committees, with two committees each operating at

Oxford, **Cambridge**, and Westminster. The committees were composed of both Puritan and high church scholars, including Lancelot Andrews, **Lawrence Chaderton, John Rainolds**, and **George Abbot**. The work of translation continued for about five years, with scholars using the Masoretic text for the Old Testament and the *Textus Receptus*, published by Erasmus, for the New Testament. Along with the Bishops' Bible, the translators relied heavily on the **Tyndale Bible**—especially in their rendering of the New Testament.

The new version of the Bible was first published in 1611 along with the apocryphal books, but it was not until the **Restoration** in 1660 that the King James Bible surpassed the Geneva Bible in popularity. It was never officially sanctioned as the authorized Bible of the **Anglican** Church, though it gradually came to replace the Bishops' Bible in most churches. With its simple, yet graceful language, the King James Version is considered one of the great works of English literature, as well as the single most important book in the development of the English language.

KING PHILIP'S WAR. King Philip's War was the bloodiest conflict between Native American Indians and English settlers. The Wampanoag chief Metacom, also known as "King Philip," attacked the village of Swansea in 1675 after colonists had executed three natives to retaliate against the killing of a "praying Indian." Soon, King Philip's attacks spread over much of New England, destroying several towns and slaying hundreds. Philip was captured and killed on 12 August 1676. The aftermath of the conflict was a severe curtailing of native territories and the near impossibility of continued evangelistic **missions**. *See also* PEQUOT WAR; ROWLANDSON, MARY.

KNEWSTUBS OR KNEWSTUB, JOHN (1544–1624). English **Nonconformist** divine. Knewtubs was born in Kirkby Stephen, Westmoreland. He attended St. John's College, **Cambridge**, graduating B.A. in 1564, and was elected a **fellow** of St. Johns in 1567. While at Cambridge, Knewstubs came under the influence of the moderate Puritan **Lawrence Chaderton**, Master of **Emmanuel College**. Knewstubs' own Puritan views became apparent when he supported a petition against the wearing of **vestments** by the clergy. While at St. John's, Knewstubs was at work on his lengthy exposition of Exodus

20; the first volume appeared in 1577 and was followed by four more volumes in the next seven years. He also distinguished himself as a principal opponent to the **Familist** movement. He preached against the Familists and served both the **Privy Council** and the diocese of Norwich by investigating the spread of Familism.

In 1579, Knewstubs was presented to the living of Cockfield, Suffolk, and was a leader of Suffolk clergy who, in 1583, protested to the Bishop of Norwich against **Archbishop of Canterbury** John **Whitgift's articles** of conformity, especially in matters pertaining to **baptism** and burial. Their appeal was denied, and Knewstubs, along with the other signatories, was suspended, though his suspension was only temporary. From 1585 to 1586, he served as chaplain to the Earl of Leicester on his expedition to the Netherlands; in 1596, he was made overseer of the Boxford grammar school. In 1603, Knewstubs was selected as one of the spokesmen for the Puritan cause at the **Hampton Court Conference**. King James rejected most of the proposals set forth by the Puritan party. In the years that followed, Knewstubs was cited twice for refusing to make the sign of the cross or wear the **surplice**, though he was not deprived of his pulpit.

Knewstubs was one of the most influential and well-connected Puritans. He preached funeral **sermons** for many other influential Puritan ministers, and he was a leading figure in the promotion of piety in the Stour Valley.

KNOLLYS, HANSERD (1598–1691). English Particular **Baptist** minister. Knollys was born in Calkwell, near Louth in Lincolnshire. His father held vicarages in Grimsby and Scartho. Knollys was educated by a private tutor, then at the Grimsby grammar school, and finally entered St. Catharine's College, **Cambridge**, where he came under the influence of Puritan teaching. He taught at the Gainsborough grammar school and, in 1629, was **ordained,** first as a deacon, then as a priest. Knollys was granted a living at Humberstone, Lincolnshire. In 1632, he married Anne Cheney, with whom he had 10 children.

Around 1636, Knollys became convinced that various practices of the **Anglican** Church were improper, including the wearing of the **surplice**, the making of the sign of the cross during **baptism**, and the administration of the Eucharist to the ungodly. He resigned his position, even after being offered a larger and more lucrative living by Bishop John Williams. Sympathetic to the Puritan cause, Williams allowed Knollys to continue to preach, but under the influence of John Wheelwright, he renounced his ordination and decided to abstain from **preaching** until he felt a clear call from Christ. When that call came, he resumed preaching with a message of "free grace."

After barely avoiding incarceration by the High Commission in 1636, Knollys fled with his family first to London and, after some time, to New England, the hard 14-week voyage claiming the life of one of his children. Knollys arrived in Boston with little money and no means of support and soon aroused suspicion of being an **antinomian**. He gathered a church at Piscataqua but was charged with sexual misconduct. His conflicts with the Massachusetts magistrates led him to migrate to Long Island, where a protest was filed against him. By 1641, he decided to return to England.

Back in London, Knollys relied on the support of friends and eventually established himself as a schoolmaster. He served briefly as a preacher in the Parliamentarian army but resigned. When he returned to London, Knollys resumed preaching without a license and was arrested for doing so on several occasions. By 1644, he had become a member of the **Independent** church established by **Henry Jacob**. Henry Jessey was the minister, and both he and Knollys came to regard infant baptism as improper. They baptized each other in 1645. In the same year, Knollys gathered his own congregation, one of the first Particular Baptist churches, supplementing his income as a customs examiner and clerk of the check. In 1658, despite having renounced his ordination as an Anglican priest some 12 years earlier, he was installed as the vicar of St. Giles in Scartho, which had been held by his father. Knollys appears to have simultaneously served this church and his Baptist church in London. Because of his connections to the **Fifth Monarchist** movement, Knollys was suspected of involvement in Venner's Rebellion (*see* THOMAS VENNER) and spent 18 weeks in Newgate Prison. Though released, he remained under suspicion and eventually fled to the continent, where he spent two or three years in the Netherlands and Germany. Most of his property was confiscated.

By 1690, Knollys was back in London and again under arrest. During his brief incarceration at Bishopsgate, he was allowed to preach to his fellow prisoners. In his later years, he continued to preach and teach; he also played a major role in the consolidating and organizing of the Baptist movement, serving at church assemblies in 1689, 1690, and 1691. His many works include *A Moderate Answer to Dr. Bastwick's Book Called Independency Not God's Ordinance* (1645), *The Shining of a Flaming Fire in Zion* (1646), and *An Exposition of the Whole Book of Revelation* (1689).

KNOX, JOHN (c. 1505, 1513, 1514–1572). Reformer, founder of the **Presbyterian** Church of Scotland. The exact date and place of Knox's birth are not known. He was most likely born in Haddington in East Lothian, the son of a farmer. He attended St. Andrews University, where he studied under John Major, though it is not known whether he graduated. At some time before 1540, he received **ordination** as a Roman **Catholic** priest, in which capacity he served as an ecclesiastical notary and private tutor to the sons of local gentry.

In 1545, Knox made his first public profession of Protestant beliefs, which he came to embrace most likely through the influence of the reformer George Wishart. Wishart had been charged with heresy in 1538 and had fled Scotland, but he returned in 1543, and two years later was burned at the stake. After Wishart's execution, Knox took refuge in St. Andrews, a Protestant stronghold. He remained in the castle as a preacher until the castle surrendered to joint Scottish and French forces in 1547; Knox served as a French galley slave for 19 months, the hardships of which permanently damaged his health. He was released in 1549, through the intervention of the government of **Edward VI**, and began to minister in England, holding appointments at Berwick-on-Tweed and Newcastle, and briefly as a chaplain in ordinary to the king. He made contributions to the second ***Book of Common Prayer*** but declined a bishopric in the Church of England.

With the accession of Queen **Mary I** in 1553, Knox fled to the continent. He accepted a call to serve as pastor to a congregation of English refugees in Frankfurt, of which **John Foxe** was a member, but a dispute over the use of the *Book of Common Prayer* led to his departure in 1555. After a visit to England and Scotland, during which he preached privately and married, Knox accepted a call to serve as minister to the English congregation at Geneva, where he became personally acquainted with John Calvin, Heinrich Bullinger, and Theodore Beza. In addition to pastoring his flock, Knox wrote prolifically, including a treatise on **predestination** and *First Blast of the Trumpet Against the Monstrous Regiment of Women*, an attack on the Catholic regent of Scotland, Marie of Guise. The book also gave offense to Queen **Elizabeth I**, who ascended to the throne of England in 1558.

In 1559, Knox returned to Scotland, where he became a champion of the Protestant cause against Marie of Guise, who was poised to stifle it with the help of troops from France. Knox was instrumental in gaining English support for the Scottish Protestants, resulting in the withdrawal of French troops in 1560. Marie died the same year, and Knox became the minister at St. Giles Cathedral in Edinburgh, in which position he became the most influential and controversial figure in Scottish religious life. He played a major role in the composition of the Scottish *Confession of Faith*, which was ratified by the Scottish Parliament. He also wrote the *Book of Discipline*, which laid out the structure of the new church, but which Parliament ultimately rejected.

When Mary Queen of Scots returned from France to assume the throne in 1561, Knox became one of her strongest opponents. On five separate occasions, Mary met with Knox for personal interviews. He acknowledged Mary's intelligence but was deeply and outspokenly antagonistic to her reign. In 1564, Knox, whose first wife had died four years earlier, married 16-year-old Margaret Stewart, a distant relation of the queen's. The marriage took place without the queen's consent and was the cause of increased royal hostility toward Knox. When Mary abdicated the throne in 1568, Knox preached the **sermon** at the coronation of her son, James IV (later **James I** of England). Knox died four years later in Edinburgh.

Knox was not only the most important figure of the **Scottish Reformation** but its principal chronicler. His *History of the Reformation of Scotland* was published in 1587. *See also* MARIAN EXILES.

– L –

LAMBETH ARTICLES. An appendix to the **Thirty-Nine Articles**. The origin of the Lambeth Articles lies in the controversy over the

Arminian teachings of two professors at **Cambridge University**, a **Calvinist** stronghold. The first of these, Peter Baro, was Lady Margaret Professor of Divinity until the uproar over his teaching of unlimited atonement led to his resignation. William Barrett of Caius College also espoused Arminian theology until his opponents brought the matter before the vice-chancellor of the University, the heads of the colleges, and finally before **Archbishop of Canterbury** John Whitgift.

Whitgift ultimately sided with the Calvinists. To settle the matter and avoid future controversies, the university heads sent **William Whitaker** and Humphrey Tyndal to meet with Whitgift and other church leaders. The conference met in London, where they adopted the Nine Articles, drafted by Whitaker, which offer a forceful statement of predestinarian teaching:

1. The eternal election of some to life, and the reprobation of others to death.
2. The moving cause of predestination to life is not the foreknowledge of faith and good works, but only the good pleasure of God.
3. The number of the elect is unalterably fixed.
4. Those who are not predestinated to life shall necessarily be damned for their **sins**.
5. The true faith of the elect never fails finally nor totally.
6. A true believer, or one furnished with justifying faith, has a full assurance and certainty of remission and everlasting **salvation** in Christ.
7. Saving grace is not communicated to all men.
8. No man can come to the Son unless the Father shall draw him, but all men are not drawn by the Father.
9. It is not in every one's will and power to be saved.

When Whitgift sent the articles to Cambridge on 20 November 1595, he made it clear that they were neither laws nor decrees because they had not been sanctioned by the queen; rather, they were to serve as clarification to already established doctrine. When **Elizabeth I** became aware of the meeting and its work, she called for the articles to be suppressed. At the **Hampton Court Conference** of 1604, Puritan representatives requested that the Lambeth Articles be added to the Thirty-Nine Articles, but **James I** refused.

LATIMER, HUGH (c. 1485–1555). Bishop of Worcester and Protestant martyr. The son of a yeoman farmer, Hugh Latimer was born at Thurcaston, Leicestershire, and educated at Clare College, **Cambridge**. He graduated B.A. and was nominated a **fellow** of Clare in 1510. He received his M.A. in 1514, but the date of his **ordination** is not known. In 1524, Latimer preached a **sermon** in which he attacked the teachings of Martin Luther's follower Philip Melancthon; however, within a year, Latimer's own theological views had shifted sufficiently for the Bishop of Ely to suspect him of Lutheranism. Latimer was forbidden to preach in the university or the diocese until he officially repudiated the teachings of Luther, after which he was allowed to preach freely. Nonetheless, he continued to court controversy: during Advent in 1529, he caused an uproar in Cambridge with his two "Sermons on the Card," in which he defended the then-illegal practice of translating the **Bible** into English.

Latimer also made enemies at Cambridge by attacking common **Catholic** practices, such as the making of pilgrimages; however, he gained the favor of King **Henry VIII** by supporting Henry's plans to divorce Catherine of Aragon and marry Anne Boleyn. In 1530, Henry invited Latimer to become a royal chaplain, but by 1531, he had left court to take the living of West Kineton (or Kington) in Wiltshire. Latimer continued to attack the teachings of the church, including the veneration of saints, the use of images, and the doctrine of Purgatory. As a result, he was excommunicated and briefly imprisoned at Lambeth in 1532, but a nominal recantation restored him to his position.

With the king's repudiation of the papacy, Latimer's influence at court grew; he became an adviser to the Henry in matters of church legislation, and, in 1535, he was created Bishop of Worcester, a position he used to advance the Protestant cause. However, his opposition to the Act of the Six Articles in 1539 led to his resignation and a yearlong imprisonment. Upon his release, he was forbidden to preach in London, at either university or in his old diocese. In 1546, he was committed to the Tower for his association with Edward Crome, until pardoned by King **Edward VI**. Upon his release, Latimer did not resume his Bishopric but continued to preach.

Shortly after the accession of Queen **Mary I**, Latimer was apprehended and taken to the Tower with **Thomas Cranmer** and **Nicholas Ridley**. Examined at **Oxford**, he was found guilty of heresy and condemned to be burned at the stake, along with Ridley, at Oxford, on 16 October 1555. "Be of good comfort, Master Ridley," Latimer reportedly said upon the scaffold; "we shall this day light a candle by God's grace in England as I trust shall never be put out."

Latimer's wit and his vivid, forceful language made him one of the most popular English preachers of the period, as well as an influential church leader, and his martyrdom helped galvanize the Protestant cause in England. *See also* MARIAN EXILES.

LATITUDINARIANISM. A body of thought that developed in the late 17th century. The Latitudinarians were a group of prominent late 17th-century scholars and churchmen who, on the one hand, sought to steer a middle course between Puritan concerns and those of the high church by stressing basic dogma and treating matters, such as church government as "things indifferent." They also attempted to reconcile the basic teachings of the Christian faith with rational thought, viewing faith and **science** as wholly compatible. Latitudinarianism was an attempt to answer challenges to the English church posed by Hobbism, Deism, Spinozism, and **Catholicism**. The Latitudinarians were also referred to as the **Cambridge Arminians**. The beliefs of the **Cambridge Platonists** are close to those of the Latitudinarians, though the two are generally viewed as separate movements.

LAUD, WILLIAM (1573–1645). Archbishop of Canterbury. Laud was born in Reading, Berkshire, in a cloth merchant's family. He studied at St. John's College, Oxford, and received ordination in the Church of England in 1601. While Puritans criticized Laud's preferences for the authority of the papacy, divine right of kings, episcopal government, and **Arminianism**, these sympathies endeared him to King **Charles I**, who came to power in 1625 and oversaw Laud's rise through the ecclesiastical ranks until he became Archbishop of Canterbury in 1633. Laud was an inveterate enemy of Puritans, especially

Presbyterians, and gained notoriety for the harsh sentences he pronounced upon them in the **Star Chamber**. One of the most shocking examples was his pronouncement against **William Prynne**, whose ears were cropped and flesh branded in 1637. In 1640, the **Long Parliament** defied the king and placed Laud under arrest. On 10 January 1645, Laud was beheaded on Tower Hill at the Tower of London.

LAWRENCE, EDWARD (1623–1695). English **Nonconformist** divine. Lawrence was born at Moston, Shropshire, and educated at the grammar school in Whitchurch. He entered Magdalen College, **Cambridge**, as a sizar (a student required to pay minimal fees), graduating B.A. in 1647-48 and M.A. in 1654. In 1648, he was presented to the vicarage of Baschurch in Shropshire, and served there, despite offers of preferment, until 1662, when he was ejected from the pulpit under the **Act of Uniformity**. Lawrence remained in Baschurch at the home of one of his parishioners until the 1665 passing of the **Five Mile Act**. He then removed to nearby Tilstock in Whitchurch parish. In 1670, he was arrested under the **Conventicle Act** for **preaching** illegally, and his belongings were confiscated. In 1671, Lawrence settled in London, and, under the **Declaration of Indulgence** in 1672, preached at a meetinghouse near the Royal Exchange until his death in 1695. His works include *Christ's Power over Bodily Diseases* (1662), *Use and Happiness of Human Bodies* (1690), and *Parents' Groans over Their Wicked Children* (1681).

LAY IMPROPRIATIONS. When **Henry VIII** established the Church of England in the 1530s, he also seized all church property in the name of the crown and then sold much of that property to noblemen and wealthy commoners. The acquisition of church lands by these laymen led to the term "lay impropriations," and the responsibility of supplying parish positions fell to these new landowners. Many chose to supply them by the most economic means possible—by underpaying parish vicars and curates and in some cases by appointing unqualified and ignorant clergy to these positions.

Many who sought to reform the church were appalled by these abuses, but then some enterprising individuals developed a way to use lay impropriations to further the Reformation cause. In 1626, several Puritans, including **William Gouge**, **Richard Sibbes**, **John**

Davenport, and **William Twisse**, established a trust for purchasing as many of these lay impropriations as possible and supplying the pulpits with Puritan ministers. Altogether, the trust raised £6,000 and purchased 13 impropriations before **Archbishop of Canterbury William Laud** called for an end to the practice in 1633. Members of the trust were brought before the exchequer; their property was seized, and they were forbidden to purchase further impropriations.

LECTURER. As demand for Puritan **preaching** increased during the late 16th and early 17th centuries, many parishes opted to call ministers to serve as lecturers. These men typically preached on Sundays, at times other than those of the usual church service, as well as on weekdays. They were supported through voluntary contributions from members of the parish and performed no other clerical or pastoral duties. Most lecturers were **ordained** ministers, and licensure by the bishop or appropriate ecclesiastical authority was required. Lectureships became one of the principal means by which the Puritan cause widened its influence and gained adherents. As such, they also posed a problem for those in authority. Accordingly, **James I** and **Charles I** both took measures to curtail lectureships during their reigns.

The term "lecturer" also carries the more common meaning of one who delivers formal discourses at a college or university.

LEE, SAMUEL (1625–1691). English and American **Nonconformist** divine. Lee was born in London, the son of a haberdasher in Fish Street. He was educated at St. Paul's School and entered Magdalen College, **Oxford**, in 1647, graduating M.A. in 1648. In 1649, he was elected **fellow** of Wadham College, and he became proctor in 1651. He served as bursar of the college in 1648, 1650, and 1654, as subwarden in 1652, and was elected dean in 1653. During his time at Wadham, he **preached** frequently in and around Oxford. In 1655, Lee became minister of St. Botolph's, Bishopsgate, where he remained until removed by the **Rump Parliament** in 1659, after which he was appointed **lecturer** at St. Helen's Bishopsgate. After the **Restoration**, Lee became a member of **John Owen**'s congregation while continuing to preach in various London churches. He also served as pastor to churches in Baker's Court, Holborn, and Newington Green.

In 1686, Lee migrated to New England with his family and was chosen minister of a church at Bristol, Rhode Island. However, in 1691, he chose to return to England. During the journey, the ship was seized by French privateers, who brought the vessel and its passengers to St. Malo. Lee was separated from his wife and daughter who were traveling with him and who were, unbeknownst to him, returned to England. Lee died and was buried in the heretics' graveyard in St. Malo.

Lee was noted for his wide learning, particularly his knowledge of languages, and his interest in natural philosophy, medicine, physics, and chemistry. In the view of **Cotton Mather**, whose third wife was one of Lee's daughters, "Hardly a more universally learned person trod the American strand." Lee wrote several religious treatises and is perhaps best known for his study titled *The Temple of Solomon* (1659).

LEIGHTON, ALEXANDER. Minister, doctor, controversialist. Leighton was born at Guily Monikie, near Dundee. He graduated M.A. from St. Andrews in 1587 and held various **lectureships** in Newcastle upon Tyne from 1603–12, but did not obtain a regular living. In 1617, he resolved to study medicine at Leiden, where he stayed at the home of Thomas Brewer, a financier of Puritan publishing. Leighton returned to London after graduating in 1619, but when he applied to the College of Physicians for a license, his application was denied. Leighton therefore set up an unlicensed medical practice. He also joined the church in Blackfriars originally established by **Henry Jacob**. During this period, he also began to publish.

Leighton's first work, *The Looking Glass of the Holy War* (1624), called for the abolition of the **episcopacy**, urged England to give military support to the Protestant cause on the continent, and opposed the marriage of Prince Charles to a **Catholic**. In his next work, *A Friendly Triall of the Treatise of Faith of Mr. Ezekiel Culverwell* (1624), Leighton defended the **Calvinist** doctrine of election. After a brief period of imprisonment, he published his third work, an antitheatrical tract titled *A Short Treatise Against Stage Players* (1625). In 1628, when **Charles I** summoned **Parliament**, Leighton organized a petition with 500 signatures for the abolition of the episcopacy. He then went to the Netherlands and began work on *An Appeale* *to the Parliament, or, Sions Plea Against the Prelacy*. In the meantime, he was invited to become minister to the English congregation at Utrecht. However, his congregation dismissed him after several months when disagreements arose over the use of ceremonies.

Leighton returned to England, where he resumed his medical practice, but, in 1630, he was arrested and thrown into prison. Tried for sedition, Leighton was represented at his trial by his wife, Isadore. When the **Star Chamber** demanded that Leighton release the names of the signatories to his petition, he refused. He was fined £10,000, his **ordination** was revoked, his nose was slit, he was branded on his cheeks (SS for "Sower of Sedition"), whipped, pilloried, and sentenced to life imprisonment. In the Fleet prison, Leighton earned money by giving medical treatment to his fellow prisoners. When Parliament ordered Leighton's release in 1642, it granted him the position of keeper at Lambeth Place, which was then being used as a military prison. Leighton died in London.

LEVELLERS. From the end of the first **English Civil War** to the early years of the **Commonwealth**, many groups with competing political aims vied for dominance. Among the most radical and influential of these were the Levellers, a number of loosely associated groups influenced by the writings of **John Lilburne**, Richard Overton, and William Walwyn. Although the principles of these groups varied, some commonly shared objectives included the establishment of a secular republic, a separation of legislative and executive power, religious **toleration**, equality of all men before the law, an extension of the right to vote to all freeborn Englishmen (excluding beggars and servants), free trade, free press, and guaranteed constitutional rights. The mainstream Leveller movement sought to distance itself from groups such as the **Diggers**, or True Levellers, who sought to abolish all property rights and establish universal communism.

The Leveller movement first began near the end of the First Civil War among members of the middle class in London who feared that **Parliament** was too yielding and complacent in its negotiations with the king. When Lilburne was imprisoned in 1615 for denouncing members of Parliament, Walwyn published *England's Lamentable Slavery*, in which he proclaimed that, as a representative body, Parliament should be directly answerable to the people. In *A Remonstrance of Many Thousands* (1616), Walwyn and Overton called for various governmental reforms, including the abolition of the House of Lords. These and other pamphlets, such as *An Arrow Against Tyrants and Tyranny*, by Overton, set forth the basic principles of the Leveller movement.

Leveller ideas also came to be embraced by many in the **New Model Army**. In March 1647, Parliament voted to disband part of the army without pay, while using the remainder to invade Ireland. Rank-and-file soldiers opposed this decision and objected that they were denied basic rights—they were not exempt from prosecution for actions performed under orders during the war, nor were there any provisions for war widows or orphans. These soldiers appointed Agitators to represent their grievances to Parliament. Soon these representatives were working with civilian Levellers to obtain their aims. They adopted *A Solemn Engagement of the Army* and *The Case of the Army Truly Stated*, a Leveller manifesto by John Wildman, which called for a new constitution. They also succeeded in forming an army council consisting of both common soldiers and senior officers, or "Grandees," such as Lord **Thomas Fairfax** and **Oliver Cromwell**. In October 1647, the Levellers and Grandees argued their positions at the **Putney Debates**.

Throughout the Second Civil War, and the subsequent trial and execution of **Charles I**, Cromwell and Fairfax were able to keep the Levellers under control, except for a minor mutiny at Corkbush Field. However, with the establishment of the **Commonwealth**, the Levellers, disappointed at the lack of significant social and political reform they had envisioned, came into direct conflict with the Council of State. Lilburne, Overton, and Walwyn were imprisoned for publishing *England's New Chains Discovered*, in which they attacked the politics of the new regime. Opposed to renewed plans under Cromwell for an invasion of Ireland, Army Levellers staged mutinies at Burford and Bishopsgate, but these were effectively put down by Cromwell and **Henry Ireton**. By 1649, the Levellers had ceased to exist as an organized movement.

The Levellers were the first organized activist political movement in England. Some Leveller groups were organized down to parish chapters; supporters and organizers held regular meetings and paid a nominal membership fee. **Women** were an active part of the movement, which made effective use of the press and even had its own newspaper, *The Moderate*, which ran from June 1648 to October 1649. The Leveller symbol was a sea-green ribbon.

LEVER (OR LEAVER), THOMAS (1521–1577). English minister. One of the most gifted and dynamic preachers of the 16th century, Lever was born at Little Lever in Lancashire and was educated at St. John's College, **Oxford**. He received his B.A. in 1541–42, and was appointed a **fellow** in 1543. In 1545, he proceeded M.A. and became a senior fellow and college preacher. At Oxford, Lever was friends with Roger Ascham, later tutor to Queen **Elizabeth I**; Lever also distinguished himself by his sometimes extreme Protestant beliefs. He was **ordained** in 1550, and preached several times before the court of **Edward VI**. In 1551, he was appointed Master of St. John's and received his B.D. in 1552.

With the death of **Henry VIII**, Lever gave his support to the cause of Lady Jane Grey. With the accession of **Mary I**, he, like many with strong Protestant convictions, fled to the continent to avoid persecution. He settled first at Zurich, then at Frankfurt, where he quarreled with **John Knox** over the use of the ***Book of Common Prayer***. Lever also spent time in Geneva, attending services and lectures by John Calvin. In 1556, he became minister to the English Protestant congregation at Arau. With the death of Queen Mary and the accession of Elizabeth, Lever returned to England, where he was appointed rector and Archdeacon of Coventry. He married and, in 1563, was made master of Shepburn Hospital at Durham. A year later, he was promoted to a stall in Durham Cathedral, but he was deprived four years later for his refusal to conform to the ceremonies of the church.

Clad in black, Lever continued to preach at Coventry and London. He was cited by the ecclesiastical court in 1571 for breach of church discipline. In 1577, Thomas Bentham, Bishop of Lichfield and Coventry, ordered him to suppress the prophesyings he had encouraged in his archdeaconry. Lever died at Ware, en route from London to Sherburn, and was buried at Sherburn Hospital. His collected **sermons** were reprinted in 1871.

Lever's works include *A Treatise of the Right Way from Danger of Synne* (1556) and *A Meditacion upon the Lordes Prayer* (1551). See also **MARIAN EXILES**.

LIGHTFOOT, JOHN (1602–1675). Preacher, Hebraist, vice-chancellor of **Cambridge University**. The son of a vicar, Lightfoot was born at Stoke-upon-Trent and educated at Morton Green, near Congelton, Cheshire. He attended Christ's College, Cambridge, where he earned a reputation for oratory. After graduating, Lightfoot was first assistant master at Repton in Derbyshire, then, having taken orders, he assumed the curacy of Norton-under-Hales in Shropshire. Here, his talent for rabbinical studies brought him to the attention of the distinguished amateur Hebraist Sir Rowland Cotton, who made Lightfoot his domestic chaplain at Bellaport. When Cotton left Bellaport for London, Lightfoot took a charge at Stone in Staffordshire, where he remained for two years. He then took up residence in Hornsey near London, primarily to make use of the library of nearby Sion College. While at Stone, Lightfoot published his first work, *Erubhin, or Miscellanies, Christian and Judaical* (1629).

In 1630, Cotton presented Lightfoot with another living—this time, the rectory of Ashley in Staffordshire, where he remained until 1642. He then removed to London to oversee publication of his second work, *A Few and New Observations on the Book of Genesis*. While residing in London, he was appointed minister of St. Bartholomew's Church, near the Exchange, and was invited to preach several times before the House of Commons. He was also an original and influential member of the **Westminster Assembly** of Divines. Along with John Selden, Thomas Coleman, and Bulstrode Whitelocke, Lightfoot maintained the **Erastian** position at the Assembly. In 1643, he published his third book, *A Handful of Gleanings out of the Book of Exodus*. He was made Master of Catharine Hall and promoted to the rectory of Much Munden in Herfordshire, retaining both positions until his death. In 1654, he was selected as vice-chancellor of Cambridge University.

Like **James Ussher**, Lightfoot is remembered for his attempts to estimate the precise moment of creation based on a careful reading of the **Bible** (near the autumnal equinox in the year 3929 B.C.). His best-known work is his commentary, *Horae Hebraicae et Talmudicae* (1658–1674).

LILBURNE, JOHN (1614–1657). **Leveller**, pamphleteer, brewer, nicknamed "Freeborn John." The son of Richard Lilburne, a gentleman, John Lilburne was born in Greenwich, and educated in the schools of Auckland and Newcastle. Around the year 1630, he was apprenticed to a clothier; at the same time, he began to read the **Bible** and Puritan writers. In 1636, he met the controversial pamphleteer **John Bastwick** and aided him in the publication of his *Litany*. Lilburne's involvement in the distribution of Puritan pamphlets brought him to the attention of the authorities; consequently, he fled England as a fugitive. When he returned in 1637, he was arrested and brought before the **Star Chamber**. Found guilty of sedition, Lilburne was fined, publicly whipped, placed in the pillory, and sentenced to prison. During his punishment, crowds cheered him as a champion of the Puritan cause. He continued to write and publish pamphlets in prison. In 1640, **Oliver Cromwell** petitioned the **Long Parliament** for Lilburne's pardon. Upon his release, he married and established a brewery.

In 1641, with the outbreak of the first **English Civil War**, Lilburn received a commission of captain in the Parliamentarian army. He fought at Edgehill and Brentford, where he was taken prisoner. The Royalists found Lilburne guilty of high treason and would have executed him, but he was instead released as part of a prisoner exchange. Elevated to the rank of lieutenant colonel, Lilburne next served in the army of Lord Manchester, at which time he became friends with several influential people, including Cromwell. He would later support Cromwell by testifying against Manchester. However, Lilburne's military career came to an end in 1645, when he refused to sign the **Solemn League and Covenant**.

An **Independent**, Lilburne opposed the establishment of **Presbyterianism** as the national church, a position that brought him into conflict with former friends, including Bastwick and fellow pamphleteer **William Prynne**. Furthermore, his involvement with the Leveller movement earned him the antipathy of Cromwell and led to his confinement in the Tower in 1645, where he continued his attacks on the monarchy, the House of Commons, and the military leadership. He spent the next several years in and out of prison. In 1648, shortly before the trial of **Charles I**, Lilburne was accused of high treason but then acquitted. In 1652, he was banished for life. When he returned to England in 1653, he was promptly imprisoned, but although he was subsequently acquitted, he spent most of the remainder of his life in prison. In his last years, he converted to **Quakerism**.

If Lilburne holds the distinction of having quarreled with virtually every major figure and institution of his time, he is also to be recognized as a forward-thinking political theorist whose ideas anticipate John Locke and Thomas Jefferson. They include many democratic principles, including the right of all people to vote for their representatives, the right against self-incrimination, and freedom of religion and press. *See also* MECHANICK PREACHERS.

LINCOLN'S INN. Lincoln's Inn is one of four Inns of Court in London, by which any barrister in England must be certified in order to practice law. The others are **Gray's Inn**, the Inner Temple, and the Middle Temple. Each of the inns has a chapel and a library. The records of Lincoln's Inn date back to 1569, when Queen **Elizabeth I** was its patron. Prominent Puritans who either studied or preached at Lincoln's Inn include **Henry Barrow**, **Thomas Fairfax**, **Thomas Helwys**, **Matthew Henry**, **Richard Sibbes**, and **John Winthrop**.

LOLLARDY. Fourteenth-century religious movement in England. The father of the Lollard movement was John Wycliffe, a professor of theology at **Oxford University**. Wycliffe's teachings challenged Roman **Catholic** theology and practice on many points: he questioned the authority of the pope and held up **Scripture** as the ultimate source of truth. Wycliffe called for various reforms of the church; he denied transubstantiation, and taught a doctrine of **predestination**.

Lollardy gained some support among members of the nobility, such as John of Gaunt, but the established church vigorously opposed it, and with the accession of Henry IV, the movement was effectively stamped out. Many of the Lollards' ideas were taken up by the great continental reformers of the 16th century, but the movement was so thoroughly suppressed in England that if Lollardy had any influence on the English Reformation, it was probably indirect.

LONG PARLIAMENT. *See* **PARLIAMENT.**

LORD'S SUPPER. *See* **SACRAMENTS.**

LOVE, CHRISTOPHER (1618–1651). Welsh **Presbyterian** divine. Love was born in Cardiff, Wales, and converted at 15 under the **preaching** of William Erbery. According to Brook, Love's father found his religious convictions objectionable and actively discouraged them so that eventually Love left home and went to live with and be educated by Erbery. He entered New Inn Hall, **Oxford**, in 1635. Though his father denied him financial assistance, he was supported by his mother and Erbery and graduated B.A. in 1639. However, his pursuit of a master's degree was hindered by his expulsion for refusing to subscribe to the canons of **Archbishop of Canterbury William Laud**. Upon leaving the university, Love was invited to act as domestic chaplain to the sheriff of London.

An ardent Presbyterian, Love refused to seek **ordination** in the Church of England. He traveled to Scotland, seeking ordination there, but was denied since his intention was to return to England rather than serve in a Scottish church. He returned to England and preached by invitation. Upon one such invitation, Love was arrested for publicly condemning the ***Book of Common Prayer*** and the rituals of **episcopacy**; however, after spending time in prison, he was eventually acquitted. Love next served as preacher to the Garrison at Windsor, where he remained during an outbreak of the plague to minister to the sick and dying.

With the establishment of Presbyterianism as the national church in 1644, Love finally received ordination; however, he continued to be the source of controversy. He preached a **sermon** before the commissioners of the Treaty of Uxbridge, openly denouncing the treaty. He served as **lecturer** at St. Ann's, Aldergate, London, and, in 1649, accepted a call to pastor the nearby church of St. Lawrence Jewry. He was also appointed to the **Westminster Assembly**, though he was not an active member.

Love opposed the execution of **Charles I**, and, in 1651 was arrested, along with six other ministers, for plotting to restore the monarchy under **Charles II**. Love pled innocent to the charges. Of the six ministers accused, only he was condemned to death for what subsequently came to be called "Love's Plot." He was beheaded on Tower Hill at the age of 33.

– M –

MAKEMIE, FRANCIS (1658?–1708). American **Presbyterian** minister. Makemie was born in Ireland and studied in Glasgow, Scotland. In 1682, he received **ordination** as a missionary from the Irish presbytery of Laggan. The following year, he came to America and traveled throughout the colonies—especially New York, Maryland, Virginia, and North Carolina—to promote the growth of Presbyterianism. From 1692–98, he lived in Barbados, and, in 1699, he returned to Virginia as a licensed preacher and mercantile trader. Makemie went to England in 1704 to recruit Presbyterian pastors to come to Maryland, a largely **Catholic** area. Only two years later, he was back in Philadelphia to organize America's first new presbytery. Makemie was arrested in New York in 1707 because his ordination was not legally recognized there, but this did not detain his later reputation as "the father of American Presbyterianism."

MANTON, THOMAS (1620–1677). English Puritan theologian and preacher. Born at Somerset, Manton studied at the school in Tiverton and then Wadham College, Oxford. At age 19, he received **ordination** as a deacon in the Church of England from Bishop **Joseph Hall** of Exeter. He did not proceed toward receiving priest's orders, however, believing them to be unnecessary for filling his responsibilities as the preacher at Culliton (or Colyton) in Devon. He preached there for three years and then at Stoke-Newington, near London, for seven more. Manton aroused suspicions from Puritan revolutionaries when he preached the funeral oration of **Christopher Love**, who had befriended the Stuart dynasty in 1651, yet his homiletic skills won the respect of **Oliver Cromwell**, who made Manton one of his chaplains.

During the **Interregnum**, Manton often preached before **Parliament**, and he wrote expositions on Isaiah chapter 53, the epistle of James, and the epistle of Jude. In 1653, he succeeded his father-in-law **Obadiah Sedgwick** as rector of St. Paul's at Covent Garden, and he remained there even after the **Restoration**, having earned King **Charles II**'s appreciation by being one of the first **Presbyterians** to greet him at Breda in 1660. Charles even requested that Oxford award Manton the D.D. degree. Yet in 1662, Manton was imprisoned for six months for not heeding the **Act of Uniformity**, and for the remainder of his life, he preached mostly from his own house under the political protection of the duke of Bedford. Late in life, he also became a close friend of **Richard Baxter**. Most of Manton's published works were posthumously printed sermons, first collected as *The Works of Thomas Manton, D.D.* (1681–1701) and later reprinted as a 22-volume set (1870–1875). Manton's erudite style strongly emphasized the holy life that results from the Christian gospel's liberation of law-condemned souls. *See also* SAINT BARTHOLOMEW'S DAY; SAVOY CONFERENCE; TRIERS.

MARIAN EXILES. Once Queen **Mary I** succeeded her half brother King **Edward VI** to the English throne in 1553, she reversed Edward's promotion of Protestantism. The daughter of King **Henry VIII** and his Spanish **Catholic** queen, Catherine of Aragon, Mary was partly motivated by a desire to vindicate the legacy of her mother, whom Henry divorced for failure to produce a male heir. Mary restored the Catholic mass, repaired the breach with the papacy, banned the ***Book of Common Prayer*** that had been authorized by Edward, and married Philip II, future king of Spain. Protestant riots, such as that led by Sir Thomas Wyatt, soon followed in 1554, as the Marian Injunctions formalized England's return to Roman Catholicism. Mary authorized the imprisonment of several recognizable Protestant leaders, including **Thomas Cranmer**, **Nicholas Ridley**, **Miles Coverdale**, and **Hugh Latimer**. Soon, many English Protestants began fleeing for safety to the Reformed cities of continental Europe. The total of Marian refugees eventually reached about 800. The religious sensitivities developed by these exiles prepared them to become the earliest English Puritans when Mary's death in 1558 freed them to return home and press anew for a Protestant restructuring.

The five cities most visited by the Marian exiles were Strasbourg, Basel, Zurich, Frankfurt, and Geneva. Strasbourg was the home of Peter Martyr Vermigli, who himself gave up a teaching position at **Oxford University** when Mary came to power. Alexander Nowell, Edwin Sandys, Edmund Grindal, Thomas Cole, and John Ponet were some of the English exiles who settled there. John Bale and **John Foxe**, who later became famous for chronicling Mary's hostilities in the *Book of Martyrs*, went to Basel. In Zurich, Ulrich Zwingli's successor Heinrich Bullinger welcomed **Lawrence Humphrey**, John Parkhurst, James Pilkington, Thomas Bentham, **Thomas Lever**, and William Cole. **William Whittingham**, Edmond Sutton, and **Thomas Wood** led the group of refugees in Frankfurt, where a dispute arose over whether the Edwardian *Book of Common Prayer* was an adequate manual for Protestant **worship**. A group from Frankfurt, including **John Knox**, moved on to Geneva to spend time with master theologian John Calvin. From 1555–60, approximately one-fourth of all the Marian exiles spent some time in Geneva. There, they developed the preferences of early **Non-Separatist** Puritanism: exaltation of the authority of the **Bible**, opposition to **prelacy** and **vestments**, **Presbyterian** church government, and worship based upon **preaching** and the metrical **Psalter**. In 1560, the Marian exiles also translated and annotated the **Geneva Bible**, which remained the preferred Bible of some Puritans even after the printing of the Authorized Version (**King James Version**) in 1611. By May 1560, nearly all the exiles had returned to England. Their experience was recorded in *Livre des Anglois or Register of the English Church at Geneva*.

During her five-year reign, the queen also executed around 280 Protestants, earning her the moniker "Bloody Mary." The first to be burned to death was **John Rogers**, at Smithfield on 4 February 1555. **John Hooper** died at Gloucester five days later. Ridley and Latimer were burned to death on 16 October 1555 and Cranmer on 21 March 1556. More than 50 **women** and even four children were among those condemned to death. At first, Stephen Gardiner, the lord chancellor, carried out most of the prosecutions, but Gardiner turned over that task to the Bishop of London, Edward Bonner, who, like his sovereign, earned the nickname "Bloody." After Queen **Elizabeth I** succeeded Mary in 1558, the Marian exiles hoped for a resumption and furtherance of the Protestant policies of Edward. Elizabeth instead preferred a "middle way" between Protestant doctrine and Catholic liturgy that disappointed those who wanted England to follow the path of Geneva. Elizabeth's appointment as the **Archbishop of Canterbury**, Matthew Parker, was among the first to describe the disaffected as "Puritans" in 1572.

MARIAN MARTYRS. *See* MARIAN EXILES.

MARPRELATE, MARTIN. In the autumn of 1588, in the wake of the English victory over the Spanish Armada, a pseudonymous pamphlet appeared around London whose purpose was to mar the respectability of English prelates. This was a seditious act because Archbishop John Whitgift had censored all printing not authorized by himself or the Bishop of London. The author's pen name was Martin Marprelate, and he issued six more pamphlets over the next several months. With biting satire, the Marprelate tracts held up a number of **Anglican** bishops to ridicule as petty antichrists and papists. Some of the criticized bishops, like Thomas Cooper of Winchester, published personal defenses, and so did Thomas Nashe and John Lyly on behalf of the crown. When Queen **Elizabeth I** prohibited anyone from owning the Marprelate tracts, she discovered that persons in her court already did so. Their popularity revealed the growing surge of Puritan dissatisfaction with church leadership, even though some early Puritan leaders, such as **Thomas Cartwright** and **Richard Greenham**, scolded them for making ecclesiastical abuses appear more comic than tragic. Ironically, Marprelate considered the bishops to be the real "puritans" because they insisted that supposedly indifferent matters of church **worship**, like the wearing of **vestments**, were actually essentials of Christian faith. The identity of Marprelate was never discovered, although the press in Fawsley, Northamptonshire, where Sir Richard Knightley permitted the tracts to be printed, was found and seized. This did not prevent their reprinting in 1637. Some have guessed that **Henry Barrow**, Job Throckmorton, Edward de Vere, or Christopher Marlowe may have helped write the tracts, and **Giles Wigginton** and John Udall denied authoring them while on trial. The Welshman John Penry was the sole person hanged in 1593 for likely involvement.

MARRIAGE. Puritans objected to the Roman **Catholic** treatment of marriage as a **sacrament**, yet they did not view the married state as inferior to celibacy as had the medieval monastics. Puritans believed that human beings were made by God to exist in concentric circles of community that rippled from the home to the church to the **Commonwealth**. Thus, Puritans in fact encouraged marriage at an early age, and they often reared large families. Marriages were more practical than romantic arrangements, although intense love did often develop between Puritan spouses. The parents of both partners would typically contribute a dowry to help the couple get off to a good start. The father was the undisputed head of the household even as Christ through his minister was the head of the church, but Puritan **women** were still afforded legal protections against verbal and physical mistreatments that were fairly progressive for the 17th century. **William Gouge** and **John Dod** advised husbands to trust their wives so that they might benefit from their wives' talents. In exchange, women were to nurture their children and frugally manage their husbands' earnings, while the men were responsible for providing for their families in both spirit and substance.

The common Puritan view of marriage is the description of Adam and Eve in **John Milton**'s *Paradise Lost*: "He for God only, she for God in him." Yet Milton also penned one of the most radical statements on marriage ever printed up until then when he said in *The Doctrine and Discipline of Divorce* (1643) that marriage should be grounded in compatibility rather than practicality. Women during the Puritan era did not generally receive a formal education, but Puritans could still appreciate the importance of literate women for securing religious and social reforms. The allegorical pilgrimage of Christiana and her children in *The Pilgrim's Progress, Part II* (1684) may have been intended by **John Bunyan** at least in part to promote female readership of devotional literature. In America some of the more influential writings on **family life** and relationships were **Samuel Willard**'s *A Compleat Body of Divinity* and **Benjamin Wadsworth**'s *The Well-Ordered Family*. They contended that God sanctified marriage in the Garden of Eden and prescribed the appropriate behavior for conducting both engagement, which often involved a series of public declarations of intent to wed, and marriage, which focused on reverence and responsibility. Despite the religious significance of marriage in Puritan culture, civil authorities usually conducted marriage ceremonies in America and eventually also in England, following the **Barebones Parliament**. Adultery was thus a civil offense, often punished in New England by ordering the guilty person to stand publicly in stocks or wear shamefully the quilted letter "A." *See also* FAMILY.

MARROW CONTROVERSY. Although the Marrow Controversy in Scotland occurred after the zenith of Puritanism in the British Isles, it was rooted in earlier Puritan discussions over the nature of **justification**. The controversy took its name from a work first published in England in 1645, *The Marrow of Modern Divinity*, by one "E. F." Most persons believed "E. F." to be **Edward Fisher** (1627–1655). The book is a dialogue between Neophytus, Nomista, and Evangelista. Evangelista explains to Neophytus the errors of Nomista, a "neonomian" who holds that faith is a "new law" that succeeds Mosaic law and must be produced on one's own in order to attain **salvation**. Evangelista, representing the author's own position, claims that the neonomian position makes of faith a meritorious work rather than a gift of God, as taught by the Protestant Reformers. In 1718, James Hog reprinted *The Marrow of Modern Divinity* in Scotland. Its chief proponent became **Thomas Boston**, who annotated yet another edition of the work in 1721 and defended his belief in *Human Nature in its Fourfold State*. Boston led a group of 12 "Marrow Men" who asserted that their opposition to **neonomianism** did not yield to the opposite error of **antinomianism**. Instead, Boston believed that his distinction of free **justification** and resultant **sanctification** was the necessary alternative to **Catholic** and **Arminian** conflations of saving grace and human response. In 1720, when William Craig denied before the Auchterarder presbytery that one must forsake **sin** before one can come to Christ, the Marrow Controversy fully erupted. That same year, Principal James Haddow of St. Andrews condemned *The Marrow of Modern Divinity*. The majority of the General Assembly of Scotland supported the neonomian position and censured the

"Marrow Men" in 1722, although they did not lose their positions in the **Presbyterian** Church.

MARSHALL, STEPHEN (1594–1655). English **Presbyterian** minister. Born at Godmanchester in Huntingdonshire and educated at **Emmanuel College, Cambridge**, Marshall began his ministerial career at Wethersfield, Essex. Although the mutual affection between Marshall and the parishioners at Wethersfield grew to be such that he pledged not to depart from them, he did in fact accept the benefice of Finchingfield in Essex after some intense soul searching in 1629. Marshall was often an object of criticism from those who bewailed his turn from **Anglicanism** to Presbyterianism, charging him in 1636 with "want of conformity" and accusing him of becoming a Puritan because he did not attain to the office of bishop as he had aspired. Others more sympathetic to Marshall's faith, such as **Richard Baxter**, praised him for an irenic spirit comparable to that of Archbishop **James Ussher** or the **Independent Jeremiah Burroughs**. Some of Marshall's friends knew him as a "Reaper in God's Harvest." In 1641, Marshall received an appointment as chaplain to the **New Model Army** regiment of **Robert Devereux**, the Earl of Essex, and in 1642, he became the **lecturer** at St. Margaret's Church, Westminster. From there, he received invitations to preach before **Parliament** alongside **Anthony Burgess**. According to Edward Hyde, the First Earl of Clarendon, Marshall exerted a greater influence on Parliament than did **Archbishop of Canterbury William Laud** on the Royalists. By declaring that Parliament's support of Puritan **preaching** should be the chariot bringing Christ to his coronation over the English Israel, Marshall won both legislative and popular favor. He joined **Philip Nye** as a representative of Parliament in negotiations with Ireland and Scotland, such as at the Uxbridge negotiations of 1645. Yet others excoriated him for treason and suggested that he took country retreats ostensibly to lament his part in inciting the regicide of King **Charles I**.

Most of Marshall's printed works were sermons, often denominating the papacy as the Antichrist. Under the pseudonym **Smectymnuus**, he and others also criticized Episcopalian polity, as it had been defended by Joseph Hall, the Bishop of Exeter, in *An Answer to a Book, Entitled "An Humble Remonstrance."* Marshall's sole original theological work, *A Defence of Infant Baptism* (1646), was written in opposition to John Tombes and the **Baptists**, who did not believe Marshall sufficiently distinguished them from more theologically extreme **Anabaptists** on the continent. Marshall again worked with Nye as one of the **triers** of ministers in 1652. Marshall spent his final two years of life in retirement at Ipswich, his most lasting achievement likely being his contributions as a divine to the **Westminster Assembly**, particularly its Shorter Catechism, and the **Solemn League and Covenant**. His body was exhumed from Westminster Abbey after the **Restoration**.

MARTEN, HENRY (1602–1680). English politician and regicide. Marten was not committed to either the theological ideas or strict standards of personal behavior upheld by most Puritan ministers, but nonetheless he was an outspoken contributor to the overall Puritan impulse to create a more perfect England. His father, Sir Henry Marten of Longworth, was a judge in the Admiralty Court, and the younger Marten also took up legal studies at **Oxford**. In 1640, Marten was elected to the House of Commons as a representative of Berkshire, but only three years later he was expelled for the vehemence of his opposition not only to the Stuart dynasty, but also to monarchy in general. For the next three years, he still served on the High Court of Justice. Upon resuming his elected office, Marten continued to urge the replacement of the crown and was a part of a group that its leader Edmund Ludlow called "Commonwealthsmen," who advocated a more republican government based upon the consent of the people. Marten eagerly signed the death warrant of King **Charles I** in 1649, but he quickly became disenchanted by the perceived unwillingness both of **Oliver Cromwell** and the **Presbyterian** church to support a completely representative government. For this reason, Marten became involved with the **Levellers** and **John Lilburne**, who had similar political views to himself. Marten had a reputation as a libertine and spendthrift during the **Protectorate**, popularized by the publication in 1662 of some of his private correspondences with Mary Ward, his mistress. Marten himself was in jail at that time, having been condemned by King **Charles II** as a regicide after the **Restoration** of 1660. Marten had actually received a death sentence but instead moved among several prisons, particularly that of Chepstow Castle, for the remaining 20 years of his life.

MARTIN MARPRELATE TRACTS. *See* MARPRELATE, MARTIN.

MARVELL, ANDREW (1621–1678). English poet and statesman. Marvell was born at Winestead-in-Holderness, in Yorkshire. His father, an **Anglican** clergyman, moved the family to nearby Hull, where Marvell attended the Hull Grammar School. In 1638, he entered Trinity College, **Cambridge**, as a sizar (a student exempted from paying most fees). He earned his B.A. in 1638 but left in 1641 without taking his M.A. From 1642–46, while England was engulfed in civil war, Marvell traveled on the continent, primarily in **Holland**, France, Italy, and Spain. In 1651, he became tutor to Mary Fairfax, the daughter of Lord **Thomas Fairfax** and future Duchess of Buckingham. Biographers speculate that Marvell wrote most of his lyric poetry while in the employ of the Fairfax family. His poem, "Appleton House," is an ode to Fairfax's Yorkshire estate. In 1653, Marvell served as tutor to William Dutton, the ward of **Oliver Cromwell**. Upon the recommendation of **John Milton**, Marvell was appointed Assistant Latin Secretary in 1657. Marvell aided Milton, who was blind, in the performances of his official duties as Latin Secretary. In 1659, Marvell was elected a Member of **Parliament** for Hull. Although Marvell lamented the death of Cromwell, he supported the **Restoration** of the monarchy. When **Charles II** ascended to the throne in 1660, Marvell retained his seat in Parliament. He intervened on behalf of Milton, sparing him from execution and ruinous fines. It was also during this time that Marvell began to write political verse satires, which earned him many enemies. The most famous of these is his poem "Rehearsal Transposed" (1672–73), against the rigid ecclesiastical policies of the Archdeacon of Canterbury, Samuel Parker. In 1677, Marvell opposed the Bill for Securing the Protestant Religion because it would have granted too much control to bishops. Marvell died of tertian fever at age 57. His housekeeper, Mary Palmer, to whom he was secretly married, published a collection of lyric poems. Though Marvell was best known in his own day for his satiric verse, his reputation today stands primarily on these posthumously published lyric poems. They include "Appleton House,"

"Bermudas," "The Gardens," and his most famous poem, "To His Coy Mistress," one of the best-known seduction poems in English literature.

MARY I (1516–1558). Queen of England from 1553–58. Mary was the daughter of **King Henry VIII** and his first wife, Catherine of Aragon. When Henry divorced Catherine in 1533 and married Anne Boleyn, Mary was deprived of her title as Princess of Wales, declared illegitimate, and made a lady-in-waiting to Henry and Anne's daughter, Elizabeth (*see* ELIZABETH I). Mary was eventually restored to her status as a princess of the realm through the influence of Henry's sixth and last wife, Katherine Parr. During the reign of her brother, **Edward VI**, Mary lived quietly while refusing to conform to the English Church. With the death of Edward in 1553, the Duke of Northumberland sought to make his daughter-in-law, Lady Jane Grey, Queen of England, but popular support for Mary prevailed, and she was crowned the same year. Both Northumberland and Lady Jane were executed.

As a devout **Catholic**, Mary hoped to restore the Roman Catholic Church in England, which her father had abolished. She repealed the Act of Supremacy and the **Act of Uniformity** passed under her father and brother, instituted strict laws forbidding Protestant heresies, and through Reginald Pole, whom she had appointed **Archbishop of Canterbury**, pursued a policy of zero tolerance for Protestant dissidents. During her reign, nearly 300 were burned at the stake, including former Archbishop of Canterbury **Thomas Cranmer** and leading churchmen, such as **John Hooper** and **Nicholas Ridley**. Many other Protestants fled the country, taking up residence in Holland (*see* DUTCH PURITANISM) and Geneva. As a result of these policies, Mary lost much of the public support that had brought her to the throne and earned the soubriquet "Bloody Mary." Several Protestant uprisings occurred during her reign, most notably "Wyatt's Rebellion," but they were easily suppressed.

Mary's subjects also vigorously opposed her marriage to the Spanish Prince Philip, son of Emperor Charles V, who did much to influence policy during Mary's reign. Mary hoped that the union would create a lasting alliance with Spain, as well as produce a Catholic heir. She falsely imagined twice that she was pregnant, and she lost Calais, the last English stronghold on the continent, because of her support of the Spanish in their war against the French. Shortly before her death at age 42, Mary reluctantly named her sister Elizabeth as her successor.

Mary's harsh suppression of Protestantism had the unintended long-term effect of intensifying English hostility toward Roman Catholicism. When the Protestant exiles (*see* MARIAN EXILES) returned to England after her death, they brought continental **Reformed theology** and polity with them, thus contributing to the rise of the English Puritan movement.

MASSACHUSETTS BAY COLONY. The Massachusetts Bay Colony was the main seat of Puritan influence in America from its founding in 1630 to the revocation of its original charter nearly six decades later. During the 1620s, following the settlement at Plymouth by the **Pilgrims**, the Dorchester Company and the New England Company hoped that founding additional colonies would be economically profitable. However, after King **Charles I** dissolved **Parliament** in 1629, several Puritans in the two companies feared that state opposition to them was imminent, and their desire to cross the Atlantic became more religious in nature. The expansion of Archbishop William **Laud**'s repression served to confirm their fear. Shareholders from the two groups merged into the Massachusetts Bay Colony and were surreptitiously able to acquire a royal charter on 4 March 1629. In April 1629, the first 400 Massachusetts settlers left England for the New World. In August 1629, according to the Cambridge Agreement, the eight Massachusetts Bay shareholders who hoped to relocate permanently to America bought out the holdings of the rest. One of these emigrants was **John Winthrop**, and in March 1630, he brought the colony charter and led 700 additional settlers to their new home. While in transit across the Atlantic aboard the *Arbella*, Winthrop preached his famous sermon, "A Model of Christian Charity," which enjoined his hearers to make of New England a "city set upon a hill."

Although the colonists celebrated the first Thanksgiving on 8 July 1630, the first winter was very difficult for them. Over 200 people died, and 200 more were ready to return to England when supply ships arrived the next spring. Yet 20,000 additional immigrants arrived over the next decade, and so a rudimentary system of government was able to form that was often free from interference by the king, who was facing impending civil war. The colonists founded and made Charlestown their first capital, but they soon moved it to Boston and surrounded it with a number of smaller hamlets like Newton (later Cambridge), Roxbury, Dorchester, Watertown, Ipswich, Concord, and Sudbury. Winthrop became the first governor of Massachusetts Bay Colony in 1630, and even though he lost the first annual colonial election to Thomas Dudley in 1634, he was voted back into office from 1637–39, 1642–43, and 1646–48. Soon, Massachusetts citizens also founded entirely independent towns like Hartford (1635) and New Haven (1639). In 1641, **Nathaniel Ward** composed the first code of laws of the colony, the Body of Liberties. In 1644, its General Court became bicameral in nature, divided into a House of Deputies and an upper house comprising of the governor and his council. Only adult males, or "freemen," were eligible to vote. Although either Winthrop or Dudley was the governor for most of the colony's first 20 years, John Haynes, **Henry Vane**, Richard Bellingham, **John Endecott**, John Leverett, and Simon Bradstreet also spent time in that capacity during the colony's history.

The preachers in Boston and surrounding towns played a vital role in maintaining the resolve and fellowship of citizens under primitive conditions. They also encouraged a **Bible**-centered pursuit of learning that gave birth to **Harvard College** in 1636. Some of these important individuals were **John Cotton**, **Thomas Hooker**, **Thomas Shepard**, **Richard Mather**, **Increase Mather**, and **Cotton Mather**. Massachusetts churches chose their own ministers and so operated according to the principles of the **Congregationalists**. Yet most of the ministers did not desire wholly to cease fellowship with any godly persons still in the Church of England, and, as in the state church back home, the American Puritan ministers benefited from a clergy tax. In the opinions of more strident **Separatists**, these clergy had insufficiently distinguished themselves from the **worship** rites of the Antichrist, and the vocal protests of **Anne Hutchinson** and **Roger Williams** led to their expulsion from the colony. Although Massachusetts ministers responded by **preaching** sermons against the declension of commitment to God and city, conflicts with Native American Indians, such as the **Pequot War** and **King Philip's War**, also tore away at the colony's peace from the outside.

Yet the intrusive policies of King **James II** were what spelled the end of the Massachusetts Bay Colony as originally conceived. Following the **Restoration** of 1660, King **Charles II** was too preoccupied with **Nonconformists** at home and war with the Dutch abroad to be very active in colonial governance. His brother James, however, forced Massachusetts into a series of mergers that effectively ended its autonomous character: from 1686–89, James consolidated Massachusetts with New York, East Jersey, and West Jersey into the Dominion of New England. Even after James fled the throne during the **Glorious Revolution**, his successors William and Mary united Massachusetts Bay under a new royal charter with Plymouth, Martha's Vineyard, Nantucket, and Maine in 1691. This led to the establishment of **Anglicanism** in the Bay, which helped to produce the end of the original Massachusetts Bay Colony in spirit, no less than constitution. *See also* NORTON, JOHN.

MATHER, COTTON (1663–1728). American Puritan minister. Mather was born in Boston, Massachusetts. His father was **Increase Mather**, and he was the grandson of both **Richard Mather** and **John Cotton**. He graduated from **Harvard College** in 1678 and began **preaching** around Boston and Dorchester in 1680. He completed the M.A. degree from Harvard in 1681 and joined his father in ministry at Boston's Old North (Second) Church in 1683. In 1689, he baptized **William Phips**, the future governor of Massachusetts. In that same year, he also issued a treatise condemning **witchcraft**, called *Memorable Providences*. Over the remainder of his career, he issued hundreds of writings on a wide variety of subjects, including biblical interpretation, ministry, slavery, government, **family life**, **science**, and ethics. His most famous work was *Magnalia Christi Americana* (1702), a history of Christianity in New England from 1620–98. Some of his other significant publications were *Wonders of the Invisible World* (1693), *Malachi; Or, The Everlasting Gospel* (1717), *Bonifacius: An Essay Upon the Good* (1720), *The Christian Philosopher* (1721), *Religious Improvements* (1721), and *Manuductio ad Ministerium* (1726). Mather also became a **fellow** of the Royal Society of London in 1713 and received a Doctor of Divinity degree from the University of Glasgow in 1724. *See also* MASSACHUSETTS BAY COLONY.

MATHER, INCREASE (1639–1723). American Puritan minister. Mather was born in Dorchester, Massachusetts, where his father **Richard Mather** was the local **Congregationalist** pastor. His mother was Katherine Holt Mather, and he had six siblings, including four who also became Puritan ministers. After completing his college degree under **Jonathan Mitchell** at **Harvard College** in 1656, he went to Trinity College in Dublin, Ireland, for the master's degree that he finished in 1658. For the next three years, Mather moved about in England, including a short stint as the governor of Guernsey. He left England after King **Charles II**'s **Act of Uniformity** and was back in New England in time to participate in debates over the **Half-Way Covenant** in 1662. At first an opponent of **baptizing** the infants of unregenerate adults, he later softened his position while still resisting **Solomon Stoddard**'s indiscriminate distribution of the **Lord's Supper** as a converting ordinance. Mather married **John Cotton**'s daughter Maria and, in 1664, became the pastor of Boston's Old North Church. In 1670, he published a biography of his own late father, *The Life and Death of That Reverend Man in God, Mr. Richard Mather*.

In 1674, the same year he became a **fellow** at Harvard, Mather issued *The Day of Trouble Is Near*, which lamented New England's spiritual decline since the time of its first settlers. Governor John Leverett disapproved of the condemnatory tenor of Mather's jeremiads, but Mather continued his call to repentance in dozens of printed works that included *First Principles*, *A Relation of the Troubles Which have hapned in New-England*, *Pray for the Rising Generation*, *Renewal of Covenant the Great Duty Incumbent on Decaying or Distressed Churches*, *A Brief History of the Warr with the Indians*, *A Discourse Concerning the Danger of Apostasy*, *The Necessity of Reformation*, and *Some Important Truths Concerning Conversion*. Mather often compared the spiritual vicissitudes of New Englanders to those of the ancient Israelites, and he interpreted Indian skirmishes and natural events as signs of God's judgment. In 1685, Mather became the president of Harvard, but he and **Samuel Sewall** left for England from 1688–91 to negotiate a new charter for Massachusetts from William and Mary. Upon his return to Boston, Mather opposed adducing spectral evidence to convict persons of **witchcraft** during the Salem witch trials. Yet Mather was not considered sufficiently modern by the new and third generation of Americans, and he resigned from Harvard under pressure in 1701. Undaunted, he continued to preach at Boston until his death and to urge moral reformation in writings like *The Duty of Parents to Pray for Their Children*. His own famous child was the Puritan historian **Cotton Mather**. *See also* MASSACHUSETTS BAY COLONY.

MATHER, RICHARD (1596–1669). English and American Puritan minister. Mather was born at Lowton, near Liverpool, in Lancashire, England. His parents were Thomas Mather and Margaret Abrams Mather. He went to the Winwick School and then to Brasen-nose College, **Oxford**. In 1618, he agreed to serve as minister and schoolmaster at Toxteth-park near his birthplace, taking **ordination** as an **Anglican** deacon in 1619, and he preached there twice each Sunday for 15 years. Mather married twice, first to Katherine Holt in 1624 and later to Sarah Hawkridge, **John Cotton**'s widow, in 1655. As he became increasingly committed to an **Independent** model of church government, Mather caught the attention of Archbishops **William Laud** and Richard Neile, and he was suspended for **Nonconformity** in 1633. After corresponding with **Thomas Hooker**, Mather committed to relocating to New England. He arrived at the port of Bristol in disguise in 1635 and sailed for Boston. His ship's survival of a violent hurricane off the Massachusetts coast was evidence to him of divine favor. In 1636, Mather became the pastor of Dorchester, where he became the patriarch of New England Puritanism's leading intellectual family. Five of Mather's sons became important Puritan ministers in their own right: Samuel in Ireland, Nathaniel and Timothy in England, and Increase and Eleazar in New England. His other children were Elizabeth and Joseph.

One of Mather's first significant contributions to colonial life was his preface to the ***Bay Psalm Book*** (1640), the first book printed in Cambridge, Massachusetts. In the 1640s, his writings were occupied mainly with defending **Congregationalism** to the Scottish **Presbyterian Samuel Rutherford**, in works like *A Discourse on the Church Covenant*, and in vindicating the **Half-Way Covenant** in *An Answer to Thirty-Two Questions*. Mather's works also became the basis for the **Cambridge Platform** of 1648. When his health began to fail, he delivered his *Farewell Exhortation* to the Dorchester church in 1657.

Mather died in 1669 in the residence of his son **Increase Mather** in Boston. Increase's biography of his father, *The Life and Death of That Reverend Man in God, Mr. Richard Mather*, is the amplest surviving insight into Mather's life and personality, particularly the priority Mather placed on the training of children and ministers. *See also* MASSACHUSETTS BAY COLONY.

MATTHEW'S BIBLE. Matthew's Bible first appeared in 1537, the same year as the second edition of the **Miles Coverdale Bible**. Through the lobbying of **Archbishop of Canterbury Thomas Cranmer**, Matthew's Bible bore the official license of King **Henry VIII**. Its editor was Thomas Matthew, a pseudonym for **John Rogers**, one of the later **Marian martyrs**. Rogers was a friend of William Tyndale and used the Pentateuch and New Testament from Tyndale's Bible for his own version; the translations of the Old Testament books Joshua–2 Chronicles may also have come from previously unpublished manuscripts of Tyndale. The books Ezra–Malachi and the Apocrypha of Matthew's Bible came from Coverdale. Matthew's Bible was first printed abroad, perhaps in Antwerp, Belgium, by Tyndale's publisher Jacobus van Meteren, and then distributed in London. Richard Taverner eliminated Rogers' copious annotations and reissued Matthew's Bible as **Taverner's Bible** in 1539.

MAYFLOWER COMPACT. On 6 September 1620, the group of Englanders later to be known as the **Pilgrims** left the port of Plymouth for the New World aboard the *Mayflower*. There were 102 people aboard ship, many of whom had been under the spiritual leadership of the **Congregationalist** pastor **John Robinson** in Leyden, **Holland**. Two travelers, **William Brewster** and **William Bradford**, had been with Robinson since his **preaching** days at Scrooby Manor in England. The ship anchored in the Massachusetts harbor on 11 November 1620. On that same day, 41 male passengers signed the Mayflower Compact. It purported to be a covenant by which the colonists, to the glory of God, would "combine ourselves together into a civil Body Politick, for our better Ordering and Preservation." Though only three paragraphs long, the Mayflower Compact was the first attempt at a written law code in the New World. On 21 December 1620, the *Mayflower*'s crew disembarked at the site that they would name Plymouth, in honor of their voyage's starting point.

MAYHEW, JONATHAN (1720–1766). American **Congregationalist** minister. Mayhew was born at Martha's Vineyard, Massachusetts, the great-great grandson of the original proprietor of Martha's Vineyard and the great grandson of Thomas Mayhew (1620–57), the Puritan minister of that hamlet who also conducted **missions** to Native American Indians. Jonathan graduated from **Harvard College** in 1744 and received a Doctor of Divinity degree from the University of Aberdeen in 1749. In 1747, he accepted appointment as the minister of West Church in Boston, in which post he remained for the rest of his life. West Church was perhaps the first Congregationalist church in its area to espouse a functionally Unitarian theology. Indeed, other ministers around Boston considered Mayhew a heretic for his subordinationist view of Jesus Christ and rejection of the **Calvinist** belief in human total depravity. He preferred a simple, moral faith based upon completely natural reason to the revealed religion of Puritan orthodoxy, and he ended up opposing the evangelistic methods of both **George Whitefield** and the Society for the Propagation of the Gospel, the very foundation that had funded the work of his great grandfather Thomas.

Mayhew's most significant historical achievement was in the area of politics, where he followed **John Wise** in drawing out the implications of Congregationalist church polity for a democratic system of government in the civic sphere. In his most famous **sermon**, preached on 30 January 1750, and entitled "A Discourse Concerning Unlimited Submission and Non-Resistance to the Higher Powers," Mayhew commemorated the centennial of King **Charles I**'s execution by rejecting all state-sponsored religion, claiming that the Son of God alone is both king and head of the church. In the fashion of John Locke, he advocated that government exists to promote the common weal and derives it authority solely from the consent of the governed. Mayhew strongly opposed the imposition on American consumer goods of the Stamp Act in 1765, and he allegedly coined the rally cry, "No taxation without representation." Also in 1765, Mayhew gave the Dudleian lecture at Harvard. Collections of his sermons remained popular in Massachusetts throughout the American Revolutionary War.

MECHANICK PREACHERS. "Mechanick" preachers first appeared in large numbers in England in the decade of the 1640s. The label was a derisive term for **Nonconformist** preachers whose lack of formal education and lawful **ordination** required them to work with their hands during the week. These preachers often, in fact, took their base heritage as a point of pride that better qualified them to speak on God's behalf to average people. They were not organized into a denominational group but gathered around them groups of widely varying theological persuasion. Even during the height of Puritan power in England, the **Interregnum**, mechanick preachers were often viewed with suspicion for their great reliance on personal inspiration from God and promotion of democratic principles. After the **Restoration**, King **Charles II** considered mechanick preachers to be such a nuisance that he pressed for the **Conventicle Act** of 1664, which required that private religious gatherings hold no more than five people. **John Bunyan**, the tinker of Bedford, was probably the most famous and among the most orthodox of the mechanicks. More radical examples might include **George Fox**, **Lodowicke Muggleton**, **Gerrard Winstanley**, and **John Lilburne**. *See also* PREACHING.

MEDE, JOSEPH (1586–1638). English theologian. Mede was born at Burdon in Essex. He studied at Hoddesdon in Hertfordshire and Wethersfield in Essex. He also taught Hebrew at the latter and became proficient as well in the Greek and Latin writings of the church fathers. He earned a bachelor's degree from Christ's College, **Cambridge**, where later, as a **fellow**, he further developed skills in philosophy, logic, mathematics, anatomy, philology, and exposition. His academic gifts were so significant that Archbishop **James Ussher** consulted him when composing his biblical chronology and asked him to become the provost of Trinity College in Dublin. Yet Mede preferred to remain at Cambridge and nurtured friendships with notable Puritans, such as **William Ames** and **William Twisse**. Mede was known for encouraging his students to admit the doubts that came to their minds while studying, and for urging that private assemblies not displace church meetings. Yet his more influential legacy was the apocalyptic key he cut in *Clavis Apocalyptica* (1627), which identified the papacy as the Antichrist and predicted that Christ might return around the year 1660 to fulfill the prophecies of Daniel and Revelation and establish a messianic kingdom. A posthumous, single-volume collection of Mede's writings first appeared in 1672, entitled *The Works of the Pious and Profoundly-learned Joseph Mede*.

MELANCHOLY. In the Puritan era, "melancholy" was an anomalous term that often included all symptoms of physical and emotional sickness for which physicians could not give an easy explanation. The evidences of melancholy could include morbid impulses, despair, obsessive behavior, temptation to suicide, fear of demons, or horrifying dreams. Some suspected melancholy to be the result of a mysterious biological imbalance. In 1621, Robert Burton's *The Anatomy of Melancholy* argued that increasing reports of melancholy were neurotic manifestations of an obsession for ecclesiastical purity. In truth, many Puritan pastors began to associate episodes of melancholy with the intense awareness of human depravity that was a requisite part of repentance for **sin**. Surviving episodes of melancholy thus became virtually an expected evidence of a person's spiritual awakening. One therefore finds episodes of melancholy in most Puritan autobiographical writings on both sides of the Atlantic, including those of **John Winthrop**, **William Perkins**, **Thomas Shepard**, **Michael Wigglesworth**, **Cotton Mather**, and **John Bunyan**. Bunyan's disquiet over an afflicted **conscience** in *Grace Abounding to the Chief of Sinners* evinces perhaps the best-known example of the whole genre of confessions of melancholy, and his depiction of a man in an iron cage in *The Pilgrim's Progress* effectively shows the sobriety with which Puritans treated the whole phenomenon.

MIDDLETON, THOMAS (1580?–1627). English playwright. Middleton was born in Newington Butts, Surrey, studied at Queen's College, **Oxford**, and, for a time, practiced law. From 1620 until his death, he was also the city chronologer of London, preceding in that position the famed Dr. Ben Jonson. Yet Middleton became better known as one of the leading dramatists of the early Stuart era prior to the closure of the **theater** during the **Interregnum**. His plays were often stories of comic characters with tragic ends. He penned dozens of works, among which some of the more successful were *The Changeling*, **Women** *Beware Women, A Chaste Maid in Cheapside, The Honest Whore, Michaelmas Terme, The Roaring Girl, A Faire Quarrel, A Game at Chess*, and *The Puritan, or the Widow of Watling Street*. Though some of Middleton's plays suggest a **Calvinist** perspective, in *The Puritan* and other plays, he criticized those who were only interested in a Puritan upsurge for possible opportunities in social advancement.

MILDMAY, WALTER (1520?–1589). English politician. Mildmay was the fifth and youngest son of Thomas Mildmay, a wealthy merchant in Chelmsford, Essex. He studied at Christ's College, **Cambridge**, but did not complete his bachelor's degree. He then followed his brother Thomas into a life of public service, becoming a surveyor of the court of argumentation of King **Henry VIII**. Mildmay's political savvy was so respected that he retained government posts during the reigns of each of Henry's children, **Edward VI**, **Mary I**, and **Elizabeth I**. During Edward's reign, he married Mary Walsingham and purchased the country estate of Apethorpe. During Mary's reign, he used his influence to protect English Protestant refugees. Under Elizabeth, he served as privy counselor, chancellor, under-treasurer of the exchequer, and a special commissioner during the trial that led to the execution of Mary, Queen of Scots. With his accumulated wealth, Mildmay became a prominent donor to his former schools at Chelmsford and Christ's College, and, in 1584, he founded **Emmanuel College** at Cambridge largely for the purpose of training ministers. Although Mildmay and his appointed headmaster **Laurence Chaderton** assured Queen Elizabeth that the religious outlook of the new college was loyal to the crown, Emmanuel College in fact went on to become an intellectual center of **Calvinistic** Puritanism. Sir Mildmay died at Apethorpe.

MILLENARIANISM. Ever since the return of the **Marian exiles** to England in 1558, many Puritans hoped that a cleansing of the Church of England might portend the second coming of Jesus and a glorious reign alongside Christ of all his saints. In 1609, Thomas Brightman published an influential reading of the book of Revelation entitled *Apocalypsis Apocalypseos*. Brightman argued for a "middle advent," meaning that the 1,000-year messianic reign on earth mentioned in Revelation chapter 20 portended the redemptive role of Puritan churches, and that, at last, Christ himself would return at the millennium's end. **John Cotton** took Brightman's millenarian scheme with him to Boston, where he used it as the basis of his **sermon** series, *The Churches Resurrection*, in 1639–40. Other attempts to decode the prophecies of Revelation and Daniel appeared throughout the reign of King **Charles I**, as hopes for a Puritan takeover of the English government continued to grow. Some of these were *Diatribe de mille annis* by Johann Heinrich Alsted, *Clavis Apocalyptica* by **Joseph Mede**, *The Personall Raigne of Christ upon Earth* by John Archer, and the anonymously written *A Glimpse of Sions Glory*. Apocalyptic fervor was most intense during the 1650s and 1660s, when a number of writings predicted Christ's return would occur. The **Fifth Monarchists** make a prime example of the widespread eschatological interests of the age. Their whole reason for being was the belief that a takeover of political power would make England the prophesied fifth and final world power that Daniel foretold would succeed the Assyrians, Babylonians, Persians, and Medes. Although millenarian intensity did not entirely disappear after the **Restoration**, as **Hanserd Knollys'** *Exposition on the Whole Book of the Revelation* made clear in 1689, fewer and fewer people were motivated to decode biblical prophecies as Puritan hegemony collapsed and the age of the Enlightenment emerged.

MILLENNARY PETITION. When King James VI of Scotland became King **James I** of England in April 1603, English Puritans believed he would support their aspiration for a more **Presbyterian/Reformed** national church. James had subscribed to the Scottish National Covenant and stated his preference for the Kirk of Scotland over the Church of England. Thus, while James was on his way to London, Stephen Egerton, **Arthur Hildersham**, and Edward Fleetwood met him to present the Millennary Petition, so named for supposedly bearing 1,000 ministers' signatures. The full title of the appeal was "The humble Petition of the Ministers of the Church of England, desiring Reformation of certain ceremonies and abuses of the Church." It asked for the king's support for reform in four areas: church service, ministers, church livings, and church discipline. King James agreed to hear out the Puritans at the **Hampton Court Conference**, but apparently he was more alarmed than conciliated by their requests; many of them, in fact, lost their positions during the course of James' reign.

MILTON, JOHN (1608–1674). English poet and statesman. Milton was born in Bread Street in Cheapside, London, the son of a well-to-do scrivener. His father gave the young Milton an excellent education: he was tutored by the gifted Puritan minister Thomas Young and entered St. Paul's School in 1620. By the time he was 15, Milton knew Latin, Greek, French, and Italian, and had begun to learn Hebrew. He had also begun to develop an interest in poetry, particularly the works of Edmund Spenser and Guillaume du Bartas.

In 1625, Milton entered Christ's College, **Cambridge**. His time there was not untroubled, for he was suspended and possibly whipped by his tutor, while his fellow students nicknamed him "the lady of Christ's" for his feminine features and austere behavior. However, he also began to blossom as a poet, both in Latin and English. He wrote his first important poem "On the Morning of Christ's Nativity," on Christmas morning, 1629. Other notable poems from this early period of Milton's career include *L'Allegro* and *Il Penseroso*, written in 1631.

In 1632, Milton left Cambridge, having earned his M.A. Although he went to Cambridge with the expectation of ultimately taking holy orders, he refused to subscribe to the ecclesiastical policies of **Archbishop of Canterbury William Laud**. Instead, he retired to his father home in Horton, Buckinghamshire, where he commenced on a rigorous course of personal study. For the next five years, Milton is said to have read everything published up to that point in English, as well as immersing himself in the classics and the **Bible**. He pursued this program with the conscious objective of preparing himself to be a poet of great importance, writing in the service of God. During this time, Milton wrote two important works, a verse masque titled *Comus*, and the pastoral elegy *Lycidas*, which commemorated the death of his Cambridge friend, Edward King.

In 1638, Milton left England for a 15-month tour of the continent. He visited France but spent most of his time in Italy, where he met such luminaries as the aging Galileo. Upon his return to England in 1639, Milton opened a school in Aldersgate, London. He also began a period of writing prose on contemporary issues. When **Joseph Hall** penned a defense of **episcopacy**, Milton joined his former tutor and the other writers known collectively as **Smectymnuus** by writing pamphlets in response, including *The Reason of Church Government* (1642). In 1634, he married 17-year-old Mary Powell, the daughter of a Royalist family. A month later, the couple separated, with Mary returning to her family in Oxfordshire. The experience led Milton to publish *The Doctrine and Discipline of Divorce* (1644), in which he argued that incompatibility is legitimate grounds for divorce. The work met with violent opposition from the **Presbyterian** clergy, and the **Westminster Assembly** demanded its public burning. It also led the House of Commons to pass an ordinance imposing increased government regulation of the press. Milton responded with *Areopagitica* (1644), a defense of free speech. The controversy marked Milton's departure from the Presbyterian cause.

With the Royalist defeat in 1645, Milton's in-laws, now financially ruined, asked Milton to take Mary back. He consented, and, over the next seven years, the couple had three daughters. When his father-in-law died, Milton also found himself the permanent host of Mary's mother and eight siblings. His collected poems appeared in 1647, the year of his own father's death. The inheritance allowed Milton to open a new school in High Holborn. Furthermore, his support for the execution of King **Charles I**, expressed in his pamphlet *Tenure of Kings and Magistrates*, now brought him official favor, and he was appointed Latin Secretary, in which his principal duty was defending the acts of the Council of State. His most famous works in this office include *Eikonoklastes* (1649) and *Pro Populo Anglo Defensio* (1650). By 1655, Milton had lost most of his eyesight, likely caused by glaucoma, and was assisted in his official capacities by **Andrew Marvell**. His first wife having died in 1652, Milton married his second wife, Catherine Woodcock, in 1656. She died two years later in childbirth and is remembered in one of Milton's most famous sonnets, "Methought I saw my late espoused saint." He married his third wife, Elizabeth Minchell, in 1663.

With the **Restoration** of the monarchy in 1660, Milton was placed under arrest. However, his life and most of his fortune were spared through the intervention of Marvell. Deeply disillusioned, Milton retired to private life. But if the Restoration meant the loss of Milton's hopes for England, it also provided the long sought opportunity to commence writing what would become the great English epic, *Paradise Lost*. It is written in the style of Homer and recounts the fall of Adam and Eve as recounted in Genesis. Then completely blind, Milton dictated the 2,000-line poem to his daughters. Milton followed the publication of *Paradise Lost* (1667) with two more verse epics on biblical subjects, *Paradise Regained* (1671), which recounts the temptations of Christ in the wilderness, and *Samson Agonistes* (1671). He died in his home in **Bunhill Fields** and is buried at St. Giles, Cripplegate, in London. *See also* SCIENCE.

MISSIONS. For the most part, Puritan missions both in England and America were really attempts to persuade persons of their need to adopt a more authentic and biblical form of Christianity. In New England, however, Puritans came into contact for the first time with persons who did not consider themselves Christians: the Native American Indians. The conduct of missions to the Indians was a biblical mandate, and so **John Cotton** encouraged **John Winthrop** to see the importance of welcoming the Indians as "partakers of your precious faith." Evangelizing the Indians could also be of eschatological significance for some like Thomas Thorowgood, who thought the Indians might be lost tribes of Israel whose Christian conversions could hail the second coming of Christ. Practically, however, missions among the Indians proved to be very difficult. Differences in religious worldviews, land disputes, and occasional armed skirmishes, such as the **Pequot War**, made missionary success problematic. One of the earliest missionaries to the Indians was John Eliot of Roxbury, Massachusetts, who employed a native Algonquin in the 1640s to translate his **sermons**. Thomas Mayhew Sr. and Thomas Mayhew Jr. pioneered mission work among the Wampanoag tribe. Hiacoomes, the first known convert of Thomas Jr., received **ordination** himself as a **Congregationalist** minister in 1670. By 1674, there were in Massachusetts two native churches and 14 Indian "praying towns." Missions nearly came to a halt, however, after **King Philip's War**

wiped out the Narragansetts in 1675–76. Yet perhaps the most successful missionary of all pursued his work over a half century later. **David Brainerd** died in 1747 at the age of 29 from tuberculosis, but the diary that **Jonathan Edwards** published after Brainerd's death records 47 baptisms by him among Indians in New York, New Jersey, and Pennsylvania.

MITCHELL, JONATHAN (1624–1668). American **Congregationalist** minister. Mitchell was born in Halifax, Yorkshire, and came to America with his family in 1635. He received his baccalaureate degree from **Harvard College** in 1647 and remained a **fellow** of the college thereafter. In 1650, he married the widow of **Thomas Shepard**, Margaret, and succeeded Shepard as minister of the Congregationalist church in Cambridge, Massachusetts. Mitchell became one of the most visible leaders of second-generation American Puritanism, most notably through his strong advocacy in 1662 of the **Half-Way Covenant**, which declared that the children of "nonconfessing" church members in good standing could still receive **baptism**. He was also the tutor and mentor of **Increase Mather**. Some of Mitchell's **sermons** were published posthumously in London. The most noted of these was "Nehemiah on the Wall," an election sermon from 1667 that defined the public welfare as the preservation of religion, life, equity, order, and peace.

MONCK (OR MONK), GEORGE (1608–1670). English soldier. Monck was born in Potheridge of Devonshire. When his father, also named George, fell on hard times financially, the younger Monck assaulted the sheriff who arrested his father for indebtedness. To avoid incarceration himself, Monck fled town and enrolled in military action. After distinguishing himself in campaigns in **Holland**, Ireland, and the **Bishops' Wars** on the Scottish border, Monck took a commission to defend King **Charles I** from the armies of **Parliament**. The Parliamentarian **John Pym** at first unsuccessfully tried to win Monck to the other side, but Monck reconsidered his position after being captured and became one of the **New Model Army**'s more skilled commanders. Eventually, **Oliver Cromwell** appointed Monck as commander-in-chief over all military forces in Scotland.

Monck ascended to national prominence in England after **Richard Cromwell**'s resignation as the lord protector in 1659 left the nation in political turmoil. The interim government, called the Committee of Safety, was composed of a few New Model Army officers whose ambitions were of concern to Parliament. Parliament's Council of State named Monck the general of all armies in England, Scotland, and Ireland in exchange for his protection. Aided by funds from a Scottish assembly, Monck's forces made it past General John Lambert's troops to arrive in London on 3 February 1660. Monck's forceful presence persuaded the Committee of Safety to dissolve itself, and when Monck restored all the **Presbyterians** who had been evicted from Parliament by **Pride's Purge**, some thought he was securing support to name himself the new lord protector. Monck did in fact persuade the **Long Parliament** at last to dissolve itself and prepare to call a new session that would presumably reinstitute a government in support of Westminster standards. Instead, Monck's wife Anne Clarges apparently convinced him that his future would be more secure if he helped restore the Stuart crown and then lived off the king's gratitude.

Monck thus corresponded with **Charles II** in France and persuaded him to make certain assurances to **Independents** in the **Declaration of Breda** that would secure the **Restoration**. Charles II received coronation on 25 May 1660 and thanked Monck with multiple titles: Baron Monck, Earl of Torrington, Captain-General of the Army, Master of the King's Horse, the first duke of Albemarle, and a Lord Proprietor of the Carolina colony in America. Monck's soldiers, dubbed the Coldstream Guards, made up the only battalion of the New Model Army to remain intact under the new king's employ. Monck's final acts of national service were the suppression of **Thomas Venner**'s London uprising in 1661, the supervision of London during the 1665 plague and 1666 fire, and the overseeing of the Second Dutch War from 1665–67. Monck received a state funeral in Westminster Abbey in 1670.

MONMOUTH REBELLION. The Monmouth Rebellion of 1685 came as part of the aftermath of the so-called Exclusion Crisis. At that time, Protestant members of **Parliament** who desired to exclude James, the duke of York, from succeeding his brother **Charles II** as king were known as Whigs. Charles had no legitimate children, and the Whigs feared James because of his outspoken Roman **Catholicism**. From 1678–81, largely under the guidance of Anthony Ashley Cooper, the First Earl of Shaftesbury, the Whigs considered various legal means to block James from succession, but Charles disbanded Parliament in 1681 before any official policy could be reached. Meanwhile, an illegitimate son of the king by Lucy Walter, James Scott the duke of Monmouth and Buccleuch (1649–85), had taken refuge on the continent following the **Rye House Plot** and was courting Whig support for a coup. Only four months after the death of his father, in June 1685, Monmouth brought 82 soldiers with him to the Beach near the Cobb at Lyme Regis, in Dorset, and asked Parliament to support his claims to be the rightful heir to the throne. Monmouth had been a captain of England's armed forces and persuaded approximately 6,000 additional men, mostly **dissenters**, to join his cause against the forces of the recently crowned King **James II**. Monmouth's soldiers were mostly untrained farmers, however, and their "Pitchfork Rebellion" failed miserably on 6 July 1685, at Sedgemoor in Somerset. Monmouth tried to flee the battlefield in disguise but was captured and beheaded on 15 July at the Tower of London. He claimed on the scaffold that he was to die a Protestant member of the Church of England. Monmouth's supporters were sorely prosecuted in ensuing months by Judge George Jeffreys, whose **Bloody Assizes** consigned 200 persons to death and 800 more to banishment in the New World. James did at last abandon his throne in December 1688 during Parliament's **Glorious Revolution**.

MUGGLETON, LODOWICKE (LODOWICK, LUDOWICK, OR LUDOVICK) (1609–1698). English **Nonconformist**. Muggleton was born on London's Bishopsgate Street and trained to become a tailor. However, in 1651, he purported to receive a series of personal visions from God, and his life took a dramatic turn. He believed that he and his cousin John Reeve were the two witnesses of divine truth mentioned in Revelation 11:3, and that he was the mouthpiece and interpreter of Reeve's special revelations. Muggleton attracted a small group of followers who were already convinced that they were living in apocalyptic times and liked Muggleton's rejection of human reason as a tool of the devil. Muggleton's first published defense of his calling, *The Transcendent Spirituall Treatise*, landed him in prison for blasphemy in 1653. Muggleton's chief theological crime in the eyes of most contemporaries was his denial of the doctrine of the Trinity. In *The Divine Looking-Glass*, he said that God has a physical body and left Elijah as viceroy of Heaven when he came to earth in the form of Jesus Christ. Yet neither his incarceration, nor the death of Reeve in 1658, nor even his disciples' repudiations of some of his teachings in 1660, broke Muggleton's convictions. He continued to publish a series of writings throughout the 1660s: *A True Interpretation of the Eleventh Chapter of the Revelation of St. John*, *A True Interpretation of All the Chief Texts . . . of the Whole Book of the Revelation of St. John*, *A Looking Glass for* **George Fox**, *An Answer to* **William Penn**, and *The Neck of the* **Quakers** *Broken*. The **Muggletonians** became obscure after the **Restoration**, yet Muggleton was again imprisoned and fined for blasphemy in 1677. A final work, *The Acts of the Witnesses*, appeared soon after his death. *See also* MECHANICK PREACHERS.

MUGGLETONIANS. The Muggletonians were among the more theologically radical of the mid-17th-century English **Nonconformists**. They took their name from **Lodowicke Muggleton**, who claimed that he and cousin John Reeve had been named by God as the two witnesses of Revelation 11:3. Reeve died in 1658, but Muggleton lived another 40 years. Muggletonians taught that the doctrine of the Trinity was an invention of human reason and therefore serviced the devil. This rejection of reason attracted the group's most famous convert, the former Ranter and Digger **Laurence Clarkson**, whose *The Lost Sheep Found* explained how internal contradictions in other sects made their logic untenable. According to Muggletonian thought, God has a physical body comparable to a human male and left Elijah to oversee Heaven when he came to earth as Jesus Christ. Muggletonians also taught not only that angels are males but that all human beings in Heaven will be transformed into males, incapable of further generation. By contrast, the first **woman** Eve was the embodiment of an evil spirit and bore her first son Cain through relations with the devil. Heaven was supposedly only about six miles above the surface of the earth, and most unlikely to be found there supposedly were the **Quakers**, the Muggletonians' fiercest polemical adversaries. Post-**Restoration** measures against Nonconformists, the rise of modern astronomy, and Muggleton's own belief that impending eschatological events made evangelism unnecessary, combined to quell the Muggletonian movement. Yet there were still enough adherents to reprint *The Works of J. Reeve and L. Muggleton* in 1832, and the last self-professed Muggletonian in England only died in 1979.

MUSIC. Whereas the Church of England employed anthems, often sung by professional singers, in its services, Puritans preferred church music whose style was less demanding and could be sung by all. The **Presbyterians** criticized the overuse of anthems for detracting from the time allowed for **sermons**, and they typically insisted that the Old Testament Psalms were to be exclusively the music of the church because they were inspired and approved by God. Psalters, or collections of Psalms set to meter, came into English Christianity through those **Marian exiles** who wanted to import Genevan **worship** into England. **William Whittingham** translated the Genevan Psalter into English in 1556 and also published about that same time the Psalter of Thomas Sternhold and John Hopkins, thereafter the standard Puritan Psalter for well over a century. Presbyterians believed that the simple tunes of the Psalter (most were in common meter) helped laypeople to memorize **Scripture**. So influential upon Puritan history was the singing of Psalms that Presbyterian soldiers during the **English Civil Wars** were known to use them as battle hymns. Also, the first book published in America was the *Bay Psalm Book*, printed in Cambridge, Massachusetts, in 1640. In 1644, the worship Directory of the **Westminster Assembly** encouraged singing the Psalms in unison. A Scottish Psalter appeared in 1650, and other English Psalters appeared from time to time throughout the latter half of the 17th century.

The preface to the *Bay Psalm Book*, probably written by **Richard Mather**, reveals that even the singing of the Psalms in Christian worship was not a matter of universal Puritan accord. Opponents of the practice, like the **Baptist** Isaac Marlow, claimed that it was inappropriate to adapt God's word to tunes invented by human beings, and that there was always the risk of believers tainting their praise of God by singing alongside persons who were in fact unbelievers. Other early Baptists like **John Smyth** and Thomas Grantham also rejected congregational singing to demonstrate a strict separation from the formal liturgies of **Anglicanism**, which they thought stifled the movement of the Holy Spirit. On the other hand, many advocates of Psalm-singing remained critical of singing freshly composed hymns whose words were not taken verbatim from the **Bible**. The first congregational hymnal printed in England appeared in 1623 from **George Wither**, titled *Hymns and Songs of the Church*, but the general acceptance of hymn-singing would not truly begin until the compositions of the **Independent Isaac Watts** showed that hymns could serve, like sermons and catechisms, as media for instruction and edification. **Benjamin Keach** also slowly introduced hymn-singing to the Baptists as a post-communion option. By 1689, the Second London Confession of the Baptists could affirm, "We believe that singing the praises of God is a holy ordinance of Christ, and not a part of natural religion or a moral duty only; but that it is brought under divine institution, it being enjoined on the churches of Christ to sing psalms, hymns and spiritual songs; and that the whole Church, in their public assemblies (as well as private Christians), ought to sing God's praises according to the best light they have received." *See also* DRAMA.

– N –

NEONOMIANISM. Neonomianism, as often suspected of **Richard Baxter** and defended by **Daniel Williams** in *The Gospel Truth*, held that the Christian gospel is a "new law" whose requirements for **salvation** are fulfilled through faith and repentance. Detractors like Isaac Chauncy and **Robert Traill** claimed that this idea was a companion of **Arminianism** and **Amyrauldianism**, and that it compromised the Reformation idea that saving faith is a wholly unmerited gift of divine grace. Neonomianism became the chief consideration of the so-called **Marrow Controversy** in the Church of Scotland. When a reprint of *The Marrow of Modern Divinity* appeared in Scotland in 1718, **Presbyterian** Church leaders at the Synod of Fife appointed a council to discredit it for espousing **antinomianism**. These individuals were mostly neonomians themselves who thought that their belief was the only antidote to an understanding of grace so unbounded that it could tolerate licentiousness. The committee issued its condemnation of the "Marrow men" in 1720 and again criticized 12 "Representers" of the Marrow position in 1722. In 1733, partly because of lingering animosities over the controversy but also to preserve the rights of elder boards to choose their own minister, Ebenezer and Ralph Erskine led the opponents of neonomianism to form the Secession Church.

NESSE, CHRISTOPHER (1621–1705). English Puritan preacher. Nesse was born at North Cave, Yorkshire. His father's name was Thomas Nesse. He studied at a private school under the guidance of the Puritan Lazarus Seaman and then at St. John's College, **Cambridge**, attaining to the Master of Arts degree. In 1644, Nesse's theological views began to merge with those of the **Independents**, and he began to preach, first at Cliffe, near Market Weighton, and later at Holderness. In 1649, he started a grammar school in Beverley, but he left the following year for Cottingham, where he resumed his **preaching**. In 1656, Nesse moved to yet another preaching appointment in Leeds. Although ejected from that position according to the **Act of Uniformity** in 1662, Nesse continued to preach where he could gather a congregation, beginning at Clayton, then Morley, and—after opening another school at Hunset—back to Leeds, and finally around London until his death. He was buried at **Bunhill Fields**, London's **Nonconformist** cemetery. Nesse's publications include *An Antidote against Arminianism*, *A Protestant Antidote against the Poison of Popery*, and *A Compleat & Compendious Church History*.

NEW ENGLAND THEOLOGY. The term "New England Theology" could be used generally to describe the **Calvinism** of the first two or three generations of American Puritans, but it refers even more specifically to a school of thought dedicated to preserving that heritage after the death of **Jonathan Edwards**. This group of New Haven theologians, so named because most were graduates of Yale, included **Samuel Hopkins**, Joseph Bellamy, Jonathan Edwards Jr., and Nathaniel Emmons. They viewed **Unitarianism**, **Arminianism**, and the **Half-Way Covenant** as the greatest threats to Edwards'

Calvinist orthodoxy. By the end of the 18th century, however, some of the later members of the "New Divinity Men" were willing to relinquish Edwards' belief in original **sin** for the idea that sin can only be a personal decision and not an inherited nature. These included Nathaniel William Taylor and Edwards' grandson Timothy Dwight. Advocates of the New England Theology drafted the Plan of Union of 1801 that temporarily united the "New Light" **Presbyterian** and **Congregationalist** churches of New England into a single denominational body supporting revivalism and religious education. The "Presbygational" experiment ended in 1837 because the Presbyterians believed the Congregationalists had become prone to emotional and theological variableness.

NEW MODEL ARMY. The **Earl of Essex** was the commander-in-chief of **Parliament**'s armies at the outset of the **English Civil Wars**. Yet Essex and several other army officers were actually politicians who were not well trained in military tactics. After Essex fled the scene of battle at Lostwithiel in September 1644, Sir **Thomas Fairfax** and **Oliver Cromwell** aspired to a completely reconstructed army, free from supervisors unequal to their task. Cromwell and his supporters among the **Independents** persuaded Parliament to pass the **Self-Denying Ordinance**, which removed all Parliamentarians from their field commands excepting Cromwell himself. The reconstructed Parliamentary army was known as the New Model Army. Fairfax was its new commander, and Cromwell was his chief lieutenant. By July 1645, the New Model Army had already routed the central and western battalions of King **Charles I**. In May 1646, Charles surrendered to the Scots; they, in turn, handed the king over to Parliament.

With Charles in custody, the soldiers of the New Model Army began to press Cromwell for the wages and religious **toleration** they had been promised. Various troops appointed "Agitators" to present their cases to the Army Council, which agreed to hear grievances in 1647 at Newmarket and Putney. At the **Putney debates**, the **Levellers** urged army leaders to implement a radically revised social program, including redistribution of wealth, but the council rejected the requests as too radical and destabilizing. Cromwell succeeded Fairfax as the army's commander in 1650; his closest adviser was his son-in-law **Henry Ireton** until Ireton's death the following year in Ireland. Following **Pride's Purge** in 1648, some remaining **Presbyterians** in Parliament feared that the rising power of Independent generals would outreach theirs, and so they attempted to disband the New Model Army. However, supervision of the army had already passed beyond their control, and, in 1653, Cromwell dismissed the **Rump Parliament** and governed alone as the lord protector.

NEWCOMEN, THOMAS (1664–1729). English **Baptist** inventor. Newcomen came from a merchant family in Dartmouth, Devon, which had lost much of its estate during the reign of King **Henry VIII**. His father Elias was also a known **Nonconformist** with Baptist sympathies, which was enough to prevent Newcomen from receiving a university education in the years following the **Restoration**. Newcomen himself preached often in Baptist churches and so should not be confused with another Thomas Newcomen who was an **Anglican** minister at Colchester earlier in the 17th century. Newcomen considered his primary trade to be that of an "ironmonger," and in his work as a smith around Cornwall and Devon, he became aware of the difficulty and expense of removing water from mines. With the help of Thomas Savery and John Calley, another Baptist, Newcomen developed the first successful atmospheric steam engine near the town of Dudley in 1712, which was 53 years before the more famous steam engine of the Scotsman James Watt. Newcomen's innovation was the injection of cold water directly into the engine's cylinder to condense the steam, and its effect was to enable mines to be drained to greater depths for easier access to their natural resources. Because of his invention, Newcomen is one of the important early figures of modern industrialization. *See also* SCIENCE.

NONCONFORMITY. Nonconformity was that expression of Puritanism whose advocates were often known as **dissenters** and who agitated for thoroughgoing liturgical reforms in the Church of England. Nonconformists did not always become **Separatists** who pursued their religion outside the state church, but they did so increasingly over the course of the 17th century. At first, during the reign of King **Edward VI**, early Nonconformists were typically distinguished by their refusal to comply with what they believed to be papal superstitions, such as wearing **vestments**, reading from the Apocrypha in **worship**, observing saints' feast days, signing the cross during **baptism**, kneeling during the **Lord's Supper**, and exchanging rings during **marriage**. Some of the early Nonconformists were **John Rogers** and **John Hooper**, both of whom were executed by order of Queen **Mary I**. The **archbishops of Canterbury** under Queen **Elizabeth I**, Matthew Parker and John Whitgift, sought to repress Nonconformists, who by that time were often critical of the whole Episcopal church structure and so were considered schismatics. **Emmanuel College** at **Cambridge** became an early hotbed of Nonconformist sentiment. After the failed attempt to persuade King **James I** to support further Protestant reforms at the **Hampton Court Conference**, some Puritans became increasingly willing to convert their Nonconformity into Separatist groups, such as the **Baptists** and the **Quakers**. Many of these groups eventually fled to **Holland** or New England to start their own congregations.

Radical Separatists like the **Fifth Monarchists** and the **Levellers** played a significant role in the **New Model Army**'s defeat of King **Charles I** during the **English Civil Wars**, but many of them found it difficult to sustain their original fervor during the **Interregnum** and so petered out. When King **Charles II** reached a settlement with **Parliament** to resume the Stuart dynasty, he issued the **Declaration of Breda** as a promise to tolerate the **preaching** of Nonconformist ministers. In actuality this did not occur, as the **Act of Uniformity** and the **Conventicle Act**, among other royal declarations, severely curtailed Nonconformist activities. **Presbyterians** and **Independents** alike, such as **Thomas Manton**, **Richard Baxter**, and **John Owen**, lobbied for the king to realize the good citizenship of Nonconformists, but to little avail. **John Bunyan**, for instance, was imprisoned in Bedford from 1660–72 for preaching without a license, and many Quakers were also jailed. In 1672, the king issued an indulgence that allowed for Nonconformists to apply for preaching licenses, and Bunyan and many others did so despite their lingering skepticism of the king's motives since the conciliatory gesture extended to Roman **Catholics** as well. During a brief renewal of prosecution against Nonconformists around 1676–78, groups of affected pastors issued defenses of their loyalty such as *The Peaceable Design; or, an Account of the Nonconformist Meetings* and *Separation* *no Schism.* King **James II** also courted Nonconformists' favor to widen opportunities for his fellow Catholics. The Act of Toleration of 1689 at last legally recognized Nonconformity, following the coronation of William and Mary.

NON-SEPARATISTS. During the Tudor dynasty, the Puritans who agitated for an increased pace of Protestant reform within the Church of England were Non-Separatists—that is, they had no ultimate desire to separate from the church but wished to purify it from the inside. After the **Hampton Court Conference** of 1604 at the beginning of the reign of King **James I**, however, an increasing number of Puritans expressed their disagreements with the state church by forming Separatist congregations and even new denominations, such as the **Baptists**, **Quakers**, and other **dissenters**. Of all Puritan groups to arise during the 17th century, the one that remained Non-Separatist the longest was **Presbyterianism**, whose leaders retained hope for realigning the national church according to their preferred polity. After the **Restoration**, however, even the **Presbyterians** became **Separatists**, and their hope for internal change within the Church of England died.

NORTON, JOHN (1606–1663). English and American Puritan preacher. Norton was born at Storford of Hertfordshire and pursued a theological education at Peter-house, **Cambridge**. He then became curate back at Storford, where he came under the influence of the preacher Jeremiah Dyke. Norton's own **preaching** was punctuated by emphases on faith, repentance, and holiness, and **William Kiffin** was one of the notable figures who claimed his preaching as a significant personal influence. Norton appeared content to remain in his own hometown, having rejected an offer from **Richard Sibbes** to become a **fellow** at **Cambridge** while agreeing to become domestic chaplain to Sir William Marsham, but the hostility of Archbishop **William Laud** toward Puritans drove Norton and **Thomas Shepard** to take the same ship bound for New England in 1635. Upon arrival, Norton was appointed the pastor at Ipswich, Massachusetts, and in 1648, he joined in the drafting of the **Cambridge Platform**. Norton remained at Ipswich until succeeding **John Cotton** as the pastor in Boston upon Cotton's death in 1652. Norton and Cotton had been close friends for a number of years, and Cotton had written the preface to Norton's *The Orthodox Evangelist* (1654). Norton wrote several other books in defense of Puritan orthodoxy, including the anti-**antinomian** *Responsio ad Gal. Appollonium* (1648), which was the first book written in Latin in America, the anti-**Socinian** *A Discussion of That Great Point in Divinity, the Sufferings of Christ* (1653), and the anti-**Quaker** *The Heart of N-England Rent at the Blasphemies of the Present Generation* (1660). It was soon after the publication of this last book that Norton and Simon Bradstreet returned to England to ask the newly crowned King **Charles II** to continue to recognize **Massachusetts Bay Colony** as a loyal colony. Norton was successful and returned to Boston in 1661, but he died suddenly only two years later. **Richard Mather** preached his eulogy.

NYE, PHILIP (1596–1672). English **Congregationalist** minister. After earning the M.A. degree at Magdalen Hall, **Oxford**, Nye served as curate of St. Michael's Church in Cornhill from 1630 to 1633. When he then relocated to **Holland** in order to flee the anti-Puritan policies of **Archbishop of Canterbury William Laud**, he met **Jeremiah Burroughs** and **Thomas Goodwin** and developed a strident preference for **Independency** that marked the rest of his career. Nye and the others returned to England about 1640 at the beginning of the **Long Parliament**. His first **preaching** post was at Kimbolton in Huntingdonshire, arranged by Lord Montagu of Kimbolton, who was the future Earl of Manchester and a personal friend of fellow Independent **Oliver Cromwell**. With Cromwell's support, Nye became one of the chief Independent leaders during the **English Civil Wars** and **Protectorate**. He joined **Stephen Marshall**'s expedition to gain Scottish support for **Parliament** in 1643 and began preaching at the rectory of Acton in the same year. He was also one of the five **dissenters** (along with Burroughs, Goodwin, **William Bridge**, and **Sidrach Simpson**) whose *Apologetical Narration* defended the Reformed orthodoxy of the **Independents** at the **Westminster Assembly**. He became one of Cromwell's **triers** of ministers in 1652 and received appointment from Cromwell to co-write (with Goodwin, Bridge, **John Owen**, **Joseph Caryl**, and **William Greenhill**) the **Savoy Declaration** of 1658.

Because Nye came increasingly to accuse **Presbyterians** of opposing **religious liberty**, they, in turn, ensured that his national influence died when Cromwell did. Nye was ejected from preaching at St. Bartholomew, Exchange, London, in 1660, and he spent his remaining years preaching for **conventicles**. His historical account of **Nonconformity** perished in the London fire of 1666, but surviving works by Nye include *Exhortation to Take the Solemn League and Covenant*, *Beams of Former Light, Discovering How Evil It Is to Impose Doubtful and Disputable Forms or Practices upon Ministers*, and *Vindication of Dissenters, Proving Their Congregations not Inconsistent with the King's Supremacy*. Nye also helped to publish sermons by **Richard Sibbes**, **Thomas Hooker**, and **John Cotton**. *See also* TRIERS.

– O –

OAKES, URIAN (1631–1681). English and American Puritan preacher and educator. Oakes was born in England but came with his family to America at an early age. He graduated from **Harvard College** in 1649 and five years later returned to his native country to serve as a private chaplain to wealthy patrons. After the **Act of Uniformity** of 1662, followed within a few years by serious personal illness and the death of his wife, Oakes was ready to return to America, and he accepted the pastorate of the **Congregationalist** church in Cambridge, Massachusetts, in 1671. In that capacity, he preached and published the jeremiad sermons upon which his literary reputation rests, including "New-England Pleaded With, and Pressed to Consider the Things Which Concern Her Peace" (1673), "The Unconquerable, All-Conquering & More-Than-Conquering Souldier" (1674), the lengthy poem "Elegie Upon the Death of the Reverend Mr. **Thomas Shepard**" (1677), and "The Soveraign Efficacy of Divine **Providence**" (1682). While serving the Cambridge church, Oakes simultaneously served as the fourth president of Harvard, first on an acting basis from 1675–79 and then full-time from 1680 until his death the following year.

ORDINATION. Disputes over the procedure and validity of ministerial ordination began in England during the reign of Queen **Elizabeth I**. Puritans who had received ordination from **Presbyterians** elsewhere in Europe began having their ordinations challenged by English church authorities. Ordination was not a **sacrament** in the Church of England as it was in Roman **Catholicism**, but it nonetheless had a very important ceremonial character as prescribed in the *Book of Common Prayer*. A prolonged controversy broke out between **Anglican** bishops like **Joseph Hall** of Exeter, who asserted that only they had the right to bestow ordination, and Presbyterian leaders, such as the five co-authors known collectively as **Smectymnuus**, who countered that bishops and elders were equivalent terms in the New Testament. The Presbyterians further argued that elders could ordain ministers without the presence of bishops. A case in point of someone personally affected by the controversy was **William Whittingham**, whom the Archbishop of York, Edwin Sandys, regularly tried for having only a Genevan ordination that was inadequate for **preaching** in England.

During the **Westminster Assembly**, the Presbyterian majority produced a Directory for public **worship** that gave instructions for ordination. The candidate was to apply for ordination, subscribe to the **Solemn League and Covenant**, receive examination in doctrine and learning, and give a public testimonial. Once accepted by one's local presbytery, the person would participate in an ordination ceremony that included a day of fasting, a **sermon**, the laying on of hands from attending elders, and various prayers and Psalms. Westminster did not question the validity of ordinations performed in the Church of England before its convocation. The minority of **Independents** at Westminster still insisted that each congregation retained a right to ordain its own minister, and, moreover, that a person should not receive ordination until offered a pastorate by a local church's membership. Many **Separatists** appear not to have had formal ordination services for their ministers at all. Following the **Restoration** and the reinstitution of the *Book of Common Prayer* in the state church, a new Ordinal in 1662 denied that all ministerial offices are equal and reemphasized that only the imposition of a bishop's hands could make an ordination legitimate.

OWEN, JOHN (1616–1683). English **Congregationalist** minister and Puritan theologian. Owen was born in Stadhampton, Oxfordshire, and received his formal education at Queen's College, **Oxford**, earning his B.A. in 1632 and M.A. in 1635. Owen received **ordination** in the Church of England while at Oxford, but he left it in 1637 over dissatisfaction with the leadership of **Archbishop of Canterbury William Laud**. After writing his first major work, *Display of Arminianism*, in 1642, Owen became for a year the pastor of a **Presbyterian** church in Fordham, Essex. Yet after reading a **sermon** by **John Cotton**, Owen rejected Presbyterian no less than Episcopalian polity and committed himself to Congregationalist principles of church government. As a leading voice of the **Independent** branch of Puritanism, he caught the attention of Lieutenant General **Oliver Cromwell**, who made him chaplain to the troops during campaigns in Ireland and Scotland from 1649 to 1651. Cromwell also named Owen to succeed the Presbyterian **Edward Reynolds** as the dean of Christ Church in 1651 and vice-chancellor of England in 1652. Owen's alma mater then conferred the D.D. degree upon him in 1653. The Cromwellian **Protectorate** was a productive period for Owen, as he preached regularly before **Parliament** and published theological writings that defended Calvinist notions of divine sovereignty and limited atonement. These included *The Doctrine of the Saint's Perseverance* (1654), *Vindiciae Evangelicae* (1655), and *On the Mortification of Sin* (1656).

Yet King **James I**'s warning of "No bishop, no king" was certainly prophetic of Owen, whose advocacy of Independency in church government—for which his inspiration of the **Savoy Declaration** (1658) may be the greatest testimony—also influenced his denunciation of the monarchy in national politics. Not surprisingly, then, upon the **Restoration** of King **Charles II** in 1660, Royalists saw to it that Owen lost all his posts. He then preached for small Congregationalist churches in London until his death, even turning down the presidency of **Harvard College** to do so. He remained ecumenical in his associations, however, maintaining friendships with Episcopalians, Presbyterians, and **Nonconformists** of Puritan persuasion. He even helped to attain the release of his friend **John Bunyan** from Bedford jail in 1672. Owen's later writings included *A Primer for Children*

(1660), the four-volume *Exposition of the Epistle to the Hebrews* (1668–1684), *Discourse on the Holy Spirit* (1674), *Christology* (1679), *Vindication of the Nonconformists* (1680), and *True Nature of a Gospel Church* (1689). A complete set of Owen's works first appeared in 23 volumes in 1820 under the editorship of William Orme. William Goold edited a revised set of 24 volumes in 1850. *See also* SAINT BARTHOLOMEW'S DAY; SAVOY DECLARATION; TRIERS.

OXFORD. *See* OXFORD UNIVERSITY.

OXFORD PARLIAMENT. *See* PARLIAMENT.

OXFORD UNIVERSITY. Oxford University is the oldest university in the English-speaking world, operating at least by the year 1096. Oxford's various colleges are individually responsible for admitting students and overseeing their tutoring, while the university as a whole dictates the content of its colleges' courses and awards degrees. In the 14th century, Oxford became a center of religious controversy when John Wyclif, the Master of Balliol College, produced an English version of the **Bible** and became outspoken in his criticisms of the papacy. During the reign of King **Edward VI** in 1548, **Archbishop of Canterbury Thomas Cranmer** brought the renowned Reformed theologian Peter Martyr Vermigli to Oxford as regius professor of divinity in the hopes of making it a center of Protestant learning. In a symbolic choice aimed at silencing Cranmer's hope, Queen **Mary I** selected Balliol College as the site for Cranmer's execution in 1556, the year after **Nicholas Ridley** and **Hugh Latimer** had also died there. Nonetheless, a number of prominent Puritans later earned their degrees from Oxford colleges, a partial list of which includes New College (**William Twisse, William Stoughton**), Wadham (**Thomas Manton**), Brasen-nose (**Richard Mather, John Foxe**), Queen's (**Thomas Middleton, John Owen**), Magdalen (**Philip Nye, Obadiah Sedgwick, Thomas Sparke, William Waller**), Christ Church (**Thomas Vincent, Nathaniel Vincent**), Trinity (**Francis Roberts**), and St. Catherine's (**William Spurstowe**).

However, Oxford became a seat of Royalist activity during the **English Civil Wars**, even after **Parliament** and King **Charles I** failed to agree to the proposed Treaty of Oxford in 1642. In 1644, Charles invited all sympathetic members of the **Long Parliament** to join him at Oxford in Christ Church Hall. Only about one-third accepted the invitation, and records of the two-year **Oxford Parliament** have not survived. Once the Long Parliament gained the upper hand in the conflict with the king and overtook the city of Oxford, it authorized seven preachers in 1646 and 10 "visitors" in 1647 to police compliance at the university with the **Presbyterians' Solemn League and Covenant**. These representatives ousted the dean and seven canons of Christ Church in 1648, but those who were displaced regained their posts after the **Restoration**.

– P –

PARKER, HENRY (1604-1652). English political theorist. Born into a prominent family in Sussex, Parker trained as a lawyer at **Oxford**. His first important writing, *The Case of Shipmony* (1640), sounded the recurrent theme of his works, which was that government exists solely for the welfare of the people. With *Discourse Concerning Puritans* (1641), written under the pseudonym Philus Adelphus, Parker accused English prelates of interfering with that welfare, and in *Observations upon Some of his Majesties Late Answers and Expresses* (1642), he heightened his rhetoric against the king. Parker did not consider himself to be a Puritan if that meant being a **Precisian** in theological matters, but he would accept the term if coming from Royalists, whom he believed in many cases to be outright irreligious. Parker came to believe that only **Parliament** truly represented the voice of the people and that its representation and governance of them should continue without interference from the crown. Although his advocacy of Parliamentary absolutism appealed more to natural law rather than legal precedents as in the case of the pamphleteer **William Prynne**, Parker's writings hardly less than Prynne's helped Parliament to justify its pursuit of outright victory over the king in the **English Civil Wars**.

PARKER, ROBERT (1564–1614). English Puritan preacher. Little is known of Parker's upbringing and education. He became the rector of North Benflete, Essex, in 1571, and then the rector of West Henningfield, Essex, in 1572. From there, he moved on to Dedham, Essex, where he was the pastor prior to John Rogers (not the Marian martyr). In Parker's first major writing, *De descensu Christi ad Infernos* (1598), he argued that Jesus Christ did not mingle with the doomed souls of Hell between his death and resurrection. By order of John Aylmer, the Bishop of London, Parker was suspended from his pastorate for refusing compliance with **Whitgift's Articles**. Specifically, Parker refused to don the **surplice** and make the sign of the cross, which he explained with the support of **William Ames** in *A Scholasticall Discourse Against Symbolizing with Antichrist in Ceremonies* (1607). However, Parker continued his **preaching** for a **Separatist** congregation in Wilton, Wiltshire. When Aylmer's successor Richard Bancroft pursued Parker, he fled to **Holland**. He moved around between Amsterdam and Leyden, where he met **Henry Jacob**, before settling in as the preacher of Doesburg. Although Parker had become a **Nonconformist**, he still preferred a system of church government closer to **Presbyterianism** than the complete autonomy argued by Jacob.

Parker's son Thomas Parker (1595–1677) also had a varied and fruitful career as a Puritan minister. After studying with **James Ussher** at Dublin, Thomas went to Leyden as well and befriended Ames. He then returned to Newbury, Berkshire, in England as the assistant to **William Twisse**. In 1634, he migrated to Ipswich, Massachusetts, and ended up as the Presbyterian pastor in the town of Newbury.

PARLIAMENT. The Parliament of England originated in the 13th century and is bicameral in nature, composed of a House of Lords and a House of Commons. These two legislative houses and the monarch form the seat of English constitutional government. Membership in the House of Lords is by hereditary nobility, while membership in the House of Commons is by election. During the 16th century, Parliament was greatly inferior in power to the monarch, who would summon the two Houses mostly for the purpose of approving new taxes. During the early 17th century, however, Parliamentarians disgruntled by the slow pace of religious reform began to assert their prerogative to convene and dismiss themselves and to cooperate with the monarch in executive decisions through a symbiosis described as "King-in-Parliament." Several conventions of Parliament, normally consisting of about 500 members, figured prominently in the history of the Puritan era; they have become known by the following respective labels.

Barebones Parliament. The Barebones Parliament was one of the manifestations of the **Long Parliament**, which met off and on from 1640–60. **Oliver Cromwell**, the general of the **New Model Army**, personally secured appointment for its 140 members. The tenure of the Barebones Parliament was only from 4 July–12 December 1653, and it is also known as the Little Parliament or the Nominated Parliament. The name "Barebones" came from one of this Parliament's leaders, a leather salesman named **Praise God Barebones**. Perhaps the chief legacy of the brief Barebones Parliament, although unpopular at the time, was the legalization of civil **marriage**. Following the last session of the Barebones Parliament, Cromwell governed England without Parliament's help as the lord protector until his death in 1658.

Cavalier Parliament. The Cavalier Parliament met from May 1661–January 1679. It offered little resistance to the policies of King **Charles II**, including the various components of the **Clarendon Code** that supported the suppression of **dissenters**.

Convention Parliament. The Convention Parliament assembled on 25 April 1660, the first Parliament to follow the **Long Parliament**. It included the House of Lords, which had been essentially defunct since the Commons' takeover of government in 1649. It agreed to the **Declaration of Breda** and welcomed King **Charles II** as the new king of England on 29 May. As a gesture of goodwill following the **Restoration**, it also repealed all laws that had been passed by previous Parliaments without royal assent. The Convention Parliament met for the last time on 29 December 1660. A second Convention Parliament convened in 1689 to oversee the succession of power from King **James II** to William and Mary.

Long Parliament. The Long Parliament convened on 3 November 1640, with **John Pym** as one of its leading spokesmen. Though not without some significant changes in its makeup from time to time, it remained seated for nearly 20 years. One of its first acts was to recall **William Prynne**, **Henry Burton**, and **John Bastwick** from their respective imprisonments. It assumed for itself increasing executive powers and often enacted its decisions without the consent of King **Charles I**. In 1641, the Parliament issued a statement of grievances against the king known as the **Grand Remonstrance**. In the same year it abolished the king's **Star Chamber** and began raising an army under the command of the **Earl of Essex** in order to secure its rule. The Long Parliament also abolished **prelacy**, forbade the wearing of **vestments**, impeached **Archbishop of Canterbury William Laud**, burned the *Book of Sports*, and passed **Sabbatarian** laws. It further declared that only Parliament could dissolve itself, which explains why it could endure as long as it did.

The Long Parliament waged the **English Civil Wars** that ended in the regicide of Charles I. Many of its original members had ambitions for a **Presbyterian** national church, and this was the motive behind calling the **Westminster Assembly** and signing the **Solemn League and Covenant** in 1643. But **Pride's Purge** in 1648 reduced the number of influential **Presbyterians** in Parliament and turned the balance of political power to Oliver Cromwell and the **Independent** leadership of the **New Model Army**. The pruned remainder of the Long Parliament after Pride's Purge became known as the **Rump Parliament**; it consisted only of Commons because the House of Lords did not meet at all from 1649–60. The Rump was in power when King Charles was executed. In 1653, Cromwell sent home the 500 members of the Rump and replaced them with 140 persons, mostly Independents, of his own choosing. This remnant of the long parliament was known as the **Barebones Parliament**; Cromwell dismissed it too at the end of 1653 and governed alone as lord protector of England. The members of the Rump Parliament briefly retook office in January 1659 during the flailing **Protectorate** of Cromwell's son Richard. On 16 March 1660, they finally agreed to dismiss themselves, thus ending the Long Parliament and preparing the way for the Convention Parliament, which reached terms with Charles II for the **Restoration**.

Oxford Parliament. After the convocation of what became the Long Parliament late in 1640, and its resultant maneuvers to check the autocratic power of the crown, King Charles I gathered a rival Parliament of Royalists at Oxford from January 1644–March 1645.

Most attendees eventually forsook the king's cause and returned to London. All records of the Oxford Parliament were burned in 1646.

Protectorate Parliament. Succeeding the Barebones Parliament of 1653 and preceding the recall of the Rump Parliament in 1659, three additional sessions of Parliament met during the years of the Protectorate. Oliver Cromwell called the first of these under the provisions of the Instrument of Government, and it met from September 1654 to January 1655. For the first time, representatives from Scotland and Ireland held seats in Parliament. However, this session was resentful of Cromwell's growing power and did not pass any of the 84 bills he proposed. In September 1656, the major generals of the New Model Army persuaded Cromwell to reconvene the Protectorate Parliament in order to raise money for fighting the Anglo–Spanish War. This session met until June 1657 and again in the first two months of 1658, with perhaps its most famous action being the mutilation of the Quaker James Nayler for riding into Bristol on a donkey and claiming to be Christ. The Protectorate Parliament met for a third time, from January to April 1659, to recognize the Protectorate of Richard Cromwell. Yet the younger Cromwell could not control a resurgent tide of royalist nostalgia, and, under pressure, he dissolved the final Protectorate Parliament and recalled the Rump Parliament.

Rump Parliament. The Rump Parliament was originally the remainder of the Long Parliament that survived Pride's Purge of leading Presbyterians in December 1648. It was seated when King Charles I was executed in January 1649. In 1653, Oliver Cromwell dismissed the majority of the Rump Parliament's members and replaced them with persons of his own choosing in the Barebones Parliament. The full Rump Parliament met again in 1659 during the final days of Richard Cromwell's rule. Its self-dismissal in 1660 simultaneously brought an end to the Long Parliament and prepared the way for the Restoration of King Charles II.

Short Parliament. King Charles I summoned the Short Parliament in April 1640 to gain financial support for the **Bishops' Wars**. Unsuccessful in accomplishing his purpose, Charles dismissed this Parliament after only a month on 5 May.

PENN, WILLIAM (1644–1718). English **Quaker** and founder of Pennsylvania. Penn was born in London, the son of Sir William Penn, the admiral who took Jamaica from the Dutch in 1635, and Margaret van der Schuren Penn. Penn's father served in the Parliamentary navy during the **English Civil Wars** and after their conclusion moved his family to Wanstead, Essex, where the younger Penn studied at the Chigwell School. Because Admiral Penn became critical of **Oliver Cromwell**, however, he decided to relocate again to Macroom Castle, near Cork, in Ireland. The Penn family then came back to London after the **Restoration** of King **Charles II**, who reciprocated the admiral's backing by supporting his son's entrance into Christ Church, **Oxford**. Yet the younger William did not remain a student at Oxford for long, being ejected for **Nonconformity**. He traveled for a time in France, studying at the Protestant academy at Saumur, before returning to London yet again in 1665 to study law at **Lincoln's Inn**. Penn's itinerant life found its spiritual center the following year when the plague of London drove him back to Cork, and he heard a **sermon** by the Quaker Thomas Loe. Immediately, Penn began writing in defense of the Quakers' exaltation of each individual's "inner light" over theological orthodoxy, even the doctrines of the Trinity and the substitutionary atonement of Christ. After writing *Truth Exalted* and *The Sandy Foundation Shaken* in 1668, Penn received imprisonment in the Tower of London, but undaunted he wrote *No Cross, No Crown* in 1669 and *The Great Case of Liberty of* **Conscience** in 1670. He was acquitted at trial that same year.

After starting married life with Gulielma Springett in 1672, Penn devoted his energies to purchasing land in America, where Quakers could **worship** freely. By 1677, Penn had become a trustee of West New Jersey, and in 1681, he purchased East New Jersey with the help of other Quakers. In that same year, he settled a debt that the king owed his father by obtaining a patent for the founding of Pennsylvania, "Penn's Woods." In 1682, Penn came to his new property to start a capital city at Philadelphia and draft a frame of government. Penn's constitution for the new colony permitted freedom of religion to all monotheists and even native Indians living in his "Holy Experiment," and he worked hard to encourage Europeans to come there to trade. After spending two years in the territory he created, Penn returned to England in 1684 to support King **James II**'s plan for a broad religious **toleration** in England that would encompass both **dissenters** and Roman **Catholics**. He expressed such views in writings like *Good Advice to the Church of England, Roman Catholic and Protestant Dissenter* and *A Perswasive to Moderation to Dissenting Christians*.

Ironically, although the successors to James II, William and Mary, did issue the **Act of Toleration** in 1689, Penn's association with James led to his imprisonment and two-year deprivation as the governor of Pennsylvania in 1692. Still, his literary output continued unabated, for works like *An Essay towards the Present and Future Peace of Europe*, *Primitive Christianity*, and *Some Fruits of Solitude* appeared over the remainder of that decade. He also married his second wife, Hannah Callowhill, in 1696. Penn came back to America in 1699 but stayed only until 1701, for concern that Pennsylvania might be made a colony of the crown precipitated his return to England. Penn moved from town to town over the next several years, even spending some time in debtor's prison. After a series of strokes in 1712, Penn was no longer the same intellectual who defended **religious liberty** and wrote more than 100 pamphlets. Upon his death in 1718, he received burial in the town of Jordans.

PEQUOT WAR. Puritans in America frequently had strained relations with the Native American Indians since their exotic appearance and unfamiliar customs made some Englishmen wonder if they were witches or possibly even demons. Indian raids beginning in the 1620s heightened the settlers' suspicions even further. The Pequots, one of the Algonquin tribes, had gained control of much of the Connecticut coastline and so were a major concern for the colonists. In 1634, leaders from both sides met for negotiations in Massachusetts, but Dutch settlers murdered the Pequot chief Tatobem. The Pequots then began killing colonists outside Saybrook and Wethersfield, Connecticut. John Mason of Connecticut and John Underhill of Massachusetts gained the support of Pequot enemies, the Mohegan and Narragansett tribes, in launching retaliation. In May and June 1637, Mason burned the Pequots' main village near present-day Groton, Connecticut, sold some captives into slavery, and forced the survivors to agree to their own disbandment as a tribe. Mason and Underhill later published accounts of the conflict. Although most colonists justified the Pequot

War as a proper application of Old Testament precedents for confronting God's enemies, the reverend **Thomas Shepard** of Cambridge, Massachusetts, feared that the war more likely signified God's judgment upon the New Englanders than upon the Pequots. *See also* KING PHILIP'S WAR.

PERKINS, WILLIAM (1558–1602). English Puritan theologian and preacher. Perkins was born in Marston Jabbet, Warwickshire, and in 1581 graduated from Christ's College, **Cambridge**. Like **Hugh Peters** after him, Perkins was for a time in his student days known for his carousing, but when he overheard a village woman using him as a cautionary illustration to improve her son's morals, he became deeply reflective upon his acts of **sin** and came to believe that unmerited grace alone could be his redemption. Thus did Perkins begin in all his teaching and **preaching** to apply a **Calvinist** emphasis on divine sovereignty to the care of individual souls, employing the aid of Ramist logic and a Reformed reading of **Scripture**. Perkins began his formal ministry by preaching to prisoners in the Cambridge jail, but when his fervent style attracted many other persons from the town, he came to the attention of St. Andrew's Church, Cambridge, and in 1584, he agreed to become its **lecturer**. Perkins held this position for the rest of his life, simultaneously serving from 1584–95 as a **fellow** of Christ's College. He did not neglect, however, to continue his preaching to the prisoners on Sunday afternoons.

Perkins' life was only one year short of matching the exact reign of Queen **Elizabeth I**, and by his preaching and teaching at **Cambridge**, he gained the reputation of being the quintessential **Non-Separatist** Elizabethan Puritan. His *A Golden Chaine* (1590) was a flow chart whose circles and variably colored lines connected scriptural terms about **salvation** in a catechetical manner that encouraged readers to locate themselves within God's self-glorifying eternal plan. Perkins also penned commentaries on Matthew 5–7, Galatians, Jude, and Hebrews 11, as well as polemical writings against Roman **Catholicism**, astrology, and **witchcraft**. He also wrote a preaching manual called *The Arte of Prophesying* (1590), devotions on the Apostle's Creed and Lord's Prayer, and theological works, such as *Manner and Order of* **Predestination**, *A Discourse of* **Conscience**, and *Whole Treatise of Cases of Conscience*.

The latter two volumes, both published posthumously in 1606, describe a process of Christian conversion that begins with seeing oneself as justly condemned before God's law but finally yields to the forensic and salvific **justification** of Christ. They are benchmarks for the many Puritan reflections on **conscience** that appeared throughout the 17th century, from **William Ames'** two books on *Conscience* to **John Bunyan**'s *Grace Abounding to the Chief of Sinners*. Perkins composed many of his works originally in Latin, and his students oversaw their translation into English, French, Dutch, and Spanish. His collected works first appeared in English translation in the three-volume set, *The Works of William Perkins* (1616–18). Perkins' fame also spread through the influence he had on Ames, his former student at **Cambridge**, and **John Cotton**, who attributed his conversion to Perkins' preaching.

PETERS, HUGH (1599–1660). English Puritan preacher. Peters was born at Fowey in Cornwall, in the southwest part of England. His father Thomas was a merchant of Dutch Reformed background, and his mother Martha came from the wealthy Treffey family. Peters entered **Cambridge** at age 14, attending first Jesus College and then Trinity College. At first, he lived as a libertine and did not follow in the direction of Puritanism trod by fellow student **Thomas Goodwin**, but after hearing **preaching** from **Richard Sibbes**, **John Davenport**, and **Thomas Hooker**, Peters began to mend his ways. In 1623, the year following Peters' completion of an M.A. degree, Bishop George Montaigne of London admitted Peters to holy orders. Peters successively became the curator of Holy Trinity Church in Rayleigh, Essex, and the preacher of St. Sepulchre's Church, London.

Peters developed into a Puritan **Nonconformist** and built a numerically successful ministry upon a theatrical preaching style that some severely scorned as buffoonery and a holdover of his profligate youth. In 1625, his marriage to the widow Elizabeth Reade also made Peters the stepfather of the wife of John Winthrop Jr. The following year, Peters' rising ministerial career was derailed when **Anglican William Laud** authorized his censure and brief imprisonment for praying at Christ Church that Queen Henrietta Maria, the wife of King **Charles I**, might renounce her **Catholicism**. Peters then fled to **Holland**, where he met Gustavus Adolphus and formed an **Independent** congregation in Rotterdam that for a time also had **William Ames** as one of its ministers. As Peters' anti-Catholicism increased during his six-year stay in Holland, so did his contacts with other important figures in early **Congregationalism**, including **William Bridge**, **Sidrach Simpson**, and Samuel Ward. In 1635, Peters followed the path of **John Robinson**'s **Separatist** group and left Holland for America, sailing on the same boat as his brothers William and Thomas, his son-in-law John Winthrop Jr., and **Henry Vane**. The family connection with Winthrop helped secure for Peters a personal assistantship (joining **Thomas Shepard** and **John Cotton**) to the elder **John Winthrop**, the governor of **Massachusetts Bay Colony**, and the pastorate of Salem, which **Roger Williams** had vacated. In 1637, Peters became an overseer (trustee) of **Harvard College** and participated in the expulsion of **Anne Hutchinson**, who had cast aspersions on his spirituality, from Massachusetts.

In 1643, Peters returned to England to plead for customs and excise relief for his colony, but he became caught up in the early events of the **English Civil Wars** and never returned. He soon began preaching not only for **Parliament** but also to soldiers under the commands of **Oliver Cromwell**, Sir **Thomas Fairfax**, and **Robert Rich**, the second Earl of Warwick. Peters so devoted himself to the cause of extirpating the king from his throne that he regularly returned to Parliament to give field reports. Following an expedition to Wales, he was even given the title of colonel and told to enlist military support. When Cromwell's wife declared Peters to be delinquent in that responsibility, Peters founded yet another Independent church to prove he had not been idle, and Cromwell himself always held Peters in high favor. Peters became chaplain to the Council of State in 1650, was involved in efforts to streamline English law in 1651, served like **Philip Nye** and **Stephen Marshall** as one of the **triers** of ministers in 1654, and preached to garrisons under the command of Colonel William Lockhart before the conflict with the Spanish at Dunkirk in 1658. Upon the **Restoration** of 1660, Peters was one of the first to be apprehended and sent to the Tower as an accused regicide.

Although the House of Commons had financially supported Peters, the House of Lords was again in ascendancy, and many did not appreciate Peters' outspoken style and rejection of a national church.

Peters pleaded not guilty to conspiring in King **Charles I**'s death, claiming in his defense that he had, in fact, personally advised Charles to resolve the national conflict peaceably, and further that he was not even present at Charles' execution as some had claimed. He also denied taking possession of some of Archbishop Laud's books after Laud was defrocked. Yet Peters was not indemnified, and within three days of his arrest, he was forced to witness the hanging and quartering of John Cook before he himself was executed at Charing Cross. The *Diary* of Samuel Pepys mentions a pamphlet published upon the occasion, entitled, "The Welsh Hubub, or the Unkennelling and Earthing of Hugh Peters that Crafty Fox." Also appearing in print before the end of 1660 were Peters' own final sermon in prison and some farewell advice to Elizabeth, his Salem-born daughter by his second wife Deliverance, called *A Dying Father's Last Legacy to an Only Child*.

PETITION OF RIGHT. As championed especially by Sir Edward Coke and **John Pym**, the Petition of Right of June 1628 was a declaration of **Parliament** that set forth the rights of English citizens in relationship to the crown. It invoked the Magna Carta as precedent. Specifically, the petition held that citizens had legal exemption from arbitrary arrest and imprisonment, taxation without Parliamentary ratification, enforced mustering of troops, and martial law. King **Charles I** agreed to accept the Petition of Right in exchange for additional subsidies from Parliament, yet he continued to tax and prosecute without its explicit approval. This hastened the onset of the **English Civil Wars**.

PHIPS, WILLIAM (1651–1695). Governor of Massachusetts. Phips was born at Woolwich, Maine, near the Kennebec River. His father helped to operate a trading post, specializing in guns and furs, for English settlers and Native American Indians. His mother remarried after his father died, and Phips was the youngest in a combined family of 26 children. Although Phips had no formal education, he learned the trade of ship carpentry and moved to Boston, where he met Captain Roger Spencer. Spencer helped advance Phips' career until Phips became a ship captain himself, mostly carrying goods between New England and the West Indies. Phips also married in 1673 to Mary Spencer Hull, the widow of Boston merchant John Hull. In 1687, Phips recovered a large amount of treasure from the shipwreck of a Spanish galleon, and, for giving one-tenth of the prize to England's King **James II**, Phips received a knighthood and the title of Sheriff of New England. Phips then returned to Massachusetts, where he led expeditions into Port Royal (in modern Nova Scotia) and Quebec in an attempt to acquire yet more loot.

In 1689, Phips received **baptism** from **Cotton Mather** in Boston's Second Church. Two years later, he joined **Increase Mather**, the president of **Harvard College**, in petitioning King William III for a new Massachusetts charter. The king not only granted the petition but made Phips the governor of the colony. When Phips arrived to take office in May 1692, the stir over accusations of **witchcraft** was beginning to grow in the town of Salem. Phips called for the Court of Oyer and Terminer to try the cases and appointed **William Stoughton**, a man of no legal training, as the chief justice. Phips permitted the use of spectral evidence in the trials, but while on a trip back to Maine, his own wife Mary was also accused of witchery. When Phips returned, he censured Stoughton's handling of the trials, forbade spectral evidence, and prohibited further cases in October 1692. He freed 49 of the 52 persons who had been imprisoned, and he manumitted the other three in May 1693. Later that year, he was recalled to England by the king for criticisms of his administration and failure to capture certain French and Indian territories. He died while still awaiting his hearing in 1695. His first biography was that of Cotton Mather, *Pietas in Patriam: Life of His Excellency Sir William Phips*.

PILGRIMS. The Pilgrims who came to America aboard the *Mayflower* in 1620 were mostly **Separatists** fleeing England for **religious liberty**. **William Brewster**, one of the leaders of the voyage, had originally been part of Richard Clifton's congregation in Scrooby, Nottinghamshire. In 1608, part of this church moved to Amsterdam, **Holland**. The following year, the group settled in Leyden under the leadership of **John Robinson**. In 1617, several members of the Robinson church secured assistance from London businessmen to gain passage to America. A group of 37 persons arrived at Southampton, England, aboard the *Speedwell*; they eventually joined with 65 others when the 180-ton *Mayflower* sailed out of Plymouth on 16 September 1620. Some few of these were not Separatists but representatives of the London Company, known to the rest as "strangers," who were overseeing their investment. John Carver, a deacon in Robinson's church, read a farewell notice from Robinson, who died before being able to cross the Atlantic Ocean himself. The ship dropped anchor at Provincetown on 19 November, but not having the legal papers to settle there, Captain Christopher Jones ordered the crew on the move again. On 21 December, the ship settled on Plymouth Harbor, and the complement disembarked on 26 December. The immigrants disregarded their charter and constituted their own tiny government under the **Mayflower Compact**, under the direction of Carver. Besides Carver and Brewster, the professional soldier Myles Standish and **William Bradford**, who coined the term "Pilgrims," offered leadership. The Pilgrims survived in part through befriending Native American Indians, such as Squanto, who taught them how to grow corn and other vegetables.

POOLE, MATTHEW (1624–1679). English **Presbyterian** scholar. Born in York and having attained an M.A. degree at **Emmanuel College, Cambridge,** Poole was named the rector of St. Michel le Querne in London in 1649. After the **Act of Uniformity** in 1662, however, this Westminster divine and papal critic fled to Amsterdam, **Holland,** where he spent the remainder of his life among fellow English Reformed refugees. Over the years 1669–1676, his Latin study of 150 biblical critics, entitled *Synopsis criticorum biblicorum*, appeared in five volumes. Poole was working on an English equivalent when he died in 1679, so some of his friends completed the work he had left unfinished by using the *Synopsis* as a basis. The result was a two-volume set, *English Annotations on the Holy **Bible***, first published in 1683 and often reprinted since under the title *A Commentary on the Whole Bible.*

POPISH PLOT. The "Popish Plot" of 1678 was an alleged conspiracy by Roman **Catholics** in England to assassinate King **Charles II** so that his brother and heir James, the duke of York, might ascend to the throne more quickly. Titus Oates disseminated word of the plot after James' secretary Edward Coleman was found with incriminating papers and a prosperous Protestant merchant in London, Edmundbury Godfrey, was found murdered. Rumor circulated that Pope Innocent XI was the mastermind of the conspiracy. Coleman was tried and executed by **Parliament** for treason, and soon afterward a number of Jesuits were put to death for abetting the plot. Parliament also passed a second **Test Act** in 1678 to outlaw the presence of any Catholics in public office. After several persons were acquitted of involvement in the plot in 1679, popular and political belief in its seriousness began to wane.

POWELL, VAVASOR (1617–1670). Welsh **Nonconformist** preacher. Powell was born at Knucklas, in Radnorshire, Wales; later, his enemies derided his parents for being an innkeeper and oatmeal dealer. Powell's uncle, the vicar of Clun, supported his studies at Jesus College, **Oxford**, but Powell moved to Clun himself as a schoolteacher without having finished his degree. He would twice marry. Powell was very intelligent and well versed in ancient languages. In 1640, he received holy orders, but he did not serve in the established church for long before becoming an itinerant preacher who was twice arrested for Nonconformity. He moved to London in 1642 but returned to Wales in 1646 as pastor in Newtown. In favor with **Oliver Cromwell** in the early 1650s, Powell was among those who oversaw the replacement of standing Welsh ministers with Puritans under the Act for the Propagation of the Gospel in Wales. Powell also founded more than 20 churches himself. It is possible that Powell came to a **Baptist** persuasion during this period of his life because he associated closely with **Calvinist** Baptist leaders like **William Kiffin** and **Hanserd Knollys** and even received rebaptism.

However, Powell's strong opposition to Cromwell's decision to become lord protector brought to him a significant turn of fortune. He believed that Cromwell became an abuser of power, little better than the recently executed King **Charles I**, and he probably wrote *A Word for God*, a Nonconformist manifesto of concerns addressed to Cromwell's close adviser **John Thurloe**. Also disappointed by the lack of outcry among Baptists, Powell joined a group of **Fifth Monarchists** who prayed for the imminent rule of King Jesus. For these political and religious views, Powell was imprisoned from 1653–54. Only three days after the **Restoration** in 1660, Powell was in prison again by order of King **Charles II**. He moved among various jails from 1660–67 and had only a brief manumission before spending his final days in the Fleet prison from 1668–70. Most of Powell's publications, such as *A Brief Narrative of the Former Propagation and Late Restoration of the Gospel in Wales*, *The Sufferer's Catechism*, and *The Bird in the Cage, Chirping* were written in prison. Published defenses of Powell like *Vavasoris Examen et Purgamen* and *The Life and Death of Mr Vavasor Powell* also remained popular for a while. Powell was buried in London's Nonconformist cemetery, **Bunhill Fields**.

PRAYER. Prayer was a vital aspect of individual Puritan devotions to God, but its role in corporate **worship** became highly debated. The bishops of the Church of England believed that approaching God properly demanded a carefully crafted litany, such as prescribed in the *Book of Common Prayer*. The first English Puritans believed the same and often requested permission to continue to use their familiar liturgy when visiting the Reformed cities of Europe. John Calvin's Geneva also used a book of worship, the *Forme and Prayers*, which cast considerable influence on **John Knox** and other **Presbyterians**. However, as Puritanism tended increasingly toward **Separatism** in Stuart England, the **Independents** and other groups began to assert that prescribed prayers were actually obstacles to the spontaneous movement of the Holy Spirit. The worship Directory of the **Westminster Assembly** reached a compromise between the Presbyterians and Independents, suggesting the kinds of prayers appropriate for worship but not the exact prescribed wording. The Westminster Confession explained, "Prayer with thanksgiving, being one special part of religious worship, is by God required of all men, and that it may be accepted, it is to be made in the name of the Son by the help of His Spirit, according to His will, with understanding, reverence, humility, fervency, faith, love and perseverance, and if vocal, in a known tongue." The Confession went on to specify against Roman **Catholic** practice that prayers were not to be offered for the dead.

After the **Restoration** and the reimposition of the *Book of Common Prayer* upon all English Christians, many **Nonconformists** like **John Bunyan** went to prison for refusing to abide by it. Even though not all Puritans approved of prescribed prayers in worship, they did tend to agree that instruction in prayer was always appropriate. Examples of prayer manuals include *A Practical Exposition of the Lord's Prayer* by **Thomas Manton**, *A Key of Heaven* by **Henry Scudder**, *Guide to Prayer* by **Isaac Watts**, and several short works by Bunyan himself. In America, prayer was particularly important for seeking God's favor and protection from all the uncertainties of living in the New World. In his historical account of the founding of Dedham, Massachusetts, for instance, John Allin hailed earnest prayers as the means by which God sealed the assurances of **Scripture** upon the hearts and minds of believers. Even as the Puritan establishment began to crack by the end of the 17th century, **Increase Mather** was still encouraging adults to nurture lives of prayer if they cared for their children's futures. *See also* PREACHING.

PREACHING. A favorite **Scripture** verse of the Puritans was Romans 10:17, which teaches that faith comes by hearing and hearing by the word of God. The exaltation of preaching therefore became a hallmark of most permutations of Puritanism, as distinguished from the greater emphasis in Roman **Catholicism** and the Church of England on the **sacrament** of the Eucharist. Preaching grew as an art form within the Church of England in the beginning of the 17th century with the learned and witty sermons of John Donne and Lancelot Andrewes, but the Puritans insisted upon a "plain style" easily understood by common people. They employed preaching manuals that enumerated the components of effective sermons: reading the biblical text, explaining its literal sense, showing its doctrinal significance, and applying it for daily Christian living. Several preaching manuals imported from Reformed cities on the continent became popular in England, such as *De formandis concionibus sacris* by Andreas Hyperius. However, no manual was more widely hailed than *The Arte of Prophesying* by England's own **William Perkins**. For Perkins, the sermon revealed God's will to human beings and at its best could simultaneously have expository, political, apologetic, and ethical purposes. Perkins also explained how sermons were the divine remedy for any **conscience** troubled by the recognition of one's unworthiness for **salvation** apart from unmerited grace. Puritans welcomed opportunities to preach in private audiences for the monarch so that they could advocate reform within the Church of England.

Leading **Anglicans**, such as **Archbishop of Canterbury William Laud**, on the other hand, thought that the Puritan love affair with the sermon stirred dissension both within the church and against the state.

The height of passion for hearing sermons was during the **Interregnum**. Puritan churches often had a high pulpit in their front center to emphasize the sermon's authority. Some wealthy officials hired personal chaplains to preach to their families, and **Oliver Cromwell** even appointed the **triers** to fill pastoral vacancies and ensure ministers' theological orthodoxy. The **Westminster Assembly**'s **worship** Directory of 1644 prescribed that sermons should proclaim the truth of God, based upon the scriptural text, for the edification of all hearers. Puritan preachers tended to preach series on books of the **Bible** or theological themes rather than a prescribed lectionary. **Thomas Manton** for instance preached nearly 200 sermons on Psalm 119 alone. Yet the preaching style of many Puritans would be unknown today were it not for the great interest in the 17th century for sermons in print. Among the more notable published Puritan preachers were **Richard Greenham, Henry Smith, William Gouge, Richard Sibbes, John Preston, Thomas Goodwin, John Owen, Richard Baxter, Matthew Henry, John Howe**, and **William Bates**. After the **Restoration**, the new king, **Charles II**, preferred moralistic and nontheological sermons that already prefigured for England the rise of Deism and its belief in an absentee God.

Puritanism in America was also predicated upon powerful preaching. Ships bearing Puritan colonists to America often featured multiple sermons, dating back to **John Winthrop**'s "A Model for Christian Charity" aboard the *Arbella* in 1630. Most solemn occasions in Massachusetts and Connecticut, such as election days and days of **prayer** and fasting, were marked by the kind of public sermons termed by historian Perry Miller as "jeremiads"—prophetic warnings against spiritual decline, girded with pleas for spiritual recovery. **John Cotton, Increase Mather**, and **Solomon Stoddard** were some of American Puritanism's more famous preachers. Although the preaching style of Stoddard's grandson **Jonathan Edwards** was unusual for Puritans since Edwards typically read his sermons straight from manuscripts, Edwards' preaching on the sovereign wonders of God was nonetheless the earliest factor of the Northeast revivals of the 1740s known as the **Great Awakening**. The Awakening was also greatly spurred by the much more animated preaching of the itinerant evangelist from England, **George Whitefield**.

PRECISIAN. "Precisian" or "precisianist" was a term of abuse first employed by Queen **Elizabeth I**'s **Archbishop of Canterbury**, Matthew Parker, to describe Puritans who were so precise in their Puritan vision for the Church of England that they refused any compromise. More specifically, a Precisian typically opposed the *Book of Common Prayer*, wearing **vestments**, and the **theater**, while asserting strict ecclesiastical discipline and a non-**Episcopal** church order. The term was most typically associated with Scotch **Presbyterians**. **Antinomianism** was likely a theological backlash against precisianism, which came in some circles to be roughly synonymous with the whole of Puritanism.

PREDESTINATION. The **Calvinist** theology that most Puritans upheld presumed that only the predestining or electing choice of God could bring **salvation** to any sinner. **Justification** was a free gift of God and not a matter of human activity or even choice because all persons have become hardened in their resistance to God and remain thus condemnable even in their best of deeds. Therefore, while God ordained **preaching** to all persons as the manner by which some of them would come to saving faith in Christ, that same faith could only become genuine and effectual in persons predestined by God through the operation of the Holy Spirit. Following John Calvin, Puritans typically believed that the doctrine of predestination was the only biblical explanation for why some sinners come to salvation when none of them could in fact be saved on their own without a special act of divine **providence**. When asked why God would then elect some to salvation but leave some to experience punishment for **sin** in Hell, Puritans could only point to the words of Paul in Romans chapters 9–11 and affirm that God is a potter who has a right to mold human clay according to God's own unsearchable wisdom.

Debates among those committed to the predestinarian theology of Calvinism arose at **Cambridge** in the 1590s. The **Thirty-Nine Articles** of the Church of England taught predestination to salvation but were unclear about whether reprobation was also an active decree of

God. Therefore, some wondered if God's decree to pass over some persons was parallel to the decree to save others. The issue was temporarily resolved in 1595 when the **Lambeth Articles**, a supplement to the Thirty-Nine Articles of the Church of England, affirmed in the words of **William Whitaker**, "From eternity God has predestined some men to life and condemned others to death." The **Irish Articles** of 1615 added that God's unchangeable counsel to save some and leave others did no violence to human wills because no fallen will could rightly please God of its own accord anyway. Mostly among continental Reformed theologians but involving some English Puritans, too, a new in-house dispute developed between those who had different conceptions of whether God's decision to save some was logically prior to his decision to permit the human fall into sin. Infralapsarians held that God's decree to redeem some sinners had to be a response to God's foreknowledge of the fall and its corrupting effects on human nature, while supralapsarians argued that God never acts contingently and so, in the order of salvation, made the decree to save some by special grace prior even to foreknowledge of why humans should become needful of salvation at all. Both sides admitted that this was largely an intellectual exercise because God is outside time and did not make his decrees in a chronological sequence anyway. No Puritan confession of faith dared make either infralapsarianism or supralapsarianism a test of orthodoxy or fellowship.

Still, such highly speculative debates seemed a wasteful use of pastoral energies to proponents of **Arminianism**, the most serious challenge to Calvinist dogma on the issue of predestination. Also known as the Remonstrants, the Arminians thought that God had decreed to predestine all those whom he foresaw would respond to the prodding of grace by placing their faith in Christ. Arminians thus exchanged the Calvinist view of predestination of individuals for the view that God predestines a category of persons into which individuals actually place themselves. England sent a small delegation to **Holland**'s **Synod of Dort** in 1619, which decided overwhelmingly in favor of the Calvinists on the issue. Calvinist Puritans in England maintained that their theology of predestination was the necessary corollary of salvation by faith alone, and they tended to associate Arminianism with works righteousness and the repressive policies of one of renowned adherents like **Archbishop of Canterbury**

William Laud. Some **dissenters**, like **John Smyth** and the General **Baptists**, adopted the Arminian position on predestination, but most, including the large majority of first generation Americans, remained Calvinistic.

PRELACY. A prelate is any high-ranking clergyman, especially the bishop over a territorial jurisdiction called a diocese, and the prelacy is the collective group of such religious officials. Puritans were so fervently critical of the prelacy of the Church of England that their disparagement was truly one of the distinguishing marks of the whole Puritan movement. Puritans strongly resented the bishops' assertion that they were the sole persons called by God to **ordain** church leaders and make church policies. Such claims appeared to the Puritans to be but variations on papal pretensions for ecclesiastical autocracy. On the other hand, the English monarchs wanted to sustain the prelacy because, as the supreme head of the church, they too were essentially prelates; so King **James I** correctively perceived, "No bishop, no king."

Presbyterian assaults on prelacy typically circulated through widely distributed tracts, such as those of **William Prynne** and the pseudonymous authors **Martin Marprelate** and **Smectymnuus**. The **Root and Branch Petition** of 1640 called for **Parliament** to abolish prelacy completely, but the **Sequestration Ordinance** of 1643 instead deprived most bishops of their livings. The Puritans' archprelate, **Archbishop of Canterbury William Laud**, was executed by Parliament in January 1645, four years before the same fate befell King **Charles I**. The **Independent John Milton** voiced his own critique of English prelates in the elegy for his late friend Edward King, entitled *Lycidas*. Yet in "On the New Forcers of **Conscience**," Milton also criticized the Presbyterian leaders of Parliament for being as narrow-minded as the "prelate lords" they had overthrown.

PRESBYTERIANS. Presbyterians were the first Puritans in England to have designs on a state church not based upon **prelacy**. Instead of governance by bishops, the Presbyterians preferred a church based upon rule by elders, or presbyters. They became convinced of the biblical nature of Presbyterianism through the writings and influence of John Calvin and his associates in Geneva, who showed the **Mar-**

ian exiles how to maintain a more democratic church government that nonetheless maintained a strong and skilled leadership. Calvin divided church leaders into ministers, teachers, elders, and deacons; the elders could also teach and help the minister to administer the **sacraments**. The elders of a church were elected by the church's membership and joined the minister to form the church's session. Session members from several churches in a particular area formed the presbytery, which bore the primary responsibility for examining the qualifications of ministerial candidates. A group of presbyteries in a larger area formed a synod, for the purpose of maintaining the church's adherence to biblical dogma and discipline. Finally, the combination of all synods was to meet in a general assembly to set the church's mission. The first presbytery in England formed in Wandsworth, near London, in 1572, but Presbyterianism never fully evolved into England's national faith.

The most distinguishing tenets of early Presbyterianism besides its method of organization were the authority of **Scripture**, the doctrine of **predestination**, and the opposition to **episcopacy**. Presbyterians justified the **baptism** of infants upon the basis of **covenant theology**, and the **music** they employed in corporate **worship** was usually metrical Psalms. Queen **Elizabeth I** repressed some of the more vocal Presbyterians in the 1590s, but they reemerged after the coronation of King **James I** to present their **Millennary Petition**. Thwarted by James dictum that eliminating bishops would inevitably lead to eliminating the king, the Presbyterians set out on a course of reform that did, in fact, later eliminate both for a time. The Presbyterians first waged a verbal war on the church's leadership through the widely circulated tracts of **William Prynne**, the pseudonymous **Martin Marprelate**, and the five authors who wrote together under the name of **Smectymnuus**. They all resisted the idea that bishops had the exclusive right to consecrate ministers and make church policy. Under the reciprocal Laudian Measures, many Presbyterians lost their livings, faced punishments doled out by the **Star Chamber**, or had their **ordination** revoked for not conforming to official church regulations.

A number of Presbyterians fled to Scotland, which had committed itself to Presbyterian ideals since the fiery **sermons** of **John Knox** sparked the **Scottish Reformation** in the 1560s. In 1637, a large majority of Scots agreed to subscribe to the National Covenant, a statement of intent to live according to Presbyterian principles. The aid of the Scottish "Covenanters," prominent among whom was **Samuel Rutherford**, would prove to be instrumental in the rise of English Presbyterian power in the 1640s. By 1643, the support of many London aristocrats secured a Presbyterian majority in **Parliament**, and these politicians sought Scottish help in their quest to force concessions from King **Charles I**. Parliament formed the **Solemn League and Covenant** with the Scottish Presbyterians in exchange for Scottish troops. These troops joined Parliament's own army, led by the **Earl of Essex** and other Presbyterian politicians. The king tried for a time to woo the Scots to the Royalist cause, but in the end it was to them that he surrendered. At first, the Presbyterians were interested only in forcing the king to share power with them and to agree to their vision for a state church. However, the **Self-Denying Ordinance** and **Pride's Purge** of 1648 squeezed many Presbyterians out of their positions of authority, both in the army and in Parliament itself. The **Independent** leadership of the **New Model Army** pressed on for the king's execution, which the Independent-led Rump Parliament approved in January 1649. The swift rise of the Independents prevented the Presbyterians from controlling the English church.

Yet the Presbyterians left a very strong theological legacy during their brief ascendancy. The **Westminster Assembly**, a convocation of mostly Presbyterian divines, first met in 1643 at Parliament's request. The Assembly would eventually produce a Directory for worship, two catechisms, and a confession of faith. The Westminster Confession temporarily replaced the **Thirty-Nine Articles** as the official doctrine of English Christianity until the coronation of King **Charles II** in 1660. The Church (or Kirk) of Scotland, however, elected to abide by the Westminster standards and stands today as the world's only Presbyterian national church. Some of English Puritanism's most outstanding preachers were Presbyterians, including **Thomas Manton**, **William Waller**, **Edward Reynolds**, **Stephen Marshall**, and **William Twisse**. When, in 1659, General **George Monck** forcibly secured the return of those expelled from Parliament by Pride's Purge, the Presbyterians were ready to compromise with Charles II and agree to the **Restoration**. The **Declaration of Breda** pledged a program of religious compromise and accommodation, but, in reality, the new king denied the Presbyterians any meaningful place in his regime and became particularly hostile toward **Nonconformists**.

Puritanism in America was largely a story of **Congregationalism**, which grew out the English Independents. **Francis Makemie** is considered "the father of American Presbyterianism" for missionary activity conducted during the 1690s, seven decades after the establishment of the **Massachusetts Bay Colony** by the Puritans. During the early decades of the 18th century, **William Tennent** and his son **Gilbert Tennent** offered theological training for Presbyterian ministers at their Log College. Supported by "New Side" Presbyterians who approved of the **Great Awakening** revivals, the Log College closed only when it was replaced by the founding of the College of New Jersey, later renamed Princeton.

PRESTON, JOHN (1587–1628). English Puritan theologian and preacher. Preston was born in Heyford, Northamptonshire, and studied at both King's College and Queen's College, **Cambridge**. After becoming a **fellow** at Queen's in 1609, he sought advancement in the Stuart court. Indeed, he won the admiration of King **James I** after arguing at a Cambridge disputation that James' hunting dogs possessed a degree of reason. Yet Preston's priorities changed to Puritan **preaching** in 1611 after hearing a sermon by **John Cotton** at St. Mary's Church, and so he used his favor with the monarch to attain academic and preaching positions from which he might best advance the Christian faith. Preston became the dean at Queen's (where he also preached at St. Botolph's Church), the preacher at **Lincoln's Inn**, a **lecturer** at Trinity Church, Cambridge (a position once held by **Richard Sibbes**), and the personal chaplain to the duke of Wales, the future King **Charles I**. Preston always denied charges from those who envied him that he rejected the ***Book of Common Prayer*** and used his oratorical skills to stir Puritan rebellion against the king. When James died in 1625, Preston perceived the disfavor with which the duke of Buckingham, Charles' other close adviser, held him, and so Preston retired from public life. But Preston's hectic speaking and writing schedule had already taken a severe toll on his health, and he died three years later at the age of 40. Preston was a **Calvinist** who frequently argued against **Arminianism**, but he also had affection for the natural theology of Thomas Aquinas. All his publications appeared posthumously. These included *The New Covenant* (1629), *The Breastplate of Faith and Love* (1630), *Life Eternal* (1631), *The Saint's Daily Exercise* (1633), *The Saint's Qualifications* (1634), *Sermons Before His Majesty* (1637), *Doctrines of the Saint's Infirmities* (1638), *Fulness of Christ for Us* (1640), and *Riches of Mercy to Men in Misery* (1658). Preston's student **Thomas Goodwin** was a principal Westminster divine.

PRIDE'S PURGE. As **Oliver Cromwell** and other **Independents** established ascendancy over the **New Model Army** in the mid-1640s, tensions arose between these Independents and the **Presbyterians** in **Parliament**. The Presbyterians became concerned about their ability to keep the army under control and a Reformed state church intact, and the Independents were alarmed that some Presbyterians in Scotland had chosen in the end to fight against them and for the king. The Independents moved more swiftly and decisively. Colonel Thomas Pride received a list of 150 members, whom he was to meet at the top of a stairwell and prevent from entering Parliament on 6 December 1648. After many of these disbarred members were temporarily held at a nearby London inn called "Hell," they agreed to leave their posts peaceably. The remaining members of Parliament, called the **Rump Parliament** after Pride's Purge, then had an Independent majority, and they secured the execution of King **Charles I** the very next month, on 30 January 1649. Oliver Cromwell's son-in-law **Henry Ireton** gave the actual orders for Pride's Purge, but Cromwell supposedly applauded it. During the chaos following the resignation of **Richard Cromwell** as the lord protector, General **George Monck** returned to Parliament the Presbyterians secluded by Pride's Purge, and their votes were enough to secure the **Restoration** of King **Charles II** on 25 May 1660.

PRIVY COUNCIL. The Privy Council was originally conceived as a body of advisers to the English sovereign concerning matters of legislation, administration, and justice. During the Tudor and Stuart dynasties, its constituents typically included the **Archbishop of Canterbury**, the Archbishop of York, and the Bishop of London, although membership could swell, depending on the desires of the monarch. Queen **Mary I** had approximately 40 members on the council, for instance, while her half-sister and successor Queen **Elizabeth I** had only 13. Sometimes the Privy Council could issue proclamations on the crown's behalf, such as when it sent invitations to the **Hampton Court Conference** on behalf of King **James I**. Yet James and his son King **Charles I** tended to govern more as absolute monarchs without relying heavily on the Council, except when Charles directed the **Star Chamber**, an offshoot of the Privy Council, to prosecute Puritans for their religious **Nonconformity**. **Oliver Cromwell** continued to employ a small privy council, which was renamed the Protector's Privy Council in 1657. This version of the Privy Council disbanded when Cromwell died in 1659, but a royal version of the Privy Council revived by order of King **Charles II** after the **Restoration**.

PROTECTORATE. The Protectorate (1653–59) was that portion of the **Interregnum** during which the **Commonwealth** of England, Scotland, and Ireland was governed first by **Oliver Cromwell** and then briefly by his son Richard under the title of "lord protector." It began in December 1653 when the Instrument of Government, a new constitution drafted by Major-General John Lambert and passed by the Council of State, first designated Oliver Cromwell as the Commonwealth's Protector. The Instrument of Government theoretically called for political power to be shared among the Protector, the Council of State, and **Parliament**, but, in practice, it accentuated the Protector's executive power, which Cromwell had already exercised *de facto* by dismissing both the **Rump Parliament** and **Barebones Parliament** earlier in 1653. In 1654–55, Cromwell convened the first **Protectorate Parliament**, which was the first Parliament to include Scottish and Irish representatives. Yet many of those elected to serve were **Presbyterians** who tended to block the ambitions of the **Independent** Cromwell; after he dissolved this Parliament, he re-divided England into 11 military districts and essentially ruled as a military governor. Cromwell permitted religious **toleration** for most Protestants and even Jews but not Roman **Catholics** or Episcopalians.

Cromwell convened the second Protectorate Parliament from 1656–58, seeking financial aid to fight the Anglo–Spanish War. Yet, he ultimately dismissed this session as well, wearying of resistance to himself and his generals from its Presbyterian members. Their defiance also militated against Cromwell taking the crown, as he had considered doing in 1657. In that same year, he was officially reinstalled as lord protector, however, and the replacement for the Instrument of Government, the Humble Petition and Advice, insisted that he be addressed as "His Highness." When Cromwell died in September 1658, his son **Richard Cromwell** became the new lord protector. Richard did not command the authority that his father did, however, and resigned the office in May 1659. Thus ended the Protectorate. General **George Monck**, a Presbyterian, then orchestrated the recall of first the Rump and then the **Long Parliament**, and, in May 1660, the **Restoration** of King **Charles II**.

PROTECTORATE PARLIAMENT. *See* PARLIAMENT.

PROVIDENCE. The providence of God, by which God was understood to conduct meticulous governance over all worldly affairs, was a central tenet of Puritan belief. It provided the assurance that all human activities were meaningful because they were caught up in the sovereign, though sometimes mysterious, will of God. One of the earliest confessional statements on divine providence to influence subsequent Puritan thought was the **Irish Articles** of 1615, which declared, "In the beginning of time, when no creature had any being, God by his Word alone, in the space of six days, created all things, and afterwards by his providence doth continue, propagate and order them according to his own will." The **Westminster Confession** of 1644 elaborated, "God the great Creator of all things, doth uphold, direct, dispose and govern all creatures, actions and things from the greatest even to the least, by His most wise and holy providence, according to His infallible foreknowledge and the free and immutable counsel of His own will, to the praise of the glory of His wisdom, power, justice, goodness and mercy." Westminster elaborated on this definition to show that providence operates through the secondary causes of nature so that the human fall into **sin** was simultaneously within the providence of God and yet attributable in its immediate culpability only to its willful agents, Adam and Eve. The clarification of God's permissive and ordaining wills could become quite elaborate in Puritan explanations of the doctrines of sin and **predestination**.

The first Puritans to come to the New World had a very strong sense that they were obeying God's providential calling to be, as **John Winthrop** famously described, a light set on a hill before all the world. **William Bradford**'s *Of Plymouth Plantation*, finished in 1645, described all of the early labors of Puritan colonists through the rubric of providence. In 1655, **Thomas Shepard** of Cambridge, Massachusetts, included instruction about providence in his primer, *The First Principles of the Oracles of God*. Shepard distinguished common providence from special providence by teaching that God's providence "is either, first, ordinary and mediate, whereby he provideth for his creatures by ordinary and usual means. Secondly, extraordinary and immediate, whereby he provideth for his creatures by miracles, or immediately by himself." In short, the Puritans' conviction about divine providence induced them to search all of life's events for indications of God's will. Further evidences of this are visible in **Mary Rowlandson**'s treatment of her captivity by Indians in *The Sovereignty & Goodness of God*, **Urian Oakes**'s examination of New England life after **King Philip's War** in *The Sovereign Efficacy of Divine Providence*, and **Roger Williams**' decision to name the Providence colony in thanksgiving for God's provision.

PRYNNE, WILLIAM (1600–1669). English **Presbyterian** pamphleteer. Prynne was one of the most controversial writers of the Puritan era, yet many of the objects of his vitriolic pen have become associated in the popular mind with the more prudish side of Puritan morality. As a barrister at law at **Lincoln's Inn**, where he probably listened raptly to the **sermons** of **John Preston** and **Richard Sibbes**, Prynne sought to expose the godlessness of drinking alcohol (*Healthes Sicknesse*), Sabbath-breaking (*Divine Tragedie Lately Acted*), and even contemporary fashions of hair dressing (*The Unlovelinesse of Lovelockes*). He was also a vocal critic of **Arminianism** (*The Church of Englands Old Antithesis to the New Arminianisme*) and an ardent defender of the doctrine of **predestination** (*The Perpetuitie of a Regenerate Mans Estate*). Prynne's *Histrio-Mastix* was a stinging series of criticisms of the godlessness of plays, dancing, and masquerades. It was predominantly for this writing that Prynne was summoned in

1633 to stand trial in the **Star Chamber** before **Archbishop of Canterbury William Laud**. Prynne had also lampooned Laud himself and the high church ceremonies he preferred in acrimonious writings like *A Brief Survey and Censure of Mr. Cozens His Couzening Devotions*, *Lame Giles his Haultiness*, *News from Ipswich*, *A New Discovery of the Prelates Tyranny*, and *God, No Imposter nor Deluder*.

The severity of Laud's sentence turned Prynne from a prolific but eccentric pamphleteer into a hero of anti-prelatical **Nonconformists**, particularly **John Lilburne**. Prynne lost his right to practice law, his degree from **Oxford**, £5,000, his freedom, and both his ears. Similar sentences befell **Henry Burton** and **John Bastwick**. Then, in 1637, the stumps of Prynne's ears were sliced off, and he was branded on each cheek and exiled to the island of Jersey. After the **Long Parliament** freed Prynne during the **English Civil Wars**, he foretold *Canterburies Doome* and received reparation of £5,000, but he refused to endorse the execution of King **Charles I**. Perhaps it was for this reason that **Charles II** did not consider Prynne among those Puritans who merited retaliation after the **Restoration**, and so the king allotted to Prynne 500 pounds per year as keeper of the records of the Tower of London. *See also* DRAMA.

PSALTER. *See* MUSIC.

PUTNEY DEBATES. As the **New Model Army**'s noose around King **Charles I** began to tighten in 1647, dissension arose within the army's ranks over what should be the future course of England after the **English Civil Wars**. The **Levellers**, led by **John Lilburne**, had joined the revolutionary cause in significant numbers because they wanted to extend the right to vote and blanket religious **toleration** to every male. On 28 October 1647, at the Church of St. Mary the Virgin in Putney, Surrey, Lieutenant General **Oliver Cromwell** agreed to hear the Levellers argue for their vision. The Levellers' spokesmen, called the Agitators, presented a document called *An Agreement of the People* that called for the dissolution of the **Long Parliament** and the election of a new **Parliament** every two years. Cromwell and his son-in-law **Henry Ireton** considered the Levellers' ideas to be too radical even for revolutionaries, for they feared that universal suffrage would leave government in the hands of unqualified persons.

The Army Council rejected the Leveller platform at the Putney Debates and even arrested Lilburne. After the trial and execution of the king in January 1649, the new heads of state largely ignored the contributions made by the Levellers to their military victory.

PYM, JOHN (1583–1643). English politician. Pym was born at Brymore House of Cannington, Somerset. His father Alexander died during Pym's first year, but his mother Phillipa's remarriage to Sir Anthony Rous, client of the Earl of Bedford, later became a doorway of opportunity for Pym's career. Pym attended Broadgates Hall (later Pembroke College), **Oxford**, and the Middle Temple, though he never practiced law. In 1604, he married Anne Hooke, the daughter of Rous's sister Barbara and a strong Puritan as well. Through the support of the Earl of Bedford, a family friend, Pym won election to the House of Commons from Tavistock, and his reputation as a reformer rose quickly. In 1625, he demanded the impeachment of the Royalist George Villiers, the Duke of Buckingham, and in 1628, he supported the **Petition of Right**, which insisted that the king's ability to levy taxes become subject to Parliamentary approval. For the next dozen years, Pym was also active in the Providence Island Company, whose purpose was to establish a Puritan colony in the Spanish-controlled West Indies.

When King **Charles I** dismissed the **Short Parliament** in 1640, Pym joined Oliver St. John and John Hampden in agitating for **Parliament**'s recall, and he insisted that in the future only Parliament could convene and dismiss itself. In 1641, Pym continued to lead Parliament in making changes that disintegrated the king's power, such as drafting the Ten Propositions and **Grand Remonstrance**, establishing control of the military following the Irish Uprising, and leading prosecution against the crown's top advisers, **Archbishop of Canterbury William Laud** and the Earl of Strafford. He also abolished the **Star Chamber**. A failed attempt by the king to impeach and arrest Pym with four other Parliamentarians in 1642 only enhanced Pym's popularity among politicians and Londoners alike, who associated Charles with **Arminianism** and papal intervention in national affairs. Pym also won Scottish **Presbyterian** support, even though he himself remained an **Anglican**, with the **Solemn League and Covenant** of 1643. Pym contracted cancer that same year and did not live to see Parliament's defeat of the king or the **Commonwealth** he had envisioned.

– Q –

QUAKERS. The Quakers (Society of Friends) gathered around the spiritual insights of **George Fox** in the 1650s. The Friends were on the left wing of Puritan **Separatism** that exalted the personal experience of God over any form of theological orthodoxy. They were better known as the Quakers from advice that Fox gave to a Justice Bennett to tremble before God. Quakers also rejected all established and formal styles of liturgy, and so in their meetinghouses they did not follow a set liturgy but awaited the quaking (stirring) of the Holy Spirit. Such inspiration could come upon **women** as well as men, and Fox's wife Margaret Fell became one of the movement's early **preachers**. Quakers did not employ water **baptism** but only baptism by the Spirit. They were "primitivists" in **worship** who had the single goal of searching directly for the divine within the human without institutionalized accretions that could get in the way. They were also recognized for their refusal to swear public oaths or remove their hats in the presence of social superiors.

Fox had his first "opening" of divine illumination in 1647, but the content of his resultant preaching was highly controversial and led to Fox's beating and imprisonment in Derby, England. He taught that every human being is naturally endowed with the "inner light" that can at any moment become aflame with the power of the Holy Spirit. The danger of this in the eyes of most Puritans particularly **Baptists**, such as **John Bunyan,** with whom the Quakers were in closest competition for converts, was that Fox's teaching minimized the authority of **Scripture** and the doctrine of **justification** by faith. The Quakers did not deny the **Bible**'s authority, but they treated it as a book of examples from "other men's words" that ultimately was subordinate to one's own personal encounter with God. This emphasis on inward experience, in turn, led to the search for what the Quaker Edward Burrough called "the Christ within." Because the Quakers believed that every person could mystically encounter Christ by means of the inner light, they downplayed the forensic, atoning effects of Christ's physical death and resurrection. John Crook confirmed this as a part of Quaker belief, and in his "Confession of the Society of Friends," Robert Barclay admitted that an explicit knowledge of Christ's death was profitable but not absolutely needful. When the Quaker James Nayler rode into the town of Bristol on a donkey in 1656 and claimed that he in fact was Christ, suspicions of Quaker excess appeared justified. Many Puritans accused the Quakers of being libertines like the **Ranters**, and the colony of Massachusetts banned Quaker meetings.

In the face of such negative publicity, Fox became a more intentional director and apologist for the Quaker movement. He set up an amicable meeting with Lord Protector **Oliver Cromwell**, disavowed Nayler's procession as representative of the whole Quaker movement, encouraged his followers to join him in practicing pacifism, and published *The Great Mystery of the Great Whore Unfolded*. From 1671–73, Fox also conducted a missionary journey in America and the West Indies, which he chronicled in his most influential writing, the *Journal*. Fox's evangelistic efforts not only appealed to society's poor and disaffected, but they won more cultured converts. Isaac Pennington, for instance, was the son of a lord mayor of London, and **William Penn** was the son of a navy admiral. Penn became the most recognizable Quaker other than Fox himself and, in 1682, founded the colony of Pennsylvania as a "holy experiment" in which Quakers could worship freely. Back in England, the Quakers were the most sorely persecuted of the **Nonconformist** groups targeted after the **Restoration** by King **Charles II**. During his reign, more than 20,000 Quakers were either fined or imprisoned, and about 450 died in jail. In fact, so many Quakers suffered from royal policies that the **Declaration of Indulgence** of 1672 was popularly known as "the Quaker Act" for the number of Quakers whom it pardoned. Quakers finally attained **religious liberty** in England from the **Act of Toleration** in 1689.

– R –

RAINOLDS (OR RAYNOLDS), JOHN (1549–1607). English Puritan theologian. Rainolds was born at Penhoe, near Exeter, in Devonshire. In his early years, he professed ecclesiastical loyalty to the papacy. Allegedly, his brother William's arguments won him to Protestantism, but ironically John's counterpoints had exactly the opposite effect, turning William to Roman **Catholicism**. At Corpus Christi College, **Oxford**, Rainolds undertook intensive study of the Greek and Latin church fathers, largely to be able to distinguish apostolic Christianity from later papal innovations. He acquired fame in debates with papists like John Hart and, after becoming Doctor of Divinity, was named divinity **lecturer** at Oxford. In that capacity, he also debated Robert Cardinal Bellarmine and thereby gained the attention of Queen **Elizabeth I**. Rainolds received from Elizabeth the deanery of Lincoln College, Oxford, but he politely declined a bishopric in order to remain in academia. And he did make that time of his life productive, publishing works like *De Romanae Ecclesiae Idolatria* in 1596 and *The Overthrow of Stage Plays* in 1599.

Then, in 1599, Rainolds gave up his deanship to become the president of Corpus Christi College. In correspondences with students, pastors, and professional colleagues, Rainolds countered Archbishop Richard Bancroft's contention that the superiority of bishops to priests and elders was grounded in the New Testament, but, nonetheless, he also encouraged peaceable conformity with **Anglican** prescriptions for **worship** and **vestments**. Thus did he urge an establishmentarian rather than dissenting course for Puritanism, such as in the posthumously published *A Defence of the Judgment of the Reformed Churches* and *A Defence of Our English Liturgy Against Rob. Browne His Schismatical Book*. Rainolds' placid demeanor and scholarly reputation precipitated his selection to lead the Puritan delegation that met with King **James I** at the **Hampton Court Conference** of 1604. Rainolds presented to the first Stuart monarch four petitions of concern, regarding the maintenance of sound doctrine, trained pastors, efficient church government, and a revised **Book of Common Prayer**. James spurned Rainolds' proposals but did take to heart his suggestion that the crown sponsor a new English translation of **Scripture**. Rainolds himself spearheaded an Oxford translation team, even hosting it in his home for a while after contracting the case of consumption that eventually took his life. He published more than 20 books and was described by one contemporary historian as the very "pillar of Puritanism." *See* DRAMA.

RAMISM. Ramism was a system of philosophical inquiry used by some Puritans that took its name from the Frenchman Pierre de la Ramée, better known as Petrus (or Peter) Ramus. Ramus taught rhetoric and logic in Paris but was murdered as part of the massacre of French Protestants on **Saint Bartholomew's Day** in 1572. His method was an intentional rejection of Scholasticism and its use of Aristotle, for Ramus believed that Aristotle's philosophy was too prone to long digressions, wordy discussions, and redundant analyses. By contrast, Ramus proposed a more practical approach to pedagogy that sought to be both spiritually and intellectually edifying. Ramus's dialectical method employed simple syllogisms to discover the "middle term" that could connect "minor" and "major" propositions and thus reveal truth. This would proceed by beginning with a general definition and then searching for specific examples of the type. For instance, the answer to the question, "Was Petrus Ramus a Protestant?" should be sought by proposing a definition for the major term "Protestant" and then determining if the minor term, Petrus Ramus, meets the definition. Ramus's *Dialectica* appeared in England in both Latin and English in 1574, and it became widely discussed and employed at **Cambridge**. Some of the persons who admitted to absorbing Ramist thought at Cambridge were Sir Philip Sydney, **John Milton**, and most particularly **William Ames**, whose writings on **conscience** were deeply indebted to the Ramist approach. Ramism remained influential in English university education until the end of the 17th century, when the writings of Francis Bacon reversed the Ramist methodology by prescribing induction from particular observations to general rules.

RANEW, NATHANIEL (NATHANAEL) (1600–1672). English Puritan preacher. Little is known about Ranew's life except that he attended **Emmanuel College** at **Cambridge** during roughly the same period as **Thomas Shepard** and **Thomas Watson**. He ministered at various Puritan churches around Essex, including Felsted and Billericay, for most of his adult life. Ranew's chief renown is his book, *Solitude Improved by Divine Meditation*, published in 1670. In typical Puritan suspicion of idleness while invoking a mystical belief that contemplation of God is a foretaste of eternal beatific vision, Ranew contended that Christian meditation bridges the spiritual disciplines of **Scripture** memorization and **prayer** and is both the duty and joy of a believer. Ranew's supporters included John Robartes, the First Earl of Radnor and Lord Lieutenant of Ireland, and his financial patrons the Earl and Countess of Warwick. Ranew helped bring into print several writings of Puritan interest, including **James Ussher**'s *A Body of Divinity*.

RANTERS. The Ranters were likely never an organized group, but Puritan writers from the mid-17th century like **John Bunyan** described them as **antinomians** and sexual libertines. One of the first and most recognizable Ranters was **Laurence Clarkson**, a former member of the **Levellers** and **Muggletonians**, who wrote *A Generall Charge* (1647), *A Single Eye All Light, No Darkness* (1650), and *The Lost Sheep Found* (1660). Clarkson taught that the **Bible** is often self-contradictory and that the true test of spiritual liberty is whether one can disobey accepted moral laws without feeling remorse. Other Ranter authors were **Abiezer Coppe**, Joseph Salmon, and Jacob Bauthumley. The Ranters rejected reason as a device of the devil and so did not come to complete theological concord even among themselves, but they generally held to a kind of pantheism that equated God with the natural world.

RAY, JOHN (1627–1705). English scientist. Ray was born in Black Notley, Essex, to a blacksmith father and an herbalist mother of modest means. He attended Trinity College, **Cambridge**, on scholarship and undertook various jobs on campus to support his mathematical and scientific studies. He became a **fellow** in 1649, a **lecturer** after completing his M.A. degree in 1651, and a junior dean in 1658. In 1660, he received **ordination** in the Church of England, but, two years later, he was forced to leave **Cambridge** for **Nonconformity**. Through the financial support of a wealthy former student named Francis Willughby, Ray spent the next 10 years traveling extensively and studying the physiology of a wide variety of fish, birds, and plants. After Willughby's death in 1672, Ray settled back at Black Notley with his wife and four daughters, continuing to write and correspond with other scientists in the Royal Society of London. Ray believed that the study of nature was a way better to know God. His studies inspired the biological classification system of Carolus Linnaeus and have earned him recognition as the father of English natural history. His notable publications are *Catalogus plantarium circa Cantbrigiam nascentium* (1660), *Methodus Plantarum Nova* (1682), *Historia Plantarum Generalis* (1686), *The Wisdom of God Manifested in the Works of the Creation* (1691) and *Three Physico-Theological Discourses* (1692). *See also* SCIENCE.

REFORMED THEOLOGY. Reformed theology was the theological system indebted above all to the Protestant Reformer of Geneva, John Calvin (1509–1564), but also to likeminded continental thinkers, such as Theodore Beza (1519–1605), Ulrich Zwingli (1484–1531), Heinrich Bullinger (1504–1575), Peter Martyr Vermigli (1499–1562), Zacharias Ursinus (1534–1583), and Francis Turretin (1623–1687). The center of Reformed theology is that all things occur for the glory of a sovereign God, and thus it places a strong emphasis on **covenant theology** and divine **providence**, a corollary of which is the doctrine of **predestination**. **Calvinism** itself was not a denomination, but it broadly and strongly influenced most Puritans, ranging from **Non-Separatists** like **William Perkins** to **Independents** like **John Owen**, but particularly the **Presbyterians** who studied with Calvin in Geneva during the reign of England's Queen **Mary I**. The annotations of the **Geneva Bible** are immersed in Reformed theology. Reformed theology permeates various statements of faith from the Puritan era as well, above all the **Westminster Confession** but also the **Savoy Declaration**, **Thirty-Nine Articles**, and others. Most Puritans in **Holland** and New England also held to Reformed theology—in America most notably **Jonathan Edwards**—but the greater allowance of human decision-making permitted by **Arminianism** arose as an internal challenge in both locations. *See also* SYNOD OF DORT.

RELIGIOUS LIBERTY. *See* TOLERATION.

REMONSTRANTS. *See* ARMINIANISM.

RESTORATION. The Restoration was the return of the Stuart dynasty to the throne of England in May 1660. Since the execution of King **Charles I** by Parliamentary order in January 1649, his son **Charles**

II had been living mostly in France and **Holland**, except for a failed attempt to rally favor in Scotland in 1650. When the unpopular **Richard Cromwell** succeeded his father Oliver as protector in 1658, some **Presbyterians** who already resented the **Independents'** inhibition of their hopes for a state church looked nostalgically to the stability of the monarchy. Sir George Booth tried and failed to oust the younger Cromwell and make way for a new king in 1659; Cromwell's adviser **John Thurloe** imprisoned **William Waller** in the Tower of London for advocating a restored monarchy without any conditions. But, in February 1660, General **George Monck**, a Presbyterian, marched from Scotland and took military control over the city of London. He returned to their livings those Presbyterian Parliamentarians evicted by **Pride's Purge**, and he began negotiations with Charles II for his return to England. Charles promised in the **Declaration of Breda** to be full and generous in his pardons, to leave untouched church lands taken during the **English Civil Wars**, and to grant freedom of **conscience** to all Protestants, except seditious sects. The reconstituted Convention **Parliament** met on 25 April 1660 and agreed to welcome Charles II as king. Charles arrived at the port of Dover on 26 May 1660; the Restoration officially occurred on 29 May when Charles processed into London on his 30th birthday. The Presbyterians were nonetheless unable by welcoming Charles finally to complete their vision for the state church, for only two years later on **Saint Bartholomew's Day**, Charles ejected 1,760 ministers and 150 college educators as enemy **dissenters**. **John Milton** lamented that the alliance of Presbyterians and Royalists had ended up dealing a serious blow to **religious liberty**.

REYNOLDS, EDWARD (1599–1676). English Puritan preacher. Reynolds was born in Southampton, England, and attended Merton College, **Oxford**, where he became probationer (divinity) **fellow** in 1620. His ability to craft sermons ameliorated the effects of his gravelly voice, and he became the preacher at **Lincoln's Inn** and rector at Braynton, Northamptonshire. By 1643, Reynolds was a completely committed **Presbyterian**, and he attended the **Westminster Assembly** as a divine. In 1646, he became a preacher at Oxford, and only two years later, he became dean of Oxford's Christ Church Cathedral and vice-chancellor of the university. When, in 1651, however, he would not sign the "Engagement" that required complicity with the regicide of King **Charles I**, he lost both positions to **John Owen**. He did return to the deanery of Christ Church in 1659 after a time as vicar of St. Lawrence's Jewry, London. Agreeable in spirit with those Presbyterians like **Thomas Manton** who welcomed the **Restoration**, Reynolds was made Bishop of Norwich and a personal chaplain by King **Charles II** in 1660. He also became a warden (trustee) at his alma mater Merton College in the same year. A six-volume collection, *The Works of Edward Reynolds, D.D.*, was already in print before Reynolds' death, and it included such writings as *Commentary on Ecclesiastes*, *The Sinfulness of Sin*, *Israel's Petition in Times of Trouble*, *Meditations on the Holy Sacrament of the Lord's Last Supper*, and *Treatise on the Passions and Faculties of the Soul*. See also SAINT BARTHOLOMEW'S DAY.

RICH, ROBERT (1587–1658). English soldier. Rich was the eldest son of Robert Rich, a descendant of King **Henry VIII**'s chancellor Richard Rich, and the First Earl of Warwick. Rich's mother was Penelope Devereux Rich, and his younger brother Henry Rich became the First Earl of **Holland**. Rich succeeded his father as the Second Earl of Warwick in 1619. He studied at **Emmanuel College, Cambridge**, and then pursued administration in several of England's colonial companies. He helped to procure the patent for the **Massachusetts Bay Colony** in 1628 and the Saybrook patent for Connecticut in 1631. He resigned from the New England Company in 1631, but he remained involved with the Bermudas and Providence Companies. A vocal opponent of King **Charles I**'s shipping regulations and **Archbishop of Canterbury William Laud**'s **worship** policies, Rich used his financial influence to support Puritan ministers and Parliamentarians, most notably **John Pym**. In 1643, **Parliament** thanked Rich for his help by naming him the lord high admiral of the navy and the governor-in-chief of all the American colonies. Rich stepped down from these positions following the king's execution in 1649.

RIDLEY, NICHOLAS (1503–1555). English bishop and martyr. Ridley came from a prominent family in Tynedale, Northumberland; his father Christopher Ridley became Lord Ridley in 1519 and was a patron of Sir Francis Bacon. Nicholas attained an M.A. degree from

Cambridge in 1525, specializing in Greek, and he also studied at the universities of the Sorbonne in France and Louvain in Belgium. In 1529, he became senior proctor at Cambridge, in which position he declared that the pope deserved no more respect from English Christians than any other foreign bishop. In 1537, he became chaplain to **Archbishop of Canterbury Thomas Cranmer**, and, in 1538, he also became the vicar of Herne in Kent. In 1540, he became a chaplain to King **Henry VIII** and Master of Cambridge's Pembroke College, followed in 1541 by being named as a canon of Canterbury Cathedral. After King **Edward VI** ascended to the English throne in 1547, Ridley's career continued to rise as well. In 1548, he helped Cranmer to compile the ***Book of Common Prayer***; in 1549, he became the Bishop of Rochester, and, in 1551, he followed the recently defrocked Edmund Bonner as the Bishop of London and Westminster.

On 9 July 1553, Ridley preached at St. Paul's Cross on the illegitimacy of Henry's daughters Mary and Elizabeth, and he preferred the recognition of a new line of succession that would place their cousin Lady Jane Grey on the throne after Edward's impending death. Lady Jane did in fact receive the crown the very next day, but she only wore it for nine days when popular support preferred the installation of Mary. Ridley participated in disputations against Roman **Catholic** officials at **Oxford** in 1554, but, for his role in supporting Jane, he was imprisoned in the Tower of London and excommunicated. On 16 October 1555, Ridley was slowly burned at the stake beside **Hugh Latimer** outside Balliol Hall, Oxford. Although Ridley had once encouraged **John Hooper** to wear the church's prescribed **vestments** at his bishop's **ordination**, Ridley's own final act of defiance was to refuse to please his accusers by donning the bishop's **surplice**, which would have been tantamount to a recantation. *See also* MARIAN EXILES.

ROBERTS, FRANCIS (1609–1675). English Puritan preacher. Roberts was born at Methley, near the town of Leeds. He studied at Trinity College, **Oxford**, and became a proponent of **Presbyterianism**, subscribing to the **Solemn League and Covenant** of 1643. In that same year, Roberts became the pastor of the St. Augustine's Church on Watling Street. He served doubly as the chaplain to the **Earl of Essex** in Dublin, and, in 1649, he became the rector at Wrington, Somerset. His theological legacy lies chiefly in his book *The Mystery and Marrow of the Bible*, a massive tome that elaborates the history of God's dealings with the human race in terms of six covenants, arranged successively through Adam, Abraham, Moses, David, the Jewish exiles in Babylon, and Jesus Christ. His additional writings include *Believers Evidences for Eternal Life*, *The Key of the Bible*, and *True Way to the Tree of Life*.

ROBINSON, JOHN (1575–1625). English Puritan preacher. Best remembered as the pastor of those Puritans who migrated to America and became known to history as the **Pilgrims**, Robinson was born in Nottinghamshire, England. He enrolled as a sizar (exempt from most student fees) at Corpus Christ College, **Cambridge**, to study with **William Perkins**, receiving first a **fellowship** and then **ordination** in the Church of England around 1597. After he recognized an anti-Puritan tenor to the early reign of King **James I**, Robinson withdrew from the state church, married, and began **preaching** at St. Andrew's, Norwich. Soon thereafter, he joined the congregation of **Separatists** that met at the Scrooby residence of **William Brewster** and also included the future **Baptist** leader **John Smyth**. Yet Scrooby Manor officially belonged to the Archbishop of York, and to evade confrontation, Robinson led about 50 persons to Amsterdam, **Holland**, in 1608. The next year, partly to avoid theological conflict with a newly arrived group led by the non-**Calvinist** Smyth, Robinson's group relocated again and settled its own congregation in Leyden (Leiden), where it eventually grew to include more than 300 people. Robinson defended his migrations in the books *Justification of Separation from the Church of England* (1610) and *Apologia* (1619), and his predestinarian theology in such works as *A Defence of the Doctrine Propounded by the **Synod of Dort*** (1624). Robinson's sermons, such as those in *Observations Divine and Moral* (1625), emphasized both divine election and lived Christian holiness. His vision of church life incorporated both the **Independency** of the **Brownists** and the orderliness of the **Presbyterians**, and so he allowed for both **Congregationalist** polity and ruling elders.

In 1617, with the threat of war with Spain looming in **Holland** and a communal life finally free of outside interference seeming possible only in the New World, several members of the Leyden congregation sold their estates to afford transportation to America. In 1620, Robinson preached a farewell sermon to those Pilgrims who, after some aborted attempts to sail from Southampton, finally left from Plymouth aboard the *Mayflower* on 16 September. Robinson read from Ezra 8:21 and encouraged the Pilgrims to take the Reformation beyond its beginnings with Martin Luther and John Calvin. **William Bradford** and **William Brewster** supervised the 35 Leyden passengers, who comprised about one-third of the ship's manifest on their three-month trek. Robinson died before completing plans to join his friends at the new Plymouth plantation. In 1658, the remainder of Robinson's group in Leyden united with the Dutch Reformed Church.

ROBINSON, RALPH (1614–1655). English Puritan preacher and theologian. Robinson was born at Heswall, Cheshire, and studied at St. Catherine's Hall, **Cambridge**, which was then known for Puritan teaching under **Richard Sibbes**. Robinson was **ordained** a presbyter at St. Mary's Church, Woolnoth Street, in London in 1642, and he served as a scribe to the first provincial assembly in London in 1647. Despite his **Presbyterianism** and support for the Puritan revolution, he did not approve the execution of King **Charles I**. Little is known about Robinson's whereabouts during the **Protectorate**, except that he wrote *Self Conduct; or, the Saint's Guidance to Glory* (1654), *The Christian Completely Armed* (1656), and *Christ All in All* (1656), a study of more than 700 pages exegeting the sole sufficiency of Christ in Colossians 3:11.

ROGERS, JOHN (1500–1555). English Puritan martyr. Rogers was likely born at Deritend. He earned a baccalaureate degree from Pembroke Hall, **Cambridge**, and also studied at **Oxford**. In 1532, he became the rector of Holy Trinity Church, Queenhithe, London. Two years later, he went to Antwerp as the chaplain to the Company of the Merchant Adventurers. In that city, Rogers met the **Bible** translator William Tyndale and married Adriana de Weyden. When Tyndale died in 1536, Rogers used the Bible of **Miles Coverdale** to complete Tyndale's translation of the Old Testament and to that added an edition of the apocryphal Prayer of Manasseh, as translated from a French edition. Enlisting the help of his wife's uncle Sir Jacobus van

Meteren, Rogers published his version of the Bible under the pseudonym Thomas Matthew, and hence it is known as **Matthew's Bible**. Although the great bulk of the translating work of Matthew's Bible belonged to Tyndale and Coverdale, Rogers did add prefaces and explanatory notes. Although King **Henry VIII** had previously banned all English translations of the Bible in his country, in 1537, he authorized the distribution of Matthew's Bible among all church parishes in England, and it, in turn, helped guide work on **Taverner's Bible**, the **Great Bible**, the **Bishops' Bible**, and the **King James Version** of the Bible.

Also in 1537, Rogers began **preaching** for a Protestant church in Wittenberg, Germany, the seat of Martin Luther's Reformation. In 1548, Rogers returned to England after the accession of King **Edward VI** to the throne. Soon thereafter, he published a translated work by the Lutheran theologian Philip Melanchthon. He also became the vicar of St. Sepulchre's Holborn, a prebendary ministry of St. Paul's Cathedral. After Queen **Mary I** succeeded her half brother in 1553, Rogers faced various trials for his outspoken preference for Edward's Protestant governance. First summoned before state authorities in August 1553, Rogers received a sentence of confinement to Newgate Prison, along with Bishop **John Hooper**, in January 1554. In January 1555, Rogers again appeared before Stephen Gardiner, the Bishop of Winchester, who enforced the anti-Protestant policies of Queen Mary and **Archbishop of Canterbury** Reginald Cardinal Pole. On 29 January 1555, Gardiner sentenced Rogers to death for rejecting the Roman **Catholic** Church and its doctrine of transubstantiation. On 4 February 1555, Rogers became the first Protestant to be burned to death by order of "Bloody Mary." The road from Newgate Prison to the place of execution at Smithfield passed by St. Sepulchre's Church, and the popular support for Rogers was so great that the French ambassador Noailles described the scene as more befitting a wedding than a funeral. Rogers refused a last-minute offer to recant for the sake of his 10 children, but instead he received his death by allegedly washing his hands in the flames, according to the hagiographer **John Foxe**, "as one feeling no smart."

ROGERS, JOHN (1572?–1636). English Puritan preacher. This Rogers was born near Essex and earned an M.A. degree from **Cambridge**. He preached at Hemingham, Norfolk, and Haverhil, Suffolk, before settling in Dedham. Known for his opposition to the wearing of papist **vestments**, he wrote *The Doctrine of Faith*, *Exposition on First Epistle of Peter*, and *A Treatise on Love*. His son Nathaniel Rogers was the assistant minister to **John Norton** in Ipswich, Massachusetts, from 1636–55.

ROGERS, RICHARD (?–1612?). English **Presbyterian** preacher. Rogers studied at **Cambridge** and ministered for most of his career at the Presbyterian church of Wethersfield in Essex. While there, Rogers wrote *The Seven Treatises* and *A Commentary upon the Whole Book of Judges*. Beginning in 1583, with an appearance before **Archbishop of Canterbury** John Whitgift, Rogers was suspended or censured on several occasions over the next 20 years for preferring the Presbyterian *Book of Discipline* to the ***Book of Common Prayer***. At last, when Richard Vaughan succeeded Bishops Bancroft and Ravio in London in 1606, Rogers was able to continue his ministry undisturbed until his death. **Stephen Marshall** became Rogers' successor, and his two sons continued Rogers' legacy. Daniel Rogers (1573–1652) studied at Christ's College, Cambridge, and ending up **preaching** in Wethersfield after Marshall. He was an outspoken objector to **Arminianism**, Roman **Catholicism**, and infant **baptism**. Ezekiel Rogers (1590–1660) first preached at Rowley, Yorkshire, but then moved to Massachusetts near his relative Nathaniel Rogers in Ipswich. In 1639, he helped to found the town of Rowley, Massachusetts, 30 miles north of Boston.

ROOT AND BRANCH PETITION. In December 1640, 15,000 citizens of London signed a petition asking the **Long Parliament** to see that **episcopacy**, "with all its dependencies, roots and branches, be abolished." The choice of wording derived from Malachi 4:1 of the Old Testament and was directed specifically against the repressive measures of Archbishop William Laud. The signatories complained that their bishops were, in fact, not called by Jesus Christ, for they refused to preach on important scriptural matters, such as original **sin**, **Sabbatarianism**, and **predestination**. Although the House of Commons did pass a Root and Branch Bill in 1641, the House of Lords refused it. However, this early sign of popular and Parliamentary unrest with the existing structures of the Church of England was a significant movement toward the **English Civil Wars**.

ROUNDHEADS. The term "Roundheads" was an appellation for the Protestant, mostly **Presbyterian**, members of **Parliament** during the **English Civil Wars** and **Protectorate** (1641–60). It was the antonym of "**Cavaliers**," which denoted the supporters of King **Charles I**. Because the males of the king's court wore their hair in long ringlets, the more austere Parliamentarians wore their hair shorter to strike an intentional contrast. Although derisive, the exact earliest use of "Roundheads" is disputed. According to John Rushworth, in his *Historical Collections of Private Passages of State, 1680–1701*, the term was first used in 1641 by a dismissed soldier of the Parliamentary army who vowed to exact revenge against the "Roundheaded Dogs." In *Reliquiae Baxterianae*, **Richard Baxter** agreed that the term dates to 1641 but attributed its first use to Queen Henrietta Maria, Charles' wife, who ascribed the label "Roundhead" to Parliamentary leader **John Pym** during the trial of Thomas Wentworth, the First Earl of Strafford.

ROWLANDSON, MARY (1637?–1710). American Puritan author. Rowlandson was born in England to John and Joan White. In 1653, the White family moved to Nashaway, Massachusetts, as one of the prominent landowning families of the town. The town's name changed to Lancaster soon after their arrival. In 1656, Mary married Joseph Rowlandson, a **Harvard College** graduate and the town minister. The couple had four children, of which the last three—Joseph, Mary, and Sarah—survived past infancy. In February 1676, Mary's husband was in Boston seeking financial assistance for his small parish when the Nipmunk and Narragansett Indian tribes attacked Lancaster as part of **King Philip's War**. She and her children were all taken prisoner and interred at various places in New England. Mary was sometimes able to see her son Joseph and daughter Mary, but Sarah died in captivity. Ransomed after 82 days for £20, Rowlandson later wrote about her experience in *The Sovereignty & Goodness of God* (1682). She described the regular relocations that her captors forced upon her, including one that brought her into direct contact with Metacom, the Wampanoag chief known as "King

Philip." Although Rowlandson was not without sympathy for her subjugators, she believed them to be largely allies of Satan, whom God had nonetheless used to show divine displeasure with New England's spiritual declension. In 1677, she and her family moved to Wethersfield, Connecticut, where the senior Joseph preached until his death the following year. Mary remarried to Captain Samuel Talcott in 1679, and he died in 1691. The anonymous friend of Rowlandson who wrote the introduction to her book was likely **Increase Mather**.

RUMP PARLIAMENT. *See* PARLIAMENT.

RUTHERFORD, SAMUEL (1600–1661). Scottish **Presbyterian** minister. Rutherford was born near Nisbet, Scotland, and attended the University of Edinburgh. He was a very talented student and stayed after his graduation to become a teacher at the university in 1623, but he was terminated three years later when his future wife Eupham Hamilton was revealed to be pregnant out of wedlock. Rutherford then became a pastor in the small village of Anwoth in southwest Scotland, where he often rose at three o'clock to begin his studies and visitations for the day. His wife and two children later died in Anwoth.

Rutherford's strongly **Calvinist** 1636 writing, *Exercitationes apologeticae pro divina gratia*, drew the concern of the ecclesiastical establishment. Finally, Rutherford's support for Presbyterianism and republicanism ran him afoul of King **Charles I**, and, in 1636, he was confined to house arrest in Aberdeen, in the northwest corner of Scotland. In Aberdeen, Rutherford kept up an ample correspondence with parishioners, friends, and politicians that became the basis for his collected letters, originally printed in 1664 under the title *Joshua Redivivus, or Mr Rutherfoord's Letters*. After other Scottish Presbyterians consolidated to oppose the king's service manual in 1638, Rutherford was able to return safely to Anwoth and assume a leadership position among the Covenanters. He was active in the Scottish General Assembly that abolished the **episcopacy** later in 1638. In 1639, he received an appointment as professor of divinity at St. Andrews College.

In 1643, Rutherford led a small Scottish delegation to the **Westminster Assembly**, and, even though he could not vote in its pro-

SACRAMENTS. Following the teachings of Protestant Reformers like Martin Luther and John Calvin, the Puritans believed that sacraments had to have explicit institution by Christ and so reduced Roman **Catholicism**'s seven sacraments to two: baptism and the Lord's Supper. As a further separation from Catholic practice, Puritans received the Lord's Supper while sitting to protest the kneeling posture in which Catholics received the mass. According to the **Westminster Confession**, "Sacraments are holy signs and seals of the covenant of grace, immediately instituted by God, to represent Christ and His benefits and to confirm our interest in Him, as also to put a visible difference between those that belong unto the Church and the rest of the world, and solemnly engage them to the service of God in Christ, according to His Word." Westminster goes on to state that the efficacy of the sacraments depends upon the working of faith by the Holy Spirit in the believer and the promise of Christ's presence as set forth in the minister's words of institution. Most Puritans held that only **ordained** ministers could administer the sacraments. Their reception was expected of Christians in obedience to **Scripture**.

Yet that very expectation became the impetus for theological controversies. In England, the earliest **Baptists** questioned the scriptural warrant for baptizing infants. The **Presbyterian** response was to emphasize that if the covenant promises of God permitted the circumcision of infants in the Old Testament, then surely the children of Christians were no less to be included in God's covenant of grace under the New Testament. According to this view, the spiritual benefits of baptism may occur after the time of its administration, so long as the infant later expresses personal faith. But when **John Smyth** nonetheless became convinced of the invalidity of his own infant baptism, he baptized himself in lieu of finding any other church body fully obedient to Scripture that could do so. The Second London Confession of 1689 spoke representatively for the various groups of Baptists when it revised Westminster's article on baptism to state that only the knowingly penitent were proper subjects for baptism, and that immersion rather than pouring or sprinkling was its proper mode. For the Baptists, baptism and the Lord's Supper were not sacraments that imparted grace but ordinances to be obeyed as symbols of one's obedience to Christ.

In America, the **Congregationalist** ministers preached so fervently on worthy participation in the Lord's Supper (1 Corinthians 11:27–30) that many adults became hesitant to receive it and began staying away from church. This meant that there were also fewer children in church, which in turned created a crisis in church membership in the mid-17th century. The solution in Connecticut and Massachusetts was the **Half-Way Covenant**. The advocates of the Half-Way Covenant, including **Thomas Hooker** and **Thomas Shepard**, began from a reading of Genesis 17:7 that God channels grace through families. Thus, they encouraged even unregenerate adults to bring their children to receive baptism and inclusion in the church. **Solomon Stoddard** of Northampton, Massachusetts, went still further to offer the Lord's Supper to those same adults, hoping that the sacrament would for them serve as a "converting ordinance." **Increase Mather** and **Edward Taylor** believed that Stoddard's policy of the Lord's Supper encouraged unworthy participation. Such disputes over the qualifications and purpose of the sacraments revealed the beginning of significant rifts within New England Puritanism's previous unanimity.

SAINT BARTHOLOMEW'S DAY. On Saint Bartholomew's Day (24 August), 1662, on the 90th anniversary of the massacre of tens of thousands of Protestant Huguenots in France, English Puritan ministers still in the Church of England had to decide whether they could reconcile themselves to the reinstitution of **episcopacy** after the **Restoration**. The **Act of Uniformity** of 1662 required such capitulation at the cost of losing one's ecclesiastical office, and Saint Bartholomew's Day was the deadline for decisions. Puritan ministers were expected on that day publicly to foreswear the **Solemn League and Covenant**, consent in all liturgical matters to the *Book of Common Prayer*, and disavow any **ordination** not conducted by bishops. Although a handful of ministers, most notably **Edward Reynolds**, did comply, around 2000 ministers did not, and so at last English **Presbyterians** joined the **Independents** and others as outright **dissenters**. Some ministers resigned their posts on the Sunday before Saint Bartholomew's Day, 17 August; these included **Richard Baxter**, **Thomas Manton**, **Edmund Calamy**, and **William Bates**. Other ministers ejected because of their refusal to submit included **John

Owen, **Thomas Goodwin**, **Anthony Burgess**, **Samuel Annesley**, and **Stephen Charnock**.

SALEM WITCH TRIALS. *See* WITCHCRAFT.

SALTMARSH, JOHN (?-1647). English Puritan writer. Born in Yorkshire, Saltmarsh graduated from Magdalen College, **Cambridge**. He became an **Anglican** minister first at Northampton, then at Braisted in Kent. He was also a chaplain for the army of Sir **Thomas Fairfax**. Saltmarsh was skeptical of both **Presbyterians** and **Independents**, and, in fact, he engaged in a written spar with the Presbyterian Thomas Edwards with pamphlets like "Groans for Liberty" and "Reasons for Unity, Love and Peace." Yet Saltmarsh was still staunchly on the side of **Parliament** against King **Charles I** during the **English Civil Wars**, claiming that the struggle with the king was really one of combating the forces of popery. On 4 December 1647, while living at Ilford in Essex, Saltmarsh told his wife that God had given him a message to deliver to Fairfax and **Oliver Cromwell** at Windsor. This message was that the war would not go well for the **New Model Army**, and Cromwell even reinforced his troops when he heard it. A week later, on 11 December 1647, Saltmarsh died at home. Saltmarsh's many writings indicate a theology of **antinomianism**, and some contemporaries believed that he had converted to the **Seekers** or even the **Familists**. Some of his other titles include "Practice of Policy in a Christian Life," "Holy Discoveries and Flames," "Free Grace," "Maxims of Reformation," "Beams of Light," "Sparkles of Glory," "The Smoke in the Temple," and "Wonderful Predictions."

SALVATION. According to most Puritans, salvation was a state of being forgiven of one's **sin** against God, made possible only through the atoning sacrifice of Jesus Christ on the cross, and applied only to those foreordained and predestined by God to respond to the **preaching** of Christ with faith. Puritans believed that the process by which the elect demonstrated their salvation consisted of several stages: justification, reconciliation, adoption, **sanctification**, and glorification. In truth, salvation and justification became approximately synonymous terms because the subsequent stages following justification were all strictly results of being saved before God and in no case factors on which salvation depended. The sharp distinction of justification and its fruits was a reaction to Roman **Catholic** teaching that an individual must further and complete the initial infusion of grace to begin a lifelong process of being saved. For the Puritans, following the Protestant Reformers Martin Luther and John Calvin, justification was not a process involving human contribution but a single declarative act of God.

The chief confession of Puritan belief, the **Westminster Confession** of 1644, declared, "Those whom God effectually calleth He also freely justifieth, not by infusing righteousness into them, but by pardoning their sins and by accounting and accepting their persons as righteous, not for anything wrought in them or done by them, but for Christ's sake alone, . . . by imputing the obedience and satisfaction of Christ unto them, they receiving and resting on Him and His righteousness by faith, which faith they have not of themselves, it is the gift of God." The American catechism of **Thomas Shepard**, *The First Principles of the Oracles of God*, taught similarly, "Justification . . . is the greatest sentence of God the Father, whereby for the satisfaction of Christ apprehended by faith, and imputed to the faithful, he absolves them from the guilt and condemnation of all sins, and accepts them as perfectly righteous to eternal life." Shepard went on to clarify that justification is perfect and complete because it rests in the righteousness of Christ, whereas **sanctification** is forever improving in this life since it is the measure of the justified person's own righteousness. **Calvinist** Puritans reserved some of their harshest condemnations for belief systems, such as **Arminianism** and **antinomianism**, which they believed either blurred or disconnected justification and sanctification. *See also* PREDESTINATION.

SAMPSON, THOMAS (?–1589). Sampson studied at both **Oxford** and **Cambridge** and apparently became a Protestant during his time at the latter. He was a nephew of **Hugh Latimer**, the former Bishop of Worcester, and he received his holy orders from **Nicholas Ridley**, the Bishop of Lincoln. In 1551, Sampson became the rector at Allhallows in London, and, in 1552, he became the dean of Winchester. He fled to Strasbourg in 1554 as one of the **Marian exiles**. He also spent time in Lausanne, Zurich, Frankfurt, and Geneva before returning to England in 1559 after the coronation of Queen **Elizabeth I**. A skilled Hebraist, Sampson may possibly have contributed to the translation of the **Geneva Bible**. Sampson became almost obsessive with determining what Roman **Catholic** and **Anglican worship** rituals could be indifferent for use by Protestants, and he regularly consulted the Reformed theologians Theodore Beza, Heinrich Bullinger, and Peter Martyr Vermigli on the matter. Even though the queen appointed Sampson as Canon of Durham in 1560 and the dean of Christ Church, Oxford, in 1561, he eventually adopted one of the hallmarks of early Puritanism by declining to wear **vestments**. For this conviction, he and **Lawrence Humphrey**, the former president of Oxford's Magdalen College, appeared on trial before **Archbishop of Canterbury** Matthew Parker in 1564. Edmund Grindal, the Bishop of London after Edmund Bonner and Parker's future successor at Canterbury, dismissed Humphrey but deprived Sampson of his office. Sampson had influential friends, however, like the Lord Burleigh, William Cecil, and the Earl of Huntington, and they helped restore him to favor. In 1567, Sampson became the Master of Wigston's Hospital in Leicester, and later he took the same title at Whittington College, London. His activity was severely limited by contraction of palsy around 1572.

SANCTIFICATION. Puritans did not believe that one's **salvation** or justification depended to any degree upon the goodness of one's works. Because all persons are corrupted by **sin**, only the grace of God bestowed through Christ upon the elect could qualify one for Heaven. However, Puritans were also strongly convinced that saved persons gave increasing evidence of their incorporation into Christ through a life of holiness. This process, never complete in this life, was that of sanctification. The **Westminster Confession** explained, "They who are once effectually called and regenerated, having a new heart and a new spirit created in them, are further sanctified, really and personally, through the virtue of Christ's death and resurrection, by His Word and Spirit in them." *The First Principles of the Oracles of God*, the catechism of Massachusetts minister **Thomas Shepard**, defined: "Sanctification, whereby the sons of God are renewed in the whole man, unto the image of their heavenly Father in Christ Jesus, by mortification, or their daily dying to sin by virtue of Christ's death: and by vivification, their daily rising to newness of life, by Christ's resurrection."

In America, the Puritan prescription for holy living and avoiding vice as public evidence of one's conversion led to an industriousness that sociologist Max Weber famously called "the Protestant work ethic." Yet the majority Puritan understanding of sanctification also became a locus of controversy when Boston's **Anne Hutchinson** declared around 1637, "I seek not for sanctification, but for Christ." Hutchinson did not believe that outward acts of piety such as reading **Scripture**, hearing **preaching**, and observing the Sabbath were necessary proofs of a person's saving familiarity with Christ. Instead, she contended that only one's own inward testimony of the Holy Spirit could be evidence for justification. To the Massachusetts establishment, her position was **antinomianism** and a recipe for libertinism. Hutchinson defended herself by appealing to the words of her minister **John Cotton**, who had argued that using sanctification to verify one's justification was akin to popery. Asked to explain himself, Cotton replied, "Let Calvin answer for me," as he sought to verify the importance of living out one's Christian duties precisely in the context of yielding to the Holy Spirit's indwelling. Governor **John Winthrop** ordered the banishment of Hutchinson from the colony for threatening public morality, yet he admitted afterward in "Christian Experience" that the process of trying her made him reevaluate his own penchant for predicating grace upon his own goodness. *See also* MASSACHUSETTS BAY COLONY; PREDESTINATION.

SAVOY CONFERENCE. The Savoy Conference of 1661 was a failed attempt to reconcile Puritan ministers to the **Restoration** of King **Charles II** and to **episcopacy** in the Church of England. It had been summoned by the king in October 1660 and convened in April 1661 at the lodging of Gilbert Sheldon at Savoy Hospital in London. Its 12 **Anglican** representatives included Sheldon, who was the Bishop of London, and Accepted Frewen, the Archbishop of York. Its 12 Puritan (mostly **Presbyterian**) representatives included **Richard Baxter, Thomas Manton, William Spurstowe,** and **Edmund Calamy**. The Puritans wanted revisions of the *Book of Common Prayer* to encompass their anti-**Catholic** sentiments, including the forbiddance of kneeling at the Lord's Supper, crossing oneself at **baptism**, and giving rings in **marriage**. The Puritans also did not want to have to wear **vestments** and reserved a right to refuse the **sacraments** to persons whose Christian faith they deemed insincere. Following the bishops' refusal to accommodate the Puritans' request, many Puritans conscientiously entered into **Nonconformity**.

SAVOY DECLARATION. On 12 October 1658, nine days after the death of **Oliver Cromwell**, representatives from over 100 **Independent** churches met at Savoy to draft a common confession of faith. Some of the leaders present were **Thomas Goodwin, John Owen, Philip Nye, William Bridge, Joseph Caryl, William Greenhill**, and the chaplain to **Richard Cromwell, John Howe**. The Independents wished to distinguish themselves from those **Presbyterians** who held out hope for a state church, yet they also still desired open communion with Presbyterians on account of their common commitment to **Reformed theology** and the **Westminster Confession**. A Latin translation of the original English pronouncement appeared in 1659. The Savoy Declaration became the basis for **Congregationalist** practice in America as well, becoming ratified by the Church of Massachusetts in 1680 at Boston, and by the Church of Connecticut in 1708 at Saybrook.

SAYBROOK PLATFORM. The Saybrook Platform of 1708 was an attempt to establish a more centralized system of church administration in Connecticut than what had been provided for in the **Cambridge Platform** of 1648. The board that drafted the document consisted of 12 ministers and four laymen. The plan for the Saybrook Platform came out of proposals made by **Cotton Mather** that never came to fruition in Massachusetts, namely the establishment of an association of elders that could enforce discipline over all the churches in a county. Advocates of the idea included Eleazar Wheelock, the founder of Dartmouth College. Opponents, such as **John Wise**, thought that the Saybrook Platform was a betrayal of **Congregationalist** polity and, in fact, a metamorphosis into **Presbyterianism**. At first, the Saybrook Platform stood alongside the **Savoy Declaration** and the 1690 Heads of Agreement as one of the foundational statements of Connecticut Congregationalism. Eventually, however, its critics triumphed and even forced the

Platform's chief author, John Woodward, from the Saybrook pulpit in 1716. By 1760, the Saybrook Platform no longer had any official ecclesiastical status.

SCIENCE. The Puritans' confidence in the desire of God to be known by human beings stirred in them a zeal to learn of God through what is revealed in "the book of nature." Although they firmly held that only **Scripture** reveals what is necessary for **salvation**, they still endorsed scientific study as a way of reversing the noetic effects of **sin**. The Puritan willingness to experiment with new political and ecclesiastical structures fostered a further eagerness to learn new scientific truths. In 1627, George Hakewill was one of the first Puritans to elucidate the Puritan affirmation of scientific investigation in *An Apologie or the Declaration of the Power and Providence of God in the Government of the World*. During a tour of the European continent, **John Milton** even conferred with the famous astronomer Galileo in Florence, Italy. The Puritan **John Ray** became the father of English botany, and another Puritan **Thomas Newcomen** invented the steam engine more than a half century before James Watt. Most of the early members of England's Royal Society were supporters of **Parliament** during the **English Civil Wars**. One of the first fellows of the Royal Society was actually **John Winthrop**, who became the governor of Massachusetts and Connecticut. Winthrop brought to the new world a telescope that he donated to **Harvard College** for the study of comets. Like a number of Puritan ministers in New England, including **Edward Taylor** and **Michael Wigglesworth**, Winthrop also served his neighborhood as a physician. **Cotton Mather** was still extolling the godly pursuit of science four decades after Winthrop's ocean voyage in his *The Christian Philosopher*, and the ethos of experimental investigation fostered by Puritanism continued to inspire such scientific worthies back in England as Francis Bacon, Isaac Newton, and Robert Boyle. Yet Puritanism's trust in the orderly constitution of God's universe may in the end have been one of the main factors in its decline, as its resulting redemption of human reason made possible the rise of Deism and the rationalist God affirmed by the likes of William Paley, Thomas Jefferson, and Benjamin Franklin.

SCORY, JOHN (?–1585). English Puritan author. Little is known about Scory's early life. He was from Norfolk and had been a Dominican friar during the reign of King **Henry VIII**. At some point, he developed Protestant sympathies, probably under the influence of Bishops **Thomas Cranmer** and **Nicholas Ridley**, each of whom he assisted as chaplain. In 1551, Scory became the Bishop of Rochester, and, in 1552, he became the Bishop of Chichester. He lost his post in 1553 after the accession of Queen **Mary I**, and in 1554, he recanted his Protestantism and received a pardon from Edmund Bonner, the Bishop of London. Yet this repudiation was either only temporary or a ruse, for Scory soon fled to the continent with other **Marian exiles**. He spent time mostly in Strasbourg and Geneva, arriving at the latter city in 1555, about the same time as the **Bible** translator **Miles Coverdale**. While in exile, Scory translated writings by the early church fathers St. Cyprian and St. Augustine—the interest in Augustine was one of the earliest evidences of Puritan attention to Augustinian understandings of original **sin** and **predestination**. Following the coronation of Queen **Elizabeth I** in 1558, Scory returned to England and participated in the Westminster Disputation with Roman **Catholic** bishops in 1559. The queen named Scory the Bishop of Hereford; in that position, he continued to defend **Reformed theology** until his death at Whitbourne more than a quarter-century later.

SCOTTISH REFORMATION. Virtually from its inception, Protestant Christianity in Scotland played an important role in the story of Puritanism, and the first great figure in that story was **John Knox**. Knox was a native Scot but was one of the many Protestants who fled England for the European continent following the accession of Queen **Mary I**. After spending time studying with John Calvin, Knox returned to England in 1558 to ask Queen **Elizabeth I** to use the Genevan church as a model for the Church of England. When she refused, Knox wrote *The First Blast of the Trumpet Against the Monstrous Regiment of Women* as a parting shot on his way back to Scotland, where he quickly organized the Scottish Church, or Kirk, as a bastion of **Presbyterianism**. Its emphases were on the authority of **Scripture** and the theology of **Calvinism**, such as **predestination**. Within a decade, many Puritan clergy, deprived of their positions by England's **Lambeth Articles**, came to Scotland to join Knox's church. In 1567, Knox preached the coronation sermon for Scotland's King James VI. James was only 13 months old, thrust onto the throne when his mother Mary, Queen of Scots, was executed as a mutineer by order of Elizabeth. James' most influential tutor throughout his youth was George Buchanan, a staunch Presbyterian. Thus, when James became King **James I** of England in 1603 and promised to unite Scotland and England, **Presbyterians** in both countries hoped for the establishment of their faith as the official polity of the Church of England. However, James disappointed the Puritans by rejecting their **Millennary Petition** following the **Hampton Court Conference**. Despite attempts by **Anglican William Laud** to take Presbyterian lands in 1625, the pace of Presbyterian hegemony still proceeded largely unabated in Scotland. And when King **Charles I** tried to impose the *Book of Common Prayer* upon the Kirk in 1637, popular riots broke out. The next year, most of the country voted to ratify the National Covenant, composed at Edinburgh's Greyfriars Church in affirmation of Presbyterianism as the Scottish national religion. Scottish Presbyterians were therefore commonly known as "Covenanters."

As the **English Civil Wars** broke out in the early 1640s, the **Parliament** under the leadership of **John Pym** began to court Scottish assistance in the struggle to overthrow King Charles. The king sent troops to Scotland to repress the mobilization of Presbyterian soldiery but was ultimately unsuccessful in what came to be known as the **Bishops' Wars**. In 1643, the Scottish Estates and Parliament agreed to abide together by the **Solemn League and Covenant**, a revision of the National Covenant. The Solemn League and Covenant was a mutual pledge to defend the Presbyterian faith against all papal, prelatical, and heretical assaults. Some **Independent** leaders in England such as **Henry Vane** insisted, however, that the wording of the Solemn League be left open to interpretation favorable to their own **toleration**. Also in 1643, **Samuel Rutherford** and George Gillespie headed a Scottish delegation to the **Westminster Assembly**. In 1644–1645, the Propositions of Uxbridge strengthened the Presbyterian leadership of Parliament.

More than 21,000 Scottish soldiers fought during the English Civil Wars. In February 1647, Scottish forces captured the king, and they received handsome payment from Parliament for his handover. But once the Independents gained the upper hand of the English rebellion's leadership in the **New Model Army**, some Scots felt betrayed and actually considered joining the Royalist cause. Aware of this disaffection, **Charles II** came out of his exile in France in 1650 and took the Solemn League and Covenant to test Scottish sympathy for supporting a restored monarchy. Yet **Oliver Cromwell**'s defeat of the younger Charles at Dunbar ended the courtship quickly. Presbyterians were, in fact, to become the loudest advocates for the **Restoration** in 1660, and General **George Monck**, a Presbyterian, was really its chief architect. But the new king did not feel beholden to his Presbyterian patrons. The Covenanters staged an uprising in 1679, supported and then repudiated King **James II** in 1685, and at last surrendered their hopes to direct the course of the Church of England in 1689–90. In 1689, the members of the Scottish Estates voted to recognize William and Mary of England as their new monarchs and then dissolved themselves. The following year, the Church of Scotland was formally constituted as a separate entity from its English counterpart, with the **Westminster Confession** rather than the **Thirty-Nine Articles** as its official doctrine. More formal political union between Scotland and England passed the Parliament of each country in 1706 and took effect in 1707. The Scots accepted invitations from the English for a few dozen seats in the new, first Parliament of Great Britain, but both sides agreed that the new political situation should not effect the national religion of either realm.

SCRIPTURE. Scripture for the Puritans was the inspired and authoritative word of God, to be obeyed without question. It was the mirror before which each person could see the salvific status of one's soul before God, and the guidebook for all human behavior both personal and corporate. Puritans scoured the **Bible** and particularly its apocalyptic texts for clues as to their own place in redemptive history. **Jonathan Edwards**' *A History of the Work of Redemption* is a prime example. They also read the Old Testament as a "type" and pattern for the conduct of a Christian commonwealth, as in **John Cotton**'s *Moses His Judicials* (1636) or **Cotton Mather**'s comparison of Governor **John Winthrop** to an American Nehemiah. The Puritan emphasis on reading and **preaching** the Bible, and seeking therein explicit warrants for doctrine and behavior, helped foster a culture of biblical literacy that encompassed all of society, from the curricula of **Oxford University**, **Cambridge University**, and **Harvard College** to relatively uneducated persons like **John Bunyan**. Multiple Bible translations proliferated during the Puritan era, but the **Geneva Bible** of 1560 and the Authorized Version, also known as the **King James Version**, of 1611 were the two most commonly used.

However, the encouragement of individual Bible reading also created the possibility for disagreements in interpretation. One of the earliest criticisms of the Puritans by the **Anglican** theologian Richard Hooker was that their confidence in understanding all parts of Scripture was a recipe for arrogance and contention. This concern seems to be at least somewhat warranted by the proliferation of Puritan and **Nonconformist** groups who often split over fine points of biblical analysis. **John Milton** ratified this fractious spirit by holding that the freedom to interpret Scripture privately was the hallmark of Protestantism and far more important than any orthodox resolution of what Scripture actually teaches. Many Puritans, therefore, tried to defend their own point of view with confessions and catechisms, or with censure of those who seemed to place personal inspiration above the majority's consensual interpretation. This is why, for example, most Puritans were skeptical of the **Quakers'** notion of the "inner light," and why **Roger Williams** and **Anne Hutchinson** were banished from Massachusetts under suspicion of **antinomianism**. Ironically, Hutchinson defended herself by continuing to employ a traditional Puritan typology, comparing herself to Daniel in the lion's den.

Although the Church of England's **Thirty-Nine Articles** and even the **Irish Articles** of 1615 still recognized the books of the Apocrypha as useful for personal edification, the Puritan confessions restricted the Christian canon to the 39 books of the Old Testament and the 27 books of the New Testament. This opposition to using the Apocrypha grew out of a desire to distance Puritan faith from **Catholic** traditions like prayers for the dead that the Apocrypha could support. Thus, the **Westminster Confession** declared in 1644 that the Apocrypha was of no authority to Christians at all. Westminster also made its understanding of Scripture an even more primal concern than the Christian doctrine of God, the Holy Trinity. It broke the standard practice of prior Christian confessions by making its first article a definition of the bounds and authority of the Bible, and most Protestant statements of faith have followed suit ever since. *See also* BISHOP'S BIBLE; GENEVA BIBLE; GREAT BIBLE; KING JAMES VERSION; MATTHEW'S BIBLE; TAVERNER'S BIBLE; TYNDALE BIBLE.

SCUDDER, HENRY (1589?–1659). English Puritan preacher. Scudder received his university education at Christ's College, **Cambridge.** This was not the Henry Scudder who fought on Long Island during the American Revolutionary War. In 1633, Scudder went to Drayton, Oxfordshire, to minister at the **Presbyterian** church. Ten years later, he received appointment as one of the divines at the **Westminster Assembly**, and he preached regularly before **Parliament** while in London. From there he moved on to a church at Collingborn-Dukes in Wiltshire. **Richard Baxter** and **John Owen** highly commended Scudder's book, *The Christian's Daily Walk in Holy Security and Peace.*

SEDGWICK, OBADIAH (1600–1658). English Puritan preacher and theologian. Sedgwick was born at Marlborough in Wiltshire; his brother John also became a Puritan preacher. At age 16, Sedgwick entered Queen's College, **Oxford**, but he finished his baccalaureate degree at Magdalen Hall. Sedgwick accompanied Lord Horatio Vere to **Holland** as chaplain, and upon his return to England in 1626, Sedgwick became the tutor of Matthew Hale, future Lord Chief Justice of England. Sedgwick soon began **preaching** at St. Mildred's on Bread Street in London. In 1639, Sedgwick followed **John Dod** as the vicar of Coggleshall in Essex, but he returned to St. Mildred's after the commencement of the **English Civil Wars**. A frequent preacher before the **Long Parliament,** Sedgwick became chaplain to the regiment of Colonel Denzil Hollis in 1642, and he received an appointment to the **Westminster Assembly** the following year. In 1646, Sedgwick began preaching at St. Paul's, Covent Garden, where his reputation for effective ministry grew considerably before he retired to his birthplace Marlborough shortly before his death. His son-in-law **Thomas Manton** took over his pastorate.

Sedgwick was the author of several popular collections of **sermons** and theological works throughout the **Interregnum**, including *The Doubting Christian Resolved* (1653), *The Humble Sinner*

Resolved (1656), *The Fountain Opened, and the Water of Life Flowing* (1657), *The Shepherd of Israel; or, an Exposition of Psalm xxiii* (1658), *Anatomy of Secret Sins* (1660), *The Parable of the Prodigal* (1660), and *The Bowels of Tender Mercy Sealed in the Everlasting Covenant* (1660). Yet this **Presbyterian**'s best-known writing was an early work, *Christ's Council to His Languishing Church of Sardis* (1640), in which, after defending his rhetorically plain style by announcing that "no preacher is so learned as he who can save souls," Sedgwick used the condemnation against vapid Christianity in Revelation 3:1–6 to encourage spiritual vitality. *See also* TRIERS.

SEEKERS. The Seekers did not comprise an organized **Nonconformist** sect so much as a loose association of persons who agreed that there was in the 17th century no wholly authentic New Testament church. Unlike other contemporary groups, such as the **Fifth Monarchists** and **Muggletonians**, however, the Seekers believed that the correct response to England's religious turbulence was not an armed assault on political authorities in the name of King Jesus. Rather, the Seekers were contemplatives who advised simply waiting on God either to purify existing church structures or to unveil a new and more perfect one. Seekers believed that the spirit of the Antichrist inspired the liturgies of the Church of England and even its Puritan alternatives, and their non-ceremonial faith anticipated that of the **Quakers**. **Richard Baxter** accused the Seekers of seeking new miracles from God in place of trusting the prescriptions for moral and doctrinal change set forth in **Scripture**. Other Puritans likened the Seekers to **antinomians** and **Anabaptists**.

Probably the earliest Seekers to fit the present definition were the brothers Walter, Thomas, and Bartholomew Legate of London. Bartholomew was executed alongside Edward Wrightman for his anti-institutional religiosity in 1612. The former Leveller William Walwyn and **John Saltmarsh** were other noteworthy Seekers; a legend holds that William Erbery even won over the daughter of **Oliver Cromwell** to Seeker beliefs. Yet the most eminent Seeker of all was **Roger Williams**. There is some question of whether Williams actively identified himself as a Seeker, but there is wide scholarly consensus that Williams became a Seeker in practice soon after founding the Providence colony as a **Baptist** in 1639. Williams believed that it was inappropriate to enforce membership in any particular church because only God can change the **conscience**, even if that meant one could not find the "right" church at all. It was as a Seeker that Williams, in *The Bloudy Tenent of Persecution*, defended his convictions against the Boston community that had once exiled him. *See also* TRIERS.

SELF-DENYING ORDINANCE. After the Earl of Essex, **Robert Devereux**, surrendered to Royalist forces at Lostwithiel in September 1644, some leaders of the Parliamentary army became concerned that inexperienced commanders were inhibiting their ability to defeat King **Charles I**. Some **Independents** also suspected that the **Presbyterian** Parliamentarians serving the army were hesitant to pursue a complete victory over the king without compromise. Sir **Henry Vane** proposed as a solution the Self-Denying Ordinance, which would prohibit members of **Parliament** from also serving as military leaders and thus leave the army in the hands of skilled professionals. The House of Commons passed the Self-Denying Ordinance in December 1644, and the House of Lords conceded to it in April 1645. The Earls of Essex, Manchester, and Warwick were among those Parliamentarians who lost their commissions. The Presbyterian **William Waller** and the Independent Arthur Haselrig resigned their commissions in order to preserve their political positions. **Oliver Cromwell** was the only person exempted from the Self-Denying Ordinance, and he became second-in-command to Sir **Thomas Fairfax** in the reorganized **New Model Army**. The army immediately won a decisive victory over the Royalists at Naseby in June 1644. The **English Civil Wars** were over in two more years when the king surrendered to Scottish forces, which, in turn, gave him to the army for trial and eventual execution.

SEPARATISM. Separatism, a term largely synonymous with **Nonconformity**, refers to that expression of English Puritanism whose advocates gradually considered the Church of England to be beyond the possibility of internal reform. The Separatist movement first gained attention during the reign of Queen **Elizabeth I** for its opposition to the **vestments** of **Anglican** clergy as anti-Christian Roman relics. The list of grievances with the state church soon expanded to include the requirements to kneel at the **Lord's Supper**, cross oneself at **baptism**, recognize the authority of the Apocrypha, honor the Episcopalian system as scriptural, celebrate feast days, and exchange rings during **marriage**. As an expression of their increasing distance from the church and even from more conservative Puritans who still desired fellowship with it, Separatists even began producing their own rival **worship** manuals to the *Book of Common Prayer*, such as the Book of Discipline published by English Separatists in Geneva. Some Separatists also insisted that foreign **ordination** also qualified them to minister to English congregations. Suppressed by Elizabeth and **Archbishop of Canterbury** Matthew Parker for being disturbers of the social order, Separatists began to meet in their own private assemblies, or **conventicles**, in homes or even outdoors. Following a convention of Separatists at Plumbers' Hall on 19 June 1567, more than 30 Separatists, including their leader Robert Hawkins, were arrested. They were released from prison in 1569.

Perhaps the most famous of the early Separatists was **Robert Browne**, who strongly criticized the polity of the established church and gathered his own congregation in Norwich around 1580. Browne went with his followers, the "**Brownists**," to **Holland** for several years before returning to England and resuming his struggle against **episcopacy** in 1586. He soon reconciled with the Anglican Church, however. Such was not the case with **Henry Barrow**, John Perry, and **John Greenwood**, who were hanged for Separatism in 1593. Nor would there be reconciliation with **John Robinson** and **John Smyth**, acquaintances who each left England for Holland to explore their Separatist beliefs in the early 17th century. Some of the followers of Robinson would later return to England as its earliest **Independents**, while others of them came to America aboard the *Mayflower* and became known as the **Pilgrims**.

While Smyth remained in Amsterdam and joined a group of Mennonites, his followers returned to London to start the first recognizable **Baptist** church in England. The Independents and Baptists became the two most influential expressions of Separatism, followed by all those religious groups which also arose during the 17th century in dissent from state-regulated worship, but which did not always share the Independent and Baptist commitment to theological orthodoxy. These included most notably the **Quakers** but also the **Seekers**, the

Levellers, the **Diggers**, the **Familists**, the **Muggletonians**, the **Ranters**, and the **Fifth Monarchists**. Because most **Presbyterians** harbored some desire for restyling the Church of England along the lines of their preferred form of polity, Presbyterianism is generally not considered an expression of Separatism.

SEQUESTRATION ORDINANCE. Under the orchestration of **John Pym**, **Parliament** passed the Sequestration Ordinance on 27 March 1643. It was ostensibly a measure to raise money for the Parliamentary army during the **English Civil Wars**. The ordinance allowed Parliament to sequester, or seize, the benefices of clergymen attested to live scandalous lives (such as by drunkenness or swearing) and the properties of Royalists. If a person were deprived of his lands, the sequestered living would come under the control of Parliamentary commissioners, who would usually siphon three-fifths for their rebellion, give one-fifth back to the person's children, and award one-fifth to the informant. Parliament agreed not to sequester properties belonging to universities. By the time of Parliament's execution of King **Charles I** in January 1649, there were virtually no Royalist-held lands left, and so the committee for sequestration dissolved. After the **Restoration**, King **Charles II** returned a number of sequestered lands to their previous owners.

SERMONS. *See* PREACHING.

SEWALL, SAMUEL (1652–1730). American Puritan judge. Sewall was born in Horton, near Bishopstoke, of Hampshire, but his father brought the family to Newbury, Massachusetts, in 1661 following the **Restoration**. Sewall graduated from **Harvard College** in 1671, became a **fellow** at Harvard in 1673, and acted as school librarian in 1674, but he would later criticize his alma mater's turn away from **Calvinist** orthodoxy. Sewall gave up a desire to be a minister after marrying Hannah Hull, the daughter of one of the colony's wealthiest merchants. Yet, he remained interested in theological matters, particularly sound **preaching**, congregational singing, evangelistic work among the Indians by the Society for the Propagation of the Gospel, and the religious instruction of children. Sewall himself had several children; his son Joseph became pastor of Boston's Old South Church in 1713 and actually conducted Sewall's second marriage to Abigail Tilley in 1719, two years after his first wife's death. Sewall held a number of positions in his long career: operator of the printing press (1681), deputy to the General Court of Westfield (1683), negotiator with England alongside **Increase Mather** (1688), member of the Governor's Council of the Commonwealth of Massachusetts (1691–1725), and chief justice of the Supreme Court of Massachusetts (1718–1728).

Sewall is best known as one of the three judges to preside over sentencing 19 persons to death during the **Salem witch trials** of 1692. In 1697, Sewall wrote a public apology for his role in the Salem trials, and he set aside a day each year of his life thereafter to fast and repent. This apology also appears in Sewall's lengthy *Diary*, whose topics range from his failed courtship of the widow Katherine Winthrop after his second wife's death, to acquaintances with New England's leading clergymen like **Samuel Willard**, **Solomon Stoddard**, and **Cotton Mather**. Sewall's other major works are *Phaenomena quaedam Apocalyptica ad Aspectum Novi Orbis Configurata* (1697), a projection of America's place in redemptive history, and *The Selling of Joseph* (1700), the first-known tract printed in America to advocate the cessation of importing African slaves. Sewall died at his Boston home in 1730, but a descendant, Samuel Edward Sewell, continued his legacy in the next century as a lawyer who was visible in the cause of ending slavery. *See also* MASSACHUSETTS BAY COLONY.

SHAW, SAMUEL (1635–1696). English Puritan preacher. Shaw was born into a blacksmith's family in Repton, Derbyshire, and should not be confused with the Samuel Shaw who served as a major in the American Revolutionary War. After graduating from St. John's College, **Cambridge**, this Shaw became the schoolmaster at Tamworth in Warwickshire in 1656. From there, he spent some time in Mosely before receiving **Presbyterian ordination** in Long Watton (or Long-Whatton), Leicestershire, in 1658. He lost his license to preach under the **Act of Uniformity** of 1662, and in 1665, while living in Cotes, he lost two daughters to plague. He wrote *The Welcome to the Plague* in reflection on these events. In 1666, Shaw arrived at Ashby-de-la-Zouch, where Arthur Hildersam had once been the minister. He preached privately in that town for two years before becoming its schoolmaster in 1668. He remained in that position until he died, having penned works both of theology, like *The True Christian's Test* and *The Voice of One Crying in a Wilderness*, and grammar, like *Words Made Visible* and *Minerva's Triumph*.

SHEPARD, THOMAS (1605–1649). English Puritan preacher and theologian. Shepard was born at Towchester, Northamptonshire, on the same day of the discovery of the **Gunpowder Plot** against King **James I**. Although the death of both his parents before he was 10 years of age had a **melancholy** effect on him, he went on to attain the M.A. degree from **Emmanuel College, Cambridge**. **John Preston** of Cambridge was influential in Shepard's Christian conversion while a student. Shepard became a **lecturer** at Earls Colne in Essex but was chased from the post by **Archbishop of Canterbury William Laud**. When Shepard relocated to Yorkshire and became the chaplain to Sir Richard Darly, the Archbishop of York, Richard Neile, would not let him preach there either. Both Laud and Neile were convinced that Shepard was a nefarious **Nonconformist**, and Laud called him a "prating coxcomb." Shepard moved on to Heddon in Northumberland, but when his eldest son died in 1635, he lost the will to remain in England, and his desire for a stealthy departure for Boston sadly prevented him and his wife from attending his son's funeral. He hoped that crossing the Atlantic Ocean would be his own personal exodus, bringing him to a better land. Yet even though Shepard soon became the pastor of the church at Cambridge, Massachusetts, sadness still attended him when both his first wife, and within a few years his second wife, the daughter of Cambridge's previous minister **Thomas Hooker**, died. Two children from that second wife also died in infancy.

Shepard's sermons understandably wrestled with grief and affliction, seeking comfort for sorrow in God's sovereign will. Other common themes of his sermons were the defense of a Sabbath rest and opposition to **Arminianism** and **antinomianism**. Related to the latter, he was complicit in the expunction of **Anne Hutchinson** from Massachusetts for emphasizing the authority of private religious experience. Shepard also preached frequently on the stages of recognizing **sin** (conviction, compunction, humiliation) and the growth of the Christian life (**justification**, reconciliation, adoption, **sanctification**, glorification). Apparently he did so with great effectiveness, for the number of converts under his ministry from among both settlers and Native Americans was as numerous as for any American Puritan preacher, including **Increase Mather** and **John Cotton**. Shepard also helped to relocate **Harvard College** to Cambridge (then called "Newtowne"), Massachusetts, and his *Theses Sabbaticae* came out of lectures at Harvard. Other writings by Shepard include his *Memoir*, *The Doctrine of the Sabbath* (1649), *The Sincere Convert* (1652), *Subjection to Christ in All His Ordinances and Appointments, the Best Means to Preserve our Liberty* (1652), *A Treatise of Liturgies* (1653), and an unusually mystical treatment of encountering God, *The Parable of the Ten Virgins* (1660). A son and grandson, both also named Thomas, followed Shepard in ministry at Cambridge. *See also* MASSACHUSETTS BAY COLONY.

SHORT PARLIAMENT. *See* PARLIAMENT.

SHOWER, JOHN (1657–1715). English Puritan preacher. Little is known about Shower's life except that his reputation grew among Puritans from being the trusted assistant to **Vincent Alsop**, the noted **Nonconformist** minister. Shower also spent some time lecturing to an English church in Rotterdam, **Holland**, and he met with the renowned Reformed theologian Francis Turretin in Geneva. Yet he was best remembered for his quarter-century of **preaching** in various London churches, especially on the theme of God's complete forgiveness of **sin** through Jesus Christ.

SIBBES, RICHARD (1577–1635). English Puritan preacher and theologian. Although Sibbes remained a member of the Church of England all his life, he became a favorite theologian of the **Nonconformists** who proliferated during and after the **English Civil Wars**. He was born the eldest son of Paul Sibbes, a wheelwright in Suffolk who dissuaded young Richard's expensive reading habits. Yet Richard was still able to attend St. John's College, **Cambridge**, because he was selected as a sizar, one who did not have to pay for tuition and food. Sibbes earned his bachelor's degree in 1599, a **fellowship** in 1601, and an M.A. degree in 1602. In 1603, he professed

Christianity under the influence of **Paul Baynes**, successor to **William Perkins** at the Church of St. Andrews in Cambridge. Sibbes then received **ordination** in the Church of England in 1607 at Norwich, became a college preacher in 1609, and from 1611–16 served as **lecturer** at Holy Trinity Church, Cambridge. Some of the future prominent persons influenced by Sibbes's ministry at Holy Trinity were **John Cotton, Hugh Peters, Thomas Goodwin**, and **John Preston**.

In 1615, Sibbes lost his fellowship, but he became lecturer at **Gray's Inn**, London, in 1617, and also master of St. Catherine's Hall, Cambridge, in 1626. Soon thereafter, Sibbes became a Doctor of Divinity, and some of his students would later become influential representatives at the **Westminster Assembly**. One former student, Preston, was **preaching** at **Lincoln's Inn** for part of the time that Sibbes was at Gray's. In 1630, Sibbes published his first and perhaps most famous work, *The Bruised Reed and Smoking Flax*, which described the elect soul distressed in **conscience** as the bruised reed on which God tenderly blows, making smoking flax to take fire for the cause of the gospel. **Richard Baxter** would later hail *The Bruised Reed* as instrumental in his conversion. Many other works of Sibbes's were published posthumously, including *The Saint's Safety in Evil Times, The Fountain Sealed, Spiritual Jubilee, The Soul's Conflict, The Returning Backslider, A Description of Christ, Christ's Exaltation, Union betwixt Christ and His Church*, and *The Glorious Feast of the Gospel*. In 1633, after the resignation of **Thomas Goodwin** and by invitation of King **Charles I**, Sibbes again added the curacy of Holy Trinity parish to his list of growing obligations.

Abstaining from marriage, Sibbes devoted all his energies not only to his own preaching and writing but also to overseeing the publication of other Puritan sermons, especially those that emphasized the indwelling, **salvation**-sealing power of the Holy Spirit and the intercessory priesthood of Christ. In these efforts, Sibbes befriended the ecclesial conservative **James Ussher** while he alarmed **Archbishop of Canterbury William Laud**, who deprived him of his fellowship at St. Catherine's. But even after his death at Gray's Inn, Sibbes would continue to inspire an upcoming generation of more aggressive Puritans, who found in his many printed sermons on spiritual warfare and Christ's defeat of the devil an encouragement for the removal of King Charles in favor of a more direct reign by Jesus. In the 1860s, James Nichol's collected *The Complete Works of Richard Sibbes* in seven volumes. *See also* LAY IMPROPRIATIONS.

SIMPSON (OR SYMPSON), SIDRACH (OR SYDRACH) (1600–1658). English **Independent** minister. Simpson completed a bachelor's degree at **Cambridge** and then became curate and **lecturer** at St. Margaret's Church on Fish Street, London. When the policies of **Archbishop of Canterbury William Laud** repressed Puritan ministers, Simpson became one of the "**five dissenting brethren**," alongside **Thomas Goodwin, Philip Nye, Jeremiah Burroughs**, and **William Bridge**, who fled to **Holland**. At first, Simpson attended the church in Rotterdam where Bridge was pastor, but he later started a separate congregation. In 1643, Simpson returned to England and received an appointment as a Westminster divine. With Goodwin and Nye, he was one of the leading advocates for the Independents among the majority of **Presbyterians**, coauthoring "An Apologetical Narration submitted to the Honourable Houses of **Parliament**." Simpson performed various duties by Parliamentary appointment during the **Interregnum**, **preaching** sermons like "Reformation's Preservation," sitting on committees, becoming an administrator at Cambridge, and acting as one of **Oliver Cromwell**'s **triers** of preachers. He also gathered an Independent church around him at Abchurch in London. Ironically, Simpson's son Sidrach shared his father's name but loathed his father's ecclesiology, becoming a well-known opponent of all **dissenters** while rector of St. Mary's Church in Stoke Newington.

SIN. Puritans typically understood sin as a rebellion against the law and will of God as revealed in **Scripture** (John 3:4). It was both a corruption of human nature resulting from the fall of Adam and an action of individual disobedience. Puritan sermons, certainly from the time of **William Perkins** on, sought to arouse one's **conscience** to the desperate and damnable condition of one's soul apart from God's unmerited grace. Such a rhetorical tactic still had its effects upon converted hearers when **Jonathan Edwards** preached "Sinners in the Hands of an Angry God" on the eve of the **Great Awakening** in America, but by the middle of the 18th century, preachers like **Urian**

Oakes were lamenting that threatened judgments against sin were no longer affecting people as they once did.

Most Puritan compendia of faith believed sin to be both original and actual. Original sin according to the Puritans was not biologically transmitted, as taught by Roman **Catholic** tradition, but rather the disobedience of Adam was charged to all his heirs as the representative of the whole human race. The **Westminster Confession** of 1644 taught that God permitted the first man to fall into sin but that the first disobedience then became part of the universal human condition. Only the imputed righteousness of the second Adam, Jesus Christ, could nullify the effects of having a sinful nature. Yet no one could accuse God of unfairness because all persons have also knowingly consented to opposing the divine will. Puritans not only preached against the traditional "seven deadly sins" (anger, pride, avarice, lust, envy, gluttony, sloth) but also such personal and societal contaminants as cursing, drunkenness, **theater** going, and contentiousness. In *A True Sight of Sin*, for instance, **Thomas Hooker** elaborated on how to recognize sin with clarity and conviction. In a catechism entitled *The First Principles of the Oracles of God* (1653), **Thomas Shepard** defined original sin as a "contrariety of the whole nature of man to the law of God, whereby it, being averse from all good, is inclined to all evil," and actual sin as "the continual jarring of the actions of man from the law of God, by reason of original sin, and so man hath no free will to any spiritual good."

Because they believed that their trans-Atlantic journeys were made to flee an increasingly sinful England, Puritan ministers in America were often sensitive to corporate hardships that could be indications of God's displeasure with their response to his deliverance. Thus, outbreaks of **antinomianism** or war with local Indians could be interpreted as warnings of God and enticements to repentance for declining from God's will. Shepard further cautioned against committing the unforgivable sin of resisting God's ministrations after having once claimed to be enlightened by Christ. The dreadful prospect of Hell as punishment for unforgiven sin began to lose its rhetorical power as the doctrine of original sin fell out of favor. In *The Reasonableness of Christianity*, for instance, John Locke contended that Adam's descendants had not contracted with their sire to represent them all before God, and so his sin's effects were only exemplary and not imputative. Without original sin with which to contend, humans were far more optimistic about directing their own futures. The perpetuation of this idea on both sides of the Atlantic through the intellectual circles of Deism and Unitarianism further enervated public interest in Puritan jeremiads against sin.

SKIPPON, PHILIP (1600?–1660). English **Presbyterian** soldier. Skippon was born to Luke and Ann Skippon in West Lexham, Norfolk. Already as a young man, he gained respect as a soldier serving with Sir Horace Vere in Bohemia and the Low Countries. He took a wife named Maria in 1622, and she would bear him seven children. In 1638, Skippon returned home to Norfolk and lived at Foulsham Hall following the death of his father, but only the next year he moved to London upon a recommendation that he serve King **Charles I** as an army commander. In fact, Skippon committed his military expertise to **Parliament**, and in 1641–42, he was given charge of leading the Trained Bands to keep Charles out of London at the battle of Turnham Green. For his success, Skippon received an appointment as sergeant major general by the Earl of Essex, **Robert Devereux**, and, in 1643, Skippon participated in some of the important conflicts of the first **English Civil War** at Reading, Gloucester, and Newbury. The last of these was at first a loss for Skippon's troops, but a second engagement at Newbury turned back toward the Parliamentary side.

After the Earl of Essex fled the battlefield at Lostwithiel, Skippon took over and reluctantly surrendered that engagement to the king, but in 1645, he was back as a Major General in the **New Model Army**, fighting the key battle of Naseby even after being wounded by a musket ball. Although Skippon preferred Presbyterianism, he cared about the morale of all his troops, and when some became disaffected by poor wages and lack of progress toward full religious **toleration**, he tried to calm tensions by writing devotional materials for his men. He was preparing to lead his company to quell uprisings in Ireland when he was called again by Parliament to secure London during the second civil war in 1648. After the execution of the king, Skippon received appointment to the High Court of Justice but never attended it. He represented King's Lynn in the House of Lords yet rarely spoke except to condemn the **Quaker** James Nayler's messianic procession into Bristol in 1656. Skippon remained commander of the London militia until his death shortly before the **Restoration**.

SLATER, SAMUEL (?–1701). English Puritan preacher. Slater was educated at **Emmanuel College, Cambridge**, and served as the minister of churches at Nayland, Suffolk, and Bury St. Edmunds. Ejected from state church office by the **Act of Uniformity** in 1662, Slater moved to London and succeeded **Stephen Charnock** at the Puritan congregation at Crosby Square on Bishopsgate Street. He attempted a revision of **John Milton**'s epic poem *Paradise Lost* for common readers. He should not be confused with the Samuel Slater who migrated from England to America and developed the first textile mill in Rhode Island in 1793.

SMECTYMNUUS. "Smectymnuus" was the pseudonym of five **Presbyterians** who published two treatises in 1641 against Episcopalian government in the Church of England. Bishop **Joseph Hall** of Exeter had contended for the divine and apostolic right of bishops not only to preach and preside over a local board of church elders, but also to assume jurisdictional authority over all church elders within a diocese. In reply, the five contributors who wrote under the name Smectymnuus produced *An Answer to a Book, Entituled, A Humble Remonstrance* and later *A Vindication of the Answer to the Humble Remonstrance*. These men selected their pen name by combining their first and last initials: **Stephen Marshall**, **Edmund Calamy**, Thomas Young, Matthew Newcomen, and **William Spurstowe**. They denied that bishops in the apostolic period had broad powers to prescribe liturgies for multiple churches, and they disagreed with Hall's claim that presbyters could not perform an **ordination** except in the presence of a bishop. *See also* SYNOD OF DORT.

SMITH, HENRY (1550?–1591?). English Puritan preacher. Records disagree on the birth and death dates of Smith, with sources suggesting either 1550 or 1560 for the former and anywhere from 1591 to 1613 for the latter. Yet it seems certain that he was born the son of a wealthy squire at Withcock in Leicestershire, was the stepson to the sister of the Lord Burleigh, William Cecil, and studied at both **Cambridge** and **Oxford**. When Smith began **preaching** at St. Clement

Danes in the Strand, John Aylmer, the Bishop of London, challenged his authority because Smith was only licensed and not **ordained**. Yet Burleigh defended him, and Smith's reputation as an orator grew to become, in Thomas Fuller's estimation, that of a silver-tongued preacher only a little below St. John Chrysostom. Smith retired from preaching around 1589 when his health became poor. There were dozens of printings in Smith's own lifetime of his sermons, which were collected for the first time by Fuller in 1675 in a single volume entitled *Sermons, with other his Learned Treatises*. A few of those many sermons, whose titles often reflect Smith's practical moral concerns, were "A Preparative to **Marriage**," "An Examination of Usury," "The Honour of Humility," "Noah's Drunkenness," "The Humility of Paul," "The Ladder of Peace," "The Art of Hearing," "The Pride," "The Poor Man's Tears," "The Godly Man's Request," "The Pilgrim's Wish," and "The Trial of the Righteous."

SMYTH, JOHN (1570–1612). English **Nonconformist** minister. Smyth enrolled as a sizar at Christ's College, **Cambridge**, in 1586. He attained the M.A. degree and became a **fellow** before receiving **ordination** as an **Anglican** priest in 1594. He began lecturing in the city of London but lost his position in 1602 for increasing indications of Nonconformity, including strong **Sabbatarian** convictions. Smyth was imprisoned for a time, but details are scarce. By 1606, Smyth had clearly become a **Separatist**, and he agreed to preach for a church in Gainsborough. His first published defenses of this decision included *The Bright Morning Starre*, *A Pattern of True Prayer*, and *The Differences of the Churches of the Separation*. Smyth feared for his congregation's safety, and so he led the group to Amsterdam, **Holland**, in 1608, to join his former Cambridge tutor **Francis Johnson** and other relocated English Separatists. **John Robinson**, the pastor of the eventual Plymouth **Pilgrims** and an acquaintance of Smyth from England, also arrived, but Smyth's religious vision was becoming divisive even among fellow **dissenters**, and he might have taken a subgroup to Leyden.

Smyth was constantly reevaluating his Christian beliefs. He changed from a **Calvinist** to an **Arminian** and began to reject the concept of original **sin**. He also believed that all aspects of a **worship** service should be spontaneous, disallowing even the public reading of **Scripture** unless from memory. Yet under the influence of a group of Dutch Mennonites, Smyth also came to question the scriptural legitimacy of infant **baptism**. Thinking that no fully biblical church existed that could properly give him a true first baptism as a believing adult, Smyth baptized himself in 1609. Robinson's followers were shocked by the audacity of Smyth's self-baptism, but then some of Smyth's own group felt betrayal when Smyth wanted to receive baptism again from the Mennonites. **Thomas Helwys**, the layman who had financed the original relocation to Holland, returned to England and founded another congregation in London in 1612.

Their emphasis on believers' baptism, combined with their insistence that government not intrude in private religion, make Smyth and Helwys the first fathers of the English **Baptist** tradition. They are often called General Baptists for their Arminian belief in Christ's general rather than individually particular atonement. Helwys continued to defend his early Baptist vision in *A Short Declaration of the Mistery of Iniquity* (1612), but Smyth did actually join and live out his days among the Mennonites. In his final years, Smyth continued to defend both his orthodox understanding of Christ's two natures and his self-baptism in writings like *Parallels and Censures, The Character of the Beast, A Dialogue of Baptism*, and *The Last Booke of Iohn Smith Called the Retraction of his Errours, and the Confirmation of the Truth*. Smyth died of consumption (tuberculosis) in 1612, having been one of the significant early proponents for religious **toleration**.

SOCINIANISM. *See* UNITARIANISM.

SOLEMN LEAGUE AND COVENANT. The Solemn League and Covenant of 1643 was based on a Reformed confession of the same name from 1590 that the majority of Scotland had adopted and to which King **Charles I**'s father King James VI (later King **James I** of England) had also subscribed. It sealed an alliance between the **Long Parliament** and Scottish **Presbyterians** that hastened the defeat of the royalist forces during the **English Civil Wars**. The Presbyterians agreed to support **Parliament**'s revolution against the king in the hope of a Presbyterian state church in exchange. Yet the **Independent** leaders of Parliament and its army carefully crafted changes to the document to allow some freedom of interpretation. Sir **Henry Vane**, for instance, believed the preamble's declaration that signatories should act "according to the word of God" could be used against Presbyterian ambitiousness if needed. After the Scottish Estates, the **Westminster Assembly**, and both Houses of Parliament all approved the amended document, it became legally binding on all adult Christians in England, Scotland, and Ireland in February 1644. King **Charles I** considered this to be treasonous, and even some Independent ministers like **Richard Baxter** believed it to be too much of an imposition. Yet, the Solemn League and Covenant was the underpinning legislative document of the **Interregnum** and **Protectorate**, and it was read aloud in every church of the **Commonwealth**. As part of a failed attempt to retake England from Scotland, **Charles II** courted Scottish support for a revived monarchy by signing the Solemn League and Covenant in 1652. Following the **Restoration**, however, Charles repealed the act, and copies of it were publicly burned.

SPARKE, THOMAS (1548–1616). English Puritan preacher. Sparke was born at South Somercoates, Lincolnshire, and attended Magadalen College, **Oxford**, where he earned a **fellowship** and studied both the church fathers and Protestant Reformers. From Oxford, Sparke went to serve at the rectory of Bleachley (Bletchley) in Lincolnshire. In 1575, he became an assistant chaplain for Bishop Thomas Cooper in London. In 1584, he joined **Walter Travers** at Lambeth in debating **Archbishop of Canterbury** John Whitgift over certain parts of the *Book of Common Prayer*. Specifically, Sparke opposed references to the Apocrypha as inspired **Scripture** and the allowance of private **baptisms**. Yet Sparke's criticisms did not take him completely in a **Nonconformist** direction, as he made evident in his book, *A Brotherly Persuasion to Unity and Uniformity*. During the reign of Queen **Elizabeth I**, he also wrote a tract whose suggestion of a possible succession to her throne placed him in some trouble. When King **James I** came to power, he included Sparke as one of but four Puritans to meet with him at the **Hampton Court Conference** of 1604.

SPURSTOWE, WILLIAM (1605?–1666). English **Presbyterian** preacher. Spurstowe was the eldest son of William Spurstowe Sr., a

London merchant. His mother, Damoris Parkhurst from Gilford, came from a well-connected Puritan family. Spurstowe began his university training at **Emmanuel College, Cambridge**, in 1623, and in 1628, he moved over to **Oxford**. In 1638, he became a **fellow** at Oxford's St. Catherine's College, while **Richard Sibbes** was the master there. In 1645, Spurstowe himself attained to master of the college. He was one of the divines at the **Westminster Assembly**, as well as one of the co-authors of the pro-Presbyterian tracts issued under the pseudonym of **Smectymnuus**. He spent some time **preaching** at the rectory of Great Hampden, Buckinghamshire, as well, but he was ejected from the state church after King **Charles II** issued the **Act of Uniformity**, even though he had opposed the execution of **Charles I**. Apart from his attendance at the **Savoy Conference**, Spurstowe spent most of his time after the **Restoration** in retirement at Hackney. His individual writings include *The Spiritual Chemist*, *The Wells of* **Salvation**, *The Wiles of Satan*, *A Crown of Life*, *The Magistrate's Dignity and Duty*, *The Doctrines of the* **Synod of Dort**, and *Death and the Grave*.

STAR CHAMBER. An outgrowth of the English monarch's royal council, the Star Chamber was in frequent use during the Tudor and Stuart dynasties as a court of law that tried enemies to the crown. It drew its name from the stars painted against a dark blue background on the ceiling of the room where it convened at Westminster. During the reign of Queen **Elizabeth I**, several persons appeared in the Star Chamber to answer to the charge of being Puritans, including Edward Deering, William Smyth, and **Thomas Cartwright**. The Star Chamber also supported **Archbishop of Canterbury** John Whitgift's censorship of the press. By the reign of King **Charles I**, the Star Chamber had become a place of severe punishments with no rights for the accused. Often, the charges leveled there were brought from the king's Council Table, without firm basis in written law. The defendants who appeared in the Star Chamber had no appeals, no juries, and no witnesses; their statements were not even admissible unless entered by an assigned lawyer who typically had no interest in absolving his client. Between 20 and 30 people of the king's appointment served at the Star Chamber, and their decisions were reached by majority vote unless the king himself were present, in which case only his decision would be valid. Some of the more notorious verdicts rendered by the Star Chamber were the cutting of an ear, splitting of a nostril, and branding of a cheek on **Alexander Leighton** in 1630, and the cropping of the ears of **William Prynne**, **John Bastwick**, and **Henry Burton** in 1633. In 1641, **John Pym** led **Parliament** to dissolve the Star Chamber, freeing the pamphleteer **John Lilburne** in the process, and the king conceded in a vain attempt to preclude his overthrow. Nonetheless, there is evidence of a meeting at the Star Chamber during the **Commonwealth** in 1655, when one John Trask was censured for observing the Sabbath day on Saturday rather than on Sunday.

STEELE, RICHARD (1629–1692). English **Presbyterian** preacher. The son of a Cheshire farmer, Steele earned an M.A. degree from **Oxford** in 1656 but was ejected from the Church of England following the **Act of Uniformity** in 1662. He moved to London and gathered **conventicles** around him. He served on the **ordination** boards for both Philip and **Matthew Henry**. He should not be confused with the Richard Steele (1672–1729) who went to Oxford from Dublin and became a politician and playwright.

STERRY, PETER (?–1672). Born in Surrey, Sterry attended **Emmanuel College** at **Cambridge**, eventually becoming a **fellow** and earning an M.A. degree there. He was an avowed Platonist who developed a mystical and philosophical style of **preaching**. He preached around London for a while and received one of the 14 appointments from the House of Lords to attend the **Westminster Assembly** in 1643. Sterry was not a Presbyterian, however, which helped to cultivate his friendship with Sir **Henry Vane** and led to his appointment as chaplain to **Oliver Cromwell**. During Cromwell's **Protectorate**, Sterry preached frequently before **Parliament** and kept official government records for the **Commonwealth**. His prominence waned after Cromwell's death, but Sterry continued to preach for London **conventicles** and to write theological tracts, such as *Discourse on the Mystery of Love and Wrath*; *The Appearance of God to Man in the Gospel*; *Discourse of the Freedom of the Will*; and *The Rise, Race, and Royalty of the Kingdom of God in the Soul of Man*.

STOCK, RICHARD (1569?–1626). English Puritan preacher. Stock was born in York and studied at St. John's College, **Cambridge**, with **William Whitaker**. After serving as a private chaplain and **preaching** around several churches in London, Stock became the assistant to Thomas Edmund at Allhallows on Bread Street in London for 16 years. Following Edmund's death, Stock remained at the church for an additional 16 years as pastor. He was buried at St. Paul's Cathedral in London. His writings include *The Doctrine and Use of Repentance* (1610) and the posthumous works *Commentary on Malachi*, *Truth's Companion*, and *A Stock of Divine Knowledge*.

STODDARD, SOLOMON (1643–1729). American **Congregationalist** minister. Stoddard was born into one of the leading mercantile families of Boston and attended **Harvard College**. He completed his degree in 1662 and became the school's first librarians in 1667. In 1672, he became the pastor of the Congregationalist church at Northampton, Massachusetts, a small town on the Connecticut River. By the time of his death around a half century later, Northampton had the second-largest church in the American colonies behind Boston. In the first three decades of the 18th century, there was likely no more influential pastor in New England than Stoddard, and his son Anthony also continued the family legacy with a 60-year pastorate of his own in Westbury, Connecticut. A good example of Stoddard's **preaching** approach, a ministry based on encouragement for doubters, is his *The Safety of Appearing at the Day of Judgment, in the Righteousness of Christ*. Yet Stoddard's long career, which included many commencement addresses at Harvard, was also marked by significant theological controversy. Some called him "Pope Stoddard" because he advocated moving toward a **Presbyterian** church polity that would allow tighter disciplinary control over the sermons of area ministers. Others criticized Stoddard for being too lax in upholding the older Puritan understanding of Christians as a regenerate people.

Like most New England churches by the time of Stoddard's ministry, Northampton practiced the **Half-Way Covenant**, whose interpretation of God's covenant promises and **baptismal** efficacy permitted baptizing the children even of parents who lacked a public conversion. Yet Stoddard also permitted adults without personal faith to receive the **Lord's Supper**, considering the sacrament a "converting ordinance" that might actually produce faith in the communicant. For this, he took strong criticisms from **Increase Mather** and **Edward Taylor** for belittling the scriptural prohibition against partaking of Christ's body unworthily. Even **Jonathan Edwards**, the grandson whom Stoddard appointed as his assistant in 1727 and who succeeded Stoddard as Northampton's pastor in 1729, agreed that Stoddard had seriously compromised the expectations of the Christian gospel on this issue. Yet Edwards nonetheless highly admired his grandfather; during the **Great Awakening**, he prayed for conversions like those of the five "harvests" of souls that Stoddard documented in 1679, 1683, 1696, 1712, and 1718.

STONE, SAMUEL (1602–1663). English and American **Congregationalist** minister. Stone was born in Hertford, England, the third son of John and Sarah Stone. He went to **Emmanuel College, Cambridge**, in 1620, and earned a baccalaureate degree. He then moved about for several years as both a private tutor and willing student, receiving **ordination** in 1626 and becoming curate at Sisted, Essex, in 1627. At this care, he married Hope Fletcher, who bore him three daughters. Because Stone developed **Nonconformist** sympathies, he joined **John Cotton** and **Thomas Hooker** aboard the *Griffin*, setting sail in 1633 for Massachusetts. At first, Hooker and Stone ministered at New Towne (later Cambridge), but, in 1636, they reached an agreement with Algonquin Indians on the Connecticut River 100 miles southwest from there to transform the Dutch settlement "House of Hope," known to the Indians as Saukiog, into the city of Hartford, named for Stone's birthplace. For 14 years, Stone served alongside Cotton, and then for another 16 years he served as pastor of the Hartford church alone. Although Stone's ministry was not without some local controversy, particularly over his willingness to baptize the children of unregenerate parents, his reputation as a doctrinal preacher and man of **prayer** led to a great outpouring of grief at his death, including the memorial sonnet "A Threnodia" by one "E. B." Stone's legacy lies principally in his co-founding of the city of Hartford and in his defense of Congregationalist polity in the writings *A Discourse upon the Logical Notion of a Congregational Church* and *A Congregational Church Is a Catholike Visible Church*.

STOUGHTON, WILLIAM (1631–1701). American Puritan politician and judge. Stoughton was born in England, but his parents Israel and Elizabeth held property rights in **Massachusetts Bay**, and they moved as a family to start the town of Dorchester when William was young. He earned a degree from **Harvard College** in 1650 and then returned to England, where he completed the M.A. at New College, **Oxford**, in 1652. Stoughton then agreed to serve as curate for a congregation in Sussex, but he lost this position after the **Restoration**, and, in 1662, he came back to Dorchester to resume **preaching**. His most notable sermon was "New England's True Interest," proclaimed during the election season of 1668, which sounded the typically Puritan theme of being a covenant people called to serve God in the wilderness. However, the remainder of Stoughton's career was notable for his involvement in the political and judicial life of the colony. From 1674–76 and 1680–86, Stoughton was the deputy president of the temporary government of Massachusetts, which placed him in charge of the colony's law courts. From 1676–79, he represented Massachusetts at the court of King **Charles II**. He was chief justice of the special Court of Oyer and Terminer that tried those accused of **witchcraft** in Salem in 1692. Stoughton permitted spectral evidence and the rumors of private conversation while disallowing counsel for the defense, yet he did not fall out of political favor—even after Governor **William Phips** called an end to the trials. Also, in 1692, Stoughton became the lieutenant governor, and from 1694 until his death he spent most of his time as the acting governor following Phips' journey to and subsequent death in England. In 1726, the town of Stoughton, Massachusetts, was named for him.

SURPLICE. *See* VESTMENTS.

SWINNOCK, GEORGE (1627–1673). English Puritan preacher. Swinnock was born in Maidstone, Kent, and raised mostly by his uncle Robert Swinnock, the mayor of the town. He graduated from **Cambridge** and became a chaplain at New College, **Oxford**. He became a **fellow** at Oxford's Balliol College in 1648 and later preached for **Presbyterian** churches in Rickmansworth, Hertfordshire, and Great Kimble, Buckinghamshire. Following the **Restoration**, he became the family chaplain for Richard Hampden.

A number of his theological works have survived, such as *The Christian Man's Calling*, *Heaven and Hell Epitomised*, *The Fading of the Flesh*, *The Incomparableness of God*, *Sinner's Last Sentence*, *Door of* **Salvation** *Opened by the Key of Regeneration*, and *The Pastor's Farewell*.

SYNOD OF DORT (OR DORDT, OR DORDRECHT). Disputes in **Holland** between **Calvinists** and **Arminians**, also known as Remonstrants, precipitated the convocation of the Synod of Dort on 13 November 1618. The main issue in dispute was whether election unto **salvation** was of specific persons granted faith, as Calvinism held, or whether, as Arminianism taught, divine election was of that group of persons who expressed faith in Christ as a precondition. With all but a handful of the 64 Dutch delegates supporting the Calvinist position, the verdict of the synod was something of a foregone conclusion. Its canons are often remembered under the English acronym TULIP: Total depravity, Unconditional election, Limited atonement, Irresistible grace, and Perseverance of the saints.

A total of 28 foreign divines also attended the synod. The English delegation sat next to the Dutch Calvinists during the proceedings and voted as a group to affirm the synod's conclusions. These men were on the whole not later known to be spokespersons for Calvinist theology, but, upon orders of King **James I**, they did wish to nurture good relations with Maurice, the Prince of Orange, who had called for the synod. They were George Carlton, **Joseph Hall**, **John Davenant**, and Samuel Ward. Carlton was the Bishop of Llandaff and the head of the group, while Hall later became embroiled in debates over **Episcopalian** government with the five authors of **Smectymnuus**. Ward was a former student of **William Perkins**, the master of Sidney Sussex College, **Cambridge**, and the nearest to being himself a Puritan. Walter Balcanqual and Thomas Goad later joined the English group. The Church of England never formally ratified the decisions of Dort, yet still they gave courage to England's Calvinist reformers and, according to **Richard Baxter**, deserve to be ranked in their influence alongside the **Westminster Confession**.

– T –

TAVERNER'S BIBLE. Taverner's Bible was edited by Richard Taverner (1505–75), who had studied Greek at both **Oxford** and **Cambridge** and had spent some time in prison by order of Thomas Cardinal Wolsey. In 1539, Taverner published *The Most Sacred Bible*, which was really a re-edition of the **Matthew's Bible** that Taverner had amended. In 1540, Taverner spent time in the Tower of London for producing his unauthorized English version of the Bible. However, through the patronage of Thomas Cromwell, the secretary of state to King **Henry VIII**, Taverner acquired posts in the courts both of Henry and his son King **Edward VI**. Although perceived as a **Nonconformist**, Taverner also received appointment as the sheriff of Oxfordshire by Queen **Elizabeth I** in 1569. His Bible, rarely reprinted, appears not to have had any significant influence on English Christianity.

TAYLOR, EDWARD (1645?–1729). American Puritan poet. Taylor was a native of England, having been born in Coventry of Leicestershire, but his reputation now rests largely on his output as a poet while in America. It seems that Taylor was a schoolteacher in his young adulthood but fled to America about 1668, like other Puritans who refused King **Charles II**'s **Act of Uniformity**. He enrolled at **Harvard College** soon after his arrival in New England, befriending Harvard President **Charles Chauncy** and fellow student **Samuel Sewall**. After graduating in 1671, Taylor accepted a ministerial call to the **Congregationalist** church at Westfield, Massachusetts, but it was another eight years before relations with the native peoples calmed to the point where Taylor could receive **ordination** and conduct his duties full-time. Like **Giles Wigginton** of Malden, Taylor also served as his town's physician. Taylor ended up **preaching** at Westfield for nearly six decades, corresponding with friends like **Increase Mather** and **Richard Baxter** and insisting against nearby pastor **Solomon Stoddard** that only regenerate believers should receive the **Lord's Supper**.

Taylor's ministry also gave cause for the writing of a number of devotional poems, many composed on Saturday evenings before leading **worship**, such as "Poems and Sacramental Meditations" and "Preparatory Meditations before my Approach to the Lord's Supper." Taylor's eschewed the typically Puritan plain style in favor of metaphysical conceits reminiscent of George Herbert, such as calling himself a crumb of earth in comparison to Christ, "Heaven's Sugar Cake." Other notable poems by Taylor include "Huswifery, "Upon Wedlock, & Death of Children," "A Fig for Thee Oh! Death," and "God's Determinations Touching His Elect." Yet because Taylor did not desire the publication of his poems in his own lifetime, it was only after the publication of *The Poetical Works of Edward Taylor* by Thomas Johnson in 1939 that Taylor achieved recognition as an eminent American Puritan poet alongside **Michael Wigglesworth** and **Anne Bradstreet**. None of Taylor's seven children by first wife Elizabeth Fitch were alive when he died in 1729, but six children from second wife Ruth Wyllys did survive him. *See also* SCIENCE.

TAYLOR, NATHANAEL (?–1702). English Puritan preacher. Little is known of Taylor's life except that he was skilled in ancient languages, preached the funeral **sermon** for the Puritan preacher **Nathaniel Vincent**, and battled the rise of late 17th century rational religion. He defended the superiority of revealed Christianity in works like *A Preservative Against Deism* and *A Discourse of the Nature and Necessity of Faith in Jesus Christ*. He may also have been the Nathanael Taylor who was the first master of Sir John Nelthorpe's school in Brigg. His descendant Nathaniel William Taylor (1786–1858) was a significant contributor to the **New England Theology** that modified the legacy of **Jonathan Edwards** with a mixture of theological rationalism and revivalism.

TAYLOR, THOMAS (1576–1633). English Puritan theologian and preacher. Taylor was born at Richmond, Yorkshire, where his father was the town recorder. He attended Christ's College, **Cambridge**, where he learned from **William Perkins** the skill of theological **preaching**, for which Taylor himself would later be known. Taylor was also exceptionally gifted academically, becoming a **fellow** and then Hebrew **lecturer** at Christ's College. Yet, as his outspoken sympathies for Puritans replaced his earlier suspicions of them, Taylor received censures from Samuel Harsnet and Mathew Wren, each at one point the Bishop of Norwich, for advocating **Nonconformity**. Wren could not prevent Taylor from earning the Doctor of Divinity degree at **Cambridge**, but upon its completion, Taylor left formal academic life for preaching responsibilities, successively in Watford of Hertfordshire, Reading of Berkshire, and Aldermanbury of London. In this last post, he served from 1625 until his death.

Taylor became so expert in explaining the spiritual similitudes of **Scripture**, like the sewer, the fisher, and the merchant, that he was hailed as "the illuminated Doctor." He even received invitations to preach at Paul's Cross before the monarchs **Elizabeth I** and **James I**. At Reading, a veritable school of disciples gathered around Taylor to imitate his effective style, even as he had once found a model in Perkins, whose collected works Taylor also helped to edit. Frequent targets of Taylor's censure in his sermons were popery, **antinomianism**, and **Arminianism**. He also published over 50 books, with titles such as *Christ's Victory Over the Dragon*, *An Exposition on the Parable of the Sower and the Seed*, *The Saint's Progress to Full Holiness*, *The Pearl of the Gospel*, *The Beauty of Bethel*, *The King's Bath*, and *Principles of Christian Practice*. One of Taylor's more noteworthy writings was *The Pilgrim's Profession*, which utilized the motif of the allegorical pilgrimage of the soul that **John Bunyan** immortalized a half century after Taylor's death. In this work, Taylor used his familiarity with the spiritual trials of one Mrs. Mary Gunter, whose funeral oration he delivered, to illustrate how Christian pilgrims must ever keep their eyes on the eternal prize promised by Christ.

TENNENT, GILBERT (1703–1764). American **Presbyterian** minister. Born in the same year as **Jonathan Edwards** in Massachusetts, Tennent was born in Armagh, Ireland, but he would later join Edwards as a leader in America's first **Great Awakening**. He came to Pennsylvania with his father **William Tennent** in 1718 and attained to an M.A. degree at Yale College in 1725. In that same year, he was licensed to preach by the presbytery of Philadelphia. He preached briefly in Newcastle, Delaware, and then moved to New Brunswick, New Jersey, where he befriended the Dutch Reformed minister Theodore Frelinghuysen. Frelinghuysen's emphasis on a deep personal piety strengthened Tennent's resolve to become one of the "New Side" Presbyterians who supported the stirring revivals of the Great Awakening. Indeed, Tennent was one of the first pastors to welcome the demonstrative English evangelist **George Whitefield**. Tennent also helped his father train ministry students at the Log College. Tennent's best-known contribution to the revivalist fervor was a sermon entitled "The Danger of an Unconverted Ministry," which he preached in Nottingham, Pennsylvania, on 8 March 1740. Tennent served among "New Side" Presbyterian churches in Pennsylvania for the rest of his life, but he came to regret any role he might have played in causing a schism between the "New Side" Presbyterians and their more staid counterparts on the "Old Side." He worked to produce a reconciliation between the two sides, which occurred in 1758.

TENNENT, WILLIAM (1673–1746). American **Presbyterian** minister. Tennent was likely born in Ireland but studied in Scotland at the University of Edinburgh. He completed an M.A. degree in 1693. He married and took orders in the Church of England in 1702, although he served in Ulster, Ireland. In 1718, he came to Pennsylvania and joined the Presbyterian church of Philadelphia, founded by **Francis Makemie**. From 1720–27, he pastored various Presbyterian churches in New York, and in 1727, he returned to Pennsylvania as pastor in Neshaminy. Along with Jonathan Dickinson, Tennent was one of America's early leading "New Side" Presbyterians, embracing the pietism and revivalism of New England Puritanism and rejecting the need for an "Adopting Act" to measure ministers' adherence to the **Westminster Confession**. To provide an alternative to **Harvard College**, whose original purpose was to educate **Congregationalist** ministers, Tennent founded the Log College at his home in 1735 to train Presbyterians. His son **Gilbert Tennent** taught alongside him. Although some "Old Side" Presbyterians at first suspected the credentials of graduates from the Log College, it only closed after inspiring the birth of the College of New Jersey, later named Princeton.

TEST ACT. Borrowing some of its thrust from the **Corporation Act** of 1661, the Test Act of 1673 was a resolution of the **Cavalier Parliament** to keep Roman **Catholics** out of public office. After the brother and heir of King **Charles II**, James the duke of York, married into an Italian Catholic family, many Protestants feared that the future king would reintroduce papal authority over English Christianity. To prevent this, the Test Act affirmed the British Empire to be the political manifestation of the Church of England and thus barred anyone from holding government office who did not receive **Lord's Supper** within the Protestant state church. The Test Act also stipulated that one could not interpret that communion through the Catholic teaching of transubstantiation. Even **Nonconformists** within **Parliament**, such as **Christopher Love**, supported the Test Act—although strictly enforced, it meant their unseating as well—because they believed the nation's freedom from the papacy was more important than the legality of their preferred style of **worship**. Charles agreed to the Test Act to avoid plunging the nation into a new civil war, but correct suspicions of his own Catholic sympathies influenced the passing by Parliament of a second Test Act in 1678 that specifically forbade Catholics from serving in Parliament or the royal court. This was about the same time of a rumored "**Popish Plot**" to bring James to the throne more quickly through the assassination of Charles. The Test Act remained in effect until 1828.

THEATER. *See* DRAMA.

THIRTY-NINE ARTICLES. Thomas Cranmer, at the time the **Archbishop of Canterbury** under King **Edward VI**, originally finished the Forty-Two Articles for the Church of England in June 1553. They constituted one of the earliest and most influential confessions of Protestant theology. Edward died in July 1553, and his half sister Queen **Mary I** executed Cranmer, but Queen **Elizabeth I** reintroduced a revision of Cranmer's document, the Thirty-Eight Articles, as the official doctrine of the **Anglican** Church in 1563. The removed articles dealt mostly with issues of eschatological debate that were no longer considered controversial. In 1571, a restored article opposing transubstantiation made the confession into the Thirty-Nine Articles. In 1630, Puritan leaders opposed the addition of a preface to the Thirty-Nine Articles by Archbishop of Canterbury **William Laud**. They believed that the preface's criticism of literal scriptural exegesis was meant to mitigate the document's **Calvinist** doctrine of **predestination**. In 1643, the Puritan-dominated **Parliament** asked the **Westminster Assembly** to review the Thirty-Nine Articles. The

Assembly revised the first 15 articles, with the biggest changes being the elimination of references to the relative authority of the Apocrypha and the early Christian creeds. In 1662, King **Charles II** restored the 1571 version of the Thirty-Nine Articles; this version with but minor changes has remained the core of Anglican theology. *See also* IRISH ARTICLES.

THURLOE (OR THURLOW), JOHN (1618–1668). English politician. Thurloe's father Thomas was the rector of Abbot's Roding in Essex. As a young man, Thurloe studied law at **Lincoln's Inn** and worked for the Parliamentarian Oliver St. John. In that capacity, he gained negotiating experience both internationally, with St. John and Sir Walter Strickland in the Netherlands, and domestically, at the peace negotiations between **Parliament** and King **Charles I** at Uxbridge. Neither of these negotiations proved successful, but Thurloe's political skills became known to **Oliver Cromwell**, who named him to several government positions during the **Protectorate**. These included appointments as secretary of state in 1652, director of spying and intelligence in 1653, and postmaster-general in 1655. Cromwell especially valued Thurloe's reconnaissance abilities because Thurloe kept an eye on **Charles II** in exile and foiled assassination plots against Cromwell by Royalists like the Sealed Knot circle. Thurloe also married twice and was a father to six children.

In 1654 and 1656, Thurloe also won election to Parliament from Ely, and in 1657, he became the governor of Charterhouse and Chancellor at the University of Glasgow as well. But even in his multiple official capacities, Thurloe could not persuade Cromwell to take the crown in 1657. Thurloe was one of the few in 1659 to hope **Richard Cromwell** could successfully follow his father as the lord protector, and he could not prevent the **Rump Parliament** from recalling Charles II to the throne. The new king arrested Thurloe and charged him with high treason even though he had not been involved in any way with the execution of Charles I. Yet Thurloe regained his freedom on the condition that he would freely share his vast political knowledge with the new regime. Many of Thurloe's letters have survived and are housed at **Oxford**'s Bodleian Library.

TOLERATION. The push for greater religious freedom in England began in earnest after Queen **Elizabeth I** succeeded her half sister **Mary I** to the throne in 1558, although some **Anabaptist** and **Arminian** groups had earlier expressed desires for greater religious toleration. During Mary's reign, 282 Protestants were executed, and many more fled to the European continent to study with the second-generation leaders of the Protestant Reformation. Once Elizabeth came to power in 1558, these **Marian exiles** returned to England and pleaded with the new monarch to reform the Church of England along the lines of John Calvin's Geneva. When the queen insisted instead on a "middle way" that could comprehend both Protestant theology and **Catholic** liturgy, a group of "Puritans" led by **William Perkins** and **William Ames** began to wish for greater freedom to include Reformed emphases within the English church. At the **Hampton Court Conference** of 1604, these Puritans offered to the newly crowned King **James I** their **Millennary Petition**, but their pleas for reform went largely unheard. From that point, Puritanism gave rise to a number of Christian groups frustrated by the pace of reform within the Church of England, who sought toleration for their own religious point of view. However, many in the established church saw religious **Separatism** as tantamount to political treason and division, and so toleration was very slow in coming.

During the **English Civil Wars**, the **Presbyterian** faction hoped that a Parliamentary victory over King **Charles I** might usher in a state church based upon governance by elders rather than bishops. However, the Presbyterians needed the cooperation of the **Independents** and other Puritan groups to defeat the king, and these groups in the end preferred toleration for themselves to complicity with a Presbyterian national church. The Independents were generally more tolerant of the multiplicity of leftwing Separatist sects, although their chief spokesperson **Oliver Cromwell** did repress politically vocal leaders of the **Levellers** and the **Diggers** after he became the lord protector of England. Some groups who began to despair of religious liberty for themselves in England fled to **Holland** and/or America.

Ironically, some of the same Independents who thought Presbyterianism no less coercive than **episcopacy** in England became architects of **Congregationalist** state churches in the American colonies, such as **Massachusetts Bay**. The earliest calls for religious liberty in

America came as reactions to such state churches from **William Penn**, who started Pennsylvania in part as a haven for his fellow **Quakers**, and **Roger Williams**, who founded Providence (Rhode Island) upon the **Calvinist** conviction that only God has the ultimate power to change one's religious beliefs anyway. In *The Bloudy Tenent of Persecution*, Williams disputed **John Cotton**'s belief that the only true religious liberty was that afforded by his established church against sectarian alternatives. Williams founded the Providence colony in 1639 while a leader of the **Baptists**—one of the first groups to argue for complete toleration for all Christians—although soon after, he became a **Seeker**. More than a century later, following the American Revolutionary Wars, Connecticut Baptists encouraged Thomas Jefferson to implement a new government based upon the separation of church and state.

Back in England, one of the chief agitators for religious liberty was **John Milton**, whose tolerance of all **dissenters** extended to include views historically considered Christian heresies, such as Arianism. Milton's defenses of freedom of religion and freedom of printed expression can be found in such works as "To Mr. Cyriack Skinner Upon His Blindness," "On the New Forcers of **Conscience**," and *Areopagitica*. When **Parliament** invited **Charles II** to take the crown in 1660 for the sake of the nation's stability, it insisted that one of the conditions for the **Restoration** would be a guarantee of toleration for **Nonconformists**. Charles' **Declaration of Breda** hence offered toleration to all those who pledged him loyalty, but his promise did not last. By 1662, hundreds of dissenters had been jailed, despite the passing of a **Declaration of Indulgence** in that same year. From 1664–73, the **Conventicle Act**, **Five Mile Act**, and **Test Act** continued to restrict free expression and political power to a powerful few. A second Declaration of Indulgence in 1672, known as the "Quaker Act" for the number of Quakers pardoned by it, also freed the Baptist **John Bunyan** after his 12 years in jail.

With a third **Declaration of Indulgence** in 1687, King **James II** extended toleration to dissenters, largely to secure greater favor for **Catholicism** in England as well. Upon his removal from the throne in 1689 and the accession of William and Mary following him, the landmark **Act of Toleration** at last no longer made religious expression a test of political loyalty. The chief drafter of the Act was John

Locke, who hoped that a generic Protestant Christianity based upon simple belief in Jesus as Messiah would forestall any repetitions of the religious wars of England's past. It would still be well over a century, however, before Catholicism, too, would be legally tolerated in England.

TRAILL, ROBERT (1642–1716). Scottish **Presbyterian** preacher. Traill was born in Else, where his father was the minister. His father signed the National Covenant in 1638 and moved to the Greyfriars Church in Edinburgh when his son was young, but he was also forced to leave Scotland with other Covenanters after the **Restoration** of King **Charles II** in 1660. Meanwhile, Robert went to study at the University of Edinburgh, but he expressed his own public commitment to the Covenanters' cause by showing support for the Rev. James Guthrie at his execution in 1661. In 1666, the same year that the Covenanters suffered a severe blow after the Pentland Rising, Traill was forced into hiding for owning private copies of a banned **Nonconformist** book, John Brown's *Apologetical Relation*. Traill joined his father in **Holland** in 1667; while there, he continued to study theology and helped see into print *Rutherford's Examination of Arminianism*. Within two years, Traill returned to England and preached for a congregation at Cranbrook in Kent. In 1677, Traill was apprehended while traveling in Scotland and sentenced to three months in the Bass Rock prison for holding **conventicles**. Upon his release, he returned for a while to Cranbrook before moving to London as pastor for a Presbyterian church. Most of Traill's publications were sermons, with the notable exception being the posthumously printed *Vindication of the Protestant Doctrine Concerning **Justification*** (1692), a condemnation of the **antinomian** doctrine of writers like **Tobias Crisp**.

TRAPP, JOHN (1601–1669). English Puritan preacher. Not much is known of Trapp's early life, except that he attained bachelor's and master's degrees from Christ's Church, **Oxford**. Around 1629, he became head schoolmaster at Stratford-on-Avon, where he been on staff for five previous years. He also was a pastor in Luddington and then Weston-on-Avon, his eventual burial place, but again the details of his ministry are few. During the **English Civil Wars**, he served as chaplain for the Parliamentary garrison in Stratford, but he suffered imprisonment in Oxford once Royalist troops secured the town. From 1646–60, by proclamation of **Parliament**, Trapp was the rector of Welford, Gloucestershire, and Warwickshire, but he lost his position after the **Restoration** to the same Dr. Bowen who had held it before him. He is best remembered for his *Annotations on the Books of the Old and New Testaments* and the witticisms sprinkled throughout his biblical commentaries, such as "Pollution is the forerunner of perdition," "Better to be pruned to grow than cut up to burn," "Unity without verity is no better than conspiracy," and, "Heresy is the leprosy of the head."

TRAVERS, WALTER (1548–1635). English Puritan preacher. Travers completed a baccalaureate degree at Trinity College, **Cambridge**, and returned to Cambridge for a divinity degree after spending some time in Geneva with the Reformed theologian Theodore Beza. In 1572, he joined England's first **Presbyterian** church at Wandsworth in Surrey, but soon he joined other English **Nonconformists**, such as **Thomas Cartwright**, in the continental city of Antwerp. There he received **ordination** as an elder and wrote extensively on church discipline, particularly *Ecclesiasticae Disciplinae et Anglicanae Ecclesiae*, printed in Geneva in 1574. Travers returned to England to serve Lord Burleigh as a domestic chaplain and the tutor to his son Robert, and he became a **lecturer** at the Temple in London. Travers was in line to become master of the Temple when Dr. Henry Alvey died in 1584, but **Archbishop of Canterbury** John Whitgift intervened and installed Richard Hooker, author of *Laws of Ecclesiastical Polity*, instead. The working relationship between Hooker and Travers was strained, and Travers and **Thomas Sparke** were dragged into public debates before Whitgift and his men in which the two Puritans argued against the canonical authority of the Apocrypha and the reception of the **sacraments** in private. At last in 1586, Whitgift secured the removal of Travers from his teaching office because his ordination was not according to the rules of the Church of England. In 1595, Travers became the provost at Trinity College of Dublin, where he taught the future Archbishop of Armagh, **James Ussher**. Travers had been dead for nine years when, in 1644, under Parliamentary declaration, his "Book of Discipline" briefly displaced the ***Book of Common Prayer***

as the requisite **worship** manual of English churches. His other writings included *A Justification of the Religion now Professed in England* and *An Answer to the Epistle of G. T. for the pretended Catholics*. See also DUTCH PROTESTANTISM.

TREATY OF NEWPORT. The Treaty of Newport was the English **Parliament**'s final attempt to negotiate a settled end to the **English Civil Wars** with King **Charles I**. Negotiations between the king and 15 commissioners from Parliament took place at Newport, on the Isle of Wight, from September to November 1648. Although both **Presbyterians** and **Independents** represented Parliament, the Presbyterians were the more eager to conduct negotiations because they hoped to persuade the king to accept a Presbyterian state church. Thus did they persuade Parliament to rescind the Vote of No Addresses from earlier that year in order to allow the talks to occur. Charles was brought from confinement at Carisbrooke Castle and appeared willing to meet the Presbyterians' request in exchange for a promise not to prosecute Royalist leaders. However, Charles secretly sent word to the Marquis of Ormond, James Butler, his general in Ireland, not to abide by any settlement reached at Newport. Eventually the Independents, such as **Henry Vane** and **Henry Ireton**, tired of the king's stalling tactic and returned him to Hurst Castle on the mainland. Within days, the Independents then staged **Pride's Purge**, the removal of Presbyterian Parliamentarians who were considered obstacles to the less-conciliatory plans of the **New Model Army**.

TRIERS (OR TRYERS). After the **New Model Army**'s victory over King **Charles I** during the **English Civil Wars**, concern arose among Protestant leaders to secure broadly consistent theological views among the ministers of the various Puritan parties. To that end, **Oliver Cromwell** appointed 38 triers of ministers on 20 March 1654, and he gave them the responsibility of ascertaining the qualifications of all new English ministers. **Parliament** agreed to abide by the decisions of the triers in 1656. The original group of triers consisted of **Independents**, **Presbyterians**, and a couple of **Baptists**, and all but eight were themselves clergymen. Some of its notable members were **John Owen, Thomas Goodwin, Stephen Marshall, Hugh Peters, Philip Nye, Obadiah Sedgwick, Sidrach Simpson, John Arrowsmith,**

Joseph Caryl, and **Thomas Manton**. An agreement of five triers was necessary for approving a candidate, while nine triers had to concur upon a rejection. There were no standard guidelines for conducting their investigations, but the triers typically required a certificate attesting to the person's holy life from three other ministers, and they tended to guard against approving ministers with tendencies toward **Arminianism** or **Socinianism**. They also appointed subcommittees to help investigate applicants outside London. Some complained that the discretionary powers of the triers made them in effect a new kind of **episcopacy**. The triers dissolved after Oliver Cromwell's death in 1659.

TWISSE, WILLIAM (1575?–1646). English Puritan preacher. Twisse was born at Spenham-Land, Berkshire, the son of a clothier, and he received his education at the Winchester school and **Oxford**'s New College. He stayed at Oxford for 16 years, part of that time as a **fellow**, rising to the M.A. degree in 1604 and the Doctor of Divinity degree 10 years later. He was a diligent student of philosophy and theology and became the personal chaplain of Princess Elizabeth, the daughter of King **James I** and the Queen of Bohemia by marriage. When political unrest forced Elizabeth's retreat, Twisse returned to England and became the curate of Newbury, very near the town of his birth. Although he had opportunities for preferment at Winchester College, the University of Franeker, and Oxford, Twisse was content to remain at Newbury and continue his **preaching** and theological writing. He wrote more than 15 books. Twisse was a strong advocate for **Sabbatarianism** in books such as *The Christian Sabbath Defended* and *Of the Morality of the Fourth Commandment*, and he refused even to read the contrary opinion set forth in and legalized by King James' *Book of Sports*. Twisse was also widely known as an inveterate enemy of **Arminianism**, and drawing upon correspondences that included Jacob Arminius himself, Twisse defended the high **Calvinist** canons of the **Synod of Dort** in such texts as *The Riches of God's Love* and *De Predestinatione et Gratia*. He even challenged his friend **John Cotton** to become more receptive to the scriptural legitimacy of a doctrine of eternal reprobation.

Because he had a widespread reputation among English Puritans both for his learning and for his humility, Twisse received an invitation from **Parliament** in 1640 to serve on a committee for introducing **worship** changes into the Church of England. And even though not all Puritans preferred Twisse's supralapsarian doctrine of election or his hope for reconciliation with King **Charles I**, both the House of Commons and the House of Lords unanimously voted to ask Twisse to preach the opening sermon of the **Westminster Assembly**. This he did in the chapel of King Henry VII in London's Westminster Abbey, on 1 July 1643. In this same church, Twisse was buried only three years later, following a great ceremony surrounding his passing. His health had been poor during the **English Civil Wars**, exacerbated by being evicted from his Newbury home by Royalist forces, for which the **Long Parliament** had offered him 100 pounds in reparation. After the **Restoration**, Twisse's body was exhumed and thrown into a common pit at the nearby St. Margaret's churchyard. His successor at Newbury, Benjamin Woodbridge, lost his position for **Nonconformity**. *See also* LAY IMPROPRIATIONS.

TYNDALE BIBLE. The Tyndale Bible was the first English version of the **Bible** to be translated completely from the original languages of Hebrew, Greek, and Aramaic. Its main translator, William Tyndale (1484–1536), had studied at both **Oxford** and **Cambridge** and was **ordained** as an **Anglican** priest in 1521. While traveling in Hamburg, Germany, in 1524, Tyndale met Martin Luther, whose German translation of the New Testament had appeared only two years earlier. Inspired by the encounter, Tyndale began his translation work on an English version of the New Testament by using the same Greek text compiled by Desiderius Erasmus that Luther had used. The printing of Tyndale's New Testament began in Cologne in 1525, but because of pressure from ecclesiastical officials, it did not reach completion until supervised by Peter Shoeffer in 1526 in the German city of Worms. The Tyndale Bible was immediately admired in England, but the bishop of London Cuthbert Tunstall purchased most of the copies to stop their dissemination, and in 1530, King **Henry VIII** expressed his fear of popular access to **Scripture** by ordering the destruction of all English Bible translations. Most copies of the Tyndale Bible did not survive, yet it still became the foundation for later English versions of the New Testament. Tyndale's knowledge of Hebrew was apparently mostly self-taught, and he was preparing his translation of the Old

Testament in Antwerp, Belgium, in 1535, when betrayed by a local man (Henry Phillips) to English authorities. Tyndale remained in jail outside Brussels for 500 days and was strangled and burned to death for heresy in 1536. In that same year, Tyndale's friends **Miles Coverdale** and **John Rogers** completed his work on the Old Testament and published the complete Tyndale Bible. **Archbishop of Canterbury Thomas Cranmer** secured royal permission to remove Tyndale's prologue and notes and reissue the Tyndale Bible with minor revisions as **Matthew's Bible** in 1537.

– U –

UNITARIANISM. Unitarianism denies the historic Christian doctrine of the Trinity, that the single essence of God is constituted by the relationships among the persons of the Father, the Son, and the Holy Spirit. During the period of the Protestant Reformation, the persons most recognized for objecting to the doctrine of the Trinity were known as Socinians. They were so named for the leadership of Faustus and Laelius Socinus, natives of Siena, Italy. In 1574, a group of Polish Socinians issued the Racovian Catechism, which became the focal document of the movement. Socinians did not affirm original **sin** or its frequent corollary, infant **baptism**. They did not completely deny the divine nature of Jesus Christ but taught against historic orthodoxy that he was a deified man rather than fully God incarnate. In 1640, the Church of England condemned adherents of Socinianism upon danger of trial in the **Star Chamber**. After 1652, Socinians in England were often called Biddellians after John Biddle, an **Oxford** graduate influenced by Jacobus Acontius and Sebastian Castello, who wrote against the divinity of the Holy Spirit. As Lord Protector of England, **Oliver Cromwell** banished Biddle to the Scilly Isles. Biddle returned to London after the **Restoration** but was imprisoned. Early English Socinianism appears to have drawn most of its membership from disaffected **Presbyterians**. Its exaltation of a religion of reason paved the way by the end of the 17th century for the non-dogmatic faith of John Locke and the Deists. Nonetheless, Unitarianism did not receive official **toleration** in England until 1813.

In Massachusetts, a new brand of Unitarianism arose which was even more willing than its European counterpart to forsake the supreme authority of the **Bible** and the miraculous birth of Christ. The Puritan emphasis on liberty of **conscience** had ended up creating in some a self-determining conscience liberated from creedal traditions. By the beginning of the 18th century, a number of **Congregationalists** had become attracted to Unitarianism's exaltation of reason over revelation and the pietistic outbursts of the **Great Awakening**. The first Unitarian congregation in America convened at King's Chapel, Boston, in 1788. Unitarianism became firmly ensconced as an intellectual force in America in 1805, when the anti-Trinitarian Henry Ware was named Hollis Professor of Divinity at **Harvard College**. The movement's most significant early preacher and theologian in the following decades was Boston's William Ellery Channing.

USSHER, JAMES (1581–1656). English theologian and preacher. Ussher himself was not a Puritan, yet the Puritans had high regard for his learning and adopted his chronology of biblical history, which dated creation to the year 4004 B.C., when they annotated the **King James Version** of the **Bible**. Ussher was born in Dublin, Ireland, to a wealthy family and was one of the very first students at Trinity College. Matriculating at the age of 13, Ussher studied with **Walter Travers**, who in turn had been a student of Theodore Beza in Geneva. Ussher graduated in 1600, received an M.A. degree the following year, and then took **ordination** as deacon and priest from his uncle, Henry Ussher, the Archbishop of Armagh and primate of Ireland. From there, Ussher accrued a number of prestigious titles, including Professor of Divinity at Trinity (1607), Doctor of Divinity (1614), Vice Chancellor of the University of Dublin (1615), the bishop of Meath (1620), privy councilor for Ireland (1623), and, following in his uncle's footsteps, the archbishop and primate of Armagh (1625).

Ussher was further known for his polemical and historical writings, such as *An Answer to a Jesuit in Ireland* (1624) and *Britannicarum Ecclesiarum Antiquitates* (1639). In 1640, Ussher left Ireland to preach at **Lincoln's Inn** in London, and he stayed in England because of the growing unrest both in England and Ireland that precipitated the **English Civil Wars**. His sympathies during that conflict were with King **Charles I** and an Episcopalian form of church government. In defense of the latter, his book *The Apostolical Institution of Episcopacy* invoked the words of St. Ignatius of Antioch, the early Christian writer whose epistles urged submission to one's bishop as unto Christ. Yet Ussher did not completely deny fellowship with those who advocated other forms of church polity, particularly **Presbyterianism**, and such a moderate temper kept him in favor even during **Oliver Cromwell**'s **Protectorate**.

Still, Ussher spurned offers to attend the **Westminster Assembly**, although his **Irish Articles** of 1615 influenced the layout and expression of its Confession. He also rejected an invitation to become a professor at the University of Leyden in **Holland** in order to devote himself, first at **Oxford** and then with the family of the Lady Peterborough at Reigate, Surrey, to writing studies of biblical theology. These included *A Body of Divinity* (1647), *Annales Vetes et Novi Testamentae* (1650–54) and *De Graeca LXX Interpretum Versione Syntagma* (1655). Ussher's influential calculation of the date of creation in *Annales* was an important consideration for Samuel Clarke's inclusion of Ussher among the Puritans discussed in his *A Collection of the Lives of Ten Eminent Divines* (1662). From 1847–64, C. R. Elrington and J. H. Todd issued a 17-volume set, *The Whole Works of the Most Rev. James Ussher, D.D.*

– V –

VANE, HENRY (1613–1662). English Puritan politician and governor of **Massachusetts Bay Colony**. Vane's father, also named Henry, was a prominent adviser to Charles, the son and eventual heir of King **James I**. From an early age, the younger Vane was interested in reading the **Bible** and Protestant theology, and he came to agree with the Puritans that the Church of England had not sufficiently pursued a reformation. Because he would not subscribe religious allegiance to the king and his church, Vane could not fulfill a desire to attend **Oxford**, and so instead his father sent him on a diplomatic mission to Vienna. In 1635, Vane's religious convictions led him to America, where he employed his mediating skills among Saybrook settlers and eventually settled in Boston. Vane was warmly received and soon even won an election for governor of the **Massachusetts Bay Colony**. Before John Locke's treatises on government and religious **toleration**, Vane conceived of politics in terms of a contract of the governed and desired that all citizens be free to pursue individual **conscience** in matters of **worship**.

Yet Vane's popularity in America quickly waned when he wished to extend that toleration to **Anne Hutchinson** after she claimed special charismatic authority from the Holy Spirit. Vane was sympathetic to her because he, too, had claimed that inward experience was more important to Christian faith than **preaching**. Concerned colonists then reelected **John Winthrop** as the governor of the colony in 1637, and Vane voluntarily returned to England before Hutchinson was finally banished from Massachusetts. Within three years, Vane entered **Parliament**, received a knighthood, and married. When the hostilities that precipitated the **English Civil Wars** began, Vane stood firmly with the insurgents against the king. He even became an officer of the **New Model Army** after other Parliamentarians like **William Waller** left it under the **Self-Denying Ordinance**.

Vane advocated the abolishment of all forms of religious establishment, for which he received the praise of **John Milton** in the sonnet, "To Sir Henry Vane the Younger" (1652). Vane retired from politics in 1654 but suffered a brief imprisonment for criticizing **Oliver Cromwell**—as he had once done to Winthrop—for failing to extend the religious liberties he had claimed to cherish. In 1656, Vane's *A Healing Question* called for a convention to form a new English constitution rooted in civil and religious liberty. Vane returned to Parliament in 1658 after Cromwell died but was sentenced to death after the **Restoration**, not because he had personally participated in the execution of **Charles I** but because his political ideas were deemed by **Charles II** to be too radical.

VENNER, THOMAS (?–1661). English revolutionary. Venner was born in England but at some point early in life came to Massachusetts, where he made a living as a wine cooper (maintainer of wooden barrels) around Salem and Boston. It is unclear how Venner's **Independent** views in religion turned toward the intensive apocalypticism of the most fervent **Fifth Monarchists**, but, before 1656, Venner came to London to plot a takeover of the government that would supposedly clear the way for Christ's millennial reign on earth. Venner briefly worked as the cooper at the Tower of London but was fired after he mentioned that the Tower could soon be destroyed. Venner then preached for **conventicles**, particularly that on Swan Alley, Coleman Street, trying to attract adherents from anyone sympathetic to his vision of theocratic government. In 1657, he planned a coup against **Oliver Cromwell**, but the protector's intelligence officer **John Thurloe** discovered the treachery and sent Venner back to the Tower as a prisoner.

Richard Cromwell, Oliver's son, freed Venner in 1659 as a gesture of goodwill, but this did not detain Venner's seditious plans. After the **Restoration** of King **Charles II** the following year, Venner desired to strike the resumed Stuart regime before it could take hold. From 1–4 January 1661, Venner and 50 supporters launched two violent attacks against the king's guards in London, saying they fought for "King Jesus, and their heads upon the gates!" Finally, the guards cornered and captured the rebels in the Cripplegate section of London. Venner and an associate were hanged on Coleman Street on 19 January 1661. Soon afterward, nine more conspirators were executed, and their heads were displayed on London Bridge. The effect of Venner's rising was that Charles, fearing further unrest and associating political instability with religious dissent, broke his assurances in the **Declaration of Breda** and sent thousands of **Nonconformists** to jail.

VENNING, RALPH (1621?–1674?). English Puritan preacher. Venning was born in Devon and attained in 1650 to the M.A. degree at **Emmanuel College, Cambridge**. He then became a **lecturer** at St. Olave's Church, Southwark, until being ejected under the **Act of Uniformity** in 1662. Alongside Robert Bragge, he continued his **preaching** at an **Independent** congregation in London. His best-known writing was *The Plague of Plagues*, a treatise on the ultimate seriousness of **sin** first published in 1669, four years after plague and fire tore through London. Venning also penned *Learning in Christ's School* and several collections of spiritual aphorisms, such as *Milk and Honey*, *Orthodoxe Paradoxes*, and *Mysteries and Revelations*. He lies buried in London's **Bunhill Fields**.

VESTMENTS. Vestments are the priestly garbs worn by Roman **Catholic** and **Anglican** clerics, over whose use considerable controversy arose during early, pre-**Separatist** Puritanism. The disputes over wearing vestments began soon after King **Edward VI** took the throne in 1547. Given that Edward granted **Archbishop of Canterbury Thomas Cranmer** permission to lead the Church of England in a more Protestant direction, some English ministers wondered if vestments were not too closely associated with the Roman mass and papal superstition to justify their continued use. These vestments typically included a gown, a square cap, a surplice (a white linen garment draped over the gown), a cope (a semicircular cloth mantle covering one's back), and a tippet (a black scarf). Although Cranmer and Nicolas Ridley, the bishop of Lincoln, believed that wearing vestments should cause no scruples of **conscience**, **John Hooper** held strongly to the contrary. After appointment as the bishop of Gloucester, Hooper delayed his installation for months while defending his right to refuse wearing all Catholic-looking vestments. He rallied support for his position from the Reformed theologians Martin Bucer, who was at **Cambridge**, and Peter Martyr Vermigli, who was at **Oxford**, both of whom believed that vestments were inventions of the Antichrist. At last in 1649, Hooper took his new post under the condition that he would only wear the prescribed vestments when **preaching** before the king or on other special occasions. Soon other bishops, like **Hugh Latimer** of Worcester and **Miles Coverdale** of Exeter, insisted on following Hooper's example, and their common stance became one of the early distinguishing features of Puritan clergy.

When Queen **Elizabeth I** came to power in 1558, she disappointed the **Marian exiles** by continuing to enforce the policy of wearing vestments. Objectors claimed a right of liberty to follow individual **conscience** in this matter, but Archbishop of Canterbury Matthew Parker, newly appointed in his post, sought strictly to enforce the royal policy. He brought charges against multiple persons, including most notably Dr. **Thomas Sampson**, the dean of Christ Church, and Dr. **Lawrence Humphrey**, the president of Magdalen College, Oxford. When tried, the accused would often appeal to statements by Protestant stalwarts like Martin Luther and John Calvin and would claim that vestments were too much of a stumbling block to lay piety to be rededicated for **Anglican** use. For instance, William Axton of Moreton Corbet, Shropshire, declared before Thomas Bentham, Bishop of Lichfield and Coventry, that vestments were the "rags of Antichrist" and thus irredeemable. In 1566, a group of censured ministers defended their stance in *A Declaration of the Doings of those Ministers of God's Word and Sacraments in the City of London which have refused to wear the Upper Apparel and Ministering Garments of the Pope's Church*. This book claimed that the surplice actually had its origins in pagan Egypt and was then used in Jewish **worship** before introduction into the church by Pope Sylvester I in the fourth century. Cambridge students and groups of laypeople also demonstrated their dislike of vestments. The controversy continued into the reign of King **James I**, after which the disaffected were more likely to leave the state church.

VINCENT, NATHANIEL (1639–1697). English Puritan preacher. Vincent was born in Cornwall, the son of the minister John Vincent and the younger brother of **Thomas Vincent**, who became best known for his benevolence work following the London fire of 1665. Nathaniel graduated from Christ Church, **Oxford**, and moved on to appointments as chaplain of Corpus Christi College, Oxford, and pastor of a church in Buckinghamshire. Following the **Restoration** and the **Act of Uniformity**, Vincent found work as a private chaplain from 1662–65 before being dragged from a London pulpit for **Nonconformity** in 1666. He was imprisoned and condemned to banishment from England, but the latter sentence was not enacted. Vincent's best-known writings are *A Discourse Concerning Love* and *The Spirit of Prayer*.

VINCENT, THOMAS (1634–1678). English Puritan preacher. Vincent was born the eldest son of the minister John Vincent at Hertford, England. His younger brother **Nathaniel Vincent** would also become a noted Puritan author. Thomas attained the M.A. degree from Christ's Church, **Oxford**, but he also became a **Nonconformist** in the process and so eventually was dismissed from the university. Often forced to move from town to town as local officials frequently suspected his religious dissent of covering political sedition, Vincent memorized the New Testament and the Psalms for fear that at some point he would be deprived of his **Bible**. And so, except for a period after the **Restoration** of 1660 when he taught at **Thomas Doolittle**'s academy in Islington, Vincent essentially became an itinerant evangelist, **preaching** by invitation from Sunday to Sunday and undertaking a personal mission of mercy to victims of the great London fire of 1665. His writings *God's Terrible Voice in the City by Plague and Fire* and *Christ's Sudden and Certain Appearances to Judgment* attempted to interpret the plague in light of God's just and redemptive **providence**. Vincent also found time to pen a number of polemical treatises in defense of Christian orthodoxy, including *An Answer to the Sandy Foundation of Wm. Penn, the Quaker* and *A Defence of the Trinity, Satisfaction by Christ, and the Justification of Sinners*. He also defended standards of the **Westminster Assembly** in *The Shorter Catechism Explained from Scripture*. Vincent's best-known work is probably *The True Christian's Love to the Unseen Christ*, an expansion on 1 Peter 1:8 that treats various spiritual disciplines, such as study, **prayer**, and obedience, as implicit means of increasing one's closeness to and love for Christ.

VINES, RICHARD (1600–1655). English Puritan preacher. Born at Blaston (or Blazon), Leicestershire, Vines excelled in Greek studies at Magdalen College, **Cambridge**, attaining an M.A. degree. He held numerous significant posts throughout his life, beginning as schoolmaster at Hinckley before becoming rector at Wedington and later simultaneously at Caldecot in Warwickshire. From there, he became **lecturer** at Nuneaton, but he had to flee to Coventry at the outset of the **English Civil Wars**. He received appointment as a **Presbyterian** divine to the **Westminster Assembly** in 1643, and he represented the Assembly in the treaties of Uxbridge and the Isle of Wight. He also helped to compose the Westminster Confession and proffered spiritual counsel to King **Charles I** on the morning of the latter's execution, 30 January 1649. Remaining active up until his death, Vines further served as Master of Pembroke Hall, Cambridge, and a preacher at St. Clement's Danes, Walton of Hertfordshire, and St. Lawrence Jewry in London. Although best remembered for his sermons, he had also penned some posthumously published theological works, such as *A Treatise on the Sacrament* and *Christ the Christian's Only Gain*.

– W –

WADSWORTH, BENJAMIN (1669–1737). American Puritan minister and educator. Wadsworth was born in Milton, Massachusetts. When Benjamin was seven years old, his father, Captain Samuel Wadsworth, died in a battle with American Indians. Wadsworth graduated from **Harvard College** in 1690 but continued to study theology, and, in 1693, he both completed his M.A. degree from Harvard and became assistant teacher at the First Church of Boston. He became the colleague pastor of the church three years later. In 1694, while on his way to a meeting of colonial leaders at Albany, Wadsworth met with representatives of the Five Nations, led by the Mohawks. Even so, he considered good soldiers one of God's blessings in preserving colonial life. Wadsworth published several **sermons**, the most famous of which was *A Well-Ordered Family* (1712), which often addressed the relations of **family life**, such as the obedience owed by wives to husbands, children to parents, and servants to masters. In 1725, Wadsworth became the eighth president of Harvard, continuing a line of early pastor-educators in that position that included **Charles Chauncy**, **Urian Oakes**, and **Increase Mather**. Wadsworth died in Cambridge, Massachusetts, in 1737, in the 12th year of his presidency.

WALLER, WILLIAM (1597–1668). English military commander. Waller was born at Knole, Kent, where his father, Thomas, was the lieutenant of Dover Castle. He attended Magdalen Hall, **Oxford**, and then traveled across the European mainland, even joining for a time the Venetian army in its struggle against the Hapsburg family during the Thirty Years War. For a time, he was also a guard for Elizabeth, the daughter of King **James I** of England, who had become the Queen of Bohemia by marriage. When civil unrest mounted in Bohemia, Waller joined a team led by Sir Horace Vere to ensure her safety. During this exercise, Waller befriended Sir Ralph Hopton, who as commander of Royalist forces during the **English Civil Wars** would become Waller's military adversary. King James knighted Waller in 1622 for his bravery, and from then until 1636 Waller lived at the manor of his first wife Jane's father at Forde House. Not much is known of Waller's life for several years after this, except that he was an investor in Providence Company and won a seat in **Parliament**, representing Andover. In 1642, Waller became the general of Parliament's "Western Association" while **Oliver Cromwell** levied his army in the east.

Waller associated the Parliamentary cause in the English Civil Wars with God and true religion, and through a succession of victories in both England and Wales, he won such nicknames as "William the Conqueror" and "the Night Owl" for his battle prowess. In late 1643, Waller suffered a heavy defeat at Roundway Down at the hands of Hopton, but the Earl of Essex, **Robert Devereux**, still promoted Waller virtually to be an equal, with his primary responsibility to track King **Charles I** himself. Although he proved victorious over Royalist forces at Arundel, Waller was unable to stifle rebellion among soldiers who disapproved his promotion of foreign mercenaries, and, after he and Essex failed to wall up Charles in Oxford, he realized that his chances for victory were poor. He was the one who suggested that the **New Model Army** replace the regional armies that had failed to end the Civil Wars, and he then complied with the **Self-Denying Ordinance**, which required members of Parliament to resign their field commissions.

For his outspoken advocacy of **Presbyterianism** over against Cromwell's own **Independency**, Waller was removed from office by **Pride's Purge** in 1648 and even imprisoned on several occasions over the next decade. Waller then worked in opposition to Cromwell's **Protectorate** and for the return of monarchy. He spent a brief amount of time in the Tower of London in 1659 for supporting the failed uprising of Sir George Booth to overthrow **Richard Cromwell**, Oliver's son and successor, and then Waller became an architect of the Stuart **Restoration**. Although reelected to Parliament in 1660, Waller preferred retirement in Osterley to serving his term.

WARD, NATHANIEL (1568–1652). English Puritan writer. Ward was the son of John Ward, Puritan preacher at Haverhill, Suffolk, where Nathaniel was born. His brothers Samuel and John themselves each became a Puritan divine. Like so many of the Puritans, Ward received his education at **Emmanuel College**, **Cambridge**, but his training was not in theology but rather law. Only after traveling to Prussia and Denmark and meeting Dr. David Pareus of Heidelberg did Ward become interested in ministry. In 1626, he began **preaching** at St. James', Piccadilly, and, two years later, he became the rector of Stondon Massey in Essex. Excommunicated by **Archbishop of Canterbury William Laud** for **Nonconformity**, Ward sailed for America in 1634. Soon after his arrival, he became the pastor of Agawam (now Ipswich), Massachusetts, and remained so for 11 years, sharing some of his responsibilities with Thomas Parker. Ward chronicled his ministry there in *The Simple Cobler of Aggawam in America* under the clever pseudonym of Theodore la Guard ("Theodore" is the equivalent of "Nathaniel" in Greek, and "la Guard" translates "Ward" in French).

Ward's contributions to Massachusetts were considerable, for besides his preaching he helped **John Cotton** to write the first body of laws produced on American soil that protected the civil rights of colonists. Whereas **John Winthrop** had attempted to govern exclusively according to Mosaic law, in *The Body of Liberties* (1641), Ward drew from his knowledge of both Mosaic and English law to draft a bill of 100 civil guarantees, including the right to legal counsel for those called to stand before magistrates. Other provisions treated property rights, protections for **women** and children, and the forbiddance of slavery. Only a short time for consideration by the various Massachusetts towns was needed before they voted the document into legislation. But like **Henry Vane** and **Hugh Peters**, Ward returned to England from America and supported **Parliament**'s cause in the **English Civil Wars**. He made clear his opposition to regicide in two writings of 1647, *A Religious Retreat Sounded to a Religious Army* and *A Word to Mr. Peters and Two Words to the Parliament and Kingdom*. Preaching in subscription to the Essex Testimony, a document defending **Presbyterianism**, Ward spent his final years at Shenfield, Essex, only a short distance from his earlier Essex pastorate.

WATSON, THOMAS (1620–1686). English Puritan writer and preacher. Watson studied at **Emmanuel College**, **Cambridge**, as other Puritans like **Thomas Shepard** had done, and he became the rector of St. Stephen's, Walbrook, in 1646. He supported the **Presbyterians** during the **English Civil Wars** but then suffered a brief imprisonment in 1651 for plotting with **Christopher Love** to bring

Charles II back to the English throne. After the **Restoration** actually did occur, King Charles II deposed Watson from St. Stephen's in 1662, but Watson continued **preaching** where he could and, in 1672, settled at Crosby Hall, home to a **Nonconformist** gathering. **Stephen Charnock**, a fellow graduate of Emmanuel and former chaplain to **Oliver Cromwell**'s son Henry Cromwell in Ireland, preached alongside Watson from 1675–80. When ill health beset Watson, he retired to Barnston, Essex, where he died while observing the instruction of Jesus in Matthew 5:6 to pray in his closet. Known for his charity even to those who persecuted him, Watson was a prolific author whose best-known works include *The Art of Divine Contentment* (1653), *The Saint's Delight* (1657), *A Discourse on Meditation* (1660), *The Beatitudes* (1660), *Jerusalem's Glory* (1661), *The Divine Cordial* (1663), *The **Lord's** Supper* (1665), *The Godly Man's Picture* (1666), *The Holy Eucharist* (1668), *The Christian Soldier, or Heaven Taken by Storm* (1669), and *A Body of Practical Divinity* (1692). This last, posthumously published volume was a collection of 176 sermons by Watson on the **Westminster Assembly**'s Lesser Catechism. It emphasized the Ten Commandments as the rule of life, the Apostles' Creed as the sum of faith, and the Lord's Prayer as a compendium of the gospel.

WATTS, ISAAC (1674–1748). English **Nonconformist** minister and hymn writer. The contributions of Watts to English hymnody are incalculable and bear the large part of his lasting international reputation. Yet Watts was also a prolific theologian and philosopher, composing at least 50 books to accompany his 700 hymns. Born the eldest of nine children in Southampton, England, Watts was raised in a Nonconformist home. His mother was also of Huguenot descent, and his father, twice imprisoned for **dissent**, was a deacon at the Above Bar **Congregationalist** Church. Watts was an excellent student and pursued Hebrew, Greek, Latin, and French at John Pinhorne's grammar school. Yet he rejected both **Oxford** and **Cambridge**, refusing to take the oaths of **Anglican** fealty they required, and continued his education at the Dissenter Academy of Thomas Rowe at Stoke Newington. In 1694, when still not quite 20 years old, Watts returned to his father's house to continue private study, and it was there that he began composing the hymns that would eventually make up *Hymns and Spiritual Songs* (1707).

At that time, metrical psalms were the standard musical form in all English churches, but Watts thought that many of these songs were difficult to sing, did not sufficiently set forth the New Testament testimony to Jesus Christ, and did not allow new poetic expression in **worship** and devotion. Challenged by a church member, "Give us something better, young man," Watts composed "Behold the Glories of the Lamb" and introduced it into worship the following Sunday. In 1696, Watts became a tutor for the family of John Hartopp and sometimes preached in the family chapel, but he preached his first public sermon for the Southampton congregation in 1698. Soon thereafter, he became the assistant to Dr. Isaac Chauncy at Mark Lane Church in London, where **John Owen** had also once preached. Watts himself became the pastor of that church in 1702 and oversaw its relocation to Bury Street.

Watts spurned marriage to devote himself entirely to being a scholarly pastor, but his short physical frame (he was barely five feet tall) was in constantly ill health because of his sedentary lifestyle. Indeed, Samuel Price had to assist Watts in his pastoral responsibilities after a severe fever afflicted him in 1712. From that time until his death more than three decades later, Watts lived with the family of Thomas Abney. But the bachelor Watts had fathered a sea change in Puritan, indeed all Christian, hymnody. Among Watts' many compositions are the songs "When I Survey the Wondrous Cross, "Joy to the World," "O God, Our Help in Ages Past," "Alas, and Did My Savior Bleed?," "Give Me the Wings of Faith," "I Sing the Almighty Power of God," "Jesus Shall Reign Where'er the Sun," "Join All the Glorious Names," and "Lord I Have Made Thy Word My Choice." His widely published *Psalms of David* sought to reclaim the psalms in Christian paraphrase, was brought to America by none other than Benjamin Franklin, and then popularized by **George Whitefield**. Watts also wrote songs especially for children, such as those in *Divine and Moral Songs for Children*. Watts' books, besides collections of hymns and sermons, included titles such as *Remnants of Time*, *The Improvement of the Mind*, *Logic*, *The World to Come*, *The Knowledge of the Heavens and the Earth Made Easy, or the First Principles of Geography and Astronomy Explained*, *Essay on the Ruin and Recovery of Mankind*, *Discourses on the Love of God*, *Catechisms*, and **Scripture** *History*.

In theological temperament, Watts was committed to the Reformed doctrine of election, yet some **Calvinists** thought his view compromised with **Arminianism** by holding both to the particular election of some individuals and a conditional election open to all. Both Calvinists and Arminians alike, including **Cotton Mather, Jonathan Edwards**, and John Wesley, were also apprehensive that Watts' writings on the Trinity equated the Son of God with the archangel Michael and thus permitted the Arian heresy of denying the Son's co-essential divinity with God the Father. Yet few if any have set forth the Christian gospel so lastingly. The University of Edinburgh awarded Watts a Doctor of Divinity degree in 1728, and upon his death 20 years later, he was buried in London's **Bunhill Fields** cemetery alongside such Nonconformist notables as John Owen and **John Bunyan**. *The Works of Isaac Watts* appeared in six volumes, edited by John Jennings and Philip Doddrige, in 1810–11. *See also* MUSIC.

WEBSTER, JOHN (1590–1661). American Puritan politician. Overlapping the years of Webster's life in the 17th century were several other notable persons by the same name, and so it is important to recognize that the John Webster treated here was not the Jacobean tragedian who wrote the plays *The White Devil* and *The Duchess of Malfi*, the leader of the **antinomian Grindletonians** in 1620s England, the author of *Metallographia* whose alchemical images may have influenced the metaphysical poetry of **Edward Taylor**, or the author of *The Displaying of Supposed* **Witchcraft**. Instead, this John Webster was born of Scottish descent in Warwickshire, England, and arrived in New Town (later Cambridge), Massachusetts, by 1633. His wife was named Agnes, and he had five children.

In 1636, Webster relocated with the Reverend **Thomas Hooker** to Hartford, where he began serving the Connecticut colony in a series of political posts. From 1639–55, Webster served as a magistrate of judge. In 1655, he was the deputy governor, and, in 1656, he was the governor. When **John Winthrop**, much better known as the multiply elected governor of Massachusetts, won election as the governor of Connecticut in 1657, Webster began serving as chief magistrate and remained in that office through 1659. While at this appointment, Webster left the **Congregationalist** church of Hartford out of disappointment that Hooker's successor as pastor, **Samuel Stone**, administered infant **baptism** to the children of unregenerate parents. Thus, Webster's disagreement was similar to that of **Edward Taylor** toward **Solomon Stoddard** in Massachusetts. Webster helped found a new church in the town of Hadley, where he spent the final years of his life. His greatest personal achievement may be his role in forming the Connecticut constitution, but his life of public service also carried on through his great-great-grandson Noah Webster, the famous lexicologist.

WENTWORTH, PETER (1524–1596). English Puritan politician. Wentworth was born in Lillingstone of Buckinghamshire, the son of Sir Nicholas and Jane Wentworth. Through his family inheritance and his two marriages, Wentworth was related by varying degrees to such notables as Sir **Walter Mildmay**, Sir Philip Sidney, the **Earl of Essex**, and two wives of King **Henry VIII**, Jane Seymour and Catherine Parr. Wentworth had a total of nine children himself. He had studied at **Lincoln's Inn** in 1542, but he did not become a public figure until nearly 30 years later, when the town of Barnstaple elected him to the House of Commons in 1571. The following year, Queen **Elizabeth I** forbade **Parliament** from intervening in the affairs of the Church of England, but Wentworth refused to cease questioning the biblical basis for **Episcopalian** church polity. For this, the queen sent him to the Tower of London in 1576 and 1587, but Wentworth defended free speech by declaring, "Sweet indeed is the name of liberty and the thing itself a value beyond all inestimable treasure." In 1592, as a representative for Northampton, Wentworth returned to the Tower for suggesting a line of royal succession that did not meet with the approval of the virgin queen. Wentworth remained in the Tower until his death and burial there in 1596. His surviving children were known to be Puritans, and his son Thomas served in Parliament during the reign of King **James I**.

WESTMINSTER ASSEMBLY. In 1643, the **Long Parliament** summoned the Westminster Assembly to revise the **Thirty-Nine Articles** along more **Calvinist** lines. Its opening meeting was in the King Henry VII Chapel of Westminster Abbey on 1 July, and **William Twisse** preached the convocation sermon. The Assembly met well over a thousand times between 1643–49; it consisted of 151 divines and 30 influential laypersons. Most of those in attendance were **Pres-**

byterians, such as Twisse, **Edward Reynolds, Obadiah Sedgwick, Stephen Marshall, William Gouge, William Spurstowe**, and **Anthony Burgess**. Presbyterians from Scotland, including **Samuel Rutherford** and George Gillespie, were also present as observers. **John Lightfoot** led a small group committed to the principles of **Erastianism**, and the **Independents** found representation in the "**five dissenting brethren**" of **Thomas Goodwin, Philip Nye, Sidrach Simpson, William Bridge**, and **Jeremiah Burroughs**. Some American **Congregationalists**, including **John Cotton** and **John Davenport**, were invited to attend, but they did not believe the transAtlantic journey to be justified if they were going to be in the minority. Neither did invited **Anglicans** like **James Ussher** usually attend the meetings.

The Assembly's members revised the first 15 of the Thirty-Nine Articles, but they stopped their work after 10 weeks, following the agreement with Scotland of the **Solemn League and Covenant**. They then turned their attention to an entirely new document that could comprehend all English, Scottish, and Irish churches. This document, patterned upon the **Irish Articles** of 1615, became the Westminster Confession. The Confession received final approval on 4 December 1646, and went to print on 29 April 1647. It had 33 articles and served as the official doctrinal statement of all churches in the British Isles until the **Restoration** of 1660. The Church of Scotland readopted it in 1690. The Confession begins with an article on the definition and authority of **Scripture**, rejecting the books of the Apocrypha as even privately edifying reading, and goes on to affirm a Calvinist doctrine of **predestination**. However, it does not mention **episcopacy** or explicitly advocate Presbyterianism. This might explain why it could exert great influence on the **Savoy Declaration** of the **Independents** and the First and Second London Confessions of the **Baptists**.

The Assembly also issued *The Directory of Public Worship* as an alternative to the *Book of Common Prayer*. The Directory suggested when **prayers** should be spoken during a **worship** service, but as a concession to the Independents, it did not insist upon exact wording. The Independents became more powerful in proportion to the ascending military career of their champion **Oliver Cromwell**, which accounts in large measure for the waning vitality of the Westminster

Assembly from the beginning of Cromwell's governance in 1649. However, the Assembly further produced a Larger and a Shorter Catechism that remain influential within Presbyterian and Reformed churches. The Shorter Catechism famously begins by declaring, "Man's chief end is to glorify God, and to enjoy Him for ever." *See also* REFORMED THEOLOGY; SYNOD OF DORT.

WESTMINSTER CONFESSION. *See* WESTMINSTER ASSEMBLY.

WHITAKER (OR WHITTAKER), JEREMIAH (1599–1654). English Puritan pastor. Whitaker was born at Wakefield in Yorkshire and studied at Sidney College, **Cambridge**. He then taught school at Oakham (or Okeham) in Rutlandshire, the town where he also married and had a son, William. After **preaching** for a while at nearby Stretton, Whitaker received appointment as one of the divines at the **Westminster Assembly** in 1643. While in London, he accepted the call as pastor of St. Mary Magdalen, Bermondsey, a **Presbyterian** church in Southwark. He also preached frequently for the Assembly and gave morning **lectures** at Westminster Abbey, often employing his skills as a translator of oriental languages, until frequent pain from ulcers and kidney stones slowed him down. **Edmund Calamy** preached the funeral oration for Whitaker, who had kept several of his sermons in print during the **Interregnum**. Whitaker's son William Whitaker (1629–72), having also developed skills as a linguist at **Emmanuel College**, **Cambridge**, succeeded his father at St. Mary Magdalen until 1662, when the **Act of Uniformity** closed the church and drove the younger Whitaker toward a more **Separatist** direction.

WHITAKER, WILLIAM (1547–1595). English Puritan scholar. This William Whitaker was born at Holme in Lancashire and should not be confused with the William Whitaker who was born at Oakham of Rutland in 1629, while his father **Jeremiah Whitaker** taught school there. Whitaker's parents were Thomas Whitaker and Elizabeth Nowell. Both were Roman **Catholic**, but Elizabeth's brother Alexander Nowell was the dean of St. Paul's Cathedral in London, and he provided for Whitaker a Protestant education. Whitaker studied at Trinity College, **Cambridge**, where he became a **fellow** and developed a reputation for translating Greek and Latin. He received a Doctor of Divinity degree from **Oxford** and then became regius professor at Cambridge. Although some envied his youth, his skill in debating theological matters with Jesuits broadened his acclaim. Whitaker later became master of St. John's College, Cambridge, and chancellor of St. Paul's. In 1589, he joined **Thomas Cartwright**, whose rhetoric he had previously criticized, in revising the Church of England's Book of Discipline toward a more **Presbyterian** polity. A contributor to the staunchly **Calvinist Lambeth Articles** in 1595, Whitaker published several **sermons** and polemical works, including *Disputations on Holy Scripture*, that were collected in Geneva in a posthumous two-volume set in 1610.

WHITEFIELD, GEORGE (1715–1770). English preacher. Although Whitefield's fame as a revivalist preacher succeeded by a short time the eclipse of Puritanism in England, his role in the **Great Awakening** nonetheless stamps him as one of the important contributors to Puritanism's last upsurge of vitality in America. Whitefield himself was conscientious of his indebtedness to Puritan theology, as evident in his reliance on the biblical commentaries of **Matthew Henry** and his penning of a preface to the collected writings of **John Bunyan** in 1767. Indeed, as early as 1829, a collection of Whitefield's own sermons published in England bore the title of *The Revived Puritan*. His important contribution to Christian history was his willingness to merge the **Calvinist** theology of the Puritans he most admired with the focus on the "new birth" and personal piety that he had learned from fellow **Oxford** students John and Charles Wesley, the founders of the Methodist movement.

Whitefield came to Pembroke College, Oxford, in 1734 from his hometown of Gloucester, where he was raised by his widowed mother (and later stepfather) as the youngest of seven children. Whitefield's father, a wine merchant and innkeeper, died while Whitefield was only two years old. Deeply impressed by the disciplined life of learning and service encouraged within the Wesleys' "Holy Club," Whitefield followed the Wesleys in attaining **Anglican ordination, preaching** at large open-air meetings, and conducting missionary journeys to America. Whitefield became widely famous for his extemporaneous preaching style which, though delivered to solicit conversions to Christ, ever remained rooted in his Calvinist conviction that saving faith only proceeds from a free and gracious gift of God. Whitefield at last purchased a tabernacle in London, from which he became known as the leader of the "Calvinist Methodists," but he preached many thousands of sermons all over England, America, Scotland, and Wales, and even Portugal and the Bermudas. Sometimes he attracted many thousands of hearers to a single service.

Whitefield made seven visits in all to America. The first of these was in 1738 to Georgia, where he founded an orphanage. His most influential tour was in 1740, when the sermons he preached in Connecticut and Massachusetts—including four at the church of **Jonathan Edwards** in Northampton—lit the spark for the series of revivals that became known as the **Great Awakening**. Whitefield's oratory was so powerful that he won the admiration even of the rationalist Benjamin Franklin, and he could supposedly reduce a congregation to tears simply by his pronunciation of the word "Mesopotamia." It was on the last of his journeys to America that Whitefield died in 1770, on an invitation to preach at the Old South First **Presbyterian** Church of Newburyport, Massachusetts. Most of his followers thereafter became **Congregationalists**.

WHITGIFT'S ARTICLES. On 23 September 1583, John Whitgift (1530–1604) succeeded Edmund Grindal as the **Archbishop of Canterbury**. Queen **Elizabeth I** directed Whitgift to curb "the obstinacy of the puritans" by eliminating private religious meetings, requiring Episcopal **ordination** and the wearing of **vestments** upon all duly recognized preachers, and enforcing the so-called "Three Articles." These articles required agreement to the queen's absolute sovereignty over all ecclesiastical and civic matters in her realm, the use of the *Book of Common Prayer* and its manner of ordination as containing nothing contrary to the word of God, and subscription to the Articles of Religion (**Thirty-Nine Articles**) agreed upon by English bishops in London in 1562. Many ministers of Puritan sympathy could agree with the first and third articles, but they could not submit to the second. Aided by John Aylmer, the bishop of London, Whitgift then launched an expansive program of suspension and imprisonment against offenders, the most noted of whom was probably **Thomas Cartwright**. Over 200 ministers in all were affected in some manner.

WHITTINGHAM, WILLIAM (1524–1579). English Puritan preacher. Born in Chester, Whittingham began his collegiate studies at Brasen-nose College, **Oxford**, then moved to All Souls College, and finally on to Christ Church after its founding by King **Henry VIII**. He completed his M.A. degree and then traveled widely across Europe during the reign of King **Edward VI**, befriending **Reformed theologians** like Peter Martyr Vermigli. Upon the accession of Queen **Mary I**, Whittingham became the leader of English Puritan refugees in Frankfurt, Germany, but he and **John Knox** relocated part of the group to Geneva to avoid a burgeoning personality conflict. There Whittingham befriended the Genevan master John Calvin himself, received **ordination** as an elder, added prefaces to tracts by one of the more famed **Marian martyrs**, **Nicholas Ridley**, translated theological writings of Theodore Beza, issued a metrical psalter, and worked on the **Geneva Bible**. Also in Geneva, he married Katherine Jacquemayne, who would bear him two children.

When Queen **Elizabeth I** followed her half sister Mary to the English throne in 1558, Whittingham returned home but soon found himself traveling again with the Earl of Bedford to France. At last Whittingham appeared to settle as a preacher in the town of Newhaven, which he also helped the Earl of Warwick to defend against the French. But Warwick persuaded the queen in 1563 to make Whittingham the dean of Durham and to invite him to preach to her personally. Whittingham's relationship with the queen even led to consideration of him as the successor to the Lord Burleigh, William Cecil, as national secretary. But the final decade of Whittingham's life was filled with far more controversy than privilege. His sympathies toward **Nonconformity** were well known, but he actually softened his opposition toward the wearing of **vestments** while in Durham. Far more serious attacks against him came from the likes of Edwin Sandys, the Archbishop of York, and **Thomas Lever**, a past acquaintance from Frankfurt, who questioned whether Whittingham's Genevan **ordination** should be valid within the Church of England. Several church trials convened to consider the case, and it was still in dispute at Whittingham's death in 1579.

WIGGINTON, GILES (1545?–1598?). English Puritan minister. Little is known about Wigginton's early years other than that he was born in the town of Oundle of Northamptonshire. He enrolled as a sizar (one required to pay minimal fees) at Trinity College, **Cambridge**, under the patronage of Sir **Walter Mildmay**, and he distinguished himself there in the study of theology, Greek, and Hebrew. He was chosen to become a **fellow** and completed work on his M.A. degree in 1572. For the remainder of his life, Wigginton was hounded and frequently imprisoned by **Archbishop of Canterbury** John Whitgift and Archbishop Edwin Sandys of York for **Nonconformity**. They intervened to prevent Wigginton's service as vicar of Sedburgh around 1581, and when Wigginton received an appointment to preach at St. Dunstan's Church in London in 1584, Whitgift forbade it and imprisoned Wigginton at Gatehouse for nearly nine weeks. In each of the next two years, Wigginton again faced the depriving of his ministry for short periods by Whitgift and Sandys. A winter imprisonment of 1586 was particularly difficult on Wigginton's health, and upon his release he preached wherever he could, including his own house, around Sedburgh.

But only the next year, 1587, Wigginton was apprehended for Nonconformity while traveling with his family in Boroughbridge, and even some of the persons who had heard him preach were excommunicated from the Church of England. In 1588, he stood trial at Lambeth Palace for writing the **Martin Marprelate Tracts**, and because his denial of authorship did not include denouncing the content of the Tracts, Wigginton went back to prison at Gatehouse. There he was accused of maintaining correspondence with revolutionaries like William Hacket, but the degree or seriousness of such communication is unclear. It is more certain that Wigginton wrote the pamphlets "A Treatise on **Predestination**," "The Fools Bolt," and "Giles Wigginton his Catechisme" during this final imprisonment. The intervention of Queen Elizabeth's secretary William Cecil, the Lord Burleigh, secured Wigginton's release and return to the Sedburgh vicarage in 1592. From this point forward in Wigginton's remaining years, again little is known.

WIGGLESWORTH, MICHAEL (1631–1705). American Puritan poet. Wigglesworth was actually born in Hedon of Yorkshire in England, but his father was a **Nonconformist** and brought the family to New Haven when his son was seven years old. Wigglesworth was frail as a child but quite intelligent, completing a degree from **Harvard College** under teachers like **Thomas Shepard** by the age of 20 and staying an additional three years at the college as a tutor to such students as **Increase Mather**. He preached at Charlestown in 1653–54, but in 1656, he accepted the position in which he would remain for nearly 50 years, the pastor of the **Congregationalist** church in the city of Malden, Massachusetts. Yet despite his vocation and a senior oration at Harvard, "The Praise of Eloquence," in which he had emphasized the transformative power of the preached word of God, Wigglesworth achieved lasting fame through his poetry. His two best-known ballads, "The Day of Doom" and "God's Controversy with New England," each appeared in 1662. "The Day of Doom" consists of 224 stanzas and predicts the sudden and terrifying day of judgment at which Christ will appear to separate the sheep from the goats: "All filthy facts and secret acts, / however closely done / And long concealed, are there revealed / before the mid-day sun." This poem can rightly be called the first American best seller, running quickly through the initial printing of 1,800 copies and sustaining 10 total editions over 140 years. "God's Controversy" is written as a first person oracle from God, warning second-generation American Puritans not to forget the religious reasons for their parents' emigration from England.

Other significant writings include Wigglesworth's personal diary and an exhortation to find blessing through suffering called "Meat Out of the Eater." In 1663, Wigglesworth fulfilled a long-held dream to study medicine and so became remembered on his tombstone as one who served Malden as a "Physician for Soul and Body too." Wigglesworth was married at different times to three **women**, including his cousin Mary Reyner and his former maid Martha Mudge. After Mudge's death and his third marriage in 1679, he also agreed to spend some of his time as a **fellow** at Harvard. Of his eight children, his son Samuel followed in his footsteps as a clergyman and poet, and his son Edward was Harvard's first Hollis Professor of Divinity. The second Hollis Professor was Wigglesworth's grandson Edward Wigglesworth, and the third Hollis Professor was Wigglesworth's great-grandson David Tappan. *See also* SCIENCE.

WILLARD, SAMUEL (1640–1707). American **Congregationalist** minister and theologian. Willard was born in Concord, Massachusetts, the son of Simon Willard, one of the town's founders and first deputy to the Massachusetts General Court. Samuel earned an undergraduate degree from **Harvard College** in 1659 and an M.A. degree a few years later. From 1663–76, Willard was the pastor of the Congregationalist church in Groton, Massachusetts, where, in 1671, he recorded investigations into the charge of **witchcraft** against Elizabeth Knapp. His marriage to Abigail Sherman equaled the length of this pastorate, for he wed her soon after his **ordination**, and she died within a year of the church's destruction during **King Philip's War**. By late 1678, a widower and father of four children, Willard succeeded Thomas Thatcher as the pastor of Boston's Old South Church. There, he married Eunice Tyng, who would bear him 14 more children.

Willard was an early advocate of the **Half-Way Covenant** and the Massachusetts Reforming Synod of 1679. He did not react favorably when Sir Edmund Andros, head of the Dominion of New England that replaced the Massachusetts charter in 1686, made him wait outside his Puritan church while **Anglican** services were conducted inside. Yet Willard remained at his Boston pastorate until his death, dealing again with witchcraft in 1692, when *Some Misallany Observations on . . . Witchcraft* granted that demon possession is possible while urging courts not to consider testimonies of supposed spectral evidence against the accused. Also in 1692, **Increase Mather** aided Willard in becoming a **fellow** and member of the governing board at Harvard. Willard became a vice-president of Harvard in 1700 and essentially served as the acting president from 1701 until his resignation shortly before his death in 1707.

Willard's first calling remained **preaching**, however, and his predominant theme was always the glory of God as "the chief end of man," as the Westminster Shorter Catechism teaches in its first question. Indeed, Willard **lectured** on the catechism every month from 1678–1707, and when these lectures were compiled in 1726 as *The Compleat Body of Divinity*, they comprised, at 914 folio pages, the largest book published in America's colonial era and American Puritanism's only systematic theology. Other titles by Willard included *Useful Instructions* (1673), A *Brief Discourse on **Justification***

(1680), *Covenant-Keeping, the Way to Blessedness* (1682), *The Character of a Good Ruler* (1694), *The Truly Blessed Man* (1700), *The Fountain Opened* (1700), and *The Child's Portion*. A favorite preacher of his friend **Increase Mather**'s son **Cotton Mather**, Willard's concerns with the proper conduct of education, **marriage**, **family life**, government, and racial relations solidified his reputation of being one of the most socially minded and pragmatic of the American Puritans.

WILLIAMS, DANIEL (1643–1716). Welsh **Presbyterian** minister. Williams was born at Wrexham, Denbighshire, in Wales, and received no formal theological training, yet he was **preaching** publicly by the age of 19. Moving to Ireland, he served as personal chaplain to the Countess of Meath in Drogheda and then as the pastor of the Presbyterian church on Wood Street in Dublin. The most frequent targets of his preaching were **antinomianism** and **Socinianism**. After nearly 20 years in Dublin, Williams went to London in 1687 to urge **dissenters** not to accept terms for religious **toleration** from King **James II** that would compromise their higher allegiance to God. Williams stayed in London to preach for the Hand Alley church on Bishopsgate Street during the **Glorious Revolution** and crowning of William and Mary. In 1691, Williams succeeded his friend and fellow moderate **Calvinist**, **Richard Baxter**, as the **lecturer** at Pinner's Hall, but he gave up that obligation to establish his own lectureship at Salter's Hall. The unschooled Williams received honorary Doctor of Divinity degrees from both the University of Edinburgh and the University of Glasgow in 1709, and when King George I became the first Hanover king in 1714, Williams led the first delegation of dissenters to meet with him. Following his death two years later, Williams was buried in London's famed **Nonconformist** cemetery **Bunhill Fields**. Known for his benevolence to charity and missionary organizations in his own lifetime, Williams' massive library remains today the centerpiece of the Center of Dissenting Studies housed at the University of London.

WILLIAMS, JOHN (1664–1729). American Puritan minister. Williams was born in Roxbury, Massachusetts. He graduated from **Harvard College** in 1683 and accepted an invitation to become the preacher at Deerfield in 1686. In 1704, Williams, his family, and dozens of citizens of Deerfield were suddenly removed from their homes during an Indian raid. Williams saw his wife, one son, and a newborn daughter slain by use of a hatchet along the forced journey to Montreal. In 1706, Williams was released along with his remaining children, except for a daughter Eunice, who married an Indian. In 1707, Williams began the work of rebuilding Deerfield and composing his memoir of his experiences, entitled *The Redeemed Captive Returning to Zion*. In his book, he vividly described the Deerfield massacre as well as his time in captivity, during which he had grudgingly yielded to attend **Catholic** mass with a group of Jesuits, even though he refused to kiss any crucifix.

WILLIAMS, ROGER (1603–1683). English **Separatist** and founder of Providence colony. Williams was born in London to a shopkeeper, James Williams, and his wife, the former Alice Pemberton. He grew up in Holborn, near Smithfield, the site of fairs and past executions of persons deemed heretics. His youthful intelligence caught the attention of Sir Edward Coke, who allowed Williams to witness the trials of **dissenters** firsthand in the **Star Chamber** and funded his studies at Sutton's Hospital (later the Charterhouse). Williams completed a baccalaureate degree at Pembroke College, **Cambridge**, in 1627 and received **ordination** as an **Anglican** minister. He did not immediately serve a particular parish, however, but agreed to become the personal chaplain for Sir William Masham of Otes in Essex County, while still working on a master's degree. In 1629, he also married Mary Barnard, who came from a Puritan family. Williams' anticlericalism soon drew notice from **Archbishop of Canterbury William Laud**, whose repressive measures against Puritans persuaded Williams to sail from Bristol for America in 1630. Williams was unable to complete his advanced degree at Cambridge, but he and his wife did arrive at Nantasket, Massachusetts, on 5 February 1631.

During the trans-Atlantic journey, Williams' **Separatism** developed into a rigid rejection of any lingering association with the Church of England, for he believed that its leadership had become hopelessly opposed to New Testament Christianity. Thus, when Williams was offered a ministerial position in Boston, he rejected it because the local church had not entirely broken fellowship with the

Church of England. He did accept a pastorate at Salem, but his scorn of the Massachusetts leadership garnered much censure from the nearby Boston elite; he soon resigned that ministry to become the assistant to Ralph Smith at Plymouth from 1631–33. Williams was opposed to enforcing the first four commandments as civil laws and to the methods by which colonial leaders had taken possession of Native American Indian lands. Although he again tried to minister at Salem from 1633–35, his outspokenness led to an appearance before the colonial court, which banished him back to England on 9 October 1635. Rather than return to England, however, Williams traveled south of the colony's border and founded his own settlement, Providence, in 1636. Williams acquired his land through negotiations with the Narragansett Indians, whose language he had learned. In 1637, Williams negotiated on behalf of all New England's European settlers during the **Pequot War**.

The distinctive feature of Providence was Williams' insistence that "God requireth not uniformity of Religion." Providence was the first government on American soil to allow complete expression of what Williams called "soul liberty"—the right to **worship** according to the dictates of one's **conscience** without fear of state reprisal. This belief that Williams shared with **William Penn**, the founder of Pennsylvania in 1681, in the end proved a more influential model for church/state relations in the United States than that originally espoused at **Massachusetts Bay Colony** by governor **John Winthrop,** who believed that God directed him to establish a city set upon a hill. This did not mean that Williams believed all religious viewpoints to be equally valid. Although Providence was the first American settlement to allow **religious liberty** to Jews and **Quakers**, Williams fiercely disagreed with their beliefs and engaged in a series of public debates with the Quakers over their alleged denial of the objective atonement of Christ. These debates were recorded and later published in 1676 as *George Fox Digg'd out of his Burrowes*. A lifelong proponent of **Calvinism**, Williams held that only God's **providence**, and not state coercion, could show the Quakers the errors of their theology.

Yet Williams' own worship preferences remained unsettled. For a short time in 1639, Williams became a **Baptist**; in that year, he founded in Providence the first Baptist church in America. Yet although he always retained the Baptist emphases on religious freedom and the separation of church and state, Williams soon distanced himself from the conviction of some Baptists that only their preferred mode of **baptism** befitted true Christians. Thus, Williams became for the rest of his life one of those **Seekers** who continually searched for the true expression of Christ's church on earth. He did remain firmly dedicated, however, to the preservation of his town. In 1644, he returned to England and employed the help of Sir **Henry Vane** in acquiring a charter that united Providence and surrounding villages into the colony of Rhode Island. While in London, he published three books in defense of his religious policies, most notably *The Bloudy Tenent of Persecution* (1644), which declared that the Boston church had moved no closer toward Christian liberty than had the Church of England from which it departed. Again in London from 1651–54 to ensure Rhode Island's continuance, Williams befriended **Oliver Cromwell** and **John Milton**, and he published *The Bloudy Tenent Yet More Bloudy* (1652), a rejoinder to **John Cotton**'s critique, *The Bloudy Tenent Washed and Made White in the Bloud of the Lamb*. From 1654–57, Williams carried the official title of President, or Governor, of Rhode Island. The outbreak of **King Philip's War** in 1675 left Williams destitute, yet even in his elderly years, he continued to serve Rhode Island as both a captain in its army and its chief negotiator with the Indians. Williams is today honored by Rhode Island with a likeness in the statuary hall of the U. S. Capitol.

WINSTANLEY, GERRARD (1609?–1676). English founder of the **Diggers**. Winstanley was born into a grocer's family in Wigan, Lancashire. In his late 20s, he moved to London as a tailor's apprentice, and in 1640, he married Susan King and moved to Walton-on-Thames to start his own business. After losing that business during the early years of the **English Civil Wars**, Winstanley became greatly disaffected with his country's entire political and economic system. In 1648, he wrote the first series of pamphlets, most notably *The Breaking of the Day of God* and *The Saints Paradice*, which set forth his radical vision for a transformed society, predicated upon the equal distribution of property among all persons. In additional writings from 1649, such as *A Watchword to the City of London and the Army, The New Law of Righteousness, A Declaration from the Poor*

Oppressed People of England, and *The True Levellers' Standard Advanced*, Winstanley traced private property rights not only to the false prerogatives of kings and clerics introduced into England by the Normans, but even to the fall against God in the Garden of Eden itself. Winstanley was essentially a pantheist who equated God with Reason and believed that Jesus Christ was "the true Leveller" who came to earth to proclaim a gospel that would subvert the established social order and restore to all persons the natural right to divide the earth as though a common treasury.

In April 1649, Winstanley joined William Everard and about 30 other persons, some of whom were disaffected soldiers from the **New Model Army**, in digging the waste ground at St. George's Hill in Surry. They planted parsnips, carrots, and beans, and staked additional claims on vacant and public properties in Kent, Northamptonshire, and Buckinghamshire. Winstanley's followers, the so-called Diggers, went beyond even the **Levellers** to advocate the complete abolition not only of private property but of wage labor. Although **Oliver Cromwell** issued a warrant for Winstanley's arrest in 1649 and ordered the dispersion of the Diggers in 1650, Winstanley continued in that same year to press his communistic agenda in new writings, such as *Several Pieces Gathered into One Volume*, *Englands Spirit Unfoulded*, and *The Law of Freedom in a Platform*, which he dedicated to Cromwell himself. Yet Cromwell's repressive measures against the Diggers proved to be the effective end of the movement. After the **Restoration**, Winstanley moved to Cobham and likely joined the **Quakers**, whose preference for interior to formal religion he had always shared. In his final years, he may have returned to London again to restart a career as a merchant. *See also* MECHANICK PREACHERS.

WINTHROP, JOHN (1588–1649). Puritan Governor of **Massachusetts Bay Colony**. Winthrop was born in Suffolk County, England. He attended Trinity College, **Cambridge**, from 1603–05, at the end of which time he married. Then, after studying at **Gray's Inn**, he served as a lawyer in London from 1613–28. His first wife Mary died in 1615 after bearing six children. Winthrop would marry thrice more and have a total of 10 more children. Influenced by his reading of Puritan preachers like **Thomas Cartwright** and **William Perkins**,

Winthrop's early journal reflects a mind of sensitive **conscience** struggling to live entirely according to God's desires rather than his own. Winthrop became convinced that God would soon punish England for failing to take the Reformation to completion, and especially after he befriended some of the trustees of the Massachusetts Bay Colony, he set his sights on moving to America. The shareholders selected Winthrop as the colonial governor even before 11 ships set sail from Southampton in 1630. Their 700 passengers were nearly seven times more than the number aboard the *Mayflower* 10 years earlier. Aboard the *Arbella*, with the Massachusetts charter in his personal possession, Winthrop delivered his immortal speech, "A Model of Christian Charity," which charged the New Englanders to shine before the world "as a city upon a hill."

During his remarkable 12 (some nonconsecutive) terms and 20 years as the governor, Winthrop welcomed **John Cotton** to preach, advised **Roger Williams** to relocate, and banished **Anne Hutchinson**. Two of Winthrops's early writings in England had been against the **antinomianism** and libertinism that he thought Hutchinson represented. Following the example of **John Knox**, Winthrop sought to govern the colony according to biblical rather than classic Greek and Roman models, and so he had to rely mostly on Old Testament examples of legal covenants. For this, he earned from **Cotton Mather** the title of *Nehemias Americanus*, the "American Nehemiah." The **worship** supported by Winthrop was strongly **Calvinist**, seeking to temper freedom of worship with the deference to appointed authority on which ordered worship relies. In 1643, Winthrop became the first president of the New England Confederation, an alliance of Massachusetts Bay, Plymouth, Connecticut, and New Haven colonies. Winthrop's intertwined vision of church and state became passé during the Enlightenment, and he once even stood trial for overstepping the limits of political authority in religious matters.

Yet his unswerving commitments to the American experiment and his dedicated leadership thereof have made Winthrop one of the most significant influences in the development of American independence. During the summer of 2004, Winthrop's lasting influence on America was evident when his "city on a hill" speech was read by Justice Sandra O'Connor during the state funeral of former Republican President Ronald Reagan. His descendant John Kerry, United States senator from the same state over which Winthrop presided as colonial governor, accepted nomination for president from the Democrat Party. *See also* SCIENCE.

WISE, JOHN (1652–1725). American **Congregationalist** minister. Wise was born in Roxbury, Massachusetts, the son of former indentured servant Joseph Wise. Wise attended local schools and earned admission into **Harvard College**, where he graduated in 1673. In 1683, he received **ordination** at the Congregationalist church of Chebacco, a parish created out of a corner of Ipswich township. In 1687, Wise briefly lost his position for protesting alongside Ipswich pastor **William Hubbard** that Governor Edmund Andros had imposed taxation without the consent of a legislature. Although none of Wise's **sermons** are extant, his reputation as a staunch advocate of democratic principles has survived primarily through his involvement in reorganizing the Massachusetts government and his two missives, *The Churches Quarrel Espoused* (1710) and *Vindication of the Government of New-England Churches* (1717). Appealing more to natural reason than to **Scripture**, Wise held that only God can wear a crown and therefore that earthly society forms only by voluntary human compact. His outspoken opposition to the centralization of church authority espoused in the **Saybrook Platform** was a primary reason for that plan's short life. Wise also served as chaplain on a failed expedition into Quebec in 1690, urged restraint during the **witchcraft** crisis of 1692, and supported the adoption of paper money in the American colonies.

WITCHCRAFT. Although witchcraft was popularly recognized as a tool of the devil throughout medieval Europe, King **Henry VIII** was the first English monarch to make witchcraft a criminal offense. Queen **Elizabeth I** and King **James I** strengthened laws against witchcraft, and witchcraft became a capital crime in 1641. Executions of witches continued in England as late as 1722. Most persons living during the Puritan era were convinced of the reality and potential hazard of witches and their black art, including such notable non-Puritans as William Shakespeare, Sir Francis Bacon, Sir Walter Raleigh, and Sir Thomas Browne.

Although there were some executions for witchcraft in Connecticut, the most notorious instance of Puritan reaction to witchcraft in America occurred in Salem (now Danvers), Massachusetts, a village founded in 1629 by Samuel Skelton and Francis Higginson. In January 1692, the daughter and ward of Rev. Samuel Parris, Elizabeth (Betty) Parris and Abigail Williams respectively, became strangely ill. Parris was age 9, while Williams was age 11. Their body aches, fever, and speaking in gibberish spread to other young girls in the town, such as Ann Putnam. The town physician, Dr. Griggs, suggested that their malady could be the result of witchcraft. Parris complained that Tituba, the family servant and a native of the Caribbean, had cast a spell over her, and Tituba, in turn, identified two elderly **women**, Sarah Good and Sarah Osborne, as her companions. Accusations and arrests multiplied. The Massachusetts colony was already in a state of unease because of local Indian conflicts and the loss of self-governance following the **Glorious Revolution** of 1688. Also, in 1689, **Cotton Mather** of nearby Boston had warned of witches whose presence foreshadowed divine judgment in *Memorable Providences, Relating to Witchcrafts and Possessions*. Mather himself was the guardian of a girl, Martha Goodwin, who had been in contact with one Goody Glover, an Irishwoman executed for witchcraft. Some interpreted the spreading accusations of witchery in Salem as evidence that God was withdrawing his favor from all New England. Hence, following a literal reading of Exodus 22:18, that witches should not be permitted to live, the Court of Oyer and Terminer first convened on 1 March 1692, to try the dozens of alleged witches who had been taken into custody.

The chief justice for the special court that oversaw the Salem witch trials was **William Stoughton**. From June–September 1692, 14 women and five men received a sentence of execution by hanging on Gallows Hill. An 80-year-old man Giles Corey was also pressed to death under stones, and a handful of other accused persons died in jail. Cotton Mather publicly defended the court's proceedings but nonetheless worked quietly to curb its zealousness. His father **Increase Mather** discouraged the use of spectral evidence (supposed out-of-body appearances by the accused) in the trials. At last, Massachusetts Governor William Phipps ordered their cessation on 19 September 1692. The 49 persons awaiting a hearing were released.

One of the judges of the Salem trials, **Samuel Sewall**, issued a public apology for his participation and set aside a day each year for fasting and repentance. The true reason for the girls' strange behavior remains a mystery, although some have suggested the deleterious effects of inhaling local ergot fungi. *See also* MASSACHUSETTS BAY COLONY.

WITHER, GEORGE (1588–1667). English Puritan poet. Wither was born to a father of the same name at Bentworth in Hampshire, and he studied at Magdalen College, **Oxford**, for two years without completing his degree. Thus, he should not be confused with the similarly named George Withers, the Doctor of Divinity who was removed from **Cambridge** for anti-papist **preaching** in 1565 by **Archbishop of Canterbury** Matthew Parker. Instead, Wither's life ran similarly to that of his contemporary John Donne as a romantic poet who developed increasingly religious interests. Wither's first major work was *Abuses, Stript and Whipt*, published in 1611 but only extant in five 1613 editions. Wither was briefly imprisoned in Southwark because certain officials believed some of the satire of *Abuses* to be directed toward them, but at that point in his life, Wither was actually a committed Stuart Royalist, even writing an elegy for the death of Prince Henry in 1612 and a poem for the marriage of Princess Elizabeth in 1613. Such devotion precipitated the admission of Wither in 1615 to **Lincoln's Inn**, where he followed up recent contributions to William Browne's *The Shepherd's Pipe* and *The Shepherd's Hunting* by penning *Fidelia*, a collection of poems that included perhaps his most famous lines, "Shall I, wasting in despair / Die because a woman's fair? / Or make pale my cheeks with care, / 'Cause another's rosy are?"

For uncertain reasons, by 1621 Wither had become an advocate of Puritan reform within the Church of England, and this set him at odds once again with authorities. He was imprisoned a second time, this time in Newgate, after the printing of *Wither's Motto*, but he persisted with *Faire-Virtue* and *Juvenilia* in 1622 and *The Hymns and Songs of the Church*, the first attempt at an **Anglican** hymnbook, in 1623. He also commemorated the London plague of 1625 with *Brittans Remembrancer* in 1628. *A Collection of Emblemes* appeared in 1634, and *Heleluiah, or Brittans Second Remembrancer*, containing the largest number of his devotional poems, appeared in 1641. Wither was still in the employ of King **Charles I** as late as the march against the Scottish Covenanters in 1639, but during the **English Civil Wars**, Wither ended up holding several different posts on the side of **Parliament** and even urged confiscation of all Royalists' properties. Yet his own house at Farnham was, in fact, burned by Royalists, and after the **Restoration**, he experienced for three years yet another imprisonment. *See also* MUSIC.

WOMEN. In Puritan culture, both English and American, women were expected to be submissive to the instructions of their husbands or fathers in accordance with a literal reading of the household codes in Ephesians chapter 5 of the **Bible**. Women were to dress modestly, covering their hair and limbs, lest they gain reputations as sexual temptresses. With a few rare exceptions among leftwing **Nonconformists**, such as the **Quakers**, women could not serve as ministers in the same churches where they were usually in the majority. Nor could women vote for or hold political office. Yet the Puritans did afford legal rights to women that were comparatively progressive for Western culture in the 17th century. Because the Puritans believed **marriage** to be a sacred covenant bound by God, wives could legally divorce husbands who neglected that covenant through adultery, desertion, or prolonged absence. Women were also protected from both physical and verbal abuse, and, in certain cases, they could hold property or receive a family inheritance.

Still, most Puritans believed that women's roles were strictly domestic and that women were divinely called to marriage and childbearing to the exclusion of theological pursuits. These expectations were spelled out in works like **Benjamin Wadsworth**'s *A Well-Ordered Family* and **Samuel Willard**'s *The Compleat Body of Divinity*. Thus, the writings of women that survive the Puritan era were usually published only much later or without their author's knowledge, like the diary of Elizabeth Wilkinson or the poems of **Anne Bradstreet** and Sarah Goodhue. Women who were too outspoken, like **Anne Hutchinson**, were shunned as **antinomian** troublemakers. The most famous attempt of Puritan culture to discipline female "weakness" occurred in the summer of 1692 with the several trials for **witchcraft** in Salem, Massachusetts. *See also* FAMILY LIFE.

WOOD, THOMAS (?–1577). English **Presbyterian** writer. Wood was a native of Leicestershire, England, who joined **William Whittingham**'s group of **Marian exiles** in moving to Frankfurt. He left England under the charge of spreading rumors that King **Edward VI** was still alive. After only a year in Frankfurt, during which time he developed a friendship with **John Knox**, Wood moved to Geneva in 1555. He received **ordination** as an elder there in 1557, and he contributed some of the marginal notes to the **Geneva Bible**. In 1563, Wood came back to London, and in 1571, he retired to his hometown, where he spent his remaining years writing letters in defense of Puritanism.

WORSHIP. The first and most common feature of Puritan worship was an opposition to the Episcopal polity of the Church of England. Puritans believed that government by bishops was not supportable by **Scripture** and limited a congregation's ability to choose its own ministers. They also associated many of the high ceremonies of the Church of England with a papist tendency to turn the rituals surrounding the Christian gospel into a distraction from a more direct proclamation of **salvation**. In reply, Puritan worship centered upon the words preached from the pulpit rather than the elements distributed from the communion altar. Puritan church buildings also tended to be iconoclastic, eliminating many of the sculptures, crucifixes, and stained glass windows that were considered to be distractions to the acquisition of faith through hearing the word of God. They also tended to forgo the wearing of **vestments**, kneeling for the **Lord's Supper**, keeping feasts for Mary and the saints, and signing the cross. In short, Puritans generally rejected any aspect of worship for which they did not find express instruction in the **Bible**.

Archbishop of Armagh **James Ussher** sought to defend the office of bishops with *The Apostolical Institution of Episcopacy*, but Ussher was also amenable to Puritan reforms and essentially defined a bishop according to a **Presbyterian** definition as the president of a board of elders. Bishop **Joseph Hall** of Exeter, however, stirred the ire of Puritans with his *Episcopacy of Divine Right*, which asserted that bishops alone have the privilege of issuing **ordination** and conducting spiritual leadership over the church. Under the pseudonym of **Smectymnuus**, five Presbyterian ministers refuted Hall's contention that the diocesan **episcopacy** was an apostolic and scriptural institution. Presbyterians still preferred a national liturgy but thought the *Book of Common Prayer* to be too formal and artificial. In 1644, the Presbyterians compromised with the **Independents** in the worship Directory issued by the **Westminster Assembly**, prescribing the ordinary prayers of a worship service but not insisting upon their exact wording. The Presbyterians' employment of **music** in their worship services usually included only metrical Psalms, but Independents like **Isaac Watts** and **Baptists** like **Benjamin Keach** eventually made hymn-singing a Puritan commonplace.

The intense dislike of imposed liturgy by the Stuart kings both before and after the **Restoration** became one of the driving forces in several **Nonconformist** expressions of worship. The early Baptist **John Smyth**, for instance, became so insistent upon the spontaneous, Spirit-led mark of true worship that he forbade even the reading of Scripture during a service unless it was previously memorized. A later Baptist, **John Bunyan**, spent a dozen years in prison following the Restoration for **preaching** without a state license and refusing to comply with the *Book of Common Prayer*. The **Quakers**' style of worship was perhaps the most reactionary of all, doing away with virtually all external acts of worship in favor of inward cultivation of the "inner light" and unprescribed utterances that could come from anyone in attendance. The distancing from "high church" worship also led most Nonconformists to reduce **baptism** and the **Lord's Supper** to memorial actions rather than sacramental means of grace. Baptists rejected infant baptism as unscriptural and insisted upon the baptism only of reasoning believers, while Quakers completely reduced baptism to a symbol of inward conversion.

Bibliography

The literature on Puritanism is quite diverse, which can be both an advantage and a disadvantage for researchers. The advantage is that one can typically find some information on virtually any aspect of Puritanism. The disadvantage is that with such a breadth of literature, one does not always find consistent answers to fundamental questions, such as the date range, ecclesiological commitments, political ambitions, or theological beliefs of "mainstream" Puritanism. On such principal issues as these, the introductory essay of this volume has proposed basic guidelines for establishing a working understanding of Puritan identity. It is hoped that with such an investigative foundation secure, the reader can better negotiate and judge between the varieties of perspectives that often arise among scholars on virtually every issue of Puritan history.

The best place to start research is reading through the primary sources of the Puritans themselves. Some major Puritan authors like John Bunyan and Jonathan Edwards fortunately have multiple writings or even collected works still in print in scholarly editions. Even when scholarly editions of Puritan authors are not available, the reprints of Puritan works by evangelical presses, such as Soli Deo Gloria Books and Banner of Truth Trust, prove to be very useful. For anyone wishing a sampling of Puritan literature, several Puritan readers are available, as listed in the "Primary Source Collections" section that follows. For a basic introduction to Puritan authors and their themes, Edward E. Hindson's *Introduction to Puritan Theology: A Reader*, David D. Hall's *Puritans in the New World: A Critical Anthology*, and Perry Miller's *The American Puritans: Their Prose and Poetry* are particularly good for the length and variety of their selections and their helpful introductions. For more in-depth investigation into specific historical events during the Puritan era, Gerald Bray's *Documents of the English Reformation* and Samuel Gardiner's *The Constitutional Documents of the Puritan Revolution, 1625–1660* stand out among several fine volumes for the thoroughness with which they present Puritanism's major theological and political documents.

In researching the biographies of individual Puritans, Benjamin Brook's three-volume *The Lives of the Puritans* remains indispensable—even though it does not typically treat Nonconformists as genuine Puritans, as does this dictionary. The British *Dictionary of National Biography* is also remarkably detailed about events in persons' lives that are often difficult to find anywhere else. When turning to introductions of the Puritan phenomenon on the whole, several books are highly serviceable, including William Haller's *The Rise of Puritanism*, Patrick Collinson's *The Elizabethan Puritan Movement*, and Sacvan Bercovitch's *The Puritan Origins of the American Self*. Christopher Hill is by all accounts the master scholar of English Nonconformity, and Perry Miller is still the starting point for serious pursuit of Puritanism in America.

To aid more specific investigation into any of the Puritan groups, the bibliography provides survey texts, thematic pursuits, and biographies of major figures for each. By using the list of sources, one may also get to know some of the representative figures for each denomination, like John Smyth and Thomas Helwys for the Baptists, Gerrard Winstanley for the Diggers, John Owen for the Independents, John Lilburne for the Levellers, George Fox and William Penn for the Quakers, and Samuel Rutherford and John Knox for the Presbyterians. There is separate attention given at the end of the bibliography to Puritans who seem to have drawn the most scholarly interest: Richard Baxter, John Bunyan, Oliver Cromwell, Jonathan Edwards, John Milton, and Roger Williams. Nonetheless, there are embedded in other sections texts either by or about many other specific Puritan individuals, including John Cotton, Edward Taylor, William Prynne, and Richard Sibbes. Some of the most respected secondary texts on the religious and social dimensions of Puritanism generally include John R. Knott's *The Sword and the Spirit*, Horton Davies' *The Worship of the English Puritans*, Edmund Morgan's *The Puritan Family*, and Margaret Olofson Thickstun's *Fictions of the Feminine*. The various writings listed in the section on women, especially those on Anne Bradstreet and Anne Hutchinson, provide a valuable perspective on an aspect of Puritan life and history that may to many persons be little known or appreciated.

For those doing research, some of the most impressive archives of Puritan-related materials can be found at Harvard University, the University of Pennsylvania, the University of Virginia, and Puritan Reformed Theological Seminary (Grand Rapids, Michigan) in the United States, and the Bodleian Library of Oxford University and the British Library in England. For those who prefer to travel by cyberspace, any number of websites can be found on virtually any search terms, but some of these are more scholarly and reliable. The Wikipedia website (http://en.wikipedia.org/wiki/Main_Page) has thorough entries for many Puritan persons and events, and "British Civil Wars, Commonwealth, and Protectorate, 1638–1660" (http://www.british-civil-wars.co.uk/index.htm) is even more specialized. Copies of many Puritan writings reside at the Christian Classics Ethereal Library (http://www.ccel.org) and "Puritan Books" (http://www.puritan-books.com). Online descriptions of "English Dissenters" (http://www.exlibris.nonconform/engdis/index.html) and "Major English Puritans" (http://members.aol.com/rbiblech/MiscDoctrine/TheMajorEnglishPuritans.htm) were helpful in the initial determinations of entries to include in this dictionary. "Puritan Studies on the Web" (http://puritanism.online.fr) should prove valuable for anyone, since it provides numerous links to primary texts, secondary articles, and government and university resources.

GENERAL

Primary Source Collections

Bray, Gerald Lewis. *Documents of the English Reformation*. Minneapolis, Minn.: Fortress Press, 1994.
DiGangi, Mariano. *A Golden Treasury of Puritan Devotion: Selections from the Writings of Thirteen Puritan Divines*. Phillipsburg, N. J.: Presbyterian and Reformed Publishing, 1999.
Gardiner, Samuel Rawson, ed. *The Constitutional Documents of the Puritan Revolution, 1625–1660*. Third Edition. Oxford: Clarendon Press, 1958.
Hall, David D., ed. *Puritans in the New World: A Critical Anthology*. Princeton, N. J.: Princeton University Press, 2004.
Hindson, Edward E., ed. *Introduction to Puritan Theology: A Reader*. Grand Rapids, Mich.: Baker Book House, 1976.
Lindley, Keith. *The English Civil War and Revolution: A Sourcebook*. London: Routledge, 1998.
Miller, Perry, ed. *The American Puritans: Their Prose and Poetry*. Garden City, N. Y.: Anchor Books, 1956.
Miller, Perry, and Thomas Herbert Johnson. *The Puritans: A Sourcebook of Their Writings: Two Volumes Bound as One*. Mineola, N. Y.: Dover Publications, 2001.
Milward, Peter. *Religious Controversies of the Elizabethan Age: A Survey of Printed Sources*. Lincoln, Neb.: Nebraska University Press, 1977.
Mitchell, Alexander Ferrier. *Catechisms of the Second Reformation*. London: James Nesbit, 1886.
Morgan, Edmund Sears. *The Founding of Massachusetts: Historians and the Sources*. Indianapolis: Bobbs-Merrill, 1964.
Murray, Iain Hamish. *The Reformation of the Church: A Collection of Reformed and Puritan Documents on Church Issues*. London: Banner of Truth Trust, 1965.
Pederson, Randall J. *Day by Day with the English Puritans*. Peabody, Mass.: Hendrickson Publishers, 2004.
Prall, Stuart E., ed. *The Puritan Revolution: A Documentary History*. Garden City, N. Y.: Anchor Books, 1968.
Rogers, Richard, and Samuel Ward. *Two Elizabethan Puritan Diaries, by Richard Rogers and Samuel Ward*. Ed. M. M. Kappen. Chicago: American Society of Church History, 1933.
Sasek, Lawrence A. *Images of English Puritanism: A Collection of Contemporary Sources*, Baton Rouge: Louisiana State University Press, 1989.
Sweet, William Warren. *The Congregationalists: A Collection of Source Materials*. New York: Cooper Square Publishers, 1964.

Related Historical Dictionaries and Encyclopedias

Abbott, Margery Post, Mary Ellen Chijioke, Pink Dandelion, and John W. Oliver. *Historical Dictionary of the Friends (Quakers)*. Lanham, Md.: Scarecrow Press, 2003.

Bailey, Michael D. *Historical Dictionary of Witchcraft*. Lanham, Md.: Scarecrow Press, 2003.

Benedetto, Robert, Darrell L. Guder, and Donald K. McKim. *Historical Dictionary of the Reformed Churches*. Lanham, Md.: Scarecrow Press, 1999.

Bennett, Martyn. *Historical Dictionary of the British and Irish Civil Wars, 1637–1660*. Lanham, Md.: Scarecrow Press, 2000.

Brackney, William H. *Historical Dictionary of the Baptists*. Lanham, Md.: Scarecrow Press, 1999.

Bremer, Francis J., and Tom Webster. *Puritans and Puritanism in Europe and America: A Comprehensive Encyclopedia*. Santa Barbara, Calif.: ABC-CLIO, 2006.

Brook, Benjamin. *The Lives of the Puritans*. 3 vols. Morgan, Pa.: Soli Deo Gloria Publications, 1994.

Buchanan, Colin. *Historical Dictionary of Anglicanism*. Lanham, Md.: Scarecrow Press, 2006.

Cross, F. L., and E. A. Livingstone. *The Oxford Dictionary of the Christian Church*. New York: Oxford University Press, 1997.

Douglas, J. D. *Who's Who in Christian History*. Wheaton, Ill.: Tyndale House, 1992.

Harris, Mark W. *Historical Dictionary of Unitarian Universalism*. Lanham, Md.: Scarecrow Press, 2004.

Holloran, Peter C. *Historical Dictionary of New England*. Lanham, Md.: Scarecrow Press, 2003.

Huussen, Arend H., Jr. *Historical Dictionary of the Netherlands*. Lanham, Md.: Scarecrow Press, 1998.

Newman, P. R. *Royalist Officers in England and Wales, 1642–1660: A Biographical Dictionary*. New York: Garland Publications, 1981.

Nicholls, C. S., and Keith Thomas. *The Dictionary of National Biography*. New York: Oxford University Press, 1996.

Palmer, Samuel. *The Nonconformist's Memorial*. 3 vols. London: J. Cundee for Botton and Son and T. Hurst, 1802.

Panton, Kenneth J. *Historical Dictionary of London*. Lanham, Md.: Scarecrow Press, 2001.

Panton, Kenneth J., and Keith A. Cowlard. *Historical Dictionary of United Kingdom: Two-Volume Set*. Lanham, Md.: Scarecrow Press, 1998.

Reid, Daniel G., Robert Dean Linder, Bruce L. Shelley, and Harry S. Stout. *Dictionary of Christianity in America*. Downers Grove, Ill.: InterVarsity Press, 1999.

Sabin, Joseph A. *A Dictionary of Books Relating to America*. Lanham, Md.: Scarecrow Press, 1966.

Thomas, Colin, and Avril Thomas. *Historical Dictionary of Ireland*. Lanham, Md.: Scarecrow Press, 1997.
Yrigoyen, Charles, Jr. *Historical Dictionary of Methodism*. Lanham, Md.: Scarecrow Press, 2005.

HISTORICAL INTRODUCTIONS

American Puritanism

Ahlstrom, Sydney E. *A Religious History of the American People*. New Haven, Conn.: Yale University Press, 1972.
Bercovitch, Sacvan. *Puritan Origins of the American Self*. New Haven, Conn.: Yale University Press, 1975.
Breitwieser, Mitchell Robert. *American Puritanism and the Defense of Mourning: Religion, Grief, and Ethnology in Mary White Rowlandson's Captivity Narrative*. Madison, Wis.: University of Wisconsin Press, 1990.
Bremer, Francis J. "The American Puritans." *Christian History* 13.1 (1994): 26–27.
Burg, B. Richard. "Ideology of Richard Mather and its Relationship to English Puritanism prior to 1660." *Journal of Church and State* 9 (August 1967): 364–377.
Cotton, John. *The New England Way: John Cotton*. New York: AMS Press, 1983.
Cowling, Cedric B. *The Saving Remnant: Religion and the Settling of New England*. Urbana: University of Illinois, 1995.
Current, Richard N., T. Harry Williams, Frank Freidel, and Alan Brinkley. *American History: A Survey*. Seventh edition. New York: Alfred A. Knopf, 1987.
Delbanco, Anthony. *The Puritan Ordeal*. Cambridge, Mass.: Harvard University Press, 1989.
Dudley, William, and Terry O'Neill. *Puritanism: Opposing Viewpoints*. San Diego, Calif.: Greenhaven Press, 1994.
Gaustad, Edwin S., and Leigh Eric Schmidt. *The Religious History of America*. San Francisco: Harper San Francisco, 2002.
Hall, David D. *Puritanism in Seventeenth-Century Massachusetts*. New York: Holt, Rinehart, and Winston, 1968.
Hall, Michael G. *The Last American Puritan: The Life of Increase Mather, 1639–1723*. Middletown, Conn.: Wesleyan University Press, 1988.
Hoffer, Peter Charles, ed. *The Marrow of American Divinity: Selected Articles on Colonial Religion*. New York: Garland 1988.
Hopley, Claire. "The Great Migrations of 1630: The Puritans." *British Heritage* 26.4 (September 2005): 20–166.
Hudson, Winthrop S. *Religion in America: An Historical Account of the Development of American Religious Life*. Third Edition. New York: Charles Scribner's Sons, 1981.

Jinkins, Michael. "John Cotton and the Antinomian Controversy, 1636–1638: A Profile of Experiential Individualism in American Puritanism." *Scottish Journal of Theology* 43:3 (1990): 321–349.

Juster, Susan. "Body and Soul: The Modernist Impulse in American Puritanism." *Reviews in American History* 21:1 (March 1993): 19–25.

King, John Owen. *The Iron of Melancholy: Structures of Spiritual Conversion in America from the Puritan Conscience to Victorian Neurosis*. Middletown, Conn.: Wesleyan University Press, 1983.

Knight, Janice. *Orthodoxies in Massachusetts: Rereading American Puritanism*. Cambridge, Mass.: Harvard University Press, 1994.

LaPlante, Eve. *American Jezebel: The Uncommon Life of Anne Hutchinson, the Woman who Defied the Puritans*. San Francisco: Harper San Francisco, 2004.

Mather, Cotton. *Magnalia Christi Americana, Books I and II*. Ed. Kenneth Ballard Murdock and Elizabeth W. Miller. Cambridge, Mass.: Belknap Press, 1977.

Middlekauff, Robert. *The Mathers: Three Generations of Puritan Intellectuals, 1596–1728*. Berkeley: University of California Press, 1999.

Miller, Perry. *Errand into the Wilderness*. Cambridge, Mass.: Belknap Press of Harvard University Press, 1956.

———. *The New England Mind: The Seventeenth Century*. New York: Macmillan, 1939.

———. *Orthodoxy in Massachusetts, 1630–1650*. Boston, Mass.: Beacon Press, 1959.

Morgan, Edmund S. *The Puritan Dilemma: The Story of John Winthrop*. Ed. Oscar Handlin. San Francisco: HarperCollins, 1958.

———. *Visible Saints: The History of a Puritan Idea*. New York: New York University Press, 1963.

Reed, Michael D. "Early American Puritanism: The Language of Its Religion." *American Imago* 37:3 (Fall 1980): 278–333.

Rutman, Darrett B. *American Puritanism: Faith and Practice*. Philadelphia, Pa.: J. B. Lippincott, 1970.

Shepard, Thomas. *God's Plot: The Paradoxes of Puritan Piety, Being the Autobiography and Journal of Thomas Shepard*. Amherst: University of Massachusetts Press, 1972.

Simmons, R. C. *The American Colonies: from Settlement to Independence*. New York: D. McKay, 1976.

Slotkin, Richard, and James K. Folsom. *So Dreadfull a Judgment: Puritan Responses to King Philip's War, 1676–1677*. Middletown, Conn.: Wesleyan University Press, 1978.

Vaughan, Alden T., and Francis J. Bremer. *Puritan New England: Essays on Religion, Society, and Culture*. New York: St. Martin's Press, 1977.

Waller, George Macgregor, ed. *Puritanism in Early America*. Boston: Heath, 1973.

Warren, Austin. *New England Saints*. Ann Arbor: University of Michigan Press, 1956.

Wentz, Richard E. *American Religious Traditions: The Shaping of Religion in the United States*. Minneapolis, Minn.: Fortress Press, 2003.

Wertenbaker, Thomas Jefferson. *The Puritan Oligarchy: The Founding of American Civilization*. New York: Scribner, 1970.

West, Thomas G. "The Transformation of Protestant Theology as a Condition of the American Revolution." In *Protestantism and the American Founding*. Eds. Thomas S. Engeman and Michael P. Zuckert, 187–224. Notre Dame: University of Notre Dame Press, 2004.

Williams, Peter W. *America's Religions: Traditions and Cultures*. New York: Macmillan, 1990.

Winslow, Ola Elizabeth. *Meetinghouse Hill, 1630–1783*. New York: Macmillan, 1952.

English Civil Wars

Ashton, Robert. "Puritans and Roundheads: The Harleys of Brampton Bryan and the Outbreak of the English Civil War." *History* 76.247 (June 1991): 310–311.

Ashton, Robert, and Raymond Howard Parry. *The English Civil War and After, 1642–1658*. Berkeley: University of California Press, 1970.

Barbary, James. *Puritan & Cavalier: The English Civil War*. Nashville, Tenn.: T. Nelson, 1977.

Barber, Sarah. *Regicide and Republicanism: Politics and Ethics in the English Revolution,* Edinburgh, Scotland, U. K.: Edinburgh University Press, 1998.

———. *A Revolutionary Rogue: Henry Marten and the English Republic*. Stroud, Gloucestershire, U. K.: Sutton Books, 2000.

Baskerville, Stephen. *Not Peace but a Sword: The Political Theology of the English Revolution*. London: Routledge, 1993.

Bennett, Martyn. *The Civil Wars in Britain and Ireland, 1638–1651*. Oxford: Blackwell Publishers, 1997.

Carruthers, Bob. *The English Civil Wars, 1642–1660.* London: Cassell, 2000.

Corns, Thomas N. *Uncloistered Virtue: English Political Literature, 1640–1660*. Oxford: Clarendon Press, 1992.

Cust, Richard, and Ann Hughes. *The English Civil War*. London: Edward Arnold, 1997.

Finlayson, Michael George. *Historians, Puritanism, and the English Revolution: The Religious Factor in English Politics Before and After the Interregnum*. Buffalo, N. Y.: University of Toronto Press, 1983.

Haller, William. *Liberty and Reformation in the English Revolution*. New York: Columbia University Press, 1955.

Haythornthwaite, Philip. *The English Civil War, 1642–1651: An Illustrated Military History*. London: Brockhampton Press, 1998.

Hill, Christopher. *The Century of Revolution, 1603–1714*. New York: W. W. Norton, 1980.

———. *Intellectual Origins of the English Revolution—Revisited*. Oxford: Oxford University Press, 2001.

———. *Puritanism and Revolution: Studies in Interpretation of the English Revolution of the Seventeenth Century*. New York: St. Martin's Press, 1997.

———. *Society and Puritanism in Pre-Revolutionary England*. New York: St. Martin's Press, 1997.

Holstun, James. *Pamphlet Wars: Prose in the English Revolution*. London: F. Cass, 1992.

Hunt, William. *The Puritan Moment: the Coming of Revolution in an English County*. Cambridge, Mass.: Harvard University Press, 1983.

Ives, E. W. *The English Revolution, 1600–1660*. London: Edward Arnold, 1968.

Jendrysik, Mark Stephen. *Explaining the English Revolution: Hobbes and His Contemporaries*. Lanham, Md.: Lexington Books, 2002.

Jessup, Frank W., ed. *Background to the English Civil War*. Oxford: Pergamon Press, 1966.

Keeble, N. H. *The Cambridge Companion to Writing of the English Revolution*. Cambridge: Cambridge University Press, 2001.

Kennedy, D. E. *The English Revolution, 1642–1649*. New York: St. Martin's Press, 2000.

Kenyon, J. P., and Jane H. Ohlmeyer. *The Civil Wars: A Military History of England, Scotland, and Ireland, 1638–1660*. New York: Oxford University Press, 2002.

Lamont, W. "Richard Baxter, 'Popery' and the Origins of the English Civil War." *History* 87.287 (July 2002): 336–352.

Lindley, Keith. *The English Civil War and Revolution: A Sourcebook*. London: Routledge, 1998.

Manning, Brian. *1649: The Crisis of the English Revolution*. London: Bookmarks, 1992.

McDowell, Nicholas. *The English Radical Imagination: Culture, Religion, and Revolution, 1630–1660*. Oxford: Clarendon Press, 2003.

McGee, J. Sears. "Sir Simonds D'Ewes and 'the Poitovin Cholick: 'Persecution, Toleration, and the Mind of a Puritan Member of the Long Parliament." *Canadian Journal of History* 38.3 (December 2003): 481–491.

Morrill, John. "Puritan Iconoclasm During the English Civil War." *American Historical Review* 110.1 (February 2005): 215–216.

Newman, P. R. *Companion to the English Civil Wars*. New York: Facts on File, 1990.

Prall, Stuart E. *The Puritan Revolution and the English Civil War*. Malabar, Fl.: Krieger, 2002.

Richardson, R. C. "Writing and Re-Writing the English Civil Wars." *Literature & History* 11:2 (October 2002): 101–107.

Roots, Ivan Alan. *Commonwealth and Protectorate: The English Civil War and Its Aftermath*. New York: Schocken Books, 1966.
Rowse, A. L. *The Regicides and the Puritan Revolution*. London: Duckworth, 1994.
Royle, Trevor. *The British Civil War: The Wars of the Three Kingdoms, 1638–1660*. New York: Palgrave Macmillan, 2004.
Seel, G. E. *The English Wars and Republic, 1637–1660*. London: Routledge, 1999.
Smith, David L. "New Perspectives on Britain's Civil Wars." *Historical Journal* 46:2 (June 2003): 449–461.
Spalding, James C. "Loyalist as Royalist, Patriot as Puritan: The American Revolution as a Repetition of the English Civil Wars." *Church History* 45 (September 1976): 329–340.
Spraggon, Julie. *Puritan Iconoclasm During the English Civil War*. Suffolk, U. K.: Boydell, 2003.
Walker, David J. "Thomas Goodwin and the Debate on Church Government." *Journal of Ecclesiastical History* 34.1 (January 1983): 85–99.
Woolrych, Austin, I. J. Gentles, J. S. Morrill, and Blair Worden. *Soldiers, Writers, and Statesmen of the English Revolution*. Cambridge: Cambridge University Press, 1998.
Worden, Blair. *Roundhead Reputations: The English Civil Wars and the Passions of Posterity*. London: Penguin Books, 2001.
Young, Peter, and Richard Holmes. *The English Civil War; a Military History of the Three Civil Wars, 1642–1651*. London: Eyre Methuen, 1974.

Dutch Puritanism

Beeke, Joel R. *Assurance of Faith: Calvin, English Puritanism, and the Dutch Second Reformation*. New York: Peter Lang, 1991.
Harrison, A. W. *The Beginnings of Arminianism to the Synod of Dort*. London: University of London Press, 1926.
Milton, Anthony. *The British Delegation and the Synod of Dort (1618–1619)*. Woodbridge, U. K.: Boydell Press, 2005.
Nobbs, Douglas. *Theocracy and Toleration: A Study of the Disputes in Dutch Calvinism from 1600 to 1650*. Cambridge: Cambridge University Press, 1938.
Sprunger, Keith L. *Dutch Puritanism: A History of English and Scottish Churches of the Netherlands in the Sixteenth and Seventeenth Centuries*. Leiden: E. J. Brill, 1982.
———. *The Learned Doctor William Ames: Dutch Backgrounds of English and American Puritanism*. Urbana, Ill.: University of Illinois Press, 1972.
Stearns, Raymond Phineas. *Congregationalism in the Dutch Netherlands: The Rise and Fall of the English Congregational Classis, 1621–1635*. Chicago: American Society of Church History, 1940.

English Puritanism

Bremer, Francis J. *Puritanism: Transatlantic Perspectives on a Seventeenth-Century Anglo-American Faith.* Boston: Northeastern University Press, 1993.

Brown, John. *The English Puritans: The Rise and Fall of the Puritan Movement.* Geanies House, U. K.: Christian Focus Publications, 1998.

Byington, Ezra Hoyt. *The Puritan in England and New England.* Boston: Roberts, 1896.

Campbell, Douglas. The Puritan in Holland, England, and America: An Introduction to American History. 2 vols. New York: Harper and Brothers, 1892.

Collinson, Patrick. *The Elizabethan Puritan Movement.* London: Jonathan Cape, 1967.

——. *Godly People: Essays on English Protestantism and Puritanism.* London: Hambledon Press, 1983.

Cragg, G. R. *Puritanism in the Period of the Great Persecution, 1660–1688.* Cambridge: Cambridge University Press, 1957.

Danner, Dan G. Pilgrimage to Puritanism: History and Theology of the Marian Exiles at Geneva, 1555–1560. New York: Peter Lang, 1999.

Dark, Sidney. *The Passing of the Puritan.* London: Skeffington, 1946.

Durston, Christopher, and Jacqueline Eales. *The Culture of English Puritanism, 1560–1700.* New York: St. Martin's Press, 1996.

Edwards, David L. *Christian England, Volume 2: From the Reformation to the 18th Century.* London: Collins, 1983.

Garrett, Christina Hallowell. *The Marian Exiles: A Study in the Origins of Elizabethan Puritanism.* Cambridge: Cambridge University Press, 1938.

Hall, Basil. "Puritanism: The Problem of Definition." In *Studies in Church History, Volume II: Papers Read at the Second Winter and Summer Meetings of the Ecclesiastical History Society.* Ed. G. J. Cuming, 283–296. London: T. Nelson and Sons, 1965.

Haller, William. *The Rise of Puritanism.* New York: Harper Torchbooks, 1957.

Henson, Hensley. *Puritanism in England.* New York: Burt Franklin, 1972.

Hill, Christopher. *The Century of Revolution, 1603–1714.* New York: W. W. Norton, 1980.

——. *Society and Puritanism in pre-Revolutionary England.* New York: Schocken Books, 1964.

Hill, Christopher; D. H. Pennington, and Keith Thomas. *Puritans and Revolutionaries: Essays in Seventeenth-Century History Presented to Christopher Hill.* Oxford: Clarendon Press, 1978.

Howard, Leon, James Barbour, and Tom Quirk. *Essays on Puritans and Puritanism.* Albuquerque: University of New Mexico Press, 1986.

Johnson, Ellwood. *The Pursuit of Power: Studies in the Vocabulary of Puritanism.* New York: Peter Lang, 1995.

Kapic, Kelly M., and Randall C. Gleason. *The Devoted Life: An Invitation to the Puritan Classics.* Downers Grove, Ill.: InterVarsity Press, 2004.

Kenyon, J. P. *Stuart England*. Second Edition. London: Penguin Books, 1985.
Neal, Daniel. *The History of the Puritans, or Protestant Nonconformists*. 2 vols. New York: Harper and Brothers, 1858.
Nuttall, Geoffrey F. *The Puritan Spirit: Essays and Addresses*. London: Epworth Press, 1967.
Packer, J. I. *A Quest for Godliness: The Puritan Vision of the Christian Life*. Wheaton, Ill.: Crossway Books, 1990.
Richardson, R. C. *Puritanism in North-West England: A Regional Study of the Diocese of Chester to 1642*. Manchester: Manchester University Press, 1972.
Ryken, Leland. *Worldly Saints: The Puritans as They Really Were*. Grand Rapids, Mich.: Academie Books, 1990.
Simpson, Alan. *Puritanism in Old and New England*. Chicago: University of Chicago Press, 1955.
Spurr, John. *English Puritanism, 1603–1689*. New York: St. Martin's Press, 1998.
Stephenson, George M. *The Puritan Heritage*. New York: Macmillan, 1952.
Tatham, G. B. *The Puritans in Power: A Study in the History of the English Church from 1640 to 1660*. Cambridge: Cambridge University Press, 1913.
Trinterud, Leonard J. *Elizabethan Puritanism*. New York: Oxford University Press, 1971.
Tyacke, Nicholas. *Aspects of English Protestantism, c. 1530–1700*. Manchester: Manchester University Press, 2001.
White, Barrington R., ed. *The English Puritan Tradition*. Nashville, Tenn.: Broadman Press, 1980.

Irish Puritanism

Coonan, Thomas L. *The Irish Catholic Confederacy and the Puritan Revolution*. New York: Columbia University Press, 1954.
Ford, Alan, and J. I. McGuire. *As by Law Established: The Church of Ireland since the Reformation*. Dublin: Lilliput Press, 1995.
Greaves, Richard L. *God's Other Children: Protestant Nonconformists and the Emergence of Denominational Churches in Ireland, 1660–1700*. Stanford, Calif.: Stanford University Press, 1997.
Gribben, Crawford. "Defining the Puritans? The Baptism Debate in Cromwellian Ireland, 1654–56." *Church History* 73.1 (March 2004): 63–89.
——. *The Irish Puritans: James Ussher and the Reformation of the Church*. Darlington, U. K.: Evangelical Press, 2003.
Herlihy, Kevin, ed. *The Irish Dissenting Tradition, 1650–1750*. Dublin: Four Courts Press, 1995.
——. *Propagating the Word of Irish Dissent, 1650–1800*. Dublin: Four Courts Press, 1998.
Kistler, Don. *The Puritan Pulpit: The Irish Puritans*. Orlando, Fl.: Soli Deo Gloria Publications, 2006.

Knox, R. Buick. *James Ussher, Archbishop of Armagh*. Cardiff: University of Wales Press, 1967.
Wheeler, James Scott. *The Irish and British Wars, 1637–1654: Triumph, Tragedy, and Failure*. London: Routledge, 2002.

Pilgrims

Bartlett, Robert Merrill. *The Pilgrim Way*. Philadelphia, Pa.: Pilgrim Press, 1971.
Beale, David O. *The Mayflower Pilgrims: Roots of Puritan, Presbyterian, Congregationalist, and Baptist Heritage*. Greenville, S. C.: Ambassador-Emerald International, 2000.
Brachlow, Stephen. "John Robinson and the Lure of Separatism in Pre-Revolutionary England." *Church History* 50 (September 1981): 288–301.
Bradford, William. *Of Plymouth Plantation*. Ed. Harvey Wish. New York: Capricorn Books, 1962.
Caffrey, Kate. *The Mayflower*. New York: Stein and Day, 1974.
Dillon, Francis. *The Pilgrims*. Garden City, N. Y.: Doubleday, 1975.
Fleming, Thomas J. *One Small Candle: The Pilgrims' First Year in America*. New York: W. W. Norton, 1964.
Philbrick, Nathaniel. *Mayflower: A Story of Courage, Community, and War*. New York: Viking, 2006.
Robinson, John. *The Works of John Robinson, Pastor of the Pilgrim Fathers*. Ed. William Allen, John Waddington, et al. Boston: Doctrinal Tract and Book Society, 1851.
Sprunger, Keith L. "Other Pilgrims in Leiden: Hugh Goodyear and the English Reformed Church." *Church History* 41 (March 1972): 46–60.
Wallace, Dewey D. *The Pilgrims*. Wilmington, N. C.: McGrath, 1977.
Yarbrough, Slayden A. "Ecclesiastical Development in the Theory and Practice of John Robinson and Henry Jacob." *Perspectives in Religious Studies* 5 (Fall 1978): 183–197.

Scottish Puritanism

Burleigh, John H. S. *A Church History of Scotland*. London: Oxford University Press, 1960.
Coffey, John. *Politics, Religion, and the British Revolutions: The Mind of Samuel Rutherford*. Cambridge: Cambridge University Press, 1997.
Cowan, Henry. *John Knox: The Hero of the Scottish Reformation*. New York: AMS Press, 1970.
Cowan, Ian Borthwick. *The Scottish Covenanters, 1660–1688*. London: V. Gollancz, 1976.

Donaldson, Gordon. *The Scottish Reformation*. Cambridge: Cambridge University Press, 1960.
Douglas, J. D. *Light in the North: The Story of the Scottish Covenanters*. Grand Rapids, Mich.: William B. Eerdmans, 1964.
Henderson, G. D. "Puritanism in Eighteenth-Century Scotland." *Evangelical Quarterly* 19:3 (July 1947): 211–221.
Kaplan, Lawrence. *Politics and Religion During the English Revolution: The Scots and the Long Parliament, 1643–1645*. New York: New York University Press, 1976.
Knox, John. *History of the Reformation in Scotland*. Ed. William Croft Dickinson. New York: Philosophical Library, 1950.
———. *The Political Writings of John Knox: The First Blast of the Trumpet Against the Monstrous Regiment of Women and Other Writings*. London: Associated University Presses, 1985.
Lachman, David C. *The Marrow Controversy*. Edinburgh, Scotland, U. K.: Rutherford House, 1988.
Lang, Andrew. *John Knox and the Reformation*. Port Washington, N. Y.: Kennikat Press, 1967.
Mason, Roger A. *Scots and Britons: Scottish Political Thought and the Union of 1603*. Cambridge: Cambridge University Press, 1994.
Matthew, David. *Scotland Under Charles I*. London: Eyre and Spottiswoode, 1955.
Morrill, J. S. *The Scottish National Covenant in Its British Context*. Edinburgh, Scotland, U. K.: Edinburgh University Press, 1990.
Mullan, David George. *Scottish Puritanism, 1590–1638*. Oxford: Oxford University Press, 2000.
Provland, William Seath. *Puritanism in the Scottish Church*. Paisley, U. K.: A. Gardner, 1923.
Stevenson, David. *The Scottish Revolution, 1637–1644: The Triumph of the Covenanters*. New York: St. Martin's Press, 1973.

Separatists, Dissenters, and Nonconformists

Davis, Arthur P. "Isaac Watts: Late Puritan Rebel." *The Journal of Religious Thought* 13 (Spring–Summer 1956): 123–130.
Dow, F. D. *Radicalism in the English Revolution, 1640–1660*. Oxford: Blackwell, 1985.
Greaves, Richard L. "Organizational Response of Nonconformity to Repression and Indulgence: The Case of Bedfordshire." *Church History* 44 (December 1975): 472–484.
———. *Saints and Rebels: Seven Nonconformists in Stuart England*. Macon, Ga.: Mercer University Press, 1985.

Hill, Christopher. *Antichrist in Seventeenth-Century England*. London: Oxford University Press, 1971.

———. *The World Turned Upside Down: Radical Ideas During the English Revolution*. New York: Viking Press, 1972.

Johnston, Warren. "The Patience of the Saints, the Apocalypse, and Moderate Nonconformity in Restoration England." *Canadian Journal of History* 38:3 (December 2003): 505–520.

Knoppers, Laura Lunger. *Puritanism and Its Discontents*. Newark, N. J.: University of Delaware Press, 2003.

Lloyd-Jones, D. Martin. *From Puritanism to Nonconformity*. Bridgend, U. K.: Evangelical Press of Wales, 1991.

MacLear, J. F. "Isaac Watts and the Idea of Public Religion." *Journal of the History of Ideas* 53:1 (January–March 1992): 25–45.

———. "Popular Anti-Clericalism in the Puritan Revolution." *Journal of the History of Ideas* 17:4 (1956): 443–470.

Manning, Brian. *The Far Left in the English Revolution, 1640 to 1660*. London: Bookmarks, 1999.

McGregor, J. F., and Barry Reay. *Radical Religion in the English Revolution*. New York: Oxford University Press, 1984.

Seaver, Paul S. *The Puritan Lectureships: The Politics of Religious Dissent, 1560–1662*. Stanford, Calif.: Stanford University Press, 1970.

Sell, Alan P. F., ed. *Protestant Nonconformists and the West Midlands of England: Papers Presented at the First Conference of the Association of Denominational Historical Societies and Cognate Libraries*. Keele, U. K.: Keele University Press, 1996.

Stell, Christopher. "Puritan and Nonconformist Meetinghouses in England." In *Seeing Beyond the Word: Visual Arts and the Calvinist Tradition*. Ed. Paul Corby Finney, 49–81. Grand Rapids, Mich.: William B. Eerdmans, 1999.

Watts, Michael R. *The Dissenters: From the Reformation to the French Revolution*. Oxford: Clarendon Press, 1978.

Zuck, Lowell H. *Christianity and Revolution: Radical Christian Testimonies, 1520–1650*. Philadelphia, Pa.: Temple University Press, 1975.

DENOMINATIONS

Baptists

Bell, Mark R. *Apocalypse How? Baptist Movements During the English Revolution*. Macon, Ga.: Mercer University Press, 2000.

Brachlow, Stephen. "Puritan Theology and General Baptist Origins." *Baptist Quarterly* 31 (October 1985): 179–194.

Brackney, William H. *Baptist Life and Thought, 1600–1980: A Source Book*. Valley Forge, Pa.: Judson Press, 1983.
Buckley, Thomas E. "Church and State in Massachusetts Bay: A Case Study of Baptist Dissenters, 1651." *Journal of Church and State* 23 (Spring 1981): 309–322.
Burdick, Oscar. "Sleuthing the Origins of English Seventh Day Baptists in the 1650s: A Bibliography." *American Theological Library Association Summary of Proceedings* 38 (1984): 134–145.
Drummond, Lewis A. "The Puritan–Pietistic Tradition: Its Meaning, History, and Influence in Baptist Life." *Review & Expositor* 77 (Fall 1980): 483–492.
Durnbaugh, Donald F. "Free Churches, Baptists, and Ecumenism: Origins and Implications." *Journal of Ecumenical Studies* 17 (Spring 1980): 3–20.
Estep, William Roscoe, and Paul Toews. *Sixteenth-Century Anabaptism and the Puritan Connection: Reflections upon Baptist Origins*. Hillsboro, Kans.: Kindred Press, 1993.
Freeman, Curtis W., and James William McClendon. *Baptist Roots: A Reader in the Theology of a Christian People*. Valley Forge, Pa.: Judson Press, 1999.
George, Timothy, and Denise George. *Baptist Confessions, Covenants, and Catechisms*. Nashville, Tenn.: Broadman and Holman Publishers, 1996.
Helwys, Thomas. *A Short Declaration of the Mystery of Iniquity*. Ed. Richard Groves. Macon, Ga.: Mercer University Press, 1998.
Lee, Jason K. *The Theology of John Smyth: Puritan, Separatist, Baptist, Mennonite*. Macon, Ga.: Mercer University Press, 2003.
Lumpkin, William Latane. *Baptist Confessions of Faith*. Chicago: Judson Press, 1959.
———. "The Bible in Early Baptist Confessions of Faith." *Baptist History and Heritage* 19:3 (July 1984): 33–41.
Manley, Kenneth R. "Origins of the Baptists: The Case for Development from Puritanism–Separatism." *Baptist History and Heritage* 22 (October 1987): 34–46.
———. *The Baptist Heritage: Four Centuries of Baptist Witness*. Nashville, Tenn.: Broadman Press, 1987.
McBeth, H. Leon. *A Sourcebook for Baptist Heritage*. Nashville, Tenn.: Broadman Press, 1990.
Parker, G. Keith. *Baptists in Europe: History & Confessions of Faith*. Nashville, Tenn.: Broadman Press, 1982.
Stassen, Glen Harold. "Anabaptist Influence in the Origin of the Particular Baptists." *The Mennonite Quarterly Review* 36:4 (October 1962): 322–348.
———. "Opening Menno Simons's Foundation-Book and Finding the Father of Baptist Origins Alongside the Mother—Calvinist Congregationalism." *Baptist History and Heritage* 33 (Spring 1998): 34–44.
Thompson, Philip E. "Seventeenth-Century Baptist Confessions in Context." *Perspectives in Religious Studies* 29.4 (Winter 2002): 335–348.

Torbet, Robert G. *A History of the Baptists*. Third Edition. Valley Forge, Pa.: Judson Press, 1987.

Diggers

Alsop, James D. "Gerrard Winstanley: Religion and Respectability." *Historical Journal* 28 (September 1985): 705–709.
Bradley, Ian. "Gerrard Winstanley: England's Pioneer Green?" *History Today* 39.8 (August 1989): 12–17.
Bradstock, Andrew. "The Earth as a Common Treasury: The Diggers and the Land Question." *Ecotheology* 1 (July 1996): 35–41.
——. *Winstanley and the Diggers, 1649–1999*. Portland, Ore.: Frank Cass, 2000.
Burgess, John P. "Biblical Poet and Prophet: Gerrard Winstanley's Use of Scripture in *The Law of Freedom*." *Journal of Religious History* 14 (June 1987): 269–282.
Gurney, John. "Gerrard Winstanley and the Digger Movement in Walton and Cobham." *Historical Journal* 37:4 (December 1994): 775–802.
Hayes, T. Wilson. *Winstanley the Digger: A Literary Analysis of Radical Ideas in the English Revolution*. Cambridge, Mass.: Harvard University Press, 1996.
Mulder, David W. *The Alchemy of Revolution: Gerrard Winstanley's Occultism and Seventeenth-Century English Communism*. New York: Peter Lang, 1990.
Rogers, Michael. "Gerrard Winstanley on Crime and Punishment." *Sixteenth Century Journal* 27:3 (Fall 1996): 735–748.
Shulman, George M. *Radicalism and Reverence: The Political Thought of Gerrard Winstanley*. Berkeley: University of California Press, 1989.
Webb, Darren. "The Bitter Product of Defeat? Reflections on Winstanley's Law of Freedom." *Political Studies* 52:2 (June 2004): 199–215.
Wellborn, Charles. "Gerrard Winstanley: A Case Study in the Relation of Religion and Culture." *Union Seminary Quarterly Review* 25 (Winter 1970): 182–190.
Winstanley, Gerrard. *The Law of Freedom and Other Writings*. Ed. Christopher Hill. Cambridge: Cambridge University Press, 1973.

Fifth Monarchists

Anderson, Philip J. "A Fifth Monarchist Appeal and the Response of an Independent Church at Canterbury, 1653." *Baptist Quarterly* 33 (April 1989): 72–80.
Brown, Louise Fargo. *The Political Activities of the Baptists and Fifth Monarchy Men in England During the Interregnum*. New York: Burt Franklin, 1964.
Capp, B. S. *The Fifth Monarchy Men: A Study in Seventeenth-Century English Millenarianism*. London: Faber, 1972.
Foster, John. "John Birchensa, Fifth Monarchy Man." *London Quarterly and Holborn Review* 176 (October 1951): 311–318.
Rogers, P. G. *The Fifth Monarchy Men*. London: Oxford University Press, 1966.

Solt, Leo F. "The Fifth Monarchy Men: Politics and the Millennium." *Church History* 30 (September 1961): 314–324.

Independents and Congregationalists

Bacon, Leonard Woolsey. *The Congregationalists*. New York: Baker and Taylor, 1904.
Cook, Sara G. "Congregational Independents and the Cromwellian Constitutions." *Church History* 46 (September 1977): 335–357.
Cooper, James F. *Tenacious of Their Liberties: The Congregationalists in Colonial Massachusetts*. New York: Oxford University Press, 1999.
Dunning, A. E. *Congregationalists in America: A Popular History of Their Origin, Belief, Polity, Growth and Work*. Boston: Pilgrim Press, 1894.
Ferguson, Sinclair B., Graham S. Harrison, Michael A. G. Haykin, Robert W. Oliver, and Carl R. Trueman. *John Owen: The Man and His Theology*. Phillipsburg, N. J.: Evangelical Press of Presbyterian and Reformed, 2002.
Goen, C. C. *Revivalism and Separatism in New England, 1740–1800: Strict Congregationalists and Separate Baptists in the Great Awakening*. Hamden, Conn.: Archon Books, 1969.
Nuttall, Geoffrey Fillingham; George Yule, and Roger Thomas. *Studies in the Puritan Tradition: A Joint Supplement of the Congregational Historical Society Transactions and the Presbyterian Historical Society Journal*. Chelmsford: J. H. Clarke, 1964.
Paul, Robert S. "Henry Jacob and Seventeenth-Century Puritanism." *Hartford Quarterly* 7 (Spring 1967): 92–113.
Shuffelton, Frank. *Thomas Hooker, 1586–1647*. Princeton, N. J.: Princeton University Press, 1977.
Youngs, J. William T. *The Congregationalists*. New York: Greenwood Press, 1990.
Yule, George. "Independents: Decentralised Calvinism in 17th Century England." *Reformed Theological Review* 15 (June 1956): 38–49.
———. *The Independents in the English Civil War*. Cambridge: Cambridge University Press, 1958.

Levellers

Aylmer, G. E. *The Levellers in the English Revolution*. Ithaca, N. Y.: Cornell University Press, 1975.
Brailsford, Henry Noel. *The Levellers and the English Revolution*. Stanford, Calif.: Stanford University Press, 1961.
Dzelzainis, Martin. "History and Ideology: Milton, the Levellers, and the Council of State in 1649." *Huntington Library Quarterly* 68:1/2 (2005): 269–287.
Gentles, Ian. "London Levellers in the English Revolution: The Chidleys and Their Circle." *Journal of Ecclesiastical History* 29.3 (July 1978): 281–309.

Glover, Samuel Dennis. "The Putney Debates: Popular versus Elitist Republicanism." *Past & Present* 164 (August 1999): 47–80.
Gregg, Pauline. *Free-born John: A Biography of John Lilburne*. London: Harrap, 1961.
Grob-Fitzgibbon, Benjamin. "'Whatsoever Yee Would That Men Should Doe unto You, Even so Doe Yee to Them:' An Analysis of the Effect of Religious Consciousness on the Origins of the Leveller Movement." *Historian* 65.4 (Summer 2003): 901–930.
Haller, William, and Godfrey Davis, eds. *The Leveller Tracts, 1647–1653*. Gloucester, U. K.: Peter Smith, 1964.
Joseph, Frank. *The Levellers: A History of the Writings of Three Seventeenth-Century Social Democrats: John Lilburne, Richard Overton, William Walwyn*. Cambridge, Mass.: Harvard University Press, 1955.
Leites, Edmund. "Conscience, Leisure, and Learning: Locke and the Levellers." *Sociological Analysis* 39 (Spring 1978): 36–61.
McDowell, Nicholas. "Ideas of Creation in the Writings of Richard Overton the Leveller and *Paradise Lost*." *Journal of the History of Ideas* 66:1 (January 2005): 59–78.
———. "Latin Drama and Leveller Ideas: Pedagogy and Power in the Writings of Richard Overton." *Seventeenth Century* 18.2 (Autumn 2003): 230–251.
Mulligan, Lotte. "The Religious Roots of William Walwyn's Radicalism." *Journal of Religious History* 12 (December 1982): 162–179.
Patton, Allyson. "John Lilburne and the Levellers." *British Heritage* 26.5 (November 2005): 12–57.
Patton, Brian. "Preserving Property: History, Genealogy, and Inheritance in 'Upon Appleton House.'" *Renaissance Quarterly* 49:4 (01 December 1996): 824–839.
Peacey, John T. "The Hunting of the Leveller: The Sophistication of Parliamentarian Propaganda, 1647–1653." *Historical Research* 78:199 (February 2005): 15–42.
———. "John Lilburne and the Long Parliament." *Historical Journal* 43:3 (September 2000): 625–645.
Seaberg, R. B. "The Norman Conquest and the Common Law: The Levellers and the Argument from Continuity." *Historical Journal* 24:4 (December 1981): 791–806.
Sharp, Andrew. *The English Levellers*. Cambridge: Cambridge University Press, 1998.
Wolfe, Don Marion. *Leveller Manifestoes of the Puritan Revolution*. New York: Humanities Press, 1967.
Wootton, David. "From Rebellion to Revolution: The Crisis of the Winter of 1642/3 and the Origins of Civil War Radicalism." *English Historical Review* 105 (July 1990): 654–669.

Muggletonians

Hill, Christopher. "John Reeve and the Origins of Muggletonianism." In *Prophecy and Millenarianism: Essays in Honour of Marjorie Reeves*. Ed. Ann Williams, 7–333. Essex, U. K.: Longman, 1980.

Hill, Christopher, Barry Reay, and William M. Lamont. *The World of the Muggletonians*. London: T. Smith, 1983.
Lamont, William M. *Last Witnesses: The Muggletonian History, 1652–1979*. Burlington, Vt.: Ashgate, 2006.
Reay, Barry G. "Muggletonians: A Study in Seventeenth-Century English Sectarianism." *Journal of Religious History* 9 (June 1976): 32–49.
Underwood, T. L, ed. *The Acts of the Witnesses: The Autobiography of Lodowick Muggleton and Other Early Muggletonian Writings*. New York: Oxford University Press, 1999.

Presbyterians

Agha, Agha Uka. "Puritan Presbyterian Polity in Elizabethan England, 1559–1593." Ph. D. diss., Drew University, 1985.
Anderson, Philip J. "Spirit and Structure in Revolutionary England, 1640–1660: Presbyterians and Congregationalists as a Case Study in Church Government." *Covenant Quarterly* 38 (February 1980): 22–39.
Beeke, Joel R. "Personal Assurance of Faith: The Puritans and Chapter 18.2 of the Westminster Confession." *Westminster Theological Journal* 55:1 (Spring 1993): 1–30.
Bolam, C. G., H. L. Short, and Roger Thomas. *The English Presbyterians: From Elizabethan Puritanism to Modern Unitarianism*. London: George Allen and Unwin, 1968.
Bozeman, Theodore Dwight. "Federal Theology and the National Covenant: An Elizabethan Presbyterian Case Study." *Church History* 61 (December 1992): 394–407.
Carlson, Leland Henry. *A History of the Presbyterian Party from Pride's Purge to the Dissolution of the Long Parliament*. Chicago: University of Chicago Libraries, 1942.
Duncan, J. Ligon, ed. *The Westminster Confession into the 21st Century: Essays in Remembrance of the 350th Anniversary of the Westminster Assembly*. Fearn, U. K.: Mentor, 2003.
Haller, William. "The Word of God in the Westminster Assembly." *Church History* 18:4 (December 1949): 199–219.
Kirby, Ethyn Williams. "The English Presbyterians in the Westminster Assembly." *Church History* 33 (December 1964): 418–427.
Lake, Peter. *Anglicans and Puritans? Presbyterianism and English Conformist Thought from Whitgift to Hooker*. London: Unwin Hyman, 1988.
Laker, Peter, and Maria Dowling. *Protestantism and the National Church in Sixteenth Century England*. London: Croom Helm, 1987.
Leith, John H. *Assembly at Westminster: Reformed Theology in the Making*. Richmond, Va.: John Knox Press, 1973.
Lingle, Walter Lee, and John W. Kuykendall. *Presbyterians: Their History and Beliefs*. Atlanta, Ga.: John Knox Press, 1978.

Mayfield, Noel Henning. *Puritans and Regicide: Presbyterian-Independent Differences Over the Trial and Execution of Charles (I) Stuart*. Lanham, Md.: University Press of America, 1988.
Parker, Kenneth L. "Thomas Rogers and the English Sabbath: The Case for a Reappraisal." *Church History* 53 (September 1984): 332–347.
Paul, Robert S. *The Assembly of the Lord: Politics and Religion in the Westminster Assembly and the 'Grand Debate.'* Edinburgh, Scotland, U. K.: T. and T. Clark, 1985.
Pearson, A. F. Scott. *Thomas Cartwright and Elizabethan Puritanism, 1535–1603*. Cambridge: Cambridge University Press, 1925.
Rutherford, Samuel. *Letters of Samuel Rutherford: A Selection*. Edinburgh, Scotland, U. K.: Banner of Truth Trust, 1973.
Trinterud, Leonard J. *The Forming of an American Tradition: A Re-examination of Colonial Presbyterianism*. Philadelphia, Pa.: Westminster Press, 1949.
Usher, Roland G., and Richard Bancroft. *The Presbyterian Movement in the Reign of Queen Elizabeth as Illustrated by the Minute Book of the Dedham Classis, 1582–1589*. London: Royal Historical Society, 1905.

Quakers

Carroll, Kenneth L. "Early Quakers and 'going naked as a sign.'" *Quaker History* 67 (Autumn 1978): 69–87.
Chu, Jonathan M. *Neighbors, Friends, or Madmen: The Puritan Adjustment to Quakerism in Seventeenth-Century Massachusetts Bay*. Westport, Conn.: Greenwood Press, 1985.
Damrosch, Leopold. *The Sorrows of the Quaker Jesus: James Nayler and the Puritan Crackdown on the Free Spirit*. Cambridge, Mass.: Harvard University Press, 1996.
Dunn, Mary Maples. "Saints and Sisters: Congregational and Quaker Women in the Early Colonial Period." *American Quarterly* 30:5 (Winter 1978): 582–601.
Dunn, Richard S., and Mary Maples Dunn, eds. *The World of William Penn*. Philadelphia: University of Pennsylvania Press, 1986.
Durnbaugh, Donald F. "Baptists and Quakers: Left Wing Puritans?" *Quaker History* 62 (Autumn 1973): 67–82.
Fox, George. *The Journal of George Fox*. Ed. John L. Nickalls. Cambridge: Cambridge University Press, 1952.
Grimes, Mary Cochran. "Saving Grace Among Puritans and Quakers: A Study of 17th and 18th Century Conversion Experiences." *Quaker History* 72 (Spring 1983): 3–26.
Hubbard, Geoffrey. *A Quaker by Convincement*. Harmondsworth, U. K.: Penguin Press, 1974.
Ingle, H. Larry. *First Among Friends: George Fox & the Creation of Quakerism*. New York: Oxford University Press, 1994.
Kent, Stephen A. "The 'Papist' Charges Against the Interregnum Quakers." *Journal of Religious History* 12 (December 1982): 180–190.

MacLear, James Fulton. "Quakerism and the End of the Interregnum: A Chapter in the Domestication of Radical Puritanism." *Church History* 19 (December 1950): 240–270.
Nuttall, Geoffrey Fillingham. *Studies in Christian Enthusiasm, Illustrated from Early Quakerism*. Wallingford, Pa.: Pendle Hill, 1948.
Penn, William. *The Peace of Europe; The Fruits of Solitude, and Other Writings*. Ed. Edwin B. Bronner. Rutland, Vt.: C. E. Tuttle, 1993.
Pestana, Carla Gardina. "The Quaker Executions as Myth and History." *Journal of American History* 80:2 (September 1993): 441–469.
Reay, Barry. *The Quakers and the English Revolution*. New York: St. Martin's Press, 1985.
Stayer, James M. "The Revolutionary Origins of the 'Peace Churches': the Peasants' War and the Anabaptists, the English Civil War and the Quakers." *Brethren Life and Thought* 30 (Spring 1985): 71–80.
Trueblood, D. Elton. *The People Called Quakers*. New York: Harper and Row, 1966.

Ranters

Barbour, Hugh. "Ranters, Diggers, and Quakers Reborn." *Quaker History* 64 (Spring 1975): 60–65.
Coppe, Abiezer. *A Fiery Flying Roll*. Exeter, U. K.: The Rota, 1973.
Davis, J. C. *Fear, Myth, and History: The Ranters and the Historians*. Cambridge: Cambridge University Press, 1986.
Ellens, G. F. S. "Ranters Ranting: Reflections on a Ranting Counter Culture." *Church History* 40 (March 1971): 91–107.
Friedman, Jerome. *Blasphemy, Immorality, and Anarchy: The Ranters and the English Revolution*. Athens, Oh.: Ohio University Press, 1987.
Hawes, Clement. *Mania and Literary Style: The Rhetoric of Enthusiasm from the Ranters to Christopher Smart*. Cambridge: Cambridge University Press, 1996.
McGregor, J. F. "Ranterism and the Development of Early Quakerism." *Journal of Religious History* 9 (December 1977): 349–363.
Morton, A. L. *The World of the Ranters: Religious Radicalism in the English Revolution*. London: Lawrence and Wishart, 1970.
Smith, Nigel. *A Collection of Ranter Writings from the 17th Century*. London: Junction Books, 1983.

RELIGIOUS THEMES

Bible

Berry, Lloyd Eason, ed. *The Geneva Bible: A Facsimile of the 1560 Edition*. Madison, Wis.: University of Wisconsin Press, 1969.

Betteridge, Maurice S. "The Bitter Notes: The Geneva Bible and Its Annotations." *Sixteenth Century Journal* 14:1 (Spring 1983): 41–62.
Coolidge, John S. *The Pauline Renaissance in England: Puritanism and the Bible.* Oxford: Clarendon Press, 1970.
Daniell, David. *The Bible in English: Its History and Influence.* New Haven, Conn.: Yale University Press, 2003.
Danner, Dan G. "The Contribution of the Geneva Bible of 1560 to the English Protestant Tradition." *Sixteenth Century Journal* 12:3 (1981): 5–18.
Doerksen, Daniel W. *Centered on the Word: Literature, Scripture, and the Tudor-Stuart Middle Way.* Newark, N. J.: University of Delaware Press, 2004.
Fienberg, Stanley P. "Thomas Goodwin's Scriptural Hermeneutics and the Dissolution of Puritan Unity." *Journal of Religious History* 10 (June 1978): 32–49.
Gordis, Lisa M. *Opening Scripture: Bible Reading and Interpretive Authority in Puritan New England.* Chicago: University of Chicago Press, 2003.
Gribben, Crawford. "Deconstructing the Geneva Bible: The Search for a Puritan Poetic." *Literature and Theology* 14:1 (March 2000): 1–16.
Hill, Christopher. *The English Bible and the Seventeenth-Century Revolution.* New York: Penguin Press, 1993.
Jensen, Michael. "'Simply' Reading the Geneva Bible: The Geneva Bible and its Readers." *Literature and Theology* 9 (March 1995): 30–45.
Knapp, Henry M. "John Owen's Interpretation of Hebrews 6:4–6: Eternal Perseverance of the Saints in Puritan Exegesis." *Sixteenth Century Journal* 34:1 (Spring 2003): 29–52.
Knott, John Ray. *The Sword of the Spirit: Puritan Responses to the Bible.* Chicago: University of Chicago Press, 1980.
MacKenzie, Cameron A. "The Coming of the Kingdom and Sixteenth-Century English Bibles." In *Looking Into the Future: Evangelical Studies in Eschatology.* Ed. David W. Baker, 144–156. Grand Rapids, Mich.: Baker Academic, 2001.
McGrath, Alister E. *In the Beginning: The Story of the King James Bible and How It Changed a Nation, a Language, and a Culture.* New York: Doubleday, 2001.
McKim, Donald K. "Ramism as an Exegetical Tool for English Puritanism as Used by William Perkins." *Society of Biblical Literature Seminar Papers* 23 (1984): 11–21.
Patterson, W. B. "James VI and I and the King James Version." *Sewanee Review* 112:3 (Summer 2004): 417–427.
Stout, Harry S. "Word and Order in Colonial New England." In *The Bible in America: Essays in Cultural History.*" Ed. Nathan O. Hatch and Mark A. Noll, 19–38. New York: Oxford University Press, 1982.

Ecclesiology

Allen, Ward. "Hooker and the Utopians." *English Studies* 51 (1970): 37–39.

Barker, William S. "Puritans and the Purity of the Church." *Presbyterion* 14 (Fall 1988): 88–97.
Bozeman, Theodore Dwight. *To Live Ancient Lives: The Primitivist Dimension in Puritanism*. Chapel Hill: University of North Carolina Press, 1988.
Brachlow, Stephen. *The Communion of Saints: Radical Puritan and Separatist Ecclesiology*, Oxford: Oxford University Press, 1988.
Bremer, Francis J. *Shaping New England: Puritan Clergymen in Seventeenth-Century England and New England*. New York: Twayne, 1994.
Calder, Isabel MacBeath. "A Seventeenth Century Attempt to Purify the Anglican Church." *American Historical Review* 53:4 (July 1948): 760–775.
Hart, A. Tindal. *The Country Clergy in Elizabethan and Stuart Times, 1558–1660*. London: Phoenix House, 1958.
Michaelsen, Robert S. "Changes in the Puritan Concept of Calling or Vocation." *New England Quarterly* 26 (1953): 315–336.
Milward, Peter. *Religious Controversies of the Elizabethan Age: A Survey of Printed Sources*. Lincoln, Neb.: University of Nebraska Press, 1977.
More, Paul E., and F. L. Cross, ed. *Anglicanism: The Thought and Practice of the Church of England Illustrated from the Religious Literature of the Seventeenth Century*. London: SPCK, 1935.
New, John F. H. *Anglican and Puritan: The Basis of Their Opposition, 1558–1640*. Stanford, Calif.: Stanford University Press, 1964.
Peterson, Mark A. "The Plymouth Church and the Evolution of Puritan Religious Culture." *New England Quarterly* 66:4 (December 1993): 570–593.
Pope, Robert G. *The Half-Way Covenant: Church Membership in Puritan New England*. Princeton N. J.: Princeton University Press, 1969.
Raath, A. W. G., and Shaun de Freitas. "From Heinrich Bullinger to Puritanism: John Hooper's Theology and the Office of Magistracy." *Scottish Journal of Theology* 56:2 (2003): 208–230.
Trevor-Roper, H. R. *Catholics, Anglicans, and Puritans*. Chicago: University of Chicago Press, 1988.
Walker, David J. "Thomas Goodwin and the Debate on Church Government." *Journal of Ecclesiastical History* 34:1 (January 1983): 85–99.
Webster, Tom. *Godly Clergy in Early Stuart England: The Caroline Puritan Movement, c. 1620–1643*. Cambridge: Cambridge University Press, 1997.
Zaret, David. *The Heavenly Contract: Ideology and Organization in Pre-Revolutionary Puritanism*. Chicago: University of Chicago Press, 1985.

Preaching

Bercovitch, Sacvan. *The American Jeremiad*. Madison: University of Wisconsin Press, 1978.

Bickel, R. Bruce. *Light and Heat: the Puritan View of the Pulpit; and, the Focus of the Gospel in Puritan Preaching.* Morgan, Pa.: Soli Deo Gloria Publications, 1999.

Bosco, Ronald A. *The Puritan Sermon in America, 1630–1750: Sermons for Days of Fast, Prayer, and Humiliation and Execution Sermons: Facsimile Reproductions.* Delmar, N. Y.: Scholars' Facsimiles and Reprints, 1978.

Bremer, Francis, and Ellen Rydell. "Performance Art? Puritans in the Pulpit." *History Today* 45.9 (September 1995): 50–54.

Brown, John. *Puritan Preaching in England: A Study of Past and Present.* New York: Charles Scribner's Sons, 1900.

Carden, Allen. "Biblical Texts and Themes in American Puritan Preaching, 1630–1700." *Andrews University Seminary Studies* 21:2 (Summer 1983): 113–128.

Chandos, John. *In God's Name: Examples of Preaching in England from the Act of Supremacy to the Act of Uniformity, 1534–1662.* London: Hutchinson, 1971.

Cohen, Charles L. "Two Biblical Models of Conversion: An Example of Puritan Hermeneutics." *Church History* 58 (June 1989): 182–196.

Coughenour, Robert A. "Shape and Vehicle of Puritan Hermeneutics." *Reformed Review* 30 (August 1976): 23–34.

Davies, Horton. "Elizabethan Puritan Preaching (I)." *Worship* 44:2 (February 1970): 93–108.

———. "Elizabethan Puritan Preaching (II)." *Worship* 44:3 (March 1970): 154–170.

Elliott, Emory. *Power and the Pulpit in Puritan New England.* Princeton, N. J.: Princeton University Press, 1975.

Guelzo, Allen C. "When the Sermon Reigned." *Christian History* 13.1 (1994): 23–25.

Holland, DeWitte Talmadge. *Sermons in American History; Selected Issues in the American Pulpit, 1630–1967.* Nashville, Tenn.: Abingdon Press, 1971.

Hoyt, Arthur Stephen. *The Pulpit and American Life.* New York: Macmillan, 1921.

Kistler, Don. *Puritan Preaching: A Study in Preaching from the Puritan Divines.* Morgan, Pa.: Soli Deo Gloria Publications, 1996.

Levy, Babette May. *Preaching in the First Half Century of New England History.* New York: Russell and Russell, 1967.

Love, Christopher. *The Mortified Christian: Showing the Nature, Signs, Necessity, and Difficulty of True Mortification, with the Right Hearing of Sermons.* Ed. Don Kistler. Morgan, Pa.: Soli Deo Gloria Publications, 1998.

McCullough, Peter E. *Sermons at Court: Politics and Religion in Elizabethan and Jacobean Preaching.* Cambridge: Cambridge University Press, 1998.

McFarland, Ronald E. "Response to Grace: Seventeenth-Century Sermons and the Idea of Thanksgiving." *Church History* 44 (June 1975): 199–203.

Morgan, Irvonwy. *The Godly Preachers of the Elizabethan Church.* London: Epworth Press, 1965.

Morrissey, Mary. "Scripture, Style and Persuasion in Seventeenth-Century English Theories of Preaching." *Journal of Ecclesiastical History* 53:4 (October 2002): 686–706.
Nichols, James. *Puritan Sermons, 1659–1689: Being the Morning Exercises at Cripplegate, St. Giles in the Fields, and in Southwark.* Wheaton, Ill.: R. O. Roberts, 1981.
Rechtien, John G. "Logic in Puritan Sermons in Late Sixteenth Century Plain Style." *Style* 13:3 (Summer 1979): 237–258.
Spalding, James C. "Sermons before Parliament (1640–1649) as a Public Puritan Diary." *Church History* 36 (March 1967): 24–35.
Stout, Harry S. *The New England Soul: Preaching and Religious Culture in Colonial New England.* New York: Oxford University Press, 1986.
Wilson, John Frederick. *Pulpit in Parliament: Puritanism During the English Civil Wars,* Princeton, N. J.: Princeton University Press, 1969.

Theology

Ahlstrom, Sydney E. *Theology in America: The Major Protestant Voices from Puritanism to Neo-Orthodoxy.* Indianapolis, Ind.: Bobbs-Merrill, 1967.
Ames, William. *The Marrow of Theology.* Ed. John Dykstra Eusden. Boston: Pilgrim Press, 1968.
Carroll, Peter N. *Puritanism and the Wilderness: The Intellectual Significance of the New England Frontier, 1629–1700.* New York: Columbia University Press, 1969.
Cartwright, Thomas. *Cartwrightiana.* Ed. Albert Peel and Leland Henry Carlson. London: Allen and Unwin, 1951.
Cragg, G. R. *From Puritanism to the Age of Reason: A Study of Changes in Religious Thought within the Church of England, 1660 to 1700.* Cambridge: Cambridge University Press, 1950.
Crampton, W. Gary, and Don Kistler. *What the Puritans Taught: An Introduction to Puritan Theology.* Morgan, Pa.: Soli Deo Gloria Publications, 2003.
Davies, Godfrey. "Arminian vs. Puritan in England, c. 1620–1650." *Huntington Library Bulletin* 5 (1934): 157–179.
Dever, Mark E. *Richard Sibbes: Puritanism and Calvinism in Late Elizabethan and Early Stuart England.* Macon, Ga.: Mercer University Press, 2000.
Dyrness, William A. *Reformed Theology and Visual Culture: The Protestant Imagination from Calvin to Edwards.* Cambridge: Cambridge University Press, 2004.
Gribben, Crawford. "The Eschatology of the Puritan Confessions." *Scottish Bulletin of Evangelical Theology* 6:4 (Winter 2002): 51–78.
―――. *The Puritan Millennium: Literature and Theology, 1550–1682.* Dublin: Four Courts Press, 2000.
Hawkes, R. M. "The Logic of Assurance in English Puritan Theology." *Westminster Theological Journal* 52:2 (Fall 1990): 247–261.

Holifield, E. Brooks. *The Covenant Sealed: The Development of Puritan Sacramental Theology in Old and New England, 1570–1720.* New Haven, Conn.: Yale University Press, 1974.

———. *Theology in America: Christian Thought from the Age of the Puritans to the Civil War.* New Haven, Conn.: Yale University Press, 2003.

Karlberg, Mark W. "Moses and Christ—The Place of Law in Seventeenth-Century Puritanism." *Trinity Journal* 10:1 (Spring 1989): 11–32.

Keddie, Gordon J. "Unfallible certenty of the pardon of sinne and life everlasting: The Doctrine of Assurance in the Theology of William Perkins (1558–1602)." *Evangelical Quarterly* 48 (October–December 1976): 230–244.

Kendall, R. T. *Calvin and English Calvinism to 1649.* New York: Oxford University Press, 1979.

Kevan, Ernest Frederick. *The Grace of Law: A Study in Puritan Theology.* London: Carey Kingsgate Press, 1964.

McGiffert, Michael. "The Perkinsian Moment of Federal Theology." *Calvin Theological Journal* 29 (April 1994): 117–148.

McKim, Donald K. *Ramism in William Perkins' Theology.* New York: Peter Lang, 1987.

Mulsow, Martin, and Jan Rohls. *Socinianism and Arminianism: Antitrinitarianism, Calvinists and Cultural Exchange in Seventeenth-Century Europe.* Boston, Mass.: Brill, 2005.

O'Donovan, Joan Lockwood. *Theology of Law and Authority in the English Reformation.* Atlanta, Ga.: Scholars Press, 1991.

Perkins, William. *The Work of William Perkins.* Ed. Ian Breward. Abingdon, U. K.: Sutton Courtenay Press, 1970.

Primus, John H. "Lutheran Law and Gospel in the Early Puritan Theology of Richard Greenham." *Lutheran Quarterly* 8 (Autumn 1994): 287–298.

Rooy, Sidney H. *The Theology of Missions in the Puritan Tradition: A Study of Representative Puritans, Richard Sibbes, Richard Baxter, John Eliot, Cotton Mather and Jonathan Edwards.* Grand Rapids, Mich.: William B. Eerdmans, 1965.

Rose, Elliott. *Cases of Conscience: Alternatives Open to Recusants and Puritans under Elizabeth I and James I.* Cambridge: Cambridge University Press, 1975.

Schneider, Herbert Wallace. *The Puritan Mind.* Ann Arbor: University of Michigan Press, 1958.

Spinks, Bryan D. *Two Faces of Elizabethan Anglican Theology: Sacraments and Salvation in the Thought of William Perkins and Richard Hooker.* Lanham, Md.: Scarecrow Press, 1999.

Stoever, William K. B. *A Faire and Easie Way to Heaven: Covenant Theology and Antinomianism in Early Massachusetts.* Middletown, Conn.: Wesleyan University Press, 1978.

Van Rohr, John. *The Covenant of Grace in Puritan Thought.* Atlanta, Ga.: Scholars Press, 1986.

Winship, Michael P. *Making Heretics: Militant Protestantism and Free Grace in Massachusetts, 1636–1641.* Princeton, N. J.: Princeton University Press, 2002.

―――. *Seers of God: Puritan Providentialism in the Restoration and Early Enlightenment.* Boston: Johns Hopkins University Press, 1996.
Yule, George. "Theological Developments in Elizabethan Puritanism." *Journal of Religious History* (June 1960): 16–25.
Zaret, David. "Calvin, Covenant Theology, and the Weber Thesis." *British Journal of Sociology* 43:3 (September 1992): 369–391.

Toleration

Coffey, John. "Puritanism and Liberty Revisited: The Case for Toleration in the English Revolution." *Historical Journal* 41:4 (December 1998): 961–985.
Fiske, John. *The Beginnings of New England: or, The Puritan Theocracy in Its Relations to Civil and Religious Liberty.* Boston, Mass.: Houghton, Mifflin, 1889.
George, Timothy. "Between Pacifism and Coercion: The English Baptist Doctrine of Religious Toleration." *The Mennonite Quarterly Review* 58:1 (January 1984): 30–49.
Grell, Ole Peter, Jonathan Irvine Israel, and Nicholas Tyacke. *From Persecution to Toleration: The Glorious Revolution and Religion in England.* Oxford: Clarendon Press, 1991.
Grisevich, George W. "Baptist–Puritan Encounter and Connecticut Religious Liberty." *Foundations* 15 (July–September 1972): 266–272.
Haller, William. *Liberty and Reformation in the Puritan Revolution.* New York: Columbia University Press, 1955.
―――. *Tracts on Liberty in the Puritan Revolution, 1638–1647.* New York: Octagon Books, 1965.
Holifield, E. Brooks. "On Toleration in Massachusetts." *Church History* 38 (June 1969): 188–200.
MacLear, James Fulton. "Restoration Puritanism and the Idea of Liberty: The Case of Edward Bagshaw." *Journal of Religious History* 16 (June 1990): 1–17.
Marriott, J. A. R. *The Crisis of English Liberty: A History of the Stuart Monarchy and the Puritan Revolution.* Oxford: Clarendon Press, 1930.
Miller, William Lee. *The First Liberty: Religion and the American Republic.* New York: Alfred A. Knopf, 1985.
Nuttall, Geoffrey Fillingham. "Law and Liberty in Puritanism." *Congregational Quarterly* 29 (January 1951): 18–28.
Polizzotto, Carolyn. "Liberty of Conscience and the Whitehall Debates of 1648–9." *Journal of Ecclesiastical History* 26:1 (January 1975): 69–82.
Porter, David. "Baptist Struggle for Religious Freedom in the Massachusetts Bay Colony, 1650–1670." *Foundations* 14 (January–March 1971): 24–32.
Ryder, Milton P. "Swimming Against the Current: The Strange Therapy of Persecution: The Price Paid for Religious Liberty by Some Early Massachusetts Baptists and the First Baptist Church." *American Baptist Quarterly* 21:1 (March 2002): 11–27.

Van Til, L. John. *Liberty of Conscience: The History of a Puritan Idea*. Nutley, N. J.: Craig Press, 1972.

Worship and Spirituality

Ball, Bryan W. "The Market Day of the Soul: The Puritan Doctrine of the Sabbath in England, 1532–1700." *Andrews University Seminary Studies* 23:1 (Spring 1985): 87–102.
Benes, Peter, and Jane Montague Benes. *New England Meeting House and Church, 1630–1850*. Boston: Boston University Press, 1980.
Cohen, Charles Lloyd. *God's Caress: The Psychology of Puritan Religious Experience*. New York: Oxford University Press, 1986.
———. *The Worship of the English Puritans*. Westminster, U. K.: Dacre Press, 1948.
Davies, Horton. *Worship and Theology in England: From Cranmer to Baxter and Fox, 1534*. Grand Rapids, Mich.: William B. Eerdmans Publishing, 1996.
Davis, James Calvin. "William Ames's Calvinist Ambiguity over Freedom of Conscience." *Journal of Religious Ethics* 33:2 (June 2005): 335–355.
Durston, Christopher. "By the Book or with the Spirit: The Debate over Liturgical Prayer During the English Revolution." *Historical Research* 79:203 (February 2006): 50–73.
Earle, Alice Morse. *The Sabbath in Puritan New England*. Detroit, Mich.: Singing Tree Press, 1968.
Gore, R. J. *Covenantal Worship: Reconsidering the Puritan Regulative Principle*. Phillipsburg, N. J.: Presbyterian and Reformed, 2002.
Hambrick-Stowe, Charles E. *The Practice of Piety: Puritan Devotional Disciplines in Seventeenth-Century New England*. Chapel Hill: University of North Carolina Press, 1982.
Morgan, Irvonwy. *Puritan Spirituality: Illustrated from the Life and Times of the Rev. Dr. John Preston*. London: Epworth, 1973.
Peterson, Mark A. *The Price of Redemption: The Spiritual Economy of Puritan New England*. Stanford, Calif.: Stanford University Press, 1997.
Pettit, Norman. *The Heart Prepared: Grace and Conversion in Puritan Spiritual Life*. New Haven, Conn.: Yale University Press, 1966.
Rust, Paul R. *The First of the Puritans and the Book of Common Prayer*. Milwaukee, Wis.: Bruce, 1949.
Spinks, Bryan D. "*The Supply of Prayer for Ships*: A Forgotten Puritan Liturgy." *Journal of the United Reform Church Society* 1:5 (1975): 139–148.
Tripp, David H. "The Ends of the Ages: Time in Christian Worship, in the Experience of the English Puritans." *Studia Liturgica* 14:2–4 (1982): 110–127.
Wakefield, Gordon S. *Puritan Devotion: Its Place in the Development of Christian Piety*. London: Epworth Press, 1957.
Walsh, James P. "Holy Time and Sacred Space in Puritan New England." *American Quarterly* 32:1 (Spring 1980): 79–95.

Young, William. *The Puritan Principle of Worship*. Vienna, Va.: Presbyterian Reformed Church, 1959.

SOCIAL THEMES

Economics

Breen, Timothy Hall. "The Non-Existent Controversy: Puritan and Anglican Attitudes on Work and Wealth, 1600–1640." *Church History* 35 (1966): 273–287.
Breslow, Marvin A. *A Mirror of England: English Puritan Views of Foreign Nations, 1618–1640*. Cambridge, Mass.: Harvard University Press, 1970.
George, Charles H. "A Social Interpretation of English Puritanism." *Journal of Modern History* 25 (1953): 327–342.
Green, Robert W., ed. *Protestantism and Capitalism: The Weber Thesis and Its Critics*. Boston: Heath, 1959.
Hertz, Karl H. "Max Weber and American Puritanism." *Journal for the Scientific Study of Religion* 1:2 (Spring 1962): 189–197.
Holstun, James. *Ehud's Dagger: Class Struggle in the English Revolution*. London: Verso, 2000.
Innes, Stephen. *Creating the Commonwealth: The Economic Culture of Puritan New England*. New York: W. W. Norton, 1995.
McCary, Fern F. "The Attitude of the English Puritan toward the Accumulation of Wealth—1564–1688." Ph. D. diss. University of Colorado, 1952.
North, Gary. "Concept of Property in Puritan New England, 1630–1720." *Westminster Theological Journal* 35 (Fall 1972): 65–67.
Solt, Leo Frank. "Puritanism, Capitalism, Democracy, and the New Science." *American Historical Review* 73 (October 1967): 18–29.
Tawney, R. H. *Religion and the Rise of Capitalism*. New York: Harcourt, Brace, 1926.
Weber, Max. *The Protestant Ethic and the Spirit of Capitalism*. Ed. Anthony Giddens. New York: Scribner, 1958.
Wright, Louis B. "The Reading of Plays During the Puritan Revolution." *Huntington Library Bulletin* 6 (1934): 73–108.

Family Life

Baskerville, Stephen. "The Family in Puritan Political Theology." *Journal of Family History* 18:2 (1993): 157–177.
Buchanan, Daniel P. "Tares in the Wheat: Puritan Violence and Puritan Families in the Nineteenth-Century Liberal Imagination." *Religion and American Culture* 8 (Summer 1998): 205–236.

Cliffe, J. T. *The Puritan Gentry: The Great Puritan Families of Early Stuart England*. London: Routledge and Kegan Paul, 1984.
Davies, Gaius. "Puritan Teaching on Marriage and the Family." *Evangelical Quarterly* 27 (January–March 1955): 15–30.
Demos, John. *A Little Commonwealth: Family Life in Plymouth Colony*. Oxford: Oxford University Press, 2000.
Durston, Christopher. *The Family in the English Revolution*. Oxford: Blackwell, 1989.
Feige, Diana, and Franz G. M. Feige. "Love, Marriage, and Family in Puritan Society." *Dialogue & Alliance* 9 (Spring–Summer 1995): 96–114.
Fishburn, Janet Forsythe. "The Family as a Means of Grace in American Theology." *Religious Education* 78 (Winter 1983): 90–102.
Graham, Judith S. *Puritan Family Life: The Diary of Samuel Sewall*. Boston: Northeastern University Press, 2000.
Johnson, J. T. "English Puritan Thought on the Ends of Marriage." *Church History* 38 (1969): 429–436.
Kishlansky, Mark A. "The Puritan Gentry: The Great Puritan Families of Early Stuart England." *Church History* 55 (March 1986): 109–110.
Lane, Belden C. "Two Schools of Desire: Nature and Marriage in Seventeenth-Century Puritanism." *Church History* 69:2 (June 2000): 372–402.
McCoy, Michael R. "Our Father/My Father: the Interpenetration of Religious and Familial Imagery in the Puritan Conception of the Father." *Perspectives in Religious Studies* 13.1 (Spring 1986): 45–54.
Moran, Gerald Francis, and Maris Vinovskis. *The Puritan Family and Religion: A Critical Reappraisal*. Notre Dame, Ind.: University of Notre Dame Press, 1980.
Morgan, Edmund Sears. *The Puritan Family: Religion & Domestic Relations in Seventeenth-Century New England*. New York: Harper and Row, 1966.
Schücking, Levin Ludwig. *The Puritan Family: A Social Study from the Literary Sources*. New York: Schocken Books, 1970.
Todd, Margo. "Humanists, Puritans and the Spiritualized Household." *Church History* 49 (March 1980): 18–34.
Westerkamp, Marilyn J. "Puritan Patriarchy and the Problem of Revelation." *Journal of Interdisciplinary History* 23:3 (Winter 1993): 571–595.

Literature

Caldwell, Patricia. *The Puritan Conversion Narrative: The Beginnings of American Expression*. Cambridge: Cambridge University Press, 1983.
Davidson, Peter. *Poetry and Revolution: An Anthology of British and Irish Verse, 1625–1660*. Oxford: Oxford University Press, 2001.
Dowden, Edward. *Puritan and Anglican: Studies in Literature*. New York: Holt, 1901.

Fisch, Harold. "The Puritans and the Reform of Prose-Style." *English Literary History* 19 (1952): 229–248.
French, J. Milton. "Notes on Two Puritan Poets, Marvell and Wither." *Notes and Queries* 174 (1938): 273–274.
Gura, P. F. "Turning Our World Upside Down: Reconceiving Early American Literature." *American Literature* 63:1 (March 1991): 104–112.
Halewood, William H. *The Poetry of Grace: Reformation Themes and Structures in English Seventeenth-Century Poetry*. New Haven, Conn.: Yale University Press, 1970.
Hamilton, Donna B., and Richard Strier. *Religion, Literature, and Politics in Post-Reformation England, 1540–1688*. Cambridge: Cambridge University Press, 1996.
Hester, M. Thomas. *Seventeenth-Century British Nondramatic Poets*. Detroit, Mich.: Gale Research, 1993.
Holstun, James. *Pamphlet Wars: Prose in the English Revolution*. London: F. Cass, 1992.
Hutchinson, Lucy. *Memoirs of the Life of Colonel Hutchinson with the Fragment of an Autobiography of Mrs. Hutchinson*. Ed. James Sutherland. London: Oxford University Press, 1973.
Keeble, N. H. *The Cambridge Companion to Writing of the English Revolution*. Cambridge: Cambridge University Press, 2001.
——— . *The Literary Culture of Nonconformity in Later Seventeenth-Century England*. Athens, Ga.: University of Georgia Press, 1987.
Kendall, Ritchie D. *The Drama of Dissent: The Radical Poetics of Nonconformity, 1380–1590*. Chapel Hill: University of North Carolina Press, 1986.
Knott, John R. *Discourses of Martyrdom in English Literature, 1563–1694*. Cambridge: Cambridge University Press, 1993.
Lerner, L. D. "Puritanism and the Spiritual Autobiography." *Historical Journal* 55 (1956–1957): 371–386.
Lowance, Mason I. *The Language of Canaan: Metaphor and Symbol in New England from the Puritans to the Transcendentalists*. Cambridge, Mass.: Harvard University Press, 1980.
Luxon, Thomas H. *Literal Figures: Puritan Allegory and the Reformation Crisis in Representation*. Chicago: University of Chicago Press, 1995.
Mahon, Vincent. "The 'Christian Letter': Some Puritan Objections to Hooker's Work; and Hooker's 'Undressed' Comments." *Review of English Studies* 25 (1974): 305–312.
Martz, Louis Lohr. *The Poetry of Meditation: A Study in English Religious Literature of the Seventeenth Century*. New Haven, Conn.: Yale University Press, 1954.
Parry, Graham. *The Seventeenth Century: The Intellectual and Cultural Context of English Literature, 1603–1700*. London: Longman, 1989.
Ritchie, Daniel E. "Robinson Crusoe as Narrative Theologian." *Renascence* 49:2 (Winter 1997): 94–110.

Rosenmeier, Jesper. "Text and Context in Mary Rowlandson's Captivity Narrative." *American Quarterly* 44:2 (June 1992): 255–261.
Sasek, Lawrence A. *The Literary Temper of the English Puritans*. Baton Rouge: Louisiana State University Press, 1961.
Sharrock, Roger. "The Trial of Vices in Puritan Fiction." *Baptist Quarterly* 14 (1951–1952): 3–12.
Sinfield, Alan. *Literature in Protestant England, 1560–1660*. Totowa, N. J.: Barnes and Noble Books, 1983.
Smith, Nigel. *Literature and Revolution in England, 1640–1660*. New Haven, Conn.: Yale University Press, 1994.
———. *Perfection Proclaimed: Language and Literature in English Radical Religion, 1640–1660*. Oxford: Clarendon Press, 1989.
Stachniewski, John. *The Persecutory Imagination: English Puritanism and the Literature of Religious Despair*. Oxford: Clarendon Press, 1991.
Stamm, Rudolf G. "Daniel Defoe: An Artist in the Puritan Tradition." *Philological Quarterly* 15 (1936): 225–246.
Stanford, Donald E. *Edward Taylor*. Minneapolis: University of Minnesota Press, 1965.
Watters, David H. *'With Bodilie Eyes': Eschatological Themes in Puritan Literature and Gravestone Art*. Ann Arbor: UMI Research Press, 1981.
Webber, Joan. *The Eloquent 'I': Style and Self in Seventeenth Century Prose*. Madison: University of Wisconsin Press, 1968.
Wilding, Michael. *Dragon's Teeth: Literature in the English Revolution*. Cambridge, Mass.: Harvard University Press, 1979.

Politics

Adair, John. *Puritans: Religion and Politics in Seventeenth Century England and America*. Stroud, Gloucestershire, U. K.: Sutton Publishing, 1998.
Baskerville, Stephen. *The Political Theology of Puritan Preaching in the English Revolution, c.1640–53*. London: University of London, 1987.
Bernstein, Eduard. *Cromwell & Communism: Socialism and Democracy in the Great English Revolution*. New York: Schocken Books, 1963.
Breen, Louise A. *Transgressing the Bounds: Subversive Enterprises Among the Puritan Elite in Massachusetts, 1630–1692*. New York: Oxford University Press, 2001.
Breen, T. H. *The Character of the Good Ruler: A Study of Puritan Political Ideas in New England, 1630–1730*. New Haven, Conn.: Yale University Press, 1970.
Burns, J. H., and Mark Goldie. *The Cambridge History of Political Thought, 1450–1700*. New York: Cambridge University Press, 1991.
Cogswell, Thomas, and Richard Cust. *Politics, Religion, and Popularity in Early Stuart Britain: Essays in Honour of Conrad Russell*. Cambridge: Cambridge University Press, 2002.

Finlayson, Michael George. *Historians, Puritanism, and the English Revolution: The Religious Factor in English Politics Before and After the Interregnum.* Toronto: University of Toronto Press, 1983.

Freeman, Thomas S. "'The Reformation of the Church in This Parliament': Thomas Norton, John Foxe and the Parliament of 1571." *Parliamentary History* 16:2 (1997): 131–147.

Mackie, J. D. *Cavalier and Puritan.* London: T. Nelson and Sons, 1930.

Morgan, Edmund S. *Puritan Political Ideas, 1558–1794.* Indianapolis, Ind.: Bobbs-Merrill, 1965.

Pearson, Andrew F. S. *Church and State: Political Aspects of Sixteenth-Century Puritanism.* New York: Macmillan, 1928.

Seaver, Paul S. *The Puritan Lectureships: The Politics of Religious Dissent, 1560–1662.* Stanford, Calif.: Stanford University Press, 1970.

———. "State Religion and Puritan Resistance in Early Seventeenth-Century England." In *Religion and the Early Modern State.* Ed. James D. Tracy and Marguerite Ragnow, 207–249. Cambridge: Cambridge University Press, 2004.

Solt, Leo F. *Saints in Arms: Puritanism and Democracy in Cromwell's Army.* New York: AMS Press, 1959.

Underdown, David. *Pride's Purge: Politics in the Puritan Revolution.* Oxford: Clarendon Press, 1971.

Walzer, Michael. *The Revolution of the Saints: A Study in the Origins of Radical Politics.* Cambridge, Mass: Harvard University Press, 1965.

Weinstein, Minna F. "Stephen Marshall and the Dilemma of the Political Puritan." *Journal of Presbyterian History* 46 (March 1968): 1–25.

Wiseman, Susan. *Drama and Politics in the English Civil War.* Cambridge: Cambridge University Press, 1998.

Woodhouse, A. S. P., ed. *Puritanism and Liberty: Being the Army Debates (1647–9) from the Clarke Manuscripts with Supplementary Documents.* Chicago: The University of Chicago Press, 1965.

Zagorin, Perez. *Culture and Politics from Puritanism to the Enlightenment.* Berkeley, Calif.: University of California Press, 1980.

———. *A History of Political Thought in the English Revolution.* London: Routledge and Paul, 1954.

Science

Cohen, I. Bernard, and K. E. Duffin. *Puritanism and the Rise of Modern Science: The Merton Thesis.* New Brunswick, N. J.: Rutgers University Press, 1990.

Hooykaas, R. *Scientific Progress and Religious Dissent.* Milton Keynes, U. K.: Open University Press, 1974.

Kemsley, Douglas S. "Religious Influences in the Rise of Modern Science: A Review and Criticism, Particularly of the 'Protestant–Puritan Ethic' Theory." *Annals of Science* 24 (1968): 199–223.

Lindberg, David C., and Ronald L. Numbers, ed. *God and Nature: Historical Essays on the Encounter Between Christianity and Science*. Berkeley: University of California Press, 1986.

Morgan, John. "Puritanism and Science: A Reinterpretation." *Historical Journal* 22 (September 1979): 535–560.

Rabb, T. K. "Puritanism and the Rise of Experimental Science in England." *Cahiers D'Histoire Mondiale* 7 (1962): 46–67.

Schaffer, Simon. "Science and Puritanism." *Social Studies of Science* 18:3 (August 1988): 551–556.

Wegter-McNelly, Kirk. "The Merton Thesis: The Influence of Puritanism on the Development of Science." *CTNS Bulletin* 21:4 (Fall 2001): 22–29.

Theater

Bawcutt, N. W. "Was Thomas Middleton a Puritan Dramatist?" *Modern Language Review* 94:4 (October 1999): 925–939.

Graves, T. S. "Notes on Puritanism and the Stage." *Studies in Philology* 18 (1921): 141–169.

Heinemann, Margot. *Puritanism and Theatre: Thomas Middleton and Opposition Drama under the Early Stuarts*. New York: Cambridge University Press, 1980.

Johnson, Odai. *Rehearsing the Revolution: Radical Performance, Radical Politics in the English Restoration*. Newark, N. J.: University of Delaware Press, 2000.

Norton, Elliot. *Broadway Down East: An Informal Account of the Plays, Players, and Playhouses of Boston from Puritan Times to the Present: Lectures Delivered for the National Endowment for the Humanities, Boston Public Library Learning Library Program*. Boston: Trustees of the Public Library of the City of Boston, 1978.

Pastoor, Charles. "Puritans and the Blackfriars Theater: The Cases of Mistresses Duck and Drake." *English Language Notes* 43:2 (December 2005): 1–12.

Pritchard, Allan. "Puritans and the Blackfriars Theater: The Cases of Mistresses Duck and Drake." *Shakespeare Quarterly* 45.1 (Spring 1994): 92–95.

Prynne, William. *Histrio-Mastix: The Player's Scourge or, Actor's Tragedy*. New York: Johnson Reprint Corporation, 1972.

Randall, Dale B. J. *Winter Fruit: English Drama, 1642–1660*. Lexington, Ky.: University Press of Kentucky, 1995.

Rice, Colin. *Ungodly Delights: Puritan Opposition to the Theatre: 1576–1633*. Alessandria: Edizioni dell'Orso, 1997.

Thompson, Elbert N. S. *The Controversy Between the Puritans and the Stage*. New York: Russell and Russell, 1966.

Tiffany, Grace. "Puritanism in Comic History: Exposing Royalty in the Henry Plays." *Shakespeare Studies* 26 (1998): 256–287.

Wiseman, Susan. *Drama and Politics in the English Civil War*. New York: Cambridge University Press, 1998.

Witchcraft

Breslaw, Elaine G. *Tituba, Reluctant Witch of Salem: Devilish Indians and Puritan Fantasies.* New York: New York University Press, 1966.
Francis, Richard. *Judge Sewall's Apology: The Salem Witch Trials and the Forming of the American Conscience.* New York: Fourth Estate, 2005.
Hall, David D. "Witch Hunting in Salem." *Christian History* 13:1 (1994): 38–40.
Hill, Frances. *The Salem Witch Trials Reader.* Cambridge, Mass.: De Capo Press, 2000.
Kibbey, Ann. "Mutations of the Supernatural: Witchcraft, Remarkable Providences, and the Power of Puritan Men." *American Quarterly* 34:2 (Summer 1982): 125–148.
Norton, Mary Beth. *In the Devil's Snare: The Salem Witchcraft Crisis of 1692.* New York: Alfred A. Knopf, 2002.
Reis, Elizabeth. *Damned Women: Sinners and Witches in Puritan New England.* Ithaca, N. Y.: Cornell University Press, 1997.
Rosenthal, Bernard. *Salem Story: Reading the Witch Trials of 1692.* Cambridge: Cambridge University Press, 1993.

Women

Bremer, Francis J. *Anne Hutchinson: Troubler of the Puritan Zion.* Huntington, N. Y.: R. E. Krieger, 1981.
Como, David R. "Women, Prophecy, and Authority in Early Stuart Puritanism." *Huntington Library Quarterly* 61:2 (Spring 1998): 203–222.
Davies, Stevie. *Unbridled Spirits: Women of the English Revolution, 1640–1660.* London: Women's Press, 1998.
Dietrich, Deborah J. "Mary Rowlandson's Great Declension." *Women's Studies* 24:5 (June 1995): 427–439.
Feroli, Teresa. *Political Speaking Justified: Women Prophets and the English Revolution.* Newark, N. J.: University of Delaware Press, 2006.
Gillespie, Katharine. *Domesticity and Dissent in the Seventeenth-Century: English Women Writers and the Public Sphere.* Cambridge: Cambridge University Press, 2004.
Gordon, Charlotte. *Mistress Bradstreet: The Untold Life of America's First Poet.* New York: Little, Brown, and Company, 2005.
Grimes, Alan Pendleton. *The Puritan Ethic and Woman Suffrage.* New York: Oxford University Press, 1967.
Haselkorn, Anne M., and Betty Travitsky. *The Renaissance Englishwoman in Print: Counterbalancing the Canon.* Amherst: University of Massachusetts Press, 1990.
Koehler, Lyle. *A Search for Power: The 'Weaker Sex' in Seventeenth-Century New England.* Urbana: University of Illinois Press, 1980.

Lang, Amy Schrager. *Prophetic Woman: Anne Hutchinson and the Problem of Dissent in the Literature of New England*. Berkeley: University of California Press, 1987.
Masson, Margaret W. "The Typology of the Female as a Model for the Regenerate: Puritan Preaching, 1690–1730." *Journal of Women in Culture and Society* 2.2 (1976): 304–315.
Piercy, Josephine Ketcham. *Anne Bradstreet*. New York: Twayne Publishers, 1965.
Plowden, Alison. *Women All on Fire: The Women of the English Civil War*. Phoenix Mill, U. K.: Sutton Publications, 1998.
Porterfield, Amanda. "Women's Attraction to Puritanism." *Church History* 60 (June 1991): 196–209.
Reis, Elizabeth. "The Devil, the Body, and the Feminine Soul in Puritan New England." *Journal of American History* 82:1 (June 1995): 15–36.
Stanford, Ann. *Anne Bradstreet, The Worldly Puritan: An Introduction to Her Poetry*. New York: Burt Franklin, 1974.
Thickstun, Margaret Olofson. *Fictions of the Feminine: Puritan Doctrine and the Representation of Women*. Ithaca, N. Y.: Cornell University Press, 1988.
Westerkamp, Marilyn J. *Women and Religion in Early America, 1600–1850: The Puritan and Evangelical Traditions*. London: Routledge, 1999.
Willen, Diane. "Godly Women in Early Modern England: Puritanism and Gender." *Journal of Ecclesiastical History* 43 (October 1992): 561–580.

MAJOR FIGURES

Richard Baxter

Baxter, Richard. *The Autobiography of Richard Baxter*. Ed. J. M. Lloyd Thomas and N. H. Keeble. Totowa, N. J.: Rowman and Littlefield, 1974.
———. *The Reformed Pastor*. Ed. William Brown. Edinburgh, Scotland, U. K.: Banner of Truth Trust, 1989.
Beougher, Tim. "The Puritan View of Marriage: The Husband/Wife Relationship in Puritan England as Taught and Experienced by Richard Baxter." *Trinity Journal* 10:2 (Fall 1989): 131–160.
Cooke, Timothy R. "Uncommon Earnestness and Earthly Toils: Moderate Puritan Richard Baxter's Devotional Writings." *Anglican and Episcopal History* 63 (March 1994): 51–72.
Davis, James Calvin. "Pardoning Puritanism: Community, Character, and Forgiveness in the Work of Richard Baxter." *Journal of Religious Ethics* 29:2 (June 2001): 283–306.
DePauley, William Cecil. "Richard Baxter Surveyed." *Church Quarterly Review* 164 (January–March 1963): 32–43.

Douglas, Walter B. T. "Politics and Theology in the Thought of Richard Baxter." *Andrews University Seminary Studies* 15:2 (Autumn 1977): 115–126.
Keeble, N. H. *Richard Baxter: Puritan Man of Letters*. Oxford: Clarendon Press, 1982.
———. "Richard Baxter's Preaching Ministry: Its History and Texts." *Journal of Ecclesiastical History* 35:4 (October 1984): 539–559.
Lamont, William M. *Richard Baxter and the Millennium: Protestant Imperialism and the English Revolution*. London: Croom Helm, 1979.
———. "Richard Baxter, 'Popery,' and the Origins of the English Civil War." *History* 87:287 (July 2002): 336–352.
Lim, Paul Chang-Ha. *In Pursuit of Purity, Unity, and Liberty: Richard Baxter's Puritan Ecclesiology in Its Seventeenth-Century Context*. Leiden: E. J. Brill, 2004.
MacGillivray, Royce. "Richard Baxter: A Puritan in the Provinces." *Dalhousie Review* 49 (1969): 487–496.
Martin, Hugh. *Puritanism and Richard Baxter*. London: SCM Press, 1954.
Packer, J. I. *The Redemption and Restoration of Man in the Thought of Richard Baxter: A Study in Puritan Theology*. Carlisle, U. K.: Paternoster Press, 2003.
Roth, Kenneth L. "The Psychology and Counseling of Richard Baxter (1615–1691)." *Journal of Psychology and Christianity* 17 (Winter 1998): 321–334.
Schlatter, Richard, ed. *Richard Baxter and Puritan Politics*. New Brunswick, N. J.: Rutgers University Press, 1957.
Wood, A. Harold. "Our Debt to Richard Baxter and the Puritans." *Reformed Theological Review* 9 (Spring 1950): 1–17.

John Bunyan

Brittain, Vera. *In the Steps of John Bunyan: An Excursion into Puritan England*. London: Rich and Cowan, 1950.
———. *Valiant Pilgrim: The Story of John Bunyan and Puritan England*. New York: Macmillan, 1950.
Bunyan, John. *Grace Abounding with Other Spiritual Autobiographies*. Ed. John Stachniewski and Anita Pacheco. Oxford: Oxford University Press, 1998.
———. *The Miscellaneous Works of John Bunyan*. 13 vols. Ed. by Roger Sharrock et al. Oxford: Clarendon Press, 1976–1994.
———. *The Pilgrim's Progress*. Ed. James Blanton Wharey and Roger Sharrock. Oxford: Clarendon Press, 1960.
Collmer, Robert G., ed. *Bunyan in Our Time*. Kent, Oh.: The Kent State University Press, 1989.
Furlong, Monica. *Puritan's Progress*. New York: Coward, McCann and Geoghegan, 1975.

Gay, David, James G. Randall, and Arlette Zinck, eds. *Awakening Words: John Bunyan and the Language of Community*. Newark, N. J.: University of Delaware Press, 2000.

Greaves, Richard L. *Glimpses of Glory: John Bunyan and English Dissent*. Stanford, Calif.: Stanford University Press, 2002.

———. *John Bunyan and English Nonconformity*. London: Hambledon Press, 1992.

Hill, Christopher. *A Tinker and a Poor Man: John Bunyan and His Church, 1628–1688*. New York: Alfred Knopf, 1989.

Johnson, Galen. "'Be Not Extream': The Limits of Theory in Reading John Bunyan." *Christianity and Literature* 49:4 (Summer 2000): 447–464.

———. "The Conflicted Puritan Inheritance of John Bunyan's Political Writings." *Baptist History and Heritage* 38:2 (Spring 2003): 103–115.

———. *Prisoner of Conscience: John Bunyan on Self, Community, and Christian Faith*. Carlisle, U. K.: Paternoster Press, 2003.

Kaufmann, U. Milo. *The Pilgrim's Progress and Traditions in Puritan Meditation*. New Haven, Conn.: Yale University Press, 1966.

Keeble, N. H., ed. *John Bunyan: Conventicle and Parnassus: Tercentenary Essays*. Oxford: Clarendon Press, 1988.

———. *John Bunyan: Reading Dissenting Writing*. Oxford: Peter Lang, 2002.

Laurence, Anne, W. R. Owens, and Stuart Sim. *John Bunyan and His England, 1628–88*. London: The Hambledon Press, 1990.

Mullett, Michael A. *John Bunyan in Context*. Pittsburgh, Pa.: Duquesne University Press, 1997.

Newey, Vincent. *The Pilgrim's Progress: Critical and Historical Views*. Totowa, N. J.: Barnes and Noble Press, 1980.

O'Donnell, Norbert F. "Shaw, Bunyan, and Puritanism." *Publications of the Modern Language Association* 72 (1957): 520–533.

Sharrock, Roger. *John Bunyan*. London: Macmillan, 1968.

———. "Person Vision and Puritan Tradition in Bunyan." *Hibbert Journal* 56 (1957): 47–60.

Sim, Stuart, and David Walker. *Bunyan and Authority: The Rhetoric of Dissent and the Legitimation Crisis in Seventeenth-Century England*. Bern: Peter Lang, 2000.

Stackhouse, Max L. "A Puritan's Pilgrimage: Beyond the Iron Cage." *Union Seminary Quarterly Review* 37:3 (1982): 205–216.

Swaim, Kathleen M. *Pilgrim's Progress, Puritan's Progress: Discourses and Contexts*. Urbana: University of Illinois Press, 1993.

Wakefield, Gordon. *Bunyan the Christian*. London: HarperCollins, 1992.

Oliver Cromwell

Abbott, Wilbur Cortez. *A Bibliography of Oliver Cromwell: A List of Printed Materials Relating to Oliver Cromwell, Together with a List of Portraits and Caricatures*. Cambridge, Mass.: Harvard University Press, 1929.

Ashley, Maurice. *Oliver Cromwell and His World.* New York: Putnam, 1972.
Boyer, Richard E., ed. *Oliver Cromwell and the Puritan Revolt: Failure of a Man or a Faith?* Boston: Heath, 1966.
D'Aubigne, J. H. Merle. *The Protector: A Vindication.* Harrisonburg, Va.: Sprinkle Publications, 1983.
Davis, J. C. *Oliver Cromwell.* London: Arnold Publishers, 2001.
Firth, Charles. *Oliver Cromwell and the Rule of the Puritans in England.* London: Oxford University Press, 1953.
Fraser, Antonia. *Cromwell: The Lord Protector.* New York: Alfred A. Knopf, 1973.
Gaunt, Peter. *Oliver Cromwell.* New York: New York University Press, 2004.
Gillingham, John. *Cromwell: Portrait of a Soldier.* London: Weidenfeld and Nicolson, 1976.
Gregg, Pauline. *Oliver Cromwell.* London: J. M. Dent, 1988.
Hill, Christopher. *God's Englishman: Oliver Cromwell and the English Revolution.* New York: Harper Torchbooks, 1970.
McMains, H. F. *The Death of Oliver Cromwell.* Lexington, Ky.: University of Kentucky Press, 2000.
Morrill, J. S., and J. S. A. Adamson. *Oliver Cromwell and the English Revolution.* New York: Longman, 1990.
Morrill, John. "Rewriting Cromwell: A Case for Deafening Silences." *Canadian Journal of History* 38:3 (December 2003): 553–578.
New, John F. H. *Oliver Cromwell: Pretender, Puritan, Statesman, Paradox?* New York: Holt, Rinehart, and Winston, 1971.
Paul, Robert S. *The Lord Protector: Religion and Politics in the Life of Oliver Cromwell.* Grand Rapids, Mich.: William B. Eerdmans, 1964.
Richardson, R. C., ed. *Images of Oliver Cromwell: Essays for and by Roger Howell, Jr.* Manchester: Manchester University Press, 1993.
Roots, Ivan Alan. *Commonwealth and Protectorate: The English Civil War and Its Aftermath.* New York: Schocken Books, 1966.
Smith, David L. *Oliver Cromwell: Politics and Religion in the English Revolution, 1640–1658.* Cambridge: Cambridge University Press, 1991.
Wedgwood, C. V. *Oliver Cromwell.* New York: Macmillan, 1956.
Woolrych, Austin. "The Cromwellian Protectorate: A Military Dictatorship?" *History* 75:244 (June 1990): 207–231.
Young, Peter. *Oliver Cromwell and His Times.* London: B. T. Batsford, 1962.

Jonathan Edwards

Brand, David C. *Profile of the Last Puritan: Jonathan Edwards, Self-Love, and the Dawn of the Beatific.* Atlanta, Ga.: Scholars Press, 1991.
Bushman, Richard L. "Jonathan Edwards and Puritan Consciousness." *Journal for the Scientific Study of Religion* 5 (Fall 1966): 383–396.

Cherry, Conrad. "The Puritan Notion of the Covenant in Jonathan Edwards' Doctrine of Faith." *Church History* 34 (Spring 1965): 328–341.
Conforti, Joseph A. *Jonathan Edwards, Religious Tradition, and American Culture*. Chapel Hill: University of North Carolina Press, 1995.
Davidson, Edward H. *Jonathan Edwards: The Narrative of a Puritan Mind*. Cambridge, Mass.: Harvard University Press, 1968.
Edwards, Jonathan. *Puritan Sage: Collected Writings of Jonathan Edwards*. Ed. Vergilius Ferm. New York: Library Publishers, 1953.
———. *The Works of Jonathan Edwards*. Ed. Perry Miller. New Haven, Conn.: Yale University Press, 1957.
Gerstner, John H. *Jonathan Edwards: A Mini-Theology*. Morgan, Pa.: Soli Deo Gloria Publications, 1996.
Hart, D. G., and Sean Michael Lucas. *The Legacy of Jonathan Edwards: American Religion and the Evangelical Tradition*. Grand Rapids, Mich.: Baker, 2003.
Hatch, Nathan O., and Harry S. Stout. *Jonathan Edwards and the American Experience*. New York: Oxford University Press, 1988.
Lee, Sang Hyun. *The Princeton Companion to Jonathan Edwards*. Princeton: Princeton University Press, 2005.
Lesser, M. X. *Jonathan Edwards*. Boston: Twayne Publishers, 1988.
Levin, David. *The Puritan in the Enlightenment: Franklin and Edwards*. Chicago: Rand McNally, 1963.
Marsden, George M. *Jonathan Edwards: A Life*. New Haven, Conn.: Yale University Press, 2003.
Parkes, Henry Bamford. *Jonathan Edwards, the Fiery Puritan*. New York: Minton, Balch, 1930.
Pauw, Amy Plantinga. *The Supreme Harmony of All: The Trinitarian Theology of Jonathan Edwards*. Grand Rapids, Mich.: William B. Eerdmans, 2002.
Scheick, William J. *The Writings of Jonathan Edwards: Theme, Motif, and Style*. College Station: Texas A & M University Press, 1975.
Smith, John Edwin. *Jonathan Edwards: Puritan, Preacher, Philosopher*. Notre Dame, Ind.: University of Notre Dame Press, 1992.
Walton, Brad. *Jonathan Edwards, Religious Affections, and the Puritan Analysis of True Piety, Spiritual Sensation, and Heart Religion*. Lewiston, N. Y.: Edwin Mellon Press, 2002.
Werge, Thomas. "Jonathan Edwards and the Puritan Mind in America: Directions in Textual and Interpretive Criticism." *Reformed Review* 23:3 (Spring 1970): 153–156, 173–183.
Wilson-Kastner, Patricia. "Jonathan Edwards: History and the Covenant." *Andrews University Seminary Studies* 15:2 (Autumn 1977): 205–216.

John Milton

Achinstein, Sharon. *Milton and the Revolutionary Reader*. Princeton, N. J.: Princeton University Press, 1994.

Armitage, David, and Armand Himy. *Milton and Republicanism*. Cambridge: Cambridge University Press, 1995.
Barker, Arthur Edward. *Milton and the Puritan Dilemma, 1641–1660*. Toronto: University of Toronto Press, 1942.
Bennett, Joan S. *Reviving Liberty: Radical Christian Humanism in Milton's Great Poems*. Cambridge, Mass.: Harvard University Press, 1989.
Berry, Boyd M. *Process of Speech: Puritan Religious Writing and Paradise Lost*. Baltimore, Md.: Johns Hopkins University Press, 1976.
Christopher, Georgia B. *Milton and the Science of the Saints*. Princeton, N. J.: Princeton University Press, 1982.
Corns, Thomas N. *A Companion to Milton*. Oxford: Blackwell Publishers, 2001.
———. "Milton's Quest for Respectability." *Modern Language Review* 77:4 (October 1982): 769–779.
Cunnar, Eugene R. "Milton, *The Shepherd of Hermas*, and the Writing of a Puritan Masque." *Milton Studies* 23 (1987): 33–52.
Daniells, Roy. *Milton, Mannerism and Baroque*. Toronto: University of Toronto Press, 1963.
Davies, J. M. Q. "'Attempting to Be More Than Man We Become Less': Blake's *Comus* Designs and the Two Faces of Milton's Puritanism." *Durham University Journal* 81:2 (June 1989): 197–219.
Emerson, Everett H. *English Puritanism: From John Hooper to John Milton*. Durham, N. C.: Duke University Press, 1968.
Fish, Stanley E. *How Milton Works*. Cambridge, Mass.: Belknap Press of Harvard University Press, 2001.
Hannay, Margaret P. "'Psalms done into metre': The Common Psalms of John Milton and of the Bay Colony." *Christianity and Literature* 32:3 (Spring 1983): 19–29.
Hill, Christopher. *Milton and the English Revolution*. New York: Viking Press, 1977.
———. *The Experience of Defeat: Milton and Some Contemporaries*. New York: Viking, 1984.
Kendrick, Christopher. *Milton: A Study in Ideology and Form*. New York: Methuen, 1986.
Lares, Jameela. *Milton and the Preaching Arts*. Pittsburgh, Pa.: Duquesne University Press, 2001.
Loewenstein, David. *Representing Revolution in Milton and His Contemporaries: Religion, Politics, and Polemics in Radical Puritanism*. Cambridge: Cambridge University Press, 2001.
Maleski, Mary A. *A Fine Tuning: Studies of the Religious Poetry of Herbert and Milton*. Binghamton, N. Y.: Medieval and Renaissance Texts and Studies, 1989.
McGuire, Maryann Cole. *Milton's Puritan Masque*. Athens, Ga.: University of Georgia Press, 1983.
McLoone, George H. *Milton's Poetry of Independence: Five Studies*. Lewisburg, N. J.: Bucknell University Press, 1999.

Meland, Bernard Eugene. "John Milton: Puritan or Liberal?" *Encounter* 33 (Spring 1972): 129–140.
Milton, John. *The Riverside Milton.* Ed. Roy Flannagan. Boston: Houghton Mifflin, 1998.
Nelson, James G. *The Sublime Puritan.* Madison, Wis.: University of Wisconsin Press, 1963.
Rowse, A. L. *Milton the Puritan: Portrait of a Mind.* London: Macmillan, 1977.
Sauer, Elizabeth. "Milton's *Of True Religion*, Protestant Nationhood, and the Negotiation of Liberty." *Milton Quarterly* 40:1 (March 2006): 1–19.
Stavely, Keith W. F. *Puritan Legacies: Paradise Lost and the New England Tradition, 1630–1890.* Ithaca, N. Y.: Cornell University Press, 1987.
Wolfe, Don Marion. *Milton in the Puritan Revolution.* New York: Humanities Press, 1963.

Roger Williams

Byrd, James P. *The Challenges of Roger Williams: Religious Liberty, Violent Persecution, and the Bible.* Macon, Ga.: Mercer University Press, 2002.
Chupack, Henry. *Roger Williams.* New York: Twayne Publishers, 1969.
Cyclone, Covey. *The Gentle Radical: A Biography of Roger Williams.* New York: Macmillan, 1966.
Garrett, John. *Roger Williams: Witness Beyond Christendom.* New York: Macmillan, 1970.
Gaustad, Edwin S. *Liberty of Conscience: Roger Williams in America.* Grand Rapids, Mich.: William B. Eerdmans, 1991.
———. *Roger Williams.* New York: Oxford University Press, 2005.
———. "Roger Williams: Beyond Puritanism." *Baptist History and Heritage* 24 (October 1989): 11–19.
Gilpin, W. Clark. *The Millenarian Piety of Roger Williams.* Chicago: University of Chicago Press, 1979.
Greene, Theodore P. *Roger Williams and the Massachusetts Magistrates.* Boston: Heath, 1964.
Hall, Timothy L. *Separating Church and State: Roger Williams and Religious Liberty.* Urbana: University of Illinois Press, 1988.
Miller, Perry. *Roger Williams: His Contribution to the American Tradition.* Indianapolis, Ind.: Bobbs-Merrill, 1953.
Morgan, Edmund S. *Roger Williams: The Church and the State.* New York: Harcourt, Brace and World, 1967.
Polishook, Irwin H. *Roger Williams, John Cotton, and Religious Freedom: A Controversy in New and Old England.* Englewood Cliffs, N. J.: Prentice-Hall, 1967.
Spurgin, Hugh. *Roger Williams and Puritan Radicalism in the English Separatist Tradition.* Lewiston, N. Y.: Edwin Mellon Press, 1989.

Williams, Roger. *The Complete Writings of Roger Williams*. 7 vols. New York: Russell and Russell, 1963.
Winslow, Ola Elizabeth. *Master Roger Williams: A Biography*. New York: Macmillan, 1957.
Wood, Timothy L. "Kingdom Expectations: The Native American in the Puritan Missiology of John Winthrop and Roger Williams." *Fides et Historia* 32:1 (Winter–Spring 2000): 39–49.

About the Authors

Galen K. Johnson holds degrees from Wake Forest University, Princeton Theological Seminary, and Baylor University (Ph. D.). He is assistant professor of theology and assistant director of honors and learning enhancement at John Brown University. His published articles have appeared in *Christianity and Literature*, *Fides et Historia*, *The Mennonite Quarterly Review*, *Islam and Christian-Muslim Relations*, *Bunyan Studies*, *Mission Studies*, *Baptist History and Heritage*, *Journal of Greco-Roman Judaism and Christianity*, and *Archiv fur das Studium dur neueren Sprachen und Literaturen*. His book reviews have appeared in *Christianity and Literature*, *Perspectives in Religious Studies*, *Calvin Theological Journal*, and *Journal of Church and State*. He is the author of *Prisoner of Conscience: John Bunyan on Self, Community, and Christian Faith*. He is the secretary for the Conference on Christianity and Literature.

Charles Pastoor received his B.A. from Calvin College, and his M.A. and Ph.D. from Baylor University. He is an associate professor in the department of English at John Brown University. His articles have been published in *Tristiania*, *Renascence*, *The Explicator*, *English Language Notes*, *Shakespearean Criticism*, and *Philological Review*.